Fables & Tales of the Unexpected
Cheque-Mate......

"In life, unlike chess, the game continues after checkmate"

Isaac Asimov: 1920-1992

The Storyteller

Captain E.S. Geary

'Shipping's Danger Man'
Lloyd's Register - Fairplay International Shipping Weekly
United Kingdom

For Jason
My son and best friend

Let parents bequeath to their children not riches,
but the spirit of reverence.

Plato: 428-348 BC

Hope you enjoy the stories
Pam, Love, Jason
Oct 2012

This book is dedicated to the memory of the late

Myles J. Tralins
My mentor ~ My friend

Always in my thoughts and
forever the elephant in the room...

CONTENTS

In life, as in chess, forethought wins.

Charles Buxton: 1823 - 1871

For Pam with best wishes.

23 october 2012

Bo Geary.

The Last Three Spins

It was a cold, wet autumn day and in spite of it being their day off the three croupiers had arranged to meet at the Pub after collecting their monthly pay checks from the Golden Nugget Casino near London's Piccadilly Circus. A few minutes after 1:00 pm Marc, David and Paul entered the White Lion Public House in Covent Garden. The loud cockney slang of the croupiers and inspectors gathered around the polished Victorian bar resonated from the elegant mahogany walls making normal conversation impossible.

The White Lion had become a gathering point for the Casino's employees where downing a few pints before or after they finished their shifts had become a sacred ritual. Without attracting the attention of their boisterous workmates the trio made their way to an unoccupied booth in the far corner of the saloon. Moments later Pat, the ever attentive barmaid appeared through the Pub's smoky haze only to confirm they'd have their regular drinks.

"Have you got it Marc?"

"Yes, I picked it up this morning."

"Are you sure it's okay?"

"Look mate, I just got it. When I return to the boat I'll try it but I am sure there will be no sweat. The key is an exact copy and it's a standard lock. Don't worry."

As the well endowed barmaid, bent over to set the drinks on the table Marc eyed the lovely breasts that exposed themselves over the top of her low cut blouse. Too bad, he thought, great body and beautiful long blonde hair which unfortunately flowed from a completely empty head.

"Hey Marc, forget about that wench. After Friday you can have any girl you want."

"Sorry Paul it's been a while since I had a good roll in the sack, so I excite easily."

In taking a swig of his whisky David said, "Okay, let's get back to the job. The only thing left to deal with was the key to the boat and that's been taken care of. You know, it's too noisy to talk here, let's finish our drinks and go to Paul's flat so we can have a look at the plan one last time."

 In the cab on the way to Hampstead the three quietly had a good laugh about becoming robbers. All in their mid 20's they had unlikely backgrounds for crime. Marc had worked in the City as a chartered accountant, but after relying on a friend's advice lost all of his money in a stock swindle. Following the intensive background checks mandated by the British Gaming Control Board through Scotland Yard and the Federal Bureau of Investigation in the United States Marc had been one of the few Americans to be approved and granted a gaming license in the United Kingdom. He'd only been a croupier dealing roulette for nine months, but because of the games' repetition and monotonous boredom his interest and attention was drawn to the large sums of cash the casino took in each night. Focusing on the casino's security procedures, particularly the flaws and weaknesses, had allowed him to formulate what he believed was a workable plan to rob the Golden Nugget Casino in London's West End.

Before leaving San Francisco and moving to London, Marc recalled seeing a movie about a Casino robbery, but even after living in London for a number of years he'd remembered the story. In recent years his life had gone through some dramatic changes. The first was losing his life savings of $500,000 in a bogus stock deal orchestrated by lawyers and stock brokers connected to the mobster Meyer Lansky who engaged in making-a-market for a worthless stock through coordinated buys and sells in Miami, New York, Chicago, Dallas and San Francisco. Once the stock's value had been sufficiently inflated it was dumped and Lansky's cohorts who had participated, all shared in the extravagant profits. Once their money was gone Diane, his elegant Roedean educated blue-blooded English wife casually advised him that she simply didn't want to be married anymore. Marc often wondered if the loss of his life savings and his wife may have actually been a blessing in disguise.

After the money was gone they were forced to sell their flat in Kensington and the country home in Berkshire subsequently taking up residency on their small yacht, after which Diane soon departed. The thought of returning to his old accounting firm and each morning having to take the 7:35 to Victoria, then an over-stuffed tube ride to Moorgate only to spend the day balancing the books of some humdrum manufacturing company in Slough before catching the 5:22 home was just unthinkable. When the Mecca Organization advertised for people to train as croupiers he applied and surprisingly was offered a job. Paul and David too, had unlikely backgrounds for crime. Paul, an Australian, was a graduate Mining Engineer who planned to travel around the world before settling down to life in Queensland as an executive with his father's mining company. His life had been shattered when both of his parents were killed in the crash of their small plane during a flight home from Canberra resulting in the mining operations being sold to pay-off its debts.

David, a Chemist, had come to Britain to gain an advanced degree in the Chemical Sciences, but instead of going back to Cape Town had decided to open a dive shop in the Seychelles. The three had diverse backgrounds from different parts of the world, but all were driven and motivated by a desire for money to facilitate their dreams. After enduring the dreariness of the English weather and a hand-to-mouth existence while eking out a living the three sought luxury and wanted to enjoy that luxury in a warm, sunny climate. As Paul opened the door to the flat the strong odor of booze filled the air.

"I know you like a drink or two Paul, but this is ridiculous," Marc said with a smirk, wrinkling his nose.

"I'm going to kill that bloody dog of yours Marc. The little bastard has knocked over the drinks trolley."

In the corner next to the window the overturned trolley lay on its side. The Waterford decanters once full were unbroken but strewn about the floor in a pool of brandy, scotch and rum.

With a laugh, David said "Seems like old Sam likes a nip or two."

Paul, seeing the funny side quipped,

"A nip or two hell, Sam's a damned alcoholic. Next time you leave your dog in my flat, you bring the booze for him."

"Sorry Paul he may have seen a cat outside the window and got a bit excited." Paul setting his briefcase on the table went to the kitchen to make some coffee while Marc and David cleaned up the mess. When Paul returned with the coffee Marc opened the briefcase and began laying a number of drawings and charts over a dry area of the floor. The dog, who had been cowering behind the settee, put his nose around the corner to see what was going on. Sam, a Labrador-Red Setter mix was an intelligent dog, but from his master's tone knew he was in trouble.

"Hey look, the boozing dog has slept it off," responded Paul gently stroking the dog's head.

"You've cost me a lot of money, you bloody mongrel," Marc said while smiling.

With no interest in animals when they went their separate ways, Diane could care less if the dog stayed with Marc. Marc dearly loved Sam and couldn't get mad at him if he tried. As Sam came scurrying towards Marc his long bushy tail sent the papers flying in all directions.

"Bloody dog, get up on the settee and be still. We've got business to discuss." Sam acknowledged the order by curling into a motionless ball in the corner of the large leather sofa. Paul returned with the coffee and handed a cup to Marc who began to grin as he recalled the film *Oceans 11* where Sammy Davis and the Rat Pack planned to rob a casino in Las Vegas.

"You know maybe like the Rat Pack we should give ourselves a name, how about the *Wheeler Dealers*?"

Smiling, Paul responded,

"Yeah, yeah, okay wise-guy let's forget the funny business. The difference between us and the Oceans 11 gang is that we're not going to get caught. Once we've melted away the media can call us anything they like. Look, let's get down to things that matter. I think we should go over the details one more time so that we all know step by step exactly how we'll successfully pull off our coup."

One of the positive elements of robbing a casino is that they're built like a big walk-in safe, fully self-contained with usually only one point of entry and exit. No windows, but if the power is cut they've got enough emergency lighting to illuminate Wembley Stadium and the Rose Bowl combined. Security is generally strict and guards plentiful. With the only exception being senior management all employees have no openings on their clothing, all pockets are required to be sewn closed and all employees even though this rarely happens, are subject to inspections. One open pocket can mean immediate dismissal. The only apparent flaw in this seemingly tight security net was the croupiers who, when they started their shifts were allowed to carry large hand bags, knap sacks or duffel bags into the casino's staff lounge. Before entering, their bags were supposed to be inspected by Security at the casino's main entrance, but only on rare occasions did the Security officers bother to inspect the contents. Unlike other casinos in London, the Golden Nugget did not have a separate staff entrance which meant that pit bosses, dealers and punters all used the same door to enter and to leave. The Golden Nuggets' second floor location overlooking Shaftesbury Avenue provided only a single street level entrance for customers and staff.

Spread on the floor of Paul's flat was a large scale plan of the Golden Nugget Casino; notes and symbols on the plan identified the precise location and linear dimensions of the restaurant, staff lounge, management office, restrooms, cashiers cage, safe, security office, gaming tables, upstairs doors, and the street level exit. An alpha-numeric character code indicated the location of each room, the number of staff that the room could hold and the number of people that would be present between 3:00 and 4:00 a.m. on Saturday the 15th, the day after tomorrow.

With the air of a General briefing his troops before battle, Marc began,

"Okay, let's go over the getaway. We've got the keys to the RIVA moored in the marina near the *Kandora*. The RIVA has Volvo gasoline engines fed by two 200 gallon fuel tanks; when the dynamite blows and ignites the petrol the flames should completely destroy what's left of the boat. The guy who owns the SUNSEEKER tied up next to the RIVA told me that the owner only uses the boat only once or twice a year, which is normally in July. The rest of the year he lives in Marbella in Spain. Apparently he claims the RIVA as a business expense because he uses it for entertaining clients when he's in London; he doesn't know it yet, but his tax deduction is going to assist in our getaway and ensure our new and permanent tax free status. Over the last number of weeks I've been able to top up the tanks with gasoline, oops sorry, petrol for you guys, a few gallons at a time in the early hours so now they're full and holding about 500 gallons. To be able to quickly secure the ketch to the RIVA for the tow I've checked the lengths of the tow lines to make sure they're all the same length and fitted each line with a heavy pelican hook. The pelican hooks will save precious time in securing the boats together for the tow out of the marina to the Thames Estuary. For the last two months I've had the *Van Dyke* moored in the marina in Kent under the name of the *Kandora*. After Diane left and the *Van Dyke* was moved, people didn't ask any questions and just assumed it had been sold because of the divorce; the *Kandora* will soon become the GABI. I've filled her with provisions, water, etc. and she's ready to go. Last month I called the people in Cardiff and over the phone was able to register the GABI on the SSR, the Small Ships Registry showing John Emory as the owner's name. Without ever seeing the yacht or knowing whether the *Kandora* or the GABI even existed the clowns in Cardiff mailed me a Certificate of Registry. When we leave the GABI will be a British yacht legally registered on the SSR. The owner of the RIVA isn't in the country, so the boat shouldn't be missed at least until he returns from Spain. The Mini-Cooper will be parked in Piccadilly somewhere close to the Regent Palace. If the BBC is correct their weather forecast for Saturday morning shows there will be no rain, a bit of fog and cold. On a Saturday, without the normal weekday traffic especially at 4:35 in the morning, it should take us only about 45 minutes to get to the marina in Kent. If it takes us say ten minutes to attach the tow lines from the RIVA to the GABI by

5:45 we should be well off the coast in the Thames Estuary. First light is 6:17 a.m. which will be enough time for us to clear the lightship on the Goodwin Sands. By 7:00 a.m. we should be in the Channel north-northwest of the French coast on a southerly heading. The fog will give us cover from the cross channel ferries or any other shipping in the channel. We'll leave the marina using the RIVA's steering compass, but with the expected fog offshore we've got the radar and navigation equipment on board. Off Cape Gris Nez we'll change course to 220° and vector southwest for the Bay of Biscay. The temporary stick-on name plates I had made for both boats should work nicely in case we're seen in the English Channel. With the new name plates we'll be nothing more that a motorboat towing a sailboat, the RIVA will have BAMBI shown on her transom towing a ketch named GABI. Once we enter the Bay of Biscay we'll keep an eye on the fuel; we've got to leave at least 50 gallons in each tank so when we cut the fuel lines the petrol will flow into the bilges allowing the fire to spread after the explosion. The dynamite charges will be placed in the main saloon and in the stern of the RIVA. We'll leave a bundle of bank notes and some of our personal gear in the bow chain locker before pulling off the temporary name plate, cutting the fuel lines and lighting the fuses. I'll drive the RIVA while you and Paul stay on the GABI during the tow. Everything we'll be taking will have already been secured on the GABI which includes our new Irish passports, clothes, foul weather gear, personal kit, and of course the duffel bags with the money. At some point after the robbery is reported the police will be looking for an American, Australian and a South African on board a RIVA motorboat, not three Irishmen on a 40 foot Ketch named the GABI. The dynamite Paul obtained through his ex-pat mining friends in Earls Court will pretty much destroy the RIVA, but should leave enough to identify the hull. Our old passports, clothing and the bank notes left onboard the RIVA will eventually be discovered in the debris and reported to law enforcement. Before we set the charges we'll need to be sure that there aren't any other ships close by or on the horizon and unless the explosion, resulting fire or smoke is seen right away we'll be well away and out of the immediate area before the wreckage is discovered.   Once the story breaks in the newspapers the Coppers, wanting to show their efficiency in solving the robbery will report that the thieves all died in the explosion and close their file while we carry on in the GABI to Corvo. We'll each stand watches of two hours and to minimize any unwanted contact with other vessels I've removed the radar reflector. We'll keep well offshore and out of the shipping lanes while we transit Biscay and the Spanish and Portuguese coasts. Corvo is a real back-water and most people don't even know it exists. When I bought the charts for the Azores the guy in the marine store in Southampton said that he'd never heard of Corvo. In my research for possible destinations I found it's only about 35 square miles and the smallest island of the Azores with a population of about 400. The inhabitants are mainly involved with agriculture, raising cattle and fishing. It has a small airport with a few TAP flights that connect to Lisbon, a couple of hours away. There's an occasional supply boat, only a few people speak English and they rarely have any visitors from the UK or Ireland. There may be the occasional English newspaper, but any papers that eventually get to the island will probably be at least a month old and would be history. Corvo is located at 39°40′N – 31°05′W and depending on the winds it shouldn't take us more than five or six days of sailing on a broad reach. So we don't attract any attention trying to use British Pounds I've changed 300.00 in sterling to escudos, the local currency. After we arrive we'll keep a low profile and cool our heels for a couple of weeks. Once the dust has settled we'll sail GABI to Ponta Delgada on São Miguel and leave her on the hook in the harbor. So the GABI can't be traced back to the Kandora, Van Dyke or any of us, I've removed her hull identification number and filed off all the serial numbers on the engine, transmission, electronics, and navigation equipment. There's no need to worry about the sails because they're all old and don't have sail numbers. After we leave the GABI we'll go directly to the airport and pay cash to purchase our tickets and hop on the first flight to Lisbon. Once we arrive in Lisbon we'll go our separate ways.   Okay, my partners in crime any questions?"

Paul and David, who had been listening intently, shook their heads. Paul, enthused with their ingenious plan, with a broad grin added, "Nope, carry on Marc."

"Good. You know the hardest thing I have to deal with is Sam. My friends Chris and Barrie who live in Essex have been sworn to secrecy, but agreed to take care of Sam until I decide where I'm going to settle, which will probably be somewhere in Mexico. Once I tell Barrie where I'm at he'll put Sam on the next plane out of Heathrow and send him to me. It'll be hard not having the little guy around, but thank goodness only a temporary situation that I'll have to deal with. Okay, that's enough of my personal stuff. Let's get into the real meat. The most important part will be how we carryout the actual heist which has to be executed with military precision. On Friday the three of us are all on the 8:00 p.m. to 3:00 a.m. shift and should arrive in the normal way, that is, I'm always early and you two just make it in time. According to Friday's shift schedule there will be two security guards, thirty-nine dealers for Roulette, Blackjack and Craps, twelve Inspectors, four Floor Managers, in addition to Cerdan the Manager, Big John the Assistant Manager, four cashiers, four waitresses, and three people in the kitchen. David, what about the gas to put everyone to sleep are you sure we can we comfortably carry the canisters in our back-packs when we report to work? Didn't you say the gas was something like ether?"

"Close, but technically it's an opiate derived incapacitating agent. I had first looked at Agent 15 or BZ, but the problem was that we've got a tight timetable and this stuff could take from 30 minutes to 24 hours to have any effect. Depending on how much of the gas was absorbed Agent 15 could last between 3 to 4 days before it wore off. Yuri, my buddy who masquerades as a commercial attaché at the Russian Embassy is in fact a covert KGB officer with the rank of major who put me on to Kolokol-1. According to Yuri, the origins and formula of Kolokol-1 has been kept under wraps so only a few people know its formula or long term affects. He said that his boss in Moscow told him that Kolokol-1 was originally developed at a secret military research facility in Leningrad, but that *incapacitating agents* in Yuri's military terminology, have had the attention of the Soviets' since the 1920's. He thinks the Kremlin may have gotten the idea of incapacitating the enemy from Hannibal who in 184 B.C. used belladonna plants to induce disorientation on the enemies he fought. Even though he doesn't have any experience with it personally, Yuri knows that some of his mates have used it in the eastern block countries when they had a problem with a comrade who didn't want to follow Moscow's line. He doesn't know why I need something to incapacitate someone and said he doesn't really want to know, but that this wonderful Soviet creation is what I should go for. In appreciation I gave him £100.00 for his help. He doesn't give a damn about mother Russia and is hoping that the Americans or the Brits will offer him a deal to defect. While he patiently waits for his offer to defect he appears to have a booming business in selling Russian military things, things that are of course not his. I think the canisters might have been a bit too big for the Embassy's diplomatic pouch, but I know because of his entrepreneurial skills he's clearly got some good contacts to get things out of Russia. I'm not sure how he was able to get the canisters to London, but a month after I gave Yuri £600.00 in cash he gave me the six canisters neatly wrapped inside an Aeroflot carry-on bag while we downed a few pints at the Prospect of Whitby in Wapping. Yuri said if I needed anything else to let him know. I said how about a MIG? Yuri smiled, said no problem, but I'd have to assemble the pieces. Everything on the formulation is hush-hush but from what I've been able to find out Kolokol-1 seems to be a derivative of Fentanly1 or maybe the extra potent Carfentanil or even 3-Methylfentanyl. The advantage of Kolokol-1 is that once it's released it takes effect very quickly and within one to three seconds will render the victim unconscious for two to six hours. Also, it's not lethal and doesn't appear to have any long term effect. Want to know more?" "No thanks David, other than one to three seconds to put everyone to sleep I'm not sure if I really understand or care what we use. What was it called Kokomo something?"

"Sorry Marc it's Kolokol-1. I didn't mean to get too technical. The stuff sounds pretty nasty, but you're right, what's important is that in one to three seconds after they inhale the stuff everyone goes to sleep and a few hours later they wake up with a mild hangover, but with no long term effects, I hope."

"That's good enough for me David. We don't want to kill anybody. With the exception of Cerdan, the others are our friends."

David got up and went into the bedroom returning a few moments later with a 2-liter size aluminum container with a small valve on top, a container that bore a striking resemblance to a miniature SCUBA diving tank.

"This is how it works. The containers each hold a little over 3kg of Kolokol-1. I've wrapped the other containers in cotton wool and then covered the cotton with muslin cloth that will also absorb the gas. It's simple, after the punters have left, the upstairs exit door is closed and the casino goes into lock-down. We open the valves to release the gas and within a minute or two, with the help of the ventilating fans, we'll have a casino full of sleeping people."

"Nice work David sounds great, but are you certain there's enough gas in six containers to fill the whole casino?"

"My calculations of dispersal show that the gas in one container will quickly cover about 15,000 square feet, we've got six. The adjoining restaurant, staff lounge and the main casino has a total area of about 50,000 square feet. With a maximum projected dispersal penetration of 90,000 square feet in the six containers we have almost twice what's needed. Also Kolokol-1 requires minimum inhalation to incapacitate. Breath it and in a few seconds you're out cold."

"It's important we have these on before we open the valves on the canisters, if we don't we'll be asleep along with everyone else," David said removing what appeared to be a vintage World War II gas mask from a bag.

Nodding in agreement Marc continued,

"I'm coming to that now. This is where our back-packs are important. The canisters will be placed on the bottom of the back-packs and hidden from view under the tightly wrapped duffel bags that we'll use to take out the money. On the top of the back-packs we'll have folded copies of today's newspapers. Just for good measure on top of the newspapers we'll put some fruit, oranges, grapes, and bananas ostensibly for our lunch break. At the end of our shift at 3:00 a.m., we return to the staff room, collect the bags and prepare for our disappearing act behind the drapes. From a little after 3:00 until 4:00 we need to be patient while we wait behind the heavy drapes until they call the last three spins. It's important that we remain motionless. There's exactly 12" between the wall and the drapes so to avoid being seen we need to position ourselves against the wall and at least 10' inside from the opening where we entered. The heavy drapes were installed as sound proofing, but in any case we need to be very quiet. An inadvertent cough shouldn't be noticed considering the punters shouting as they win or lose and the normal noise of the casino, but if one of us moves causing the drapes to move we could have a real problem as any movement behind the drapes might be noticed by a dealer or a pit boss. When we leave the Casino the money in the duffel bags must be covered with the newspapers. It's important too that once the duffel bags are full as tempting as it might be, we shouldn't try and over fill the bags. We take only £10's and £20's and no small notes or US currency under $20.00. It's unlikely, but just in case one of the security guards wants to take a quick look in our bags when we leave all he'll see is newspapers. Now, let's look at the Casino layout. You know Paul, maybe you should have been an architect instead of a mining engineer your drawings and the details are outstanding."

Pointing with a pencil Marc continued,

"Here we have the long heavy drapes that hang from the ceiling to the floor surrounding the entire gaming area. The drapes will provide cover after we leave the staff room, but only if we remain still, maybe frozen would be a better word. The roulette tables are located in a row along the center of the room in four lines with the blackjack tables shown here in the upper left hand corner. The cash point is here and in the far left hand corner the crap tables. In the back of the room we have the security office and next to that, the staff lounge. All the gaming tables are positioned in such a way that the dealers are facing towards the center of the casino floor with the drapes at their backs. There's a distance of about six or seven feet between the dealers and the drapes. The openings where we slip behind the drapes are to the left and right of the entrance to the staff lounge. Because the closest blackjack tables are situated on both sides twenty feet away if we move quickly we shouldn't be seen, also being a Friday the place will be jammed with people. We've gone over this before, but let's do it again; a little after 3:00 when our shift is over we'll all leave the staff lounge together. I'll come out of the staff lounge with my back-pack, but just before reaching the cash point quickly check to be sure there's no one behind me, bend over like I'm picking something up, but instead of getting up, slip behind the drapes to the left side. David a few moments later you'll leave the staff room, check to be certain no one is behind you, but instead of going out and turning left towards the cash point and main exit, bend over and move to the right, staying close to the wall on the right side as you slip behind the drapes. Casino regulations say when the dealers shift is over they are to leave the staff lounge by passing in front of the cash point then proceed directly to the main exit, but as it's very busy on Fridays, I'm *betting* no one will notice. Sorry for the pun. Paul, you'll also make the same move as David and also slip behind the drapes to the right. It's important you stay together as you'll be directly below the ceiling circulation fans for the air conditioning units which will accelerate the dispersal of the gas. I'll do the same and release my canisters on the other side of the room. Paul when you make your move be sure to check that the emergency door leading to the staff lounge, security office and staff restaurant is open. It's normally open, but as you leave be sure to check it so the gas can spread into all the areas. Before we leave we must set our watches exactly with the staff lounge clock. Let's take security next. A few minutes before 4:00 from behind the drapes we'll all be able to hear the call for the last three spins. We won't be able to see the exit door, but will be able to hear it being closed around 4:15. When the punters are gone the only voices we'll hear will be those of the croupiers and pit bosses as the casino is shut off from the rest of the building. Usually by 4:20 downstairs at the entrance after one of the security officers has bolted the street level door the entire casino will be cut off from the outside world. After the door has been closed each table's cash box will have been placed on the table, opened and the money laid out in rows of five by denomination while the dealers stand by their tables and wait for the cash count, the cashiers will have opened the main safe. We'll check our watches and at exactly 4:22 put on the gas masks, carefully take the canisters from the back-packs, open the valves, and gently place them on the floor with the tops protruding through the opening below the bottom of the drapes. Just to double-check I've clocked it for the last two weeks and it only takes four or five minutes for the punters to leave the first floor and walk down to the front entrance on Shaftesbury Avenue. Restaurant staff is next on the list. The main restaurant has very few customers after 2:00 and closes completely at 3:00, by 3:20 the takings are brought to the cash point and the staff waiters and cocktail waitresses will have left. The two restaurant cleaners, who remain to clean the ashtrays and pick up the empty glasses, are always gone by 3:30. If any of the restaurant staff still happen to be around they'll get gassed with the rest. If Yuri is right by 4:25 the gas will have taken effect and everyone will be sleeping like babies. The only people still conscious in the Golden Nugget casino will be the three of us and the two security guards stationed downstairs at the main door. In the normal scenario after the cash is counted the croupiers pick up their things in the staff lounge and by 4:45 begin leaving from the casino's entrance downstairs. It's important that we have the cash from the tables, cashiers cage and from the safe in the duffel bags no later than 4:40 and be gone. To keep to the normal procedures we shouldn't leave any earlier, if we are any later the guards downstairs may become suspicious and wonder why no other croupiers are coming out. If one of them calls upstairs and gets no answer and sets off the alarm before we get out, we're dead meat. Well that's it, any questions?"

"Marc where do we leave the car?"

"This is important, Paul. We've got to be sure to leave the car parked on the street close to the Regent Palace Hotel, somewhere around Brewer Street where parking late at night is allowed on the single yellow line."

Marc, emphasizing the single yellow line,

"We don't want to get to the car at 4:45 in the morning and find that because it was parked illegally it's been towed away or maybe been clamped."

"It shall be done Admiral," said Paul saluting in a subservient manner.

Marc smiled,

"Hey Paul, as a military exercise shouldn't I be referred to as a General?"

"Well Marc, I think because we're leaving by boat Admiral is clearly more appropriate."

"Aye, aye, mate. Okay, let's go over it one more time just to be sure we haven't forgotten anything. I've got the key to the RIVA, Paul's stowed the dynamite on the GABI, and we're okay with the gas canisters, duffel bags, passports, and provisions for the yacht. I think that covers everything. Oh yeah passports, I picked up our new Irish Passports and they are on the boat now. Well gentlemen tomorrow we start the day as struggling croupiers, but the following day we'll be three Irishmen on the high seas maybe about a £1,000,000.00 richer. Let's all hope that it's a winning night for the Golden Nugget."

The midday sun shrouded by clouds was barely visible when Marc and Sam returned to the *Kandora*. The lovely little yacht was rolling slowly from side to side, gently pitching and tugging at her mooring lines. Her tender movements seemed to indicate that she too was anxious to make the voyage to warmer shores.

After spending the night at Paul's flat Sam was pleased to get back to his floating home, but before jumping on the boat Sam bolted running up and down the quayside taking a pee or two. Deciding a short nap was in order both were soon fast asleep. It was about 6:00 p.m. when Sam's barking awoke Marc.

"Shut up you little bugger or I'll throw you overboard."

Marc peered through the porthole. With a knot in his stomach and fear running through his body he jumped from his bunk. There across the water he saw Mac the marina mechanic and his helper climbing onboard the RIVA - their escape boat.

Marc quickly dressed and walked across the jetty. To Mac and the people at the Marina, Marc was known as John Emory, a yachtsman and Canadian writer visiting the U.K. on his way to Sweden.

"Good afternoon, Mr. Emory."

"Good afternoon Mac. First time I've seen anyone around the RIVA since I've been here are you getting her ready for a trip?"

"Her owner is coming back from Spain for a business meeting and wants to use her while he's here." Marc's heart started pounding. "When is he coming back?"

"He told me that he'd be here Thursday, next week." Marc resumed normal breathing.

"Strange though, I thought I had drained and cleaned the fuel tanks and only put in 50 or 60 gallons, but now I've found they're completely full. I must be getting old to forget something like that."

"Hey Mac, you look after lots of boats. What's a full tank here or there? Can't do any harm."

"Yeah, guess you're right."

"See you Mac, have a good day."

"Thanks. See you later Mr. Emory."

With that, Marc went back to the KANDORA and tried to forget about this near disaster.

After pondering the terrible possibility if the owner had returned this week Marc made himself a strong coffee spiced with a shot of Mount Gay rum. The rest of the day was un-eventful; Marc tidied things up around the boat and let Sam out for a run while he waited for Barrie to pick up the dog to take him to his temporary home in Essex. The following day the train was on time and the journey into town as boring as usual. Marc thought to himself that this was probably the best journey he'd ever had on British Rail because it would be his last. During the journey he gave the back-pack a final check for the fruit he'd packed and the tightly rolled duffel bag containing the canisters closing it as the train pulled into Victoria Station. At the W.H. Smith newsagents shop in the station Marc bought copies of the Daily Express, The Times and The Evening Standard.

The normal ritual of a visit to the White Lion Pub was skipped. When he arrived at the casino he exchanged the normal niceties with his fellow dealers and Big John, the Casino's Assistant Manager. Reaching the second floor were the casino was located he was somewhat concerned at the small number of people milling around the tables. Even though only 5:30 p.m., it was a Friday and still early. A few dealers were milling about the staff lounge and Paul and David hadn't arrived yet, which was right according to the plan.

By 7:50 p.m. Marc was becoming concerned until three minutes to 8:00 when Paul and David entered the staff lounge with back-packs, canisters, duffel bags, fruit, and newspapers. The three didn't engage in conversation, but after a brief hello all proceeded to their assigned tables in the Pit. The night seemed to drag by, but hour after hour an increasing number of punters filled the casino. The roulette tables were three deep with people shouting for wheel checks to play. At short time later the crap tables became unusually busy with a gregarious group of high rollers shouting 7 or 11 for the benefit of an enthusiastic throng of supporters.

A casino is a beehive of activity with a multitude of diverse peoples some winning, others losing, but all immersed in the exciting and exhilarating atmosphere of a place where it's all happening. Paul and David were scheduled for the last break of the hour from fifteen minutes past the hour while Marc was on second break, from thirty minutes past the hour to fifteen minutes before the hour. Marc, while passing David and Paul on one of their breaks both indicated everything was a go by giving the thumbs up sign. A quick check of the trio's back-packs at 2:00 a.m. showed the canisters and expandable duffel bags were secure and had not been disturbed.

Much like a first night performance Marc had butterflies in his stomach, but fortunately this would only be a *one* night performance. Finishing his stint on the table and leaving for a break Marc looked around to size things up, so far luck had been with them and everything was coming together as planned. The casino was packed and apparently from the look and demeanor of Cerdan the casino manager, it was proving to be a good night for the house. Some rather unpleasant Arab, probably a wealthy Oil Baron, between midnight and 2:00 a.m. had lost over £200,000. From the amount of money that had been gambled over the green felt, a good night for the house meant a good night for Marc and his buddies as they might easily walk away with even more than

£1,000,000.00. At 2:30 a.m. Marc came out for his last break of the evening and was again checking his back pack when Ray, one of the security guards entered the staff room.

"What's ya' got in there lad, the Crown Jewels?"

"No Ray nothing as dramatic as that, it's only my uneaten lunch. You know with what they pay you here you've got to be frugal." Marc chuckled to himself. If only Ray knew. At 2:45 a.m. Marc went back to deal his last game of roulette. It was a very quiet game with only one or two people at his table; the high-rollers were all huddled over the Crap tables or playing Black Jack or Baccarat. Boring as hell, he thought. He spun the ball, cleared the table, collected or paid out over and over again. Twenty-five, red odd; seventeen pieces green; place your bets; no more bets; seventeen black odd; eight pieces green; place your bets. He repeated the calls over and over again. Seemingly mesmerized he hadn't paid attention to the time. Picking up the little white ball to spin again he was interrupted.

"Hey, don't spin up" said Carol, another dealer approaching the table.

"It's 3:00 o'clock time for you to go luv."

Marc raising his hands over his head clapped them together and left the pit making his way quickly back to the staff lounge. He was just behind David and Paul, who too were ending their shift.

Turning slightly, David said softly, "Everything okay Marc?"

"All systems go," Marc responded with firm assurance and a thumb's up. Back in the staff lounge, a dozen or so dealers were reading newspapers, drinking coffee or waiting to use the public telephone.

"Okay, we're ready let's go," said Paul nervously.

David gave an appropriate nod, the three smiled, checked their watches and at precisely 3:10 a.m. they left the staff lounge. As Marc, the last to leave went out the door the staff public telephone rang.

"Curse that damned Alexander Graham Bell," he said quietly returning quickly to answer the phone.

"Hello, Golden Nugget."

"May I please speak to Joan Sims?"

"Sorry, she's on the table. Call back in fifteen minutes."

Without a further word, Marc slammed the phone back into the receiver. Calm down, calm down, you're too jumpy, he said to himself. Walking down the passage leading to the casino he saw it was packed with excited punters and very busy. About ten feet from the staff lounge he glanced up at the ventilating units and the small openings in the drapes then quickly checked to ensure that there was no one behind him. The punters all seemed glued to the games, cards on the table or the movement of the little white balls spinning at high speed around the fast moving roulette wheels. Stooping slightly he quickly disappeared behind the heavy drapes holding his breath hoping he hadn't been noticed. If someone had seen him he surely would be caught within minutes. Still nervous he became more confident as the noise of the casino became barely audible through the thick and bulky drapes. He checked his watch, 3:11 a.m. and felt relieved, no one had seen him. Now, if the others had concealed themselves, they'd be home free. Carefully he peaked through a small opening, but could only see the back's of the dealers and the edges of the blackjack tables. Even though the opening in the drapes was small he could feel the air conditioning fans from above blowing cold air past him. Bloody cold, he thought. My God, suppose I sneezed and someone heard me! What a cheerful thought.

From where Marc was standing he couldn't see if Paul and David had made it to their positions, but with no commotion from the floor assumed they had secreted themselves behind the drapes to his right. It was 3:50 when Marc looked at his watch and thought to himself, only a few minutes to zero. Standing immobile he had become quite cold in his confined isolation that reeked of cigarette and cigar smoke along with an accumulation of dirt and grime, but was able to smile knowing that his hiding place had been chosen well. It was evident that no one may have looked or been behind the heavy drapes in years. He tried to pass the time by listening to the conversations between punters, but the thickness of the drapes only allowed a muffled sound to filter through. When the noise began to die down Marc peaked through a small opening to see the punters getting up from the tables and moving like cattle in the direction of the exit.

His heart started to pound knowing it would soon be show-time.

He carefully reached for the duffel bag and removed the two canisters placing them upright on the floor. Slowly slipping the mask over his head he wiggled it about to ensure it made a good seal. Suppose he didn't have it on correctly and went to sleep, my God, what a terrible thought. He couldn't see, but heard the security guard slipping the heavy bolt across the door. Show-time! After checking his watch Marc laid the two canisters horizontally and opened the valves allowing the gas to flow into the casino through the opening below the bottom of the drapes. Quietly to himself he said, *Time to go to sleep; all of you please go to sleep.* Again peering through the small gap in the drapes he thought, *Good God, how slow time passes when you are waiting for something to happen.* He had been uncomfortable having to stand motionless in one position for an hour behind the filthy drapes, but then for a third of maybe £1,000,000.00, it was worth it. He must have been day dreaming for the next thing he knew, the drapes were pulled open and standing before him like a monster from space, was a figure frantically waving his arms emitting barely audible sounds from behind a mask.

"Marc, c'mon, let's get cracking."

Paul was inside the cashier's cage near the vault while Marc and David were busy cleaning the tables of the rows of cash, quickly placing them into the duffle bags. Bodies littered the room. Croupiers that had been preparing to cash in lay motionless between the roulette tables or were slumped over the stilled wheels. It had taken Paul only a few minutes to empty the vault and he was now helping in clearing the cash from the tables. Neat piles of carefully stacked bank notes filled the large duffel bags leaving only a space for the newspapers to cover their takings.

The casino was in shambles. Chairs and stools, had been overturned or pushed aside while unconscious bodies were strewn amongst opened cash boxes and the occasional £10 or £20 note inadvertently dropped in haste due to the restricted vision of the gas masks. Making his way to the exit door Marc glanced back to see Paul rushing back to the cashier's cage. Once outside the upstairs door they ripped the gas masks from their faces which gave a short pop of air like a punctured rubber tire. They then stuffed the masks in a waste bin near the door.

"What the hell did you go back for, Paul?" Marc asked in a demanding tone.

"I went back for two things a wrapped package of $20,000.00 in US dollars that I forgot and this bag of coins. I also put a pound in Cerdan's pocket." Cerdan, the abrasive casino manager had never been a favorite of the trio.

"He can use it for cab fare home." Paul said grinning from ear to ear.

The three, wearing overcoats which covered their green shirts, rapidly descended the stairs to the main lobby. Bill one of the guards at the downstairs entrance remarked,

"You three are the first out. Must have been a very good night, it's probably taking them a bit longer to count all that money." Bill then gave a deep laugh. The three smiled and looked at each other.

"Good-night Bill" said Marc with a brisk wave.

The trio moved slowly while Crossing Shaftesbury Avenue struggling with the heavy duffel bags stuffed with money. Once in the shadows of Brewer Street still dragging the bags they broke into a quickened run, upon reaching the car the duffel bags were thrown in the back seat.

"Okay, let's get out of here," said Marc gasping for air.

Moments later they passed Piccadilly Circus driving well within the speed limit. The city's lights reflected a buttery haze nestled over the metropolis that gave the appearance of a warm blanket which had been put in place by angels to keep the city warm at night.

The classic architecture of Westminster with the spires of the Houses of Parliament piercing the heavens elegantly silhouetted against the forthcoming dawn made this city unique in the entire world. Going through the railway arches in Vauxhall, they came upon a group of society's castoffs clustered together for collective warmth in the wintry early morning mist.

"Marc stop the car for a moment."

Paul then reaching into his duffel bag took out the bag containing the coins and threw it towards the collection of men and women huddled against the cold that had moved inquisitively closer to the stopped car.

"Happy Christmas, mates! Okay Marc, let's get going," shouted Paul. "Right on, Santa Claus any more stops you want to make?" chided David. There was momentary silence then they all laughed. Having made good time through the South London suburbs they soon reached the motorway to Kent.

The smoldering remains of the Mini Cooper lay partially wrapped around a telephone pole just off the motorway, the wreckage barely visible because of the thick morning fog. The three bodies inside the twisted mass of steel had been burned almost beyond recognition. Three large duffel bags that the fire brigade had removed from the car had been blackened and seared by the intense flames and heat, but the tightly packed bundles of bank notes inside remained intact. The police inspector shook his head then turning to the newspaper reporter while pointing towards the money filled duffel bags now in the boot of the police Jaguar,

"It appears they managed to get six gas canisters past security into the casino in these bags. After the gas took effect and put everyone to sleep they used the bags to take away what the Casino said was close to £1.5 million in stolen money. What happened next, we're not certain of, but it appears that they made a serious mistake. When the gas was released into the casino low levels were apparently absorbed by the material of the duffel bags and in their clothing. Seems like when they were outdoors the gas that had been absorbed by their clothing wasn't immediately evident, but on a cold foggy morning with the heater on and all the windows in the car closed, it must have taken about 30 minutes, but eventually, the three were put to sleep.

The car had been traveling at a pretty good clip when the driver lost consciousness and crashed killing all three."

19:01

The traffic was heavy as Jerry Rosen made his way along Ashford Avenue in San Juan's Condado section of Puerto Rico. Having lived in Buenos Aires Rosen was always annoyed and impatient with the inconsiderate Puerto Rican drivers who ignored red lights or squeezed their cars through any open space cutting in front of other drivers. The afternoon air of the Condado was balmy and filled with the fragrance of fresh flowers. The Christmas winds that develop to strong forces as they pass through the Caribbean between December and mid January had subsided which meant that Rosen could have a pleasant weekend on his 58' Bertram while reading the documents he was on his way to collect from his PLO contact.

A young Palestinian entered the Condado Plaza Hotel taking a seat near the escalators on the ground floor just as Rosen's Mercedes 450 SL approached the hotel's valet parking. As Rosen entered the hotel the Palestinian picked up the brown Samsonite briefcase beside him and went directly to the men's toilet at the eastern corner of the lobby. Before doing what men normally do when standing in front of a urinal the Palestinian placed his Samsonite briefcase on the floor between them. Finishing the task Rosen zippered up his trousers, stooped, picked up the briefcase and left. The Palestinian waited a moment zippered his trousers and left the restroom before disappearing into the boisterous crowd of New York tourists that now filled the lobby.

During the years since its creation the State of Israel had developed a strong and dominant military machine in addition to an influential and powerful central government presently under the leadership of the clever, dedicated and universally respected Golda Meir. The Minneapolis native had come to Israel at the suggestion and prodding of her friend and mentor David Ben-Gurion, a charismatic leader whose priorities were always focused on the needs of the Jewish people and the young State of Israel. Unbeknownst at the time the diminutive housewife from Minnesota was to impact her new country with positive, creative and imaginative thinking. Her constructive approach to governance would be remembered and reflected in the Israeli administration for decades to come. The Kremlin had a less than positive view. With its pro-western stance in the middle-east Moscow believed that the State of Israel was a serious threat to Soviet interests and influence, a threat that had to be eliminated. Because of their Jewish heritage, hard-line communist sympathies and thorough indoctrination the KGB considered Abraham and Vida Schlomo as perfect candidates to operate covertly as KGB moles under the cover and guise as immigrants to Israel.

The Schlomo home in Leningrad had first been bombed by the Germans, what remained was destroyed by the advancing allied troops. While being born into the faith and seemingly believed to be practicing Jews, Abe and Vida were also avowed communists. During their intensive KGB indoctrination sessions in Moscow they had met and befriended a young Palestinian. Abe and Vida soon found that their new Palestinian friend was not only cleaver, but had the ability and following to create havoc that could destroy the State of Israel and establish and promote Communist ideology throughout the Moslem world of the Middle East.

Yasir Arafat spent many hours with Abe and Vida discussing and promoting the cause of his Palestine Liberation Organization, a terrorist group which he ran from a base in Lebanon. The PLO had been founded in 1964 and was dominated by the anti-Israel guerilla organization al-Fatah, a group led by its chairman Yasir Arafat. Arafat's Intifada in Gaza and the West bank was focused on dissolving the state of Israel with the ultimate goal of establishing an independent Palestinian state.

Arafat frequently made reference to the unfortunate and premature demise of the Third Reich before it could achieve its goal of the Final Solution. The need to destroy the new State of Israel before it gained further territory or military advantage was always the primary topic of their conversations. Their friendship developed to such a degree that Arafat, as a result of his frequent visits to Moscow eventually moved in with the Schlomo family. Even though continually prodded by the KGB, it was not until after the birth of their first son, Abe Jr. and then Joseph, named after the Russian tyrant Stalin that Abe and Vida began to finalize the KGB's plan for them to leave mother Russia. Whether it was Beria of the KGB, Arafat or the Schlomo's who first conceived the strategy to infiltrate the Knesset is unknown. Funded by the KGB, Abe and his family would immigrate to Israel. Under the guise of a learned academic Abe would become a KGB mole with specific assignments of espionage for the PLO and their mentors in the Kremlin. Having gained the reputation as a respected professor of Political Science at the University of Moscow Abe became a recognized expert in Political Strategy for third world countries, at least from the Soviet perspective. Their travel documents were expediently sanctioned by the various government Ministries in the Kremlin and as returning Jews their immigration was promptly approved by the Israeli government. Within a week of receiving their travel documents the Schlomo's flew to Vienna where they boarded an EL AL flight to David Ben-Gurion Airport and their new home in Israel.

They were fortunate when upon their arrival in Tel Aviv the Schlomo's found that the Israeli government had provided the family with a comfortable flat in the northern suburbs, an area where Conrad Hilton would later build the tallest hotel in the city. Abe's first job was an appointment in the Ministry of Finance where he held a low level position dealing with farm policies. His assent to Assistant Secretary of Agricultural Trade was as a result of what was recognized as his brilliant negotiations involving a substantial export order of Israeli 'Jaffa' oranges to Russian fruit wholesalers. Abe's performance was applauded by his superiors who brought about his promotion which increased his access to the corridors of power.

While being attentive to his work Abe remained focused on his primary goal; influence and access to the inner circle of power within the Israeli government. As he had never actually been told exactly what the KGB or his PLO handlers had in mind he often wondered what his ultimate mission would be. The news came exactly one week after his son Joseph's birthday, a contact identified only as Benjamin, would be at a public telephone booth located near the Hertz Rental counter adjacent to the arrivals area at Ben-Gurion Airport.

Abe was told that Benjamin would be in the first telephone booth at exactly 1800 hours where he would remain until 1805 hours. He would be wearing a tan suit and would walk with a cane whose top would be adorned with the head of a duck. At the appointed hour his contact would leave a small white envelope in the telephone booth, the envelope would contain a coded cassette tape. If there were any problems or if it appeared that either party was being watched or followed Benjamin would keep the tape and Schlomo would be contacted again.

After collecting the envelope and listening to the message later that evening, Abe carefully noted the phrases recorded on the cassette which he later de-coded. The PLO plan was to kill Golda Meir. After memorizing the instructions the cassette was burned. On August 23rd, the Prime Minister would be opening the new Genetics Lab and Research Centre built near Iksal with funds provided by a group of British Zionists lead by Lord Marks of Marks and Spencer Fame. As a government official Abe was included as a guest at the opening festivities. The Prime Minister and her official party would be arriving at the function at 5:15 p.m. The reception was to be held in the facility's conference hall that had a large plate-glass window situated on its west side. The window overlooked an expansive low-lying landscape with small bushes and scrub, the surrounding area and entry to the Iksal complex was tightly monitored, secured and protected by the IDF. Abe was assigned the task of drawing the Prime Minister to the exposed window and keeping her there engaged in conversation between 5:45 and 6:00 p.m.

———

Lying in the prone position Mustapha Abu Sulah adjusted the sling and tri-pod of his Russian RPG-7 while squinting through its scope. Even though he was 400 metres away Sulah's camouflage made him virtually undetectable in the barren landscape surrounding the Research Centre. In spite of the distance the weapon's high powered optical scope gave him a clear view of the people standing next to the Centre's large window. Now positioned Sulah waited.

Having gained the reputation and status of being affectionate and caring Golda Meir was not just the Prime Minister of the Jewish State, but revered and respected as the young country's mother figure. She didn't hate Arabs but couldn't understand their reluctance to accept the fact that the Jews and the State of Israel were here to stay. Mrs. Meir was confident that Jews would someday overcome the oppression and prejudices they had endured for 2000 years and do so through education, devotion and strength. She once told the Catholic educated U.S. Ambassador that Christians were taught to turn the other cheek when confronted, Jews were taught to respond. When Jews get sick they relied on chicken soup, when they were attacked they relied on the Israeli Defense Force. Both made Jews feel better.

Having arrived a bit early on August 23rd Abe was looking about the room identifying and noting the various Ministers and members of the Knesset in attendance. Mrs. Meir was in a corner of the room speaking with Moshe Dayan the flamboyant IDF General idolized by all Israelis. Both were laughing with Dayan waving his arms as if to illustrate some military strategy that had provided yet another victory over the enemy who Dayan frequently described as mentally retarded camel traders. Schlomo positioned himself next to the Prime Minister and graciously thanked her for the complimentary letter she had sent to his superiors congratulating him on a recent project successfully completed in Aquaba.

It took only a moment for Abe Schlomo to convince the Prime Minister to join him at the refreshments table near the window for a glass of the punch that had been spiked with a generous portion of Sabra. Abe looked at his watch; the time was exactly 5:44 p.m. After accepting the glass of punch from Schlomo, the Prime Minister turned and began to walk away to rejoin the colorful General.

"No, please Mrs. Meir just a moment I would like you to stay, I have………"

Moments later the wall and roof of the building were blown away by the RPG that blew pieces of concrete, shards of glass and debris throughout the room. On his regular hourly patrols the IDF sentry had been through the area a number of times since reporting to duty at noon, but this time his attention had been attracted and drawn to a flash of what appeared to be a mirror. Through his 40mm image stabilizing binoculars Corporal Barzov saw the reflection was from the lens of the scope on Mustapha's RPG-7; Barzov's Uzi rang out its bullets ripping through Mustapha's body shredding it with the efficiency of a Shafra in the slaughtering of a lamb at Ramadan.

What Abe Schlomo hadn't known at the time was that if the rocket propelled grenade Mustapha fired in his last throes of life had hit its target instead of the roof above the window it would have killed him as well as Mrs. Meir. The subsequent investigation by the Mossad could not directly connect the PLO gunman with Abe Schlomo, but there were questions. In a review of the time line of the assassination attempt which placed the Prime Minister in the line of fire at the window, and Mrs. Meir's report of Schlomo's efforts to keep her there when the RPG was fired, provided enough circumstantial evidence for the Mossad to declare Schlomo as an enemy of the State of Israel. There was no publicity, no trial and therefore no appeal. The Schlomo family was to be deported.

They were told they could return to Russia or relocate to any other country that would approve their residency. While the Schlomo's preferred America or England, neither country would have them. Because of the Iksal incident the Israelis, through diplomatic channels, had branded the Schlomo's as terrorist sympathizers with connections to the PLO. Their options of relocation were limited. Their applications for residency in Canada, Uruguay, Peru, and Brazil were all denied. The Russians were silent. Well-placed PLO operatives in a number of countries exerted great efforts, but all had failed in their efforts in seeking residency status for the Schlomo Family.

As time was running out the Schlomo's found the only country that would accept and approve their application was Argentina. Not speaking the language made the first year in their adopted country difficult. The family was fluent in Russian, Hebrew and English, but soon mastered Spanish as a result of intensive language courses which they all attended. Abe was offered a number of menial jobs in Buenos Aires, but eventually accepted a position with RTV Argentina as a television proof reader.

While at RTV Abe met and became friendly with Max Blume the owner of TeleAd a large advertising group based in Buenos Aires. In addition to their presence in Argentina TeleAd had offices operating in a number of other South American countries. Impressed with Abe's creative talents and management skills while at RTV, Blume asked Abe to join TeleAd offering him the position as senior vice-president of marketing. While Abe and Vida slowly adjusted to their new home their two sons Abe Jr. and Joseph were quicker in adapting to the slower pace of the South American lifestyle. After gaining a fluency in Spanish Abe Jr. and Joe soon became acclimatized and adjusted to the Latin customs and the laid-back environment of their new home.

Abe Jr., the apple of his dad's eyes, after completing his studies at university was offered a position to join his father at the TeleAd advertising agency; while Joe seemingly happy, pursued his studies in law. Unbeknownst at the time Joe wasn't as happy as everyone had believed. Much like his parents he longed to participate and support the PLO or other terrorist and communist sponsored activities that were on the increase throughout the world.

When Joe announced to his parents that he was planning to immigrate to South Africa and work with PLO supporters such as Oliver Tambo and Nelson Mandela of the ANC his parents first objected, but subsequently wished him well. Recognizing his talents of subversion Joe Schlomo was later to become one of the leaders of the African National Congress. Following his arrest and release from detention he was expelled from South Africa, but continued his ANC activities from Lusaka in Zambia.

TeleAd grew and prospered. Laundered funds provided by Hezbollah operatives in Cuidad del Este, Paraguay channeled through a Lebanese bank in London allowed Abe Sr. to purchase TeleAd. As the major shareholder with control of the board of directors he elevated himself to Chairman while Abe Jr. was appointed Managing Director. A short time after taking control of TeleAd Abe and his wife Vida were killed in a mysterious automobile accident while returning from a holiday in Mar de Plata, a seaside town South of Buenos Aires. While he couldn't prove it, Joe Schlomo always believed the death of his parents had not been an accident, but an assassination carried out by the Mossad.

Pedro Hestres, a PLO asset based in Buenos Aires had carried out various assignments for the Abu Nidal Faction of the PLO and had been instrumental in the Schlomo's move to Argentina. A short time after the death of his parents Pedro Hestres contacted Abe Jr. and said it was important they meet right away telling him to be at the Cafe de la Paz at 5:00 p.m. After greetings were exchanged Hestres got right to the point,

"Abe its common knowledge in Jerusalem that Moshe Dayan and Golda Meir often joked about the failed assassination attempt by claiming that each had been the chosen target. You may not be aware and even though it's been a number of years the Mossad has always considered the Schlomo family to be dangerous, wherever they where. There's no question that the Mossad would eventually eliminate your parents. The PLO has learned that the mysterious automobile accident that killed your parents was not an accident; their death was simply the final chapter of a Mossad mission. I've received other information from a contact in Nablus that you and your family are in danger. From what we've learned the Israeli's are planning to hit you next."

"Pedro, this seems a bit bizarre." Rubbing his temples Abe Jr. asked. "Why would the Mossad want to kill us?"

"Fact is we really don't know. Chairman Arafat believes it may be a grudge. Could be that someone in the Mossad was disciplined after the Iksal incident and gets upset knowing that there's still members of the Schlomo family that are still living."

"What are we to do? I think I can take care of myself, but my concern is for my wife and sons."

"We're going to change your identity and you're going to leave Argentina. After a short holiday in Miami you'll be moving to Puerto Rico."

"Puerto Rico?" With a perplexed look on his face Abe Jr. asked,

"Why there? I'm not sure what my wife and kids will have to say about moving. With all their friends, schools, I don't know......"
"Abe there's really no other option. You move to Puerto Rico or stay here and all of you will probably be dead within a year. The Commonwealth of Puerto Rico is an island and as a U.S. territory most of the Puerto Ricans speak Spanish and English. You all speak English and are fluent in Spanish so you'll easily fit into the Anglo-Hispanic culture of the island. You and Carmen will become Jerry and Connie Rosen. The boys will be Benjamin and Andrew. We've arranged to get you American passports which show that all of you were born in New York, but have been living in Argentina for the last number of years. You will also be provided with birth certificates, Social Security cards and Puerto Rican driver's licenses with your new identities and the address of your new home in San Juan. Oh and here are the keys to your new home. It's fully furnished; the only thing needed is food. I'm sure you'll like it. You shouldn't have any problems as you'll easily blend into the mixed population of what's called The Enchanted Island."
Still in a bit of a daze,
"Okay Pedro, I'll break the news to Carmen. How long do we have before we have to make the move?"
"Considering the imminent danger you should start making arrangements right away."
To sell their two cars and the condominium Abe placed ads in the English newspaper the Buenos Aires Times and the Spanish paper La Nación. The advertising agency was sold to a management consortium made up of TeleAd employees. While TeleAd had been easy to sell what had not been easy was getting paid for it in American dollars. After disposing of their worldly possessions Abe made arrangements with the new owner to stay in their condominium until the day they were to leave.
Abe and Carmen's most difficult part of the move was explaining to the boys why they all had new names; Abe and Carmen overcame the questioning explaining that this was something that adults did when they moved to a new country. The explanation was apparently accepted as Benny and Andy never again brought up the subject. After an 8 hour flight they arrived in Miami on a

warm sunny day in September. With American passports they cleared immigration and customs without being challenged. After a 10 minute ride on the hotel shuttle the Rosen family checked into the Marriott airport hotel. At the Marriott the boys, Benny and Andy apparently unfazed by the long flight asked,

"Can we see Mickey Mouse?"

"Sure, why not. But Mickey lives in Orlando so tomorrow we'll rent a car and drive up to meet Mickey and his friends who live at Disney World."

When renting a car at Hertz the new Mr. Rosen had to pay over $700.00 in cash as a deposit before he was allowed to take the car. He made a mental note that the first thing he had to do in Puerto Rico was open a bank account to get a credit card. Jerry and Connie had a pleasant weekend with Benny and Andy who thoroughly enjoyed their visit to meet Mickey and his friends. They drove back to Miami with intermittent stops at various fast food establishments before reaching the Marriott in an exhausted state. The following afternoon they boarded an American Airlines flight that put them in San Juan 2 hours later.

The address shown on their Puerto Rican driver's licenses hadn't meant much to the Rosen's until after arriving in San Juan they told the taxi driver where they wanted to go. Thanks to Pedro the Rosen's found that their new home was a luxurious four bedroom penthouse on Calle Marseilles overlooking the Laguna Del Condado. Jerry, Connie and their two children became regular members of the Synagogue in Santurce and soon became pillars of the Jewish Community.

After the family had settled in Jerry began compiling a list of names, addresses and companies while gathering other pertinent details of Zionist sympathizers that were then sent to the leader of the Abu Nidal Cell in Queens, New York. He was a bit disappointed when he found that high profile targets in Puerto Rico were limited, while New York offered endless opportunities for harassment of the Jews and other Zionist sympathizers.

Enjoying a good life Jerry and Connie Rosen soon gained recognition from their peers in San Juan as the ideal Jewish couple. They had a beautiful home in a desirable section of San Juan and for the weekends, Jerry purchased a 58' Bertram sport-fisherman which he appropriately re-named *Shalom*. He kept the yacht at the Villa Marina Yacht Harbour in Fajardo a convenient drive some 40 miles east of San Juan.

On one of the family's visits to Samana, a small fishing village located on the eastern tip of the Dominican Republic, Jerry hid Paco, a young Dominican on board the *Shalom* and brought him back to Puerto Rico to work as a deck hand on the boat. Within a short time the Dominican had become a virtual slave. Paco had made numerous attempts to illegally enter the U.S., but each time after successfully crossing the Mona Passage the boat he was on had been intercepted by the Border Patrol or the Coast Guard before reaching the coast of Puerto Rico. He was arrested and spent the night in a jail in Mayaguez before being sent back to Santo Domingo.

With no formal education Paco probably would be considered stupid by any standard, smelled like an un-flushed toilet and had to be told twice before he'd understand even the simplest of instructions. However, he was happy to work for Rosen for a bunk in the crew quarters, a diet of rice and beans, and $25.00 a week for which he always kept the boat spotless.

It was only a few days after an Abu Nidal agent assassinated Meir Kahane in New York that Rosen received a telephone call from New York, asking if he knew of a doctor in San Juan by the name of Paul Shelton.

"My wife and I both know Paul and Lyn because we're members of the same synagogue in Santurce. They've been to our home and spent a number of weekends as guests on our boat. Interestingly, Paul liked our boat so much I think it may have been the reason that he eventually bought his own motor yacht."

The caller, a PLO operative then said,

"You will receive your instructions by courier. The courier will be in the lobby of the Condado Plaza Hotel on Ashford Avenue at precisely 4:30 pm tomorrow; he can be identified as he will carry a copy of the Financial Times of London under his left arm. The paper will be different from other newspapers because it's printed on pinkish paper. The courier will be carrying a tan Samsonite briefcase. Once you make eye contact you will say nothing and walk slowly to the men's rest room on the eastern side of the lobby. The transfer of the briefcase will take place while you are both standing at the urinals. The courier will set his briefcase on the floor between you, when he leaves you will pick up the briefcase and leave the restroom. When you get home you will de-code the documents. Please continue to check your phones daily to insure they're clean and sweep your home for bugs. The details of your rendezvous in Sint Maarten and the collection of the explosives will be explained in documents. If there are any changes or developments I will contact you within 48 hours. Please do not attempt to make contact with the numbers that you have in New York as we aren't certain whether the phones may have been compromised."

That evening Jerry began reading the papers in the briefcase.

Paul Shelton: born New York 1942, parent's Irving & Golda, a lay Rabbi, both prominent leaders of the Jewish community in the Eastern United States. Married: wife Lyn age 36, two children, one girl, Alexis age 14 and one boy, Michael age 11, members of Beth Israel temple in San Juan.

Even though Jerry believed he knew more about Paul and Lyn than anyone else inside or outside of the Abu Nidal faction or the PLO he continued to read the de-coded message.

Assignment 19:01 was displayed in bold type and contained explicit details of the Shelton's and their event scheduled for January 19th when Paul and Lyn would host a Bat Mitzvah for their daughter Alexis at the El San Juan Hotel.

Paul Shelton was widely known both in the United States and Israel because of his efforts in organizing the sale of over 16 million dollars of Israeli State bonds in the United States. He was a personal friend of every Prime Minister from David Ben-Gurion who he'd met as a child, to Yitzhak Shamir. Paul Shelton, a Jewish-American doctor born in trendy Westchester had moved to Puerto Rico after completing his studies in New York. Shelton had met the striking Ms. Lyn Chevon, who at the time was living in New York and struggling to further her career as a model. Assisted in part from a small inheritance received on the death of his parents Paul and Lyn had become a perfect example of cosmopolitan elegance and charm.

Paul's practice grew while Lyn set aside her modeling aspirations to raise their children and assist in running the business side of his medical practice. While being a practicing physician Paul's real flair was in his business dealings. His father, though not overly successful in his commercial dealings, had provided Paul with a sound business sense and the ability to recognize a *deal*. Having gained a respectable standing in business circles and widening contacts within the Jewish community propositions flowed to his offices in San Juan on a regular basis. The flamboyant doctor and his striking Mrs. had developed a flair for *doing deals* and were fluent in Spanish, French and Dutch. Their linguistic skills also included flawless Oxford English intentionally acquired during annual stays at their Tudor Mansion located in the Sussex Downs south of London.

Jerry's mind wandered as he thought of the numerous television stations, ad agencies and commuter airlines that were included in Shelton's holdings. Shelton was handsome, had a good-looking wife and two good looking bright children. He also had the panache for making vast sums of money that flowed like a fast moving river into his coffers. Unfortunately he was a Jew and worse yet a Zionist whose money allowed the Israeli government to steal Palestinian territory while financing the IDF who killed those who dared to protest against what many deemed as the illegal Israeli occupation of their land.

Assignment 19:01 could prove to be the highlight of Jerry's activities with the PLO. If he could pull it off he'd be responsible for delivering a tremendous psychological blow to the Zionists and Israeli sympathizers throughout the United States. It would be a public relations coup for the PLO while he would walk away unscathed to continue his life of deception with no one knowing who was responsible.

Other than Paco getting seasick Rosen's trip from Fajardo to Sint Maarten in the Dutch West Indies was uneventful. The *Shalom* ran beautifully moving effortlessly through the 4' to 6' seas of the Anegada Passage between the British Virgin Islands to the draw bridge that when opened, allowed entry to the Simpson Bay Lagoon on the island of Sint Maarten.

Shortly after entering Simpson Bay and dropping anchor near Snoopy Island a man in a Boston Whaler approached the Bertram and called out Jerry's name. Over the transom a small package was handed over which Jerry carefully placed in a larger box that had been lined with bubble-wrap packing material. Jerry later learned that the small cylinders secured inside the package contained enough plastic explosives to blow up not only the ballroom of the El San Juan Hotel, but probably the entire west wing and the first four floors of the building.

After a pleasant weekend sampling the finer restaurants of Marigot on Sint Maarten's French side, early on Monday morning Jerry edged the *Shalom* through the entrance that leads from the lagoon to the open sea. After clearing the small harbor near the Pelican Bay Beach Club, Jerry set a direct course due west towards Fajardo. With the explosives on board he was pleased the seas were relatively calm and down hill with the wind and wave action gently pushing the Bertram westerly on its 270° course towards Puerto Rico.

After parking his car Jerry made his way into the lobby of the El San Juan passing the potted plants and the dark polished mahogany that adorned its interior. Passing the reception desk he turned to the right and then left. After passing the restrooms he approached the wide staircase leading to the ballroom. As he entered through the large ornate doors a cleaning lady was coming out. They exchanged smiles and a cordial, *gracias, de nada* while Jerry held the door as she departed. The entrance foyer had two levels. To the left twelve steps down lead to the lower gallery where three sets of double doors provided access to the main ballroom. Bearing to the right at the end of the lower gallery another set of double doors lead to a large room adjacent to the main ballroom. Before leaving Jerry carefully penned a sketch of the area while making a note of the various access and emergency doors.

Later at home while studying the penciled sketches and notes he had made of the ballroom and adjacent rooms, Jerry determined that the table for the gifts would most likely be placed at the point of entry to the ballroom where the guests would be greeted by Alexis and her parents, Paul and Lyn Shelton. Following tradition a large photograph of their daughter would be placed near the gift table next to a book for the guests to sign.

No doubt to avoid the embarrassment of forgetting someone Jerry learned through a contact at the Synagogue that Lyn had been carefully preparing the guest list for months. In early June Paul made arrangements for a private visit by Moshe Arens, the Israeli Defense Minister to attend the Bat Mitzvah which would coincide with his planned visit to Washington and a scheduled meeting with the U.S. Secretary of State. Accompanying Mr. Arens would be two members of the Knesset and Harold Saks. Saks, the British Member of Parliament from Chelsea had recently been successful in pushing a bill through the House of Commons providing a direct grant to Israel of £12 million pounds to acquire a new British designed missile system. Lyn's guest list included the Magnin's of San Francisco, six pro Israeli Senators, four Jewish Congressmen and prominent Jewish leaders from a number of major cities in the United States. The list of those attending the Bat Mitzvah was virtually a Who's Who of Judaism. The list also included Paul's old friend Elizabeth Taylor, Mr. and Mrs. Jerry Rosen, and Mike Kelly, a marine surveyor and his son Joshua.

Carefully removing the cylinder containing the plastic explosives Jerry gently wrapped them in a Harrods gift box that was roughly the size of a shoe box. He connected the wires from the timing device to the detonation caps and covered the top with cotton wool. He neatly wrapped the present in the distinctive Harrods green paper, but without a card identifying the giver. He laughed to himself as he thought of his sweet revenge, a little pay back for what the Israelis had done to his parents. He only wished that Golda Meir hadn't died so she could be told of the murder of at least 200 influential Jews. He grinned and laughed aloud when he also thought of the personal revenge in killing Kelly, that bastard marine surveyor. Although a Catholic, Mike Kelly had become a close friend of the Shelton's and was also a Zionist sympathizer.

Mike, who would be at the Bat Mitzvah with his son Joshua, had caused Rosen endless problems when he wouldn't go along with his request to add a few thousand dollars to his recent insurance claim. Kelly reported the attempted fraud to the underwriter who promptly denied the claim and cancelled his insurance policy. Rosen simply wanted to upgrade the Bertram after it had been only slightly damaged in last year's hurricane, but Kelly wouldn't go along. January 20th would be get-even-time.

––––––

As the Rosen's approached the entrance to the ballroom they were almost blinded by the lights of the film crew that Paul had engaged to record the historic event. Many guests were now milling about in both the upper and lower galleries. Carefully placing the *present* on the gift table near the door Jerry and Connie congratulated Alexis and her proud parents and asked if the Arens party had arrived.

"Alexis I hope you like the present, I'm sure you'll really get a bang out of it," he said smiling while turning to kiss Lyn on the cheek.

Lyn smiled, "Thanks Jerry, we're pleased you're here. I know you'll enjoy meeting the guests and the other important people we've invited. You're a bit early, but we expect the Arens party and the other guests will arrive about 6:30 p.m."

Thank God of that thought Jerry as the timing device was set to detonate at exactly 19:01. The gallery will be filled with people and we'll be conveniently on the other side of the hotel at the far end of the casino. Unbeknownst to Rosen, ten of the guests, four in tuxedos and six in evening gowns were agents of the Mossad. At precisely 18:35 Moshe Arens, Minister of Defense for the State of Israel entered the ballroom of the El San Juan accompanied by a further five Mossad agents who were his security detail. The group included Dominique Levi and Ari Barzion the agent in charge of security when cabinet level Ministers traveled abroad.

"Mazel Tov my dear Doctor. Paul it's great to see you. *Simchas* are always so wonderful with friends," said a beaming Arens.

"Elizabeth Taylor, Elizabeth Taylor, like where is the lady?

Paul, you I like, Elizabeth Taylor I love?"

"Sorry Moshe she's running a bit late. Her plane was delayed leaving Kennedy so it had a late arrival in San Juan. She's staying in the hotel and will be down shortly."

The room was alive with the laughter of happy people mingled with the voices of the troupe of Broadway dancers singing to the sound tracks of current hits as the champagne flowed.

At 37 Dominique Levi was strikingly beautiful. Through her training she had become a clever and skillful agent of the Mossad which came about in part, through her father who had been the naval attaché at the Israeli Embassy in Rome. During his posting at the embassy he had met Dom's mother who was visiting Rome with her father, a Rabbi who provided spiritual guidance to a large Jewish congregation in Genoa. Following her mandatory service with the Israeli Defense Force Dominique Levi had been hand picked for special training with the Mossad.

Dom, as she was known to her colleagues, was a tall, elegant and gracious woman who on the firing range could hit 9 out of 10 targets with either an Uzi or a P38. She had also qualified as a black belt instructor of Judo. In addition to being attractive she had gained a reputation of being perceptive and smart as a result of her earlier success with Israel's subversive Mirage Mission in Switzerland and collaboration with Daniel Kalen. Working with the agents of the Knesset's Security Group she developed a keen sense of humor as a result of the prodding of whether she had attained her nickname from her given name or from the Dom Perignon champagne she so adored.

As the Arens party slowly worked the crowd greeting friends old and new, Dom tilted her head slightly to the side beckoning Ari Barzion's attention. The two then moved to the lower gallery standing alongside a large serving table that had a center piece sculptured in ice that bore a striking resemblance to a circumcised penis. The table displayed an array of delectable foods along with an exquisite platter of peppered smoked salmon positioned next to a chilled silver urn of the finest caviar.

"You know its times like this when it's truly nice to be Jewish," Barzion said turning his head and smiling at his beautiful colleague.

As part of the security team it was Dom Levi's task to make certain the facilities of the hotel were secure and safe. Amongst other responsibilities this included checking all access points, the hotel staff, invited guests, and so on. At first glance the name Rosen hadn't meant anything to Dom, but when Jerry and Connie entered the ballroom she frowned, thinking that their faces looked familiar.

After a quick scan on her pocket data terminal Dom found photos and the profile of the Schlomo's now surfacing as Jerry and Connie Rosen. The pair, PLO sympathizers were last known to be living in Buenos Aires, their present location was unknown. Dom's attention was further aroused when she saw Rosen instead of personally handing the present to Alexis, which is traditional at such ceremonies, gently set the Harrods's box on the gift table like it contained loose eggs. The Rosen's having been identified as the Schlomo's, at Dom's direction were now being kept under close surveillance by three Mossad agents.

After the Rosen's left the reception area Ari and Dom discreetly scanned all the gifts on the table with their Mark II scanners, finding them to be clean Dom then scanned the unmarked Harrods's box left by Rosen which gave an indication of explosive material. Not knowing the method or the precise time of detonation Dom and Ari knew that when the Rosen's left the festivities they would have little time to get the box and its explosive contents out of the building. Ari instructed two of his agents to carefully remove the Harrods's box and take it from the ballroom using the emergency exit leading to the beach. From their Mossad profile it was clear that the Rosen's weren't suicide bombers so as long as both he and his wife remained they were confident the explosives wouldn't detonate.

The IDF Mark II scanner is about the size of a pack of cigarettes and has a 2.2" screen with a gradient detection scale much like a thermometer. The scanner was able to determine the presence and level of explosive material such as C4 and with the exception of lead encapsulation, detection levels could be determined with up to one inch of shielding. The device had been used successfully by the Israelis for over a decade and had become an important instrument for covert bomb detection. Ari and Dom agreed that the Defense Minister and his party should be quickly but quietly ushered out of the ballroom before being advised of the situation.

At 18:55 Jerry and Connie left the ballroom walking down the steps and then turned towards the hotel's main lobby with the Mossad agents following close behind. When the Rosen's reached the main lobby they could either proceed straight to the casino or turn right towards the Hong Kong Village leading to the hotel's exit. Reaching the lobby the Mossad agents lunged forward grabbing Jerry's and Connie's arms while forcibly moving them towards the exit.

The Mossad agents who had removed the Schlomo's gift from the hotel were now standing on the beach. After yelled orders from Ari the explosive gift was thrown seaward into the surf as the agents dropped face down in the sand and covered their heads. The Mossad agents were uninjured in the explosion, but its force rattled the windows of the hotel and the adjacent apartment buildings. In spite of being curious why the Arens party had been strangely ushered out of the ballroom by their security people, then the explosion on the beach Paul and Lyn remained smiling as they graciously moved hand in hand through the ballroom.

"You know Lyn everything has been spectacular. This will be a night we will all remember forever, everything has just been wonderful." Standing behind Paul and Lyn, Ari and Dom looked at each other, smiled and toasted themselves, "Cheers," gently touching their glasses before finishing the last of their champagne.

———

A short time later two Puerto Rican police officers stood over the bodies of Jerry and Connie Rosen found lying face down in an alley adjacent to the hotel. Seeing the bullet holes that had entered through the back of their heads Lt. Rolando Silva moved the motionless bodies to reveal that the upper part of their foreheads had been blown away as the bullets exited their skulls. Sergeant Sanchez noted that the lady carried no hand bag; both the man and the woman had had their rings and watches removed, as evidenced by the suntan lines. With no handbag for the female and the male victim's wallet missing the bodies couldn't immediately be identified. Not knowing that silencers had been used Sanchez thought it was strange that no one had heard any shots being fired, but believed any gun fire may have been masked by the earlier explosion.

The Puerto Rican Police determined that this was clearly a case of a robbery committed on tourists, something which is quite common especially at night along the islands beaches. The police report would indicate a robbery-homicide.

Later that night Ari and Dom walked along the waterfront in Old San Juan. Approaching the cruise-ship dock they watched as the mooring lines were being cast off from the Cunard Countess. The duo then passed a homeless soul sleeping in the shadows; next to the motionless form they placed a zip-lock bag containing money and two gold Rolex watches, one for a man and one for a woman. As they approached the departing ship they paused momentarily before emptying the contents of a man's wallet and a woman's hand bag into the black waters of San Juan Bay.

Goodbye My Love

Sam was a tall, handsome and energetic man who even though 63 appeared 20 years younger. He was trim, athletic and an avid sailor. After completing his studies at Columbia and graduating cum laude, he went directly to the Navy rapidly rising to the rank of Commander. Shortly after attaining the rank of Captain he fortuitously met and married the daughter of his Commanding Officer at the Coronado Naval Base in San Diego, California. Ms. Beverly Adams was a beautiful bride who complimented the young Captain with her elegance and charm, refined sophistication and graciousness acquired during her attendance at finishing schools in Switzerland and at Roedean in England. As a result of Sam's successful naval career the two had traveled extensively while enjoying the luxury afforded to naval officers of command rank. As a result of prudent investments the years had been good to Sam and Bev. Their net worth had increased even more when she inherited a princely sum following the untimely death of her parents. The only thing missing were the children that Sam so badly wanted, but that Bev couldn't provide due to a botched abortion she had as a young teenager.

———

As the plane touched down at Tortola's Beef Island airport in the British Virgin Islands both Sam and Bev were captivated by the beauty of the crystal blue water and white sand beaches that fringe the small islands and cays of this tropical paradise. The taxi ride from the airport took Captain and Mrs. Brown over the Queen Elizabeth II Bridge past the Go Vacations Charter Base through the settlement of East End to the rolling hills overlooking Road Harbour and Road Town, the principal city of this British Caribbean dependency. As they walked down the dock at Village Cay towards the *Spirit*, they saw Marty Gold and Inga

Wolfson who would be their crew for the delivery of the *Spirit* back to her home port of Miami. Marty and Inga had known Sam and Bev for a number of years having been neighbors of the Browns while they were living in Falmouth, Massachusetts. After 20 years as an admiralty lawyer with Goldman and Thomas LLP in Boston Marty had retired. On his last trip to Europe he met Inga, a glamorous Danish flight attendant with the Scandinavian Airlines System. Soon after she was transferred to the SAS Base at JFK Inga moved in with Marty and regularly commuted between New York and Boston on her layovers.

"Hi Marty, hello Inga, been on board yet?"

"No Sam we just got here." replied Marty.

"We had to take the Bomba Charger from St. Thomas because we missed the last Air BVI flight to Beef."

Together the four walked down the dock to the 43 foot sailboat *Spirit* and went aboard as the sun began to set on this warm winter day in the Caribbean.

The wind was driving the heavy snow across the road as Sam drove the last mile into the suburbs of Boston. The offices of Fidelity Insurance were cold, but the glowing warmth of the receptionist brought a broad smile to Sam's face.

"May I help you Sir?"

"Yes please, I've got an appointment with Bob Delgado about some life insurance."

"Just a moment please," as the receptionist then dialed a number.

"Mr. Delgado, I have a gentleman here to see you, he said you're expecting him. May I have your name sir?" "Sam Brown."

"Of course, yes, Mr. Delgado. You may go in Mr. Brown."

The documents appeared to be seemingly endless, with form after form requiring completion and signature.

"Okay Mr. Brown that's one million each for the term life policies for you and Mrs. Brown. The medicals are fine; we'll mail you the policies the early part of next week."

"No need to mail them, I'll be in Boston next Thursday and I'll stop by and collect them." Sam hoped that the insurance agent hadn't noticed his anxiety. After gathering Bev's medical records he then worked to perfect her signature so that it wouldn't be questioned on the life insurance application. If the plan was to work Bev couldn't know that her husband had insured her life.

He also didn't want the policies mailed to his home in case Bev got to the mail before him. Even though the insurance broker's office was cold Sam was perspiring. Over the last number of months Sam had carefully planned the death of his wife and finally everything was falling into place. It was all coming together because of Sam's friend Rod Sheldon, a Podiatrist in Boston who owned a 43 foot ketch that was in charter service in the Virgin Islands. The previous summer Rod had invited Sam and Bev to Newport to sail with him on a boat he had chartered. During the Newport charter Rod had mentioned that he planned to hire a skipper to bring his boat, the *Spirit,* back to Miami the following season. Having been unhappy with the charter company and their seemingly endless bills for repairs he decided to pull the boat. Sam offered his services and jumped at the chance to act as the delivery skipper. The thought of an ocean voyage with a woman he had grown to hate would present the opportunity for the perfect crime.

Although childless the couple had been happy in the early days of their marriage. Sam however, had never forgiven Bev for not telling him she couldn't have children until a year after they were married. Both began to drink heavily and had engaged in numerous affairs between drinking binges that sometimes lasted days on end. Many times smelling of booze Sam had been cautioned by his navy superiors about reporting for duty while under the influence. Fortunately his wit and charm and his father-in-law being an admiral had always kept him clear of harms way or worse yet, a Court Martial.

At one point Sam thought seriously of divorcing Bev, but when her parents died leaving their only offspring an accumulated $9.8 million dollars he no longer thought of divorce, but rather how he could get rid of his wife and keep her inheritance. An inheritance he'd lose if he divorced her. His idea of an additional million dollar life policy would simply be the frosting on the cake. Sam's plan would be like any successful naval engagement; precise timing and sound logistical tactics with uncomplicated execution. He'd also ensure he had people as crew on board who knew them both and who could attest to Bev's accidental death. Marty and Inga were reasonably experienced sailors as well as being friends and would be perfect witnesses to Bev's unfortunate, but accidental death. For Bev's last few days on earth Sam would be remembered as a kind, gentle and loving husband for the world and his crew to see.

Sam smiled as he poured over the charts plotting the voyage from the Virgins north to Miami carefully analyzing each of the prospective ports of call. Thinking to himself, *First stop Mayaguana? Yes, that's good, small population and few other cruising boats to contend with. I'll say the stop was needed for emergency repairs. Let's see. Before we leave Village Cay I'll disconnect the navigation and the compass lights and add a little sand in the tank to clog the fuel line. I'll use the engine to leave the harbor then we'll be under sail until we reach Mayaguana. After starting the Spirit's Perkins diesel on the approach to Mayaguana it'll probably only run about 30 minutes before it dies. Hmmm, the radio and flares have got to go. Yes, that should do it.* As Sam's finger moved up the chart, he quietly called out the names of the various islands and cays all located due north of the Dominican Republic; let's see we'll pass midway between West Caicos and Little Inagua through the Seal Cays then set a course to Abraham's Bay on Mayaguana.

His mind was running like a computer, calculating distances, location of reefs and the chance of rescue if something went wrong. If he pressed on further north to Exuma there would be more boats and people and the possibility that if Bev didn't drown right away, she might be rescued by BASRA, the Bahamas Air Sea Rescue folks, who had a presence in the Exuma's. That leaves either Acklins Island or Diana Reef off Fortune Island south of Long Cay. The chart shows that the reef south west of Acklins has shallow water extending out about 3 miles and the island is sparsely populated. Sam decided that Acklins would be a perfect spot to scuttle the *Spirit* as Bahamas Air had flights in and out of Acklins on Wednesdays and Saturdays. With careful planning he could carry out the perfect crime, step ashore and be on his way home within 24 hours as a single man with a net worth of almost $11 million dollars.

———

"Sam this thing's a peace of junk." Marty said standing in the cockpit of the boat.

"Christ, look at the sails, they're stained and look like they're a 100 years old."

Marty was a weekend sailor on Long Island Sound and had a reasonably good knowledge of boats, but clearly wasn't impressed with the *Spirit*. The boat had foul odors coming up from the bilges and from the heads that appeared to have never been correctly flushed. Leaving the boat they decided to have dinner at Spaghetti Junction, a small popular bistro across from the marina. After a number of Margaritas, a bountiful meal and two bottles of superb Beaujolais they staggered back to their rooms at Village Cay. Sam had made an extra effort to get two of the 'B' rooms that face the town, instead of the 'A' rooms that overlook the marina.

After Bev had fallen into a drunken slumber and began her normal snoring, Sam slipped into his Bermuda shorts, made his way to the dock and boarded the *Spirit* which didn't look quite so bad in the dim lights of the dock. While gently tugging her frayed mooring lines the little ketch also appeared to be anxious in anticipation of fleeing the Virgins for the high seas.

On deck Sam unfurled the jib and pulled the main sail open looking closely at the clew, the head and other vital parts of the sails.

The running rigging looked tired, but Sam felt certain that it should hold up for her last voyage. The standing rigging and the swaged fitting holding the wire in place was rusted, but in not pushing her hard hoped it wouldn't prematurely fail. He quickly stowed the main and used the roller furling to return the jib. Down below he found the electrical wires to the navigation lights were badly corroded; a slight tug broke the connections. They would leave in daylight, but most of the passage to Mayaguana would be during the hours of darkness. He wouldn't need the compass light as his plan was to sail the *Spirit* to Acklins by celestial navigation, tugging on the compass light it pulled free.

The VHF radio didn't come to life when he turned it on because the fuse was blown. To be on the safe side he removed the coaxial antenna wire and just to be sure cut the end that made contact with the female receptacle. He found four ocean service life jackets stuffed under the forward v-berth that were wet from bilge water and mildewed from the lack of ventilation. Sam placed three of the life jackets back into their musty compartment and put one in the cockpit locker. He found three flares swollen from water beneath the galley sink and left them where he found them. As Sam strolled back to his room, he laughed as he read a "Trip Survey" that had been carried out for Rod by a local surveyor who described the *Spirit - in good condition fully sound and ready for sea.* This is really silly. Sam wondered if the surveyor had ever bothered to go on board the boat.

The next morning, Marty and Inga were in the restaurant having breakfast when Sam and Bev came down from their room. Small talk was exchanged and it was decided that Marty and Inga would pick up the last provisions at Bobby's Supermarket before they cleared customs and set sail. Sam was insistent that they depart Road Town at least by noon, not necessarily because he wanted to leave in daylight, but to prevent the crew from finding out they had no compass or navigation lights. The *Spirit* cast off her lines and set sail from Village Cay at 10:30. At 7:00 p.m. in the failing light Sam asked Inga to go below and turn on the navigation lights.

"Sam, is it the one that says "NAV?"

"Yes, please switch it on," responded Sam.

"Marty please help her out," Sam called out to his mate who had been napping on the foredeck. Going below Marty shouted,

"Sam the switch is on are the lights on?"

"No, Marty take a look to see if the fuse is blown."

"Nope, fuse is ok, I'll check the bulbs." Marty began looking for a flashlight and eventually found a plastic one that emitted about as much light as the glow of hot coals. After removing the cover and checking the compass light and navigation lights mounted on the bow, Marty called out,

"The bulbs are okay, but the wires are completely corroded and broken off."

"Marty not to worry, don't forget I taught celestial navigation at the academy, I'll steer by the stars tonight and we'll fix them in the morning. Sailing without the navigation lights won't be a problem we'll just keep an eye out for other vessels that might not see us."

Marty, Inga and Bev couldn't see the small smile that filled Sam's face. The sun slowly came up on the horizon as Sam rubbed the sleep from his eyes. The forward cabin was quiet with Marty and Inga fast asleep. During the night while Sam kept the *Spirit* on her northwesterly course he'd heard Inga moaning and groaning as Marty brought her to numerous peaks of orgasmic sensation. Both must have been exhausted by the time they finished and soon fell asleep in blissful exhaustion. Lucky bastard as Sam thought of his wife's idea of sex as something to be undertaken at regular intervals of maybe once a month.

Sam was again thinking about his new life as a wealthy widower, the first thing would be a visit to Jackie O's in Acapulco. He'd cozy up to the first senorita, take her back to the Hilton and screw her brains out until he was exhausted, and he wouldn't care if the senorita was a matron from Milwaukee or a young hooker from the Hyatt. The soothing gentle roll of the boat moving through the turquoise seas and gentle breeze brushing his face was mesmerizing; with his eyes closed he continued fantasizing of the future, his future. His thoughts were interrupted by Marty shouting through the open hatch,

"God damn it this stupid stove doesn't work."

"Did you pump it Marty? Alcohol stoves need to be pumped before they work," yelled Sam.

"Holy Christ we're on fire, we're on fire!" The fear penetrated the air.

"Sam come quickly the curtains are on fire."

On Sam's suggestion Marty had apparently pumped the stove, but had pumped it too much allowing alcohol to flood the surface around the burners; when he lit it the flames ignited the curtains.

"Where's the fire extinguisher?"

"I don't know, grab a bucket of water and throw it over the curtains," Sam said.

Letting go of the wheel the sails luffed and the *Spirit* stalled. Inga took the wheel while Sam and Marty dealt with the smoldering remains of the fire and its aftermath of charred cupboards and the burnt remnants of the Nylon curtains. It took a little more than an hour to clean up the mess in the galley and dry the stove before having coffee and a sparse breakfast of hard boiled eggs and soggy bread. As Sam came back up on deck he immediately sensed something was wrong.

"Damn it the sun's on the port side! Inga, what the hell have you done? You've turned us around and put us on a course back to the Virgin Islands!"

"Oh, sorry Sam, it's just with all the confusion..."

"Oh forget it," Sam said rolling his eyes looking to the clouds. After getting the *Spirit* back on course it was mid morning as they rounded the headland entering the open bay that Mayaguana called its harbor. Sam pressed the start button to fire up the Perkins diesel, but the only response was a subdued click.

"Marty it looks like we've got dead batteries to boot. I'll bring her around and when she's pointing into the wind, drop the hook."

After making a wide swing about a half mile from the shore with the boat pointing into the wind he heard the clang and rattle of the anchor chain feeding out over the bow roller. After the anchor was set, Sam furled the jib and stowed the main, leaving the mizzen in place to stabilize the boat while she swung in the offshore breezes. As Bev had been unusually quiet the last 24 hours, Sam guessed she probably had her nose stuck in a book. He thought of the many times they had gone to bed and he had exerted considerable effort trying to arouse his wife only to be told that she wanted to read. While privately infuriating, Sam always managed a subdued chuckle at the sarcastic remarks at the officers club about his 100 lb. 5'2" wife who was endowed with a bosom that if activated might easily feed the 6th fleet. Following many years of infrequent and pointless penetration of her innermost parts and sterile fondling of her breasts Sam simply had lost interest.

With the lowering of the sails Bev climbed the companionway steps from the aft cabin asking,

"Are we there yet?"

Turning, Sam said, "We're at Mayaguana in the lower Bahamas we'll stop here to fix the navigation lights and get the batteries charged."

The anchorage was deserted with only a few small buildings visible on the distant shoreline. Marty struggled to put the heavy batteries in the badly leaking Avon inflatable then began rowing to shore in hopes of finding someone to charge the two 6D batteries. After Marty left Sam gave a credible theatrical performance of trying to fix the navigation lights. Inga and Bev who had known each other more as acquaintances rather than close friends hadn't said much to one another since leaving Road Town. Once the boat stopped moving and was swinging on the hook the two didn't stop talking, much like two hens cackling away on the foredeck. In true Danish fashion Inga had stripped off her clothes and was sitting cross legged with her back leaning against the mast. The 55 year old Bev believing that nudity had no place in modern society had obviously been influenced by her younger friend and with the desolation of Mayaguana was now laying flat on her back covered only by a thin layer of tanning cream.

Sam surreptitiously occupied himself below deck, not repairing things, but just giving the appearance of being busy. Rummaging through the forward cabin Sam found his crew's toiletries and clothing neatly folded along with an expensive Nikon camera. Inga's cosmetic bag in addition to her make-up contained a very large vibrator with two sets of extra batteries. Sam laughed and thought to himself, I guess the vibrator was insurance in case Marty couldn't perform - Inga would get herself off.

As Sam continued his sweep through the *Spirit* he found the forward seacock was leaking. The bilges around the mast step had an accumulation of water that was almost a foot deep. The boat had two bilge pumps, but with a limited capacity of only 750 gallons per hour may have been better suited for a fish tank. The forward pump didn't work, but after reconnecting its broken ground wire it started pumping. Sam wanted to lose the boat and kill his wife, but on his schedule. The last thing he wanted was a premature flooding that he couldn't control. Even though Sam had put sawdust in the fuel tank to stop the engine it was apparent that it wasn't necessary because the ships batteries wouldn't hold enough power to start the engine even if the fuel hadn't been contaminated by sand. About four hours later having been unable to find someone to charge the batteries Marty returned to the boat.

It was just after midday when they decided to have lunch. The preparation of lunch proved to be an interesting experience when it was found that the refrigeration on the boat wasn't working and the food in the fridge while not totally bad was warm. The boat's cold-plate refrigeration system was powered by the batteries which were only charged when the engine was running. As they had been under sail and hadn't used the engine it allowed the refrigeration system to drain whatever power was left in the batteries. The fresh milk had to be thrown away leaving the four to devour what was left of the salami and cheese before it went bad; the chicken and ham they had planned to cook during the voyage was fed to the fish. Sam assured his crew that the remaining canned foods, bread, dried fruits and oatmeal would sustain them until they reached the lower Bahamas where they would restock with enough provisions to reach Miami. Over their meager lunch Marty insisted that they discuss the remainder of the voyage.

"Sam I know you're an expert in navigation, but these waters are extremely dangerous night or day. The local fellow who tried to help me find someone to charge the batteries said we should stay the night here and leave in the morning. He said to try and pass Acklins Island at night would be very dangerous, because of the strong current many boats end up on the reef. The local fellow suggested that we leave at first light and take an offshore course directly to the island of San Salvador." Marty had a grim look on his face.

Sam smiled. "Marty, I've taken destroyers with a 30' draft through the Marianas and most of the South Pacific. I'm sure I can take a 43' sailboat with a 5' draft through a five mile channel in the Bahamas, trust me."

"But Sam, we have no engine, no batteries, no compass or navigation lights, and we're in a boat that's rapidly falling apart." Marty appeared distraught.

"Marty I want to be home by New Years. If we go on the outside we'll lose two days in this hulk."

Sam was adamant; no one was going to change his very carefully laid plans. About 4:00 p.m. Marty and Inga struggled with the anchor and after bringing it up, lashed it on the foredeck. Bev was reading in the cockpit, after the anchor was stowed and the sails filled she went below to continue reading in the aft cabin. As the *Spirit* left the protected lee of the island and picked up the wind she heeled 15° to port and on a broad reach began to pound in the increasing swells. Two frigate birds played tag with the wind tell-tales on the shrouds while a group of dolphins leaped and frolicked back and forth in front of the bow. Marty offered to take the helm and steer the first watch and Sam agreed.

Sam didn't mind Marty doing the watch during the afternoon and early evening hours, but after sunset he would take the helm. It was important that Sam maintain the course to Acklins so the *Spirit* would hit the reef at the precise time and at exactly the right place. In spite of the large swells and the set and drift of the current Marty did an admirable job of steering keeping the *Spirit* on course. The sky was clear and even though he'd brought his sextant Sam kept his eyes to the sky monitoring their position while telling Marty every now and then to make minor course corrections to port or starboard. After the sun had set Sam relieved Marty and took over the helm. Marty, pleased to be relieved immediately went below to resume playing games with Inga who he frequently referred to as his *Danish Delight*. Looking at his watch the glow of the luminescent face told him that within 4 hours he would be abeam of Acklins reef where a 90° swing to port would bring about the end of the *Spirit* and make him a wealthy widower.

———

The first indication of shallow water was the loud scrapping of the keel as the *Spirit* slid over the first coral head. In hitting the reef the ability to steer was immediately lost. With both hands Sam held tightly to the steering pedestal as the bow dipped and another wave crashed over the bow quickly flooding the forward cabin through its open hatch. The bow of the *Spirit* rose and again plummeted into the darkness while making a violent roll to starboard as it impacted another coral head only inches below the surface. The brutal pounding and impact with the coral head destroyed the rudder. As the rudder was torn off a large portion of the hull and transom was sheared away leaving a gapping hole in the stern. The flow of water entering through the shredded fiberglass opening quickly flooded the aft cabin.

The *Spirit*, now loosely wedged between two coral heads in the blackness of the night was being beaten to death by the raging seas. The sails, once taut were flapping and flailing wildly against the rigging and emitting a continuous high pitch whine as a result of the relentless winds. Emerging from the forward cabin Sam could hear Marty and Inga as they began making their way through the waist deep water and debris floating in the main saloon. Grasping his shoulder which had either been broken or dislocated when he was thrown from his bunk, Marty was clearly in pain while Inga appeared to be unhurt. Sam couldn't actually see them, but could hear them shouting while struggling and making their way towards the cockpit. As the *Spirit* violently rolled and heeled to port Marty yelled in pain as he fell into the cockpit and was thrown against the steering pedestal. The port rail was now awash allowing water to fill the cockpit. Playing the role of a true thespian Sam shouted toward the direction of the aft cabin, "Bev, Bev, are you okay?"

"Sam I've hurt my back. Help me, please help me."

Carefully making his way down the companionway Sam found Bev huddled in the corner of the partially flooded cabin next to the aft head. She screamed as he grabbed her arm trying to pull her diminutive body towards him. Over the noise and chaos Sam shouted, "Bev we're sinking you've got to get up to the cockpit. Hang on to me!"

Sam's mind was racing, just his luck, the stupid bitch would stay down here, end up injured, but not dead and I'll be stuck with her forever in some nursing home. Sam forcefully dragged his wife into the cockpit while the *Spirit* continued to be pounded and battered by the angry seas. Sam couldn't see a thing, but outboard of the wheel was able to grab the lifeline attached to the starboard entry gate which was still above water. Grasping tightly Bev's nails dug into her husband's arm puncturing the skin. The water was cold and the wind chilled it even further.

The salt was burning Sam's eyes and his muscles ached with the strain. Bev was tiring as Sam felt her grip loosen. Sam moved his hand along the starboard gate until he found the gooseneck fitting that connected the lifeline to the gate. Knowing that a sudden jerk would release the lifeline across the gate he slipped off the safety latch of the gooseneck leaving the lifeline connected. With the safety latch removed Sam then positioned Bev so her back was leaning against the lifeline across the gate. Sam grabbed her right hand and told her to hold tightly to the stanchion next to the gate. Bev was shivering violently and her hand was icy cold, she was in an advanced stage of hypothermia. Sam shouted into the darkness,

"Marty have you got the life jackets? Quickly get me one for Bev!"

Marty, never having looked or been asked about them didn't know where the life jackets were. Sam put on the life jacket he had left in the cockpit before leaving Tortola. With the interior now flooded it would be impossible to get to the three life jackets under the forward v-berth. Marty was shouting something, but Sam couldn't understand what he was saying. A few minutes passed and Bev's body became limp in Sam's arms. Another large wave slammed against the *Spirit* violently rolling her from a port list that totally submerged the starboard rail. Sam released his hold on Bev and with a slight nudge pressed her body against the gated lifeline. The gooseneck opened releasing the lifeline.

As Bev's body disappeared into the raging sea Sam gently whispered, "Goodbye my love."

Then waiting an appropriate moment Sam yelled,

"My God, Bev's been thrown over board!"

For the desired effect he repeated his distressful call a couple of times, just to make certain the message was heard by Marty and Inga.

"I'm going in after her!" shouted Sam in the most convincing voice possible.

"Don't be a fool you'll get killed, stay with the boat and once its light we can see where we are and then look for Bev,"

Marty responded yelling like a madman with fear in his voice. Sam smiled and to himself said, *sounds good to me!*

Sam smiled again as he thought about where they were - 22° 38' 45.24" N – 76° 51' 28.66" W and the carefully planned disposal of his wife on the reef of Acklins Island just south of the Devil's Backbone near what's called the Settlement. From the local airport Bahamas Air provides service twice a week to Nassau on Wednesdays and Saturdays. It's now about 0300 hours on Wednesday morning, sunrise at 0617. Hmm, maybe an hour to the beach, a good breakfast, fill out the police report and yes, I should be able to catch today's flight at 2:15 p.m. They were all cold from being soaked while hanging on to the steering pedestal in the strong winds and battering seas that had pounded the *Spirit*. The keel had been torn off and the lower section of the hull lost to the ravages of the coral heads. The masts and sails were still up but only the deck and top sides of the hull resembled a boat.

The large swells had pushed the remnants of the hull over the outer reef and she was now just inside the reef. What remained of the *Spirit* was now tightly wedged between two coral heads. The sea around them was littered with coral heads in depths of 6' to 10' below the surface. Because of the pain from his injured shoulder Marty was almost helpless so Sam and Inga unlashed the Avon inflatable and pushed it over the side; the partially inflated Avon bounced and thrashed about in the boiling seas. Inga, Marty and Sam slid into the inflatable before pushing it away from the *Spirit* with the three occupants holding tightly to the Avon's safety line. As they drifted towards the beach the short choppy seas soon smoothed to a long rolling swell. In the pitch blackness time was incalculable, but eventually the partially inflated Avon reached the beach and slid to a stop. The three weary occupants struggled to their feet, walked to the edge of the green turtle grass, dropped to their knees and slowly rolled onto their backs.

Police Constable Jeremy Romney had been on his regular early morning patrol along the Southern coast of Acklins when he saw a yacht whose sails were flapping in the wind. At first PC Romney hadn't given much thought to seeing the sails as many boats pass Acklins Island on their voyages between the West

Indies and Florida. However, a closer look showed that the sails were not outside, but inside the reef. Twenty minutes later Romney found Sam, Marty and Inga walking along the road adjacent to what the locals call Maria's Beach. During the drive back to the Settlement on Acklins Island where Romney's police station was located the shipwrecked trio told the constable of the grounding and that Bev Brown, one of the persons on board was missing.

"I'll need a written statement of what happened. In the meantime I'll ask some local fisherman who live in the area to look for your wife Mr. Brown. Mr. Gold we don't have a medical doctor on Acklins, but my neighbor Johnny Gumbs worked with a vet in Nassau and can have a look at your shoulder. Maybe Johnny can wrap it up till you can see a doctor in Miami."

Marty clearly wasn't enthusiastic about the attention from Johnny Gumbs, but rather than show his displeasure said,

"Thanks Constable my shoulder is getting better so I'll wait till I get back to the States to have it looked at."

The process of providing a statement to Romney proved to be a challenging experience. The information from Sam, Marty and Inga was limited; there was an error in navigation by a retired navy officer who was skippering and the boat hit the reef, Bev was washed overboard and the three survivors floated ashore in a dinghy.

Even though the statements were brief in content they took an unimaginable amount of time because Romney completed and wrote each statement by hand. The statement's had almost been completed when they were interrupted by a local who entered the room. The man told PC Romney that the missing lady had been found, but that she was dead. He said her body had been found in a cove near a fisherman's house a mile down the coast where it had been washed ashore.

"Oh my God no, no, it can't be. Are they sure she's dead?"

Sam was pleased with his response. He appeared distraught. His grief-stricken facial expression and tone reflected the sorrow and anguish expected of a forlorn husband. Sam thought to himself, *you're good, you're really good. That was a great performance by a now grieving widower. If I keep this up who knows maybe*

*I'll have a new calling as an actor, the Merry Widower playing
Macbeth or maybe Moses parting the waters.*
On the other hand Romney wasn't convinced that this was just an
accident. Thinking to himself, *why would an experienced naval
officer end up on a well known charted reef? His behavior
seemed staged and disingenuous.*
In spite of Romney's personal thoughts,
"I'm very sorry for your loss Mr. Brown. We've finished with the
Statements so let's drive to the fisherman's house so you can
identify the body."
Bev's body had been laid out on the porch of the fisherman's
wooden shack. Her eyes were closed and with the exception of
the purplish discoloration of her face she appeared to be sleeping.
Sam continued his mournful performance, but in spite of trying
couldn't bring tears to his eyes. Instead he began rubbing his eyes
to make them red. Marty and Inga gasped in horror then quickly
looked away.
"Constable, because of Marty's injury and my dead wife I would
like to leave immediately and get Bev back to the States so the
funeral arrangements can be made. In any case there's nothing
more we can do here and no way to preserve her body so the
sooner it's moved the better."
"I'm sorry Mr. Brown, but I first need to obtain Nassau's
permission for you to leave and take the body back to the States.
This is necessary in all cases of a death."
While PC Romney was adamant in his obligations to conform to
regulations, Sam was distraught learning he would be unable to
leave.
"There's a Bahamas Air flight leaving today at 2:15 and as we've
completed the statements there's no reason why we shouldn't be
on it," pleaded Sam.
Romney, after contacting his superiors in Nassau permitted
Marty and Inga to leave on the afternoon flight that Sam too had
planned to be on. In frustration Sam was forced to wait until
Friday morning before the officials in Nassau eventually
provided the necessary authorization and permission for Sam and
Bev's body to be flown out of Acklins. After enduring the
unexpected delay and not wanting to wait for the Bahamas Air

flight on Saturday, once he received permission to leave Sam used Romney's telephone to hastily arrange the charter of a single engine Comanche from a company that operated out of Fort Lauderdale.

Having maintained his composure during the 48 hours he had been forced to endure Sam was pleased when he saw the Comanche land and taxi to the small building that Acklins called an Airport. The aft seats had been removed to accommodate the pine box that a local carpenter had assembled to serve as Bev's coffin.

———

When Romney and a U.S. Coast Guard officer from Miami arrived to inspect the wreckage of the chartered Comanche it was nose down in four feet of water, the cockpit was submerged. When the engine failed just after take-off the pilot had apparently attempted to land in the shallow water off the end of the dirt runway, but the undercarriage struck a partially submerged coral head. The pilot had been seriously injured on impact and being unable to release his seat belt had subsequently drowned. PC Romney identified the passenger who had been sitting in the right hand seat as Mr. Samuel Brown of the United States, a retired naval officer. However, the cause of Mr. Brown's death was not from drowning but from decapitation. The Coast Guard Situation Report indicated that a pine box which had been used as a casket had been improperly lashed and secured in the aft part of the aircraft, on impact the casket had catapulted forward and neatly separated Mr. Browns head from his body. The following month the insurance company agreed to give what was left of the *Spirit* to PC Romney in return for him taking the responsibility of removing the wreck. In the course of stripping the wreck of her hatches, masts, rigging and gear for salvage PC Romney found a diary carefully enclosed in a sealed Ziploc bag.

The cover read, *Beverly Brown - My Diary*. Romney took the Diary back to his office and was troubled by what he read. Three months earlier Beverly Brown had written *I believe that Sam may wish to kill me; Sam received confirmation of an insurance policy issued by the Fidelity Life Insurance Co. of Boston, Mass. The policy indicates a limit of one million dollars on my life, with a double indemnity clause. Why??* Romney suspected all along that Sam Brown wasn't being as truthful as he appeared considering the circumstances surrounding the tragic loss of his wife while the others survived. Even though he viewed the death as suspicious without firm proof he couldn't charge or hold him. After reading the Diary and thinking about the way Sam Brown died Romney smiled and thought *if he was responsible for his wife's death I wonder if this was her way of getting even?*

The First Factor

With a slow turn the VC10 effortlessly banked on its final approach to Jan Smuts Airport on the outskirts of Johannesburg signaling that the long flight from London was finally reaching its conclusion. Peering through the plane's window it wasn't difficult to see why they called Jo'burg the city of gold. The sun's reflection from the mine dumps located near the city appeared as a golden buttery haze that bathed the land as far as the eye could see. As if to arouse his slumbering passengers the crisp and cultured public school accent of the Captain broke the silence.

"This is the Captain speaking. On behalf of all the crew I would like to thank you for being the guest of British Overseas Airways. It's been our pleasure to have you on board. I hope you enjoyed the trip and that we will again have the pleasure of seeing you on another BOAC flight. Crew please prepare for landing."

Even with the overnight stop in London it had been a long 24 hours flying time from San Francisco and while BOAC may like to see him again soon Guy hoped it would be some time before he had to undergo the rigors of numerous time zones and the confinement of any long-haul flight. Being in First Class made the flight bearable. Sitting next to a beautiful South African from London made the flight pleasurable. His traveling companion, Rona Tannenbaum was a magnificent creature that he later learned was the idol of all white South African movie goers. It wasn't hard to see why. She stood an imposing 5'10" with a figure that would stop traffic on any continent.

While leafing through the magazines on the plane he had seen the September issue of Panorama that featured the star and her latest film. In addition to rave reviews of the motion picture the article included a photographic montage of its star and her eye-pleasing physical attributes while prominently noting her recent divorce from Abe Silver, the British now resident South African movie mogul. Engaging in small talk over a bottle of excellent Laurent Perrier following a stop in Rome and another after leaving

Nairobi, Guy became focused on developing a relationship with this spectacular woman.

South Africa, best described as an industrial colossus was the only white ruled independent African nation on the continent. The country covered a total area of 447,445 square miles and had a population of over 28 million people of all races. The country's story began in 1652 when the Dutch East Indies Company set up a supply station in Cape Town to serve their ships transiting to and from the Far East. Later to escape British encroachment the Boers known as Afrikaners moved northeast on the Great Trek which is often compared to the American Pioneers moving westward. South Africa was originally inhabited by the peaceful Khoisan and Bantu tribes, but unlike the American pioneers the Boer's had no warring tribes to fight.

In the 1800's huge deposits of diamonds and gold were discovered. The discovery generated an economic interest by the British which subsequently lead to the Boer Wars. Britain eventually seized control of the country in 1902 and in 1910 the Union of South Africa was created. At the turn of the century Winston Churchill, then a young British journalist chronicled the Boer Wars in the British press as a front line war correspondent. In 1948 under the leadership of General Jan Smuts the Nationalist Party institutionalized the policy of APARTHEID. Not realizing it at the time Smuts gave a name to a policy that would lead to the expansion of a doctrine that in later years would provide an unprecedented turn in world opinion against his country.

APARTHEID sharply curtailed the rights and movement of non-whites with a policy to create a national program that introduced *separate development* of the entire non-white population. The Apartheid Policy set aside 13% of the country for development of what was identified as the Homelands where it was envisaged that the blacks would live and work separately from the whites. The plan was to eventually declare the independence of the Transkei region followed by Bophuthatswana and later Venda. Millions of tribal members would be stripped of their South African Citizenship and made citizens of the new homelands, regardless of where they lived. While the Homelands policy would create hardships and hate the Afrikaners deemed it was necessary if they were to retain control.

In the Union of South Africa the administrative capital was established in Pretoria, legislative in Cape Town and Judicial in Bloemfontein. South Africa's commercial center was and continued to be located in Johannesburg. Its religions and languages were as diverse as the country itself, with Christians, Jews, Muslims, and Hindus speaking Afrikaans, English, Zulu, Xhosa, Sotho, and a conglomeration of other African languages. The diversities from the never ending stream of migrant workers from North of the Limpopo had been visibly woven into the tapestry that created the country. These migrants seeking a better life were also aware that their earnings paid in South African Rand had greater value than the national currencies to the north. The Rand was a currency backed by gold, gold that was either in the treasury or waiting to be mined less than a mile from the Central Bank.

While operationally located in Johannesburg, the headquarters of the South African Special Branch was based in Pretoria, a town of some 550,000 blacks and whites. Situated some 50 miles Northeast of Johannesburg, both cities are located in the State of the Transvaal. The operational functions of the Special Branch were planned and carried out principally by a group of fanatical hard liners of the BROEDERBOND, or Brotherhood. The Special Branch was often compared to Hitler's Nazi SS because of the backing and support it received from Dr. Balthazar Johannes, a Nationalist Party leader who had been imprisoned during World War II for being a Nazi sympathizer.

White supremacy was the order of the day and liberals were not tolerated in any form, white or black. House arrest meant no trial and banishment to total isolation for an undetermined period of time at the pleasure of the government. The Communist Party was outlawed, but played its damning role through outlets such as the Zambia based, African National Congress and FRELIMO, the communist backed rebels who were causing grief to the Portuguese government in Mozambique and later Angola.

Ian Smith or Smithy as he was known to the Afrikaners to the South was a former RAF fighter pilot who was concerned with the black movements' successful expansion as a result of the

ANC's worldwide public relations effort. The ANC efforts brought about a seemingly endless supply of arms and funding being provided by amongst others, Russia and China.

In an effort to stem the expansion of Black Nationalism Smithy proclaimed a Unilateral Declaration of Independence in Southern Rhodesia in 1961. The infamous Sharpeville massacre of 1959 in the Black township of Vereeniging was the first of many actions by the South African government that began the country's descent into an abyss. The killing at Sharpeville had adversely affected any reasonable resolution being achieved in Southern Africa. In spite of the ANC's rapid and expanding influence White South African's continued to believe that their beloved country was secure. With the white dominated Smith Government strongly in place in Rhodesia and the Portuguese firmly in control in Angola and Mozambique the Afrikaners were confident that their well trained, superbly equipped and highly motivated South African Defense Force could meet any challenge. From the Simons Town Naval Base the South African Navy and the British Royal Navy controlled the vital sea lanes around the Cape of Good Hope.

The South African Air Force had air superiority with state-of-the-art aircraft and equipment all supplied by the United States, Britain, France, and other western countries who were committed to preventing a communist backed takeover of the Cape's sea lanes. The United Nations conveniently provided a visible forum for governments to condemn and decry the inhumanities of Apartheid while safely distancing them from the regime in Pretoria. At the same time these governments were providing the latest in military hardware to insure that the South African Defense Forces were amongst the best equipped armed forces in the world.

———

After landing at Jan Smuts and taking Guy's hand Rona leaned over and in a low voice said,

"You go first and I'll follow a minute or two later. It's not a good idea for us to be seen together when we leave the plane or as we pass through Customs and Immigration. Sorry Guy, I can't explain things now please just trust me."

Guy's first reaction was to think, *you're kidding, come on. Why not be seen together?* What's up? Is it that she doesn't want to have to provide an explanation of being seen with an unknown stranger or maybe have to deal with an ex-husband that's at the airport to meet her?

Before leaving the plane Rona kissed him on the cheek gave him a note with her address and phone number and said, "Call me later."

It wouldn't be until sometime later that Guy would learn that his beautiful traveling companion wasn't just a film star, but the leader of the SABRA Faction. Under her code name *Raven* she was the mastermind and principal strategist of the SABRA, a left-wing Jewish group that supported and covertly worked with both the outlawed African National Congress and the Pan Africanist Congress in their acts of sabotage against the government.

After passing through Customs Guy briefly turned to see Rona being escorted by two uniformed officers to an unmarked room with frosted glass just inside the immigration hall. Even though a bit unnerved by her *let's not be seen together,* he had Rona's address and telephone number which assured him that he'd be seeing her again.

His immigration entry documents had fortunately been completed by the South African authorities before he'd left the United States. Fortunate because the immigration officer who took his papers had the demeanor of a disgruntled SS officer who had just received orders to report to Stalingrad in February 1943 as the German Army was being annihilated by Soviet forces.

"Why are you coming to South Africa? Are you a journalist? Maybe a left-wing journalist who's planning to write another biased story about our Apartheid Policy that you Americans have labeled as racist? Tell me why you are here? You're a journalist."

"No, I am not a journalist. I am not a journalist. I am a computer engineer involved in the marketing of computer systems. As you will see from the papers issued by the South African Consul General in Los Angeles I have been given permission to immigrate to South Africa as a permanent resident. My entry papers clearly show I am involved only in computer systems. I am not a journalist."

After repeatedly denying that he was a journalist a senior immigration officer who had been listening to the heated exchange took Guy's passport and papers from the desk officer and pulled him to one side.

"You know my friend we have to be very careful about certain people who wish to enter South Africa, especially those from Britain and the United States. You have your racial problems in America, but here we are outnumbered seven to one by the blacks.

There are far too many left-wing journalists and communists who write biased stories about our country so we must be very diligent in screening those who are allowed to enter; we put the troublemakers back on the plane before they can cause problems."

His thick Afrikaans accent made it necessary for Guy to listen carefully to each word, but the message was clear. With the snap of his finger the senior immigration officer dismissed him with, "Okay, you can go." At the same time pointing in the direction of Customs.

As the luggage from the aircraft's hold began its journey around the baggage conveyor he noticed Rona across the hall. Having been able to sort out whatever problem she had had with immigration Rona was now walking towards customs. Guy pondered the options, could it be that she had been taken aside by the two oversized immigration officers who wanted a private conversation with the star or maybe even a signed photo? From their size it was clear that male Afrikaners always eat their *Wheaties* or whatever they eat in South Africa as they all seemed to be related to the Jolly Green Giant. Most were big burly six footers that could easily wrestle a rhino and probably did so when they weren't verbally thrashing selected arriving passengers. Guy looked across the baggage hall at Rona, but the moment they made eye contact, she turned away. Guy thought to himself ...strange, I wonder what's going on. After picking up his luggage he proceeded to customs.

"Do you have anything to declare?"

"No nothing."

After a cursory look in his briefcase with the assurance that he had nothing to declare in his checked luggage he breezed through Customs. Guy wondered if the customs officer who swiftly waved him through got lucky last night or maybe he was just friendly to the few Americans that passed through Jan Smuts Airport. Whatever the reason passing through Customs was quick and painless.

––––––––

It was September 3rd, but the trip and Guy's meticulous planning had begun in earnest many months before. Guy was born, raised and went to school in Santa Clara, California. After five arduous years he had graduated with honors from San Jose State College with a master's degree in Business Administration. The degree had assured him a position with International Business Machines Corporation, the computer giant identified on the stock exchanges throughout the world as IBM. Guy's entry level position with IBM was in the accounting department at their recently opened plant in San Jose, California. After only a few weeks he found that the job and many of his fellow workers bored him. From 8 to 5 the work was monotonous and dull; balancing accounts payable, payroll and verifying supplier's invoices, tasks that were all tedious and mundane. The required uniform of the day was dark conservative suits, dark conservative ties and dark conservative hats that were to be worn when they ventured beyond the dark conservative doors of the dark conservative plant into the bright real world beyond.

Thinking to himself, good God, all these people ever seem to talk about is their IBM family, their medical plans and the wonderful retirement benefits they will be granted after providing twenty years of dedicated service. Still loosely tied to the conservative mode the only people within IBM who appeared to be masters of their own destiny was the sales force. After three arduous years of difficult conformity Guy decided that if he was to maintain his sanity he had to break out and get into the sales and marketing side of the business. In concert with the prescribed *IBM Way* he requested permission to submit his application for a position in sales. He was willing to sell anything IBM produced. Computer systems, accounting machines, data entry machines, even typewriters. Irrespective of the product he was confident that he possessed the personality, enthusiasm and the technical proficiency to become a star performer.

Guy's superior arranged a meeting with Harvey Hawthorne, manager of the personnel department. The interview seemed to go well. Harvey, having spent 15 years with IBM in New York had moved west with his wife Gladys, Harvey Jr. and little Melanie whose photograph was astutely displayed on Harvey's desk. A photograph most likely put on view to confirm to his fellow workers his dedication as a devoted family man. Two other 5" x 7" photographs were also prominently positioned on Harvey's small desk; one was showing the Hawthorne family standing next to a small inflatable swimming pool and the other while posed in a formal setting in front of a fireplace with Rover, the family Labrador laying at their feet. Not exactly a Norman Rockwell original, but something that indicated to all visitors that Harvey was a conservative family man who worked for a conservative family company. Even though it was Guy who was being interviewed Harvey did most of the talking; first about his wonderful family then about the security provided by the wonderful IBM family. It became apparent that there were only two things important to Harvey, first the IBM family then his own family. Without any real explanation he stressed the importance of the company's motto THINK then embarked on a dissertation about his family followed by his aspirations within the IBM family.

The Hawthorne's lived in a conservative 3-bedroom house in a conservative sub-division near the conservative town of Campbell, drove a conservative 4-door Chevrolet and regularly worshiped as members of the local Assemblies of God Church. Each year the Hawthorne family spent their two week vacation visiting the Indian burial grounds near King City, but really looked forward to the time when Harvey would retire so they could cash out his pension, buy a camper and see the Grand Canyon.

Guy, thought to himself, Harvey is really boring. Quickly accessing the situation Guy decided he'd go with the flow and tell

Harvey anything necessary hoping it would result in a transfer to the sales division. When Harvey finished his obviously often repeated flowery dissertation Guy began by elaborating his praise and great affection for IBM, the IBM Family and his overwhelming desire to become one of IBM's outstanding leaders in sales. With boundless admiration he applauded the wonderful job security that the organization provided, finishing with his over-whelming desire to embark on a long career with the company. Restraining himself from a subtle smirk he said he was envious of Harvey, his wonderful family and his accomplishments with the company that he had so loyally served for fifteen years.

Guy had smiled at the correct time, appropriately admired Harvey's drab little family and said how he envied him to be able to visit the Indian burial grounds on an annual basis. After leaving the interview he went into the men's rest room brought the fingers and palms of both hands together and looking up quietly said,

"Sorry God, but it was important that I score some good points in the interview. I really want to get into the sales side and hope you'll forgive me for being a little bit untruthful with Harvey, but I had to convince that brainwashed little vegetable that old Tom Watson himself would do hand-stands to get me on the front line to sell the products that had made him and IBM's shareholders so rich. AMEN."

After his meeting with Harvey Guy decided that a small celebration would be in order. Stopping by her desk on his way out he suggested that Yvette join him for dinner. Yvette, who shared a striking resemblance to Brigitte Bardot in addition to her good looks, was also the only brains in the steno pool. That night at Giorgio's they drained the wine cellar's supply of its finest Napa Valley Chardonnay before returning to her townhouse where they romped in exploration of each others private parts, promptly destroying the satin sheets on her waterbed. With a chuckle he thought, too bad before the fun and games began she hadn't said she was having her period as they might have salvaged at least the upper one. After leaving the untidy heap of blood stained sheets in a bed where it appeared that the occupants may not have survived they proceeded to the shower.

Looking at the bed Yvette smiled,

"Hey, the sheets can be replaced, multiple organisms are irreplaceable."

It took Harvey the bore, a week to send Guy a short rejection notice to inform him that the company did not consider him suitable for a sales position, but eminently qualified for the accounting position he presently held. Guy was furious. What an asshole! The rejection letter had barely dropped on his desk before he was on the phone to personnel. Harvey wasn't there. A nameless assistant answered the phone and obviously reading from his file unsympathetically advised him that *they* didn't believe he was suitable for a sales position and therefore wouldn't recommend his transfer.

Out loud he said, "That's bullshit!"

He then called Arnold Brown his superior and arranged to meet him in 20 minutes.

"Guy, I think you'd make a great salesman. I know you really want to make the move to sales so don't get upset. I'll call the department head and see if he'll reconsider your application which I'll personally recommend. It's a long shot but it might just work."

The meeting was short. Arnold Brown was a company man and with nineteen years at *Big Blue* wasn't about to upset the apple cart for somebody with only three years under their belt, even if he too thought the transfer was a good idea. Arnold called the head of personnel and secured another appointment, but instead of Harvey he met with a Michael Reynolds. After reading his original application he reluctantly agreed to give Guy the sales/marketing appointments test, a test he hadn't been offered in his first interview.

Michael explained that this wasn't normally done at such an early stage, especially when someone had been deemed unfit in their first interview, but said he'd schedule the test next week. No doubt to impress him, Arnold later told Guy that he'd *pulled some strings* to arrange the test. Pulled some strings my foot, even having only three years with *Big Blue* Guy knew that pulling any strings in IBM rarely happens. Even though always business-like, Arnold did display some feminine *limp-wrist* tendencies and was quietly believed to be a closet gay. Guy wondered if Arnold's contact in personnel might also be gay who he promised a date if he would arrange the test. Could also be that Arnold might even be planning to hit on Guy because he knew that Bill, Guy's younger brother was gay. Guy never did find out about Arnold's preferences, but he did take the exam scheduled for the following Friday. During the week to prepare himself for the test he read every piece of IBM's sales literature he could lay his hands on. By Friday he had devoured all the available material and that afternoon took the test. Being the eternal optimist he arranged to have dinner Friday night with Yvette.

The dinner at the Bold Knight would be to celebrate what he believed would be his successful passing of the test. Without an explanation Guy told Yvette the dinner would be a foursome. After completing the test in less time than the prescribed two hours he turned it in to the receptionist at personnel. Hmm, what a sweet little morsel, Guy thought to himself as he smiled when he handed the test to the outstretched pretty white hand that showed no evidence of a wedding ring. How did I miss that little beauty the last time around, your slipping Young!

As Guy wheeled his Alfa Spider through the last of the Friday night commute traffic he thought of the move and his new career in sales. He liked the idea of the outdoors, no more stuffy office, no more endless mindless reports and no more of the volumes of columns of figures that took hours to produce and which most likely would be filed away never to be seen again. As he swung into the entrance drive of the Bold Knight he saw Yvette just getting out of her little Volvo grasping the waiting hand of Sam the Car Valet. A Volvo? Yvette always amazed him because at times she could be so practical.

Sam on the other hand was a rakish good looking brute who could never be considered practical. He had gone to college with Guy earning a degree in business, but soon found that he didn't like the life of mind-numbing conformity. He was a surfer at heart and after finishing college spent his days looking for the big rollers off Santa Cruz while listening to Herb Alpert and the

Tijuana Brass. At night he made an honest living parking cars at the Bold Knight. Sam's dad, Louie Demarcas had a very successful trucking business in addition to making a buddle of money on the side from his nefarious activities as a Mafia Capo. The Demarcas family lived in an enormous mansion on the eastside of town near the country club. It was no secret that his dad had bought him the Porsche 911 Turbo and continued to give him the same $1,500.00 per month allowance that he received while going to college.

Guy watched as Sam the blond 6'2" hunk took Yvette's hand to help her from the car while focusing on the micro mini skirt that exposed the best pair of legs in Santa Clara County.

"Hi Guy, thought you wouldn't be back till the next harvest of the grapes," Sam said grasping the door handle of the Alfa.

"Sorry Sam, we can't wait for the harvest. Yvette and I are anxious to start working on the in-house stuff tonight. Oh, by the way, I really hope you get lucky tonight, so that hard-on you just grew doesn't have to be taken into your own hands!"

Yvette, who was standing nearby giggled at the comment. Guy too was in high spirits and in the mood to celebrate his successful passing of the exam.

Yvette with a quizzical look asked, "Guy you told me that our dinner tonight was a foursome. Who else is coming?"

"Be patient sweetheart we'll see the other two in a few minutes."

The foursome was completed when the waiter carefully set two bottles of a vintage Cabernet Sauvignon on the table.

"Why two bottles?" Yvette quipped with a puzzled look.

"They only had two bottles of the '59 left in the cellar so I wanted to be sure no one else got the other one. In any case we're celebrating and I'm thirsty so let's enjoy another night of reckless abandon!"

The next few days dragged by. Receiving no word on the results of the test made it difficult for Guy to concentrate on his work. Guy saw Arnold in the cafeteria and he was pleasant as usual, if he knew the results of the test he hadn't let on what they were. Finally ten days later the mail room messenger dropped off his stack of incoming correspondence and right on the top was the envelope marked "Confidential" with a return address from the personnel office downtown. Guy tore the envelope open and knew from the first two words knew it was bad news. *We regret to inform you the results from the Sales/Marketing Aptitude Test indicate that you are unsuited for transfer to the Sales Department as a trainee.*

Guy was devastated. He could not believe that a company such as *Big Blue* couldn't recognize the talent they had within their ranks. Quietly he murmured,

"Damn it there must be a way."

Guy was at a complete loss as to what to do. He really didn't want to leave the company, but couldn't bear the thought of twenty years looking at rows and rows of boring figures written in neat columns on mundane reports. IBM was considered a big plum for the commercial and economic sector of Santa Clara County and that night in the San Jose Evening News Guy saw an article about Thomas Watson Sr., the founder of IBM who had recently passed away. The article said that Tom Junior was planning a trip to San Jose to get a better grasp of the west coast operations and would be visiting their offices the following week. Like a lighting bolt from the heavens Guy got a terrific idea. Why not corner Tom Junior during his visit when his guard was down, preferably when he was alone and make his pitch for the transfer? To meet his military obligations Guy had spent the last few years serving his country during which time he received instructions in how to be a good warrior along with the training to fly single engine observation aircraft. His first tour of duty was in the Army Reserve as a Military Police Officer. When the Air Force Reserve established an Air Police wing he was transferred as a result of his training skills. In addition to mastering the proficiency required by the armed forces for criminal investigations, crowd control and interrogation, he had also received training in tactical maneuvers and strategy. Using his knowledge of theoretical strategy he felt confident that he could work out a plan to meet and grab the attention of IBM's *numero-uno* for a brief moment to present his case for a move to the sales division. Over a glass of wine that night Guy told Yvette of his plan. Yvette obviously wasn't sure,

"Do you really think it'll work? Watson is rarely alone when he travels and he's only going to be in San Jose for the day. I haven't seen his schedule, but Jennifer may be able to get me a copy of Watson's itinerary, can't promise, but I'll try. If I can get it you mustn't tell anyone as we all could be fired."

Two days later as they were leaving the building Jennifer, the plant manager's secretary in the Executive Office surreptitiously passed Yvette a copy of Watson's confidential itinerary for his one-day visit. Guy was dismayed in reading Watson's 9 to 5 schedule as it appeared he'd be shadowed virtually every minute by the local hierarchy, including the luncheon which was to be a closed-door affair in the executive dining room. The schedule was disappointing in that every moment *Junior* would be surrounded by his New York entourage and the local chain-of-command. Guy's brain went into overdrive as he pondered his options. It appeared that the only opportunity to get Watson alone might be if he was in a restroom taking a pee and unless his followers had to go at the same time, he'd be unaccompanied. Thinking out loud, let's say, if from a distance I follow him until nature called, I then might just have a chance to make the pitch when his pants were unzipped. Depending on how much coffee he'd had and how bad he had to go I'd probably have less than sixty seconds to impress *Junior* with my overwhelming desire to be an IBM Salesman.

There's a chance that he might even be impressed with my creative approach. In considering his rest-room idea as workable, Guy began drafting what he would say. After considering a number of approaches he settled on, *Mr. Watson, I hope you will forgive this somewhat unorthodox meeting with you, but I am at wits end in my efforts to make a valuable contribution to the firm. My name is Guy Young; I am an accountant here in the card processing plant in San Jose. I have a burning desire to transfer into sales and I feel I can do an outstanding job for the company if I am given the chance. I have been interviewed by personnel and taken the company test for salesman. They tell me I am unsuited for sales. I feel they are wrong and appeal to you to help me secure the transfer I have requested. I will not let you or the company down and would be grateful if you would assist me. If after six months my superiors in sales are not satisfied with my performance I'll return to accounting or resign whichever you prefer. Please give me this opportunity. I personally feel that this great company that was built by your father will further grow and expand under your guidance and leadership by opening doors and providing opportunities to deserving employees who can make a positive contribution to the company.* AMEN, Guy thought to himself. Over lunch the next day Yvette was made privy to the details. She thought it was a great idea, but added that her friends who had met or been around the founder's son said he was a somewhat cold and unsympathetic money man who never really enjoyed personal contact with his minions in the field.

"Thanks Yvette that's not very encouraging, but what the hell, I've got nothing to lose."

Yvette had given Guy the itinerary under a veil of secrecy over a quiet dinner at her apartment. The next few days Guy rehearsed his lines as if auditioning for a Broadway Play. The following Wednesday was D-Day. The day before *Junior's* arrival the plant was spruced up like a hospital room, fresh flowers were placed everywhere and literally dozens of THINK signs were polished and prominently displayed on every desk.

On the day of his planned assault, Guy put on his conservative black suit, which he hadn't worn since his grandfather's funeral which was adorned by a very conservative blue tie. Learning that Tom Junior liked black suits and blue ties he knew the suit and tie would add a nice touch to the operation. He spit shined his black dress shoes with an even higher gloss than his days in boot camp.

The standard operating procedure when a high ranking guest visited was to serve them coffee in the executive lunch room during which time the plant manager and his followers would expound the virtues of the management team followed by an inspection of the troops. Guy figured that if Watson's bowels worked along the lines of regular folks he'd probably be ready to relieve himself about 11:00 A.M., more or less about an hour after the first cup of Folgers finest had touched his regal lips.

Staying well back, Guy stalked his leader with the precision of a Green Beret allowing just enough distance to keep his prey in sight along with the closest restroom. The first false move towards a door marked Gentlemen saw beads of sweat appear on Guy's forehead. He had to keep cool he said to himself, gently wiping his brow with the Kleenex tissues brought along for the purpose.

Tom Watson was an imposing man standing over six feet tall impeccably dressed in a dark suit and blue tie. He moved in strides comparable only with that of Lord Mountbatten reviewing the Coldstream Guards at Buckingham Palace. When the first suggestion became evident, Guy couldn't hear the words, but the hand movements indicated it was apparent that His Excellency was excusing himself for a visit to pass the coffee that had been introduced to his system but an hour before. Those accompanying him nodded acknowledging his temporary absence and graciously turned no doubt to quietly discuss how thing were going and anxious to analyze the pleasure or displeasure of what their leader had seen so far. Guy wondered whether the boss was about to do a stand up, or drop his pants for a number two, but now realizing he hadn't planned on the possibility of him dropping his pants. Good God what should he do if Watson was behind a closed door in the sitting position when he entered – continue the pitch or abort the mission?

Oh well, too late now. Like a Lion ready to pounce for the kill Guy sprang into action, he cleared the distance between him and the Gentleman's rest rooms in seconds. Watson was alone when he entered and was standing in front of a urinal doing what all men do in similar circumstances. Guy strode into the rest room and standing at the urinal next to Watson, with passionate enthusiasm began dispensing his personal appeal. Watson finished his task, zippered his trousers and without looking up walked to the sinks to wash his hands. Guy remained at the urinal. Through the reflection in the mirror Watson looked at Guy. Momentarily pausing he then spoke with the pompous air of Julius Caesar on the podium in Rome.

"My boy IBM has these tests and qualifying criteria to guide management in the selection of the right people for the many positions within our company. If personnel have told you that you're unsuited for sales it's in your best interest and the best interest of IBM that you remain where you are. Be content, do your job and the company will look after you."

With that a now relieved Thomas Watson, Jr., Chairman of the Board of International Business Machines left the washroom. Realizing that his sales career with IBM had ended even before it began Guy's head dropped to witness his expended urine as it disappeared down the drain much like his objective. The brief encounter with Watson even though somewhat clever and imaginative obviously had had little effect on this captain of industry.

The encounter did not go completely unnoticed as evidenced by the numerous requests from all levels, at what may have been said during Guy's seemingly coincidental meeting with this almost god like creature in the rest room. Knowing that his short-lived career with IBM would soon be coming to a close he decided to get creative. As the financial media had been riff with take-over rumors he left his peers and masters in an apprehensive silence by simply saying they had briefly discussed the possible sale of the IBM plant to their arch rival, the Remington Rand Univac Division. Guy said he was sorry, but it would be inappropriate and improper for him to discuss or divulge the substance of their brief meeting without Watson's approval.

Having been denied a transfer to sales he knew it was time to move on and turned to that bastion of business knowledge and lucrative opportunities, The Wall Street Journal. Over the next few weeks he read that Remington's Univac Division was indeed biting at the heels of *Big Blue.* As a result of their new and innovative products Remington was becoming a serious threat. At the same time the Journal reported that an even greater threat was coming from Tom Watson Sr.'s old nemesis, The National Cash Register Company of Dayton, Ohio. Guy was not a vindictive type, but what better way to prove a point than to join the competition. He had pleaded with IBM to simply give him a chance, but his appeal had been rejected at all levels. He was convinced that NCR would be good for Guy Young and that Guy Young would be good for NCR.

One month later he was employed as a trainee salesman with NCR learning the intricate workings of Integrated Data

Processing Systems. Three months to the day after joining NCR as a trainee he was appointed as a territory sales representative and six months after that he was elevated to the position of Division Manager at the NCR office in San Francisco. In strong competition against IBM Guy prevailed in selling the superior NCR systems; he had proved his point and it didn't take IBM long to realize they'd made a terrible mistake. He soon became one of NCR's top ten producers in the United States, winning trips all over the country and making money beyond his wildest dreams. As a result of his success he moved from his apartment in San Jose to a Penthouse in the Marina section of San Francisco and replaced his Alfa Romeo with a new black Aston Martin.

Guy had always had a passion for good music and applied his talents as an aspiring drummer with a group that did gigs at Pedro's, a small jazz bistro in the North Beach Section of the city. When he was at *Big Blue* earning a paltry salary, the drinks and the extra $150.00 per week earned at Pedro's was always helpful. After moving to NCR he still received the money from Pedro's, but now did the gig just for the kicks. He may not have been the best stick man around, but the bistro's customers liked the group's cool sounds. While he met a large number of interesting people with his new job at NCR, Pedro's was a great place to meet even more neat people in the Bistro's laid-back environment.

Pedro had originally asked that they do four gigs a week, but because of their daytime work pressures the group had to limit the nights they played to Friday's and Saturday's. The jazz group consisted of Bob Coles, who strummed a mean bass, but paid his mortgage with a position as a vice president with Bank of America. Sam Moore who had the hottest keyboard ivories in town during the day drove a Muni Bus, and Bernie Swartz who played a mean Sax was a trial lawyer and clearly didn't need the money. Possibly as a result of thunderous opening or closing arguments in court Bernie had lungs that made his alto sax purr like a cat at Fisherman's Wharf. Life was good.

Guy was doing what he liked to do, both at work and at play and generally enjoying life.

At first it had only been a casual glance, but Guy noticed the increased attention from this attractive lady who was always alone, but frequently engaged in animated conversation with the bistro's owner while he tended the bar. One night just before closing time after the band finished their last performance of a Miles Davis classic Pedro formally introduced Guy to Veronica. She was a quiet type, didn't drink much, used little makeup, and was always fashionably dressed. When he inquired she said that Gucci was her family name.

Veronica was of a slender build, stunningly attractive with long natural blond hair. She was about 5'2", had flashing blue eyes and a personality that radiated her charm. Pedro's, a small intimate bistro tastefully decorated in the theme of a sidewalk café in the south of France had become a favorite of San Francisco's patricians because of its extensive menu of reasonably priced Mediterranean delicacies and good music. The polished mahogany bar could seat about fifteen in addition to tables that could accommodate another thirty.

Veronica, who generally came in about 10:00 p.m. on Friday and Saturday nights always took a seat at the end of the bar near the band. The first time Guy noticed this lovely creature he had inquisitively looked for a wedding ring but saw none. Not that a wedding ring meant anything, but he was just being careful in case their might be a Mr. Veronica lurking somewhere in the shadows. Guy loved women, but because of his strict Catholic upbringing always stayed well clear of the potential problems of frustrated married women that were readily available in the bistro. Entertainers being in the limelight always seemed to receive particular attention by these enthusiastic and eager ladies. Even though as flattering as it might be, a relatively good looking single male doesn't need to fool around with trouble when available single women are always plentiful.

Their initial eye contact brought frequent smiles then after a few nights developed into brief exchanges during the breaks. Veronica said that like Guy she was a native Californian who was single and didn't work because she had a private income. Not wishing to make a move prematurely when she didn't offer her phone number he didn't ask for it. Initially their conversations were limited to small talk between two self confident individuals who were obviously attracted to one another.

On a subsequent Saturday night Veronica suggested after Pedro's closed they might have coffee at the Denny's Restaurant nearby, a suggestion to which Guy quickly agreed. As they entered the all night restaurant, Guy was impressed by the almost regal bearing of this self assured female who moved with the grace of a Princess Royal at Court.

It was just after 2:30 a.m. and Denny's was busy bustling with the night people of San Francisco. Finding a small booth in a corner they ordered coffee from a disinterested waitress who appeared to wish she were someplace else, perhaps home in bed. Engaging in small talk Guy found that his princess was thirty two, had attended a finishing school in England followed by three years at the Sorbonne in Paris where she studied the old masters. She liked to travel, had hoped one day she could learn to fly and loved the large yachts she'd seen at the St. Francis Yacht Club. Guy told her about himself and his love of airplanes and boats and that he was involved with Offshore Power Boat Racing. Taking a photo from his wallet he showed her a picture taken by helicopter of the Stiletto, his 38' Magnum Offshore Racer during recent races in the Sacramento Delta. Her only comment was, "Isn't it a bit small."

Their relationship blossomed with Guy and Veronica seeing each other on a regular basis. Friday and Saturday nights after leaving Pedro's they went to Guy's place for coffee then met two or three times a week at his Penthouse to make love before going their separate ways. In spite of their time together it seemed that Guy actually knew very little about his new found lover. She either came to his Penthouse or they would meet in some quiet cafe like the Place Pigalle, another French bistro near the Penthouse. On other occasions they'd have a late night snack at the Blue Fox in the City's Financial District.

Even though he'd frequently asked where she lived she hadn't told him. She'd cut-off his inquisitiveness by simple saying that she lived near Nob Hill. He checked, but found there was no Gucci listed in the phone book with an address on or near Nob Hill or any of the other affluent areas of Twin Peaks or Pacific Heights. Guy was surprised that if she was single and really lived in the City why they never met where she lived nor did she ask to be collected at her home.

The following week Veronica was visibly upset when Guy told her that they would have to temporally forgo their lovemaking sessions for a few days because of a training course that he was obliged to attend in Newport Beach. To calm her he promised he'd be back the following Friday and ready to make up for lost time.

The flight to Los Angeles was short and uneventful during which time he sipped a rum and coke while giving the flight attendants a coy once-over, but none warranted serious attention. As the pilot announced their final approach to LAX Guy looked out the window for a glimpse of the thick smog covering the city sometimes referred to as Tinsel Town. Taking a deep breath of the cabin air he thought it might be the last reasonably clean air until he reached the Inn at Newport Beach where the seminar was being held.

The congestion on Century Boulevard was terrible, but nothing compared to the San Diego Freeway which was bumper to bumper. It took his limo 2 hours to reach Highway 55 and the Newport Beach turnoff. During the journey Felix the driver told Guy he was from Jamaica and even though he missed his family in Montego Bay he'd quickly adjusted to living in California because of the opportunity of making money that wasn't available back home. The limo and chauffeur had been provided and paid for by NCR, but Guy gave Felix an extra $30.00 as a tip. As Guy entered the hotel lobby he was greeted by a piercing voice,

"Bloody hell mate it's about time you got here. We've been sinking a few pints while waiting till we saw your smiling face coming out of that block long limo. I guess when the higher-ups anoint you with a big title you don't have to ride in the steamy little airport vans like us working class lads."

The voice was unmistakably that of Angus MacFarlane an NCR super salesman based in Seattle, Washington. In his initial training classes with NCR Angus was the instructor during which time they had become good friends. Having once served as a sergeant-major with the Royal Marines he liked training to what he often referred to as his *new recruits*. Even though NCR frequently offered him promotion Angus looked upon management and its inherent responsibilities with disdain choosing to remain a front line salesman with occasional assignments as an instructor. Following his retirement from the British military in the late 1950's Angus enrolled at Edinburgh University. His first job was as a computer salesman with International Computers and Tabulators or ICT as it was known in the United Kingdom where he soon became a star performer. Having received a university degree in accounting and business management and tiring of the terrible weather in Scotland he decided to immigrate to the United States. Sitting next to Angus was a small, wiry little man that he introduced as Ian Cowan who Angus said was known to his friends as Haggis. Angus went on to say that Ian had earned this nickname due to his fondness for that solely Scottish delicacy of oatmeal and blood stuffed into a sheep's intestine. According to Angus, Haggis was known to habitually introduce this appalling mixture to his body's digestive system along with substantial amounts of ale or Scottish malt whisky.

Guy was anxious to check in and get to his room so he could change and shower, Angus however, insisted that they have at least one drink in the bar before he went up.

"Give me 5 minutes. I'll check-in, get my key and meet you in the bar before going to my room."

Magnificently located on the coast south of Los Angeles the Inn at Newport was the perfect venue to hold one of the sometimes tedious conferences put on by the company. It was fortunate that Angus was in attendance as his wit and charm would liven the meeting and offset the boredom. Beautifully situated alongside the Pacific Ocean the Inn was a stones throw from some of California's nicest marinas which were always filled with fantastic boats that were usually adorned with some of the best looking women in the United States. After the drinks Guy excused himself and made his way to the desk to check for any messages. While at the desk Guy hadn't noticed the tall brunette that had quietly slipped behind him. Moving closer she pinched him on the buttocks while at the same time blowing in his ear and whispering in a low sultry voice,

"Hey good looking how about coming up to my room to see my etchings?"

Guy turned his head slightly and looking into her flashing brown eyes said,

"Screw the etchings can't I just come up and fool around with the artist?"

Dangling her key the beautiful Samantha simply said, "1102."

Putting his arm around her diminutive waist he gave her a brief kiss on the cheek, brief just in case there were prying eyes observing their contact. Guy would save the wet and passionate, down the throat tongue job for later.

Samantha Brown was a magnificent creature. Her shoulder length natural mahogany hair framed a tanned face that would compliment the covers of Cosmopolitan or Vogue. Her gracious, alluring features put the finishing touches to a 5'9" body that could easily bring tears to the Goddess Venus de Milo. When entering, a room would fall silent, its occupants mesmerized by her sensuous movements. Sam was not only majestically beautiful she was smart. With a mind that could challenge Einstein, a sense of humor comparable to George Burns and a wit equal to Carol Burnett she could accomplish any task set before her.

Unlike many of her peers, her career had not commenced with IBM as she had gone directly from college to a position with NCR. As a result of her initial interview NCR immediately recognized her superior qualities and she was hired without hesitation. In spite of being a liberated woman in an industry controlled by men Sam had risen rapidly within the company. Guy, as an enlightened liberal had always understood and appreciated the immense difficulties that an intelligent, charming and elegant woman would have in the chauvinistic environment filled with insecure males such as existed in the U.S. computer industry. The Walter Mitty's within NCR or any other organization while fantasizing the seduction of this striking lady had to conceal the threat she posed to them and the male dominated society they so badly wished to perpetuate for eternity. Guy had met Sam during training sessions when both were enthusiastically clawing their way up NCR's chain-of-command. Soon becoming friends, a mutual respect for each other quickly followed. Sam was born and raised in San Diego where her extended family lived and her career began in NCR's San Diego branch. Recognizing her accomplishments through frequent promotions she rapidly moved from strength to strength. Her success in San Diego brought about the offer of a managerial position and subsequent transfer to one of NCR's significantly larger offices in Dallas, Texas. Sam's accomplishments in San Diego brought her fame and fortune, but Dallas is where she really made her mark. She did to Texas what Santa Ana and his Mexican Army did to the Alamo. Moving from success to success Sam was happy in Dallas, but deeply longed to return to California where she would be closer to her family and the sailboat she kept moored in a marina on Mission Bay.

When the opportunity arose, she seized it without hesitation and accepted a lateral move to NCR's branch in Los Angeles. During her ascent to prominence she had graciously and frequently assisted Guy with complex programs or specialized applications where she possessed unique expertise. Sam was brilliant and always anxious to provide help when he needed it.

At 34 she was unlike most of the other women that Guy knew. Sam adored male companionship, enjoyed a good time in the company of intellectually stimulating friends, but wasn't seeking marriage as she remained focused solely on her career. She had frequently visited San Francisco for lovemaking sessions, sessions that sometimes continued during the drive from the city back to the airport. On one occasion after Guy's fingers had induced a breathtaking climax both were frantically trying to locate her panties in the airport parking lot 40 minutes before her scheduled departure. The Aston Martin was an extraordinary car with or without M's gadgets and as far as he knew even James Bond had never attempted front seat fornication or in the heat of the moment had he? Guy thought of Ian Fleming and knowing of his love of women thought maybe he had had another idea of GOLDFINGER when he originally penned the story.

———

"Sorry love can't make it right now, Angus MacFarlane is waiting for me. Let's plan to meet later and discuss art appreciation, your place or mine?" Guy said with a wink. With that Sam turned and blew him a kiss as she sensuously moved across the lobby. The message light on the bedside telephone was flashing like a beacon in the night as Guy entered his darkened room. After switching on the light and opening the drapes he kicked off his shoes and loosened his tie. Dropping on the bed he pressed the message button on the phone. The operator responded,

"Messages for 1027, Mr. Young welcome to the Inn. Mr. MacFarlane in 902 would like you to call him as soon as you arrive. Veronica called and said she misses you and will be glad when you get back, she didn't leave a call-back number. Those are the only messages I have for you sir."

"Thank You."

After removing his clothes he showered and slipped into his tan Topsider deck shoes, cotton khakis and the Pierre Cardin shirt that Veronica had recently given him. Remaining on the bed he turned on the TV to see what was happening in the world, but soon dozed off. He was awoken when the phone came to life with its short bursts demanding attention. The clock on the TV indicated it was 7:05 p.m.

Picking up the phone and before he could say anything the voice on the other end shouted,

"Get your bloody ass down here lad, we can't start the festivities without your good self in attendance." The Scottish jargon made it unmistakably clear it was Angus.

"Okay, okay give me a couple of minutes. I'll be right down. No need to ask where, I'll see you in the bar."

The bar was filled with people. After a quick glance around the room he saw Angus in one corner waving his arms in the air to attract Guy's attention.

"It's about time what have you been doing up there, knocking off some little bird before cocktails?" said Angus in his normally boisterous tone.

"Mind your own business you bloody Scot. After our drinks earlier I figured I'd take a quick nap before we got going again."

They all laughed as Guy sat down. Angus wasn't biased and

favored any drinking establishment that served beer which had its origins in the British Isles. The wild Scot was particularly pleased that the Inn had Worthington E on tap as that was one of his favorites. From their raucous demeanor and red faces it was apparent that Angus and his friend Ian, or Haggis as he preferred to be called had consumed substantial portions of the warm British brew prior to Guy's arrival. Angus had acquired the reputation of having at least one hollow leg to accommodate the vast amount of beer he could drink in one sitting, but always dismissed his excessive consumption levels noting that Scotland produced men not the little boys found on this side of the Pond. Fortunately Angus had a very understanding wife who graciously tolerated his drinking habits and somewhat unorthodox behavior.

"Mate, I'd like you to meet my friend Haggis who's visiting from South Africa. We go back many years."

"It's probably the beer, but thanks, don't you remember you introduced Haggis to me earlier."

Haggis, who Angus later said was normally quiet and somewhat subdued, after drinking for the last couple of hours was no longer quiet or subdued. Now boisterous and laughing loudly he was amused at the rather crude jokes that Angus continuously presented from a never ending inventory. After the jokes had run their course Angus then began speaking about Haggis and their friendship over the years. When Angus and his little lady as he affectionately referred to his wife Dora had come to the United States, Ian and his wife had immigrated to the Republic of South Africa. They lived in a pleasant flat in the centre of Johannesburg and had accepted a sales position with the South African subsidiary of ICT. Ian kept his British Passport as opposed to Angus who had become a naturalized U.S. Citizen. While Angus may have become a U.S. Citizen, as evidenced by his new passport, it was quite obvious that his loyalties still remained with the Queen.

Haggis, after another sip of his Worthington E said,

"Angus has told me about your meteoric rise in the company and that you are considered a marketing genius at NCR."

"Well, I don't know if I'd go that far, but things have been good. In developing the specialized programs for the auto industry and

the legal profession I've made a little money while having a good time in the process,"
Guy said in an attempt at modesty.
"Come on lad you've made a fortune at the same time you were getting laid more times in a week than most mere mortals experience in a year," Angus gleefully added. While Guy had indeed achieved a certain level of success, Angus was by far the best and highest paid front line salesman at NCR. The clever Scot disdained management and repeatedly declined the frequent offers of promotion by insisting he couldn't afford to take a cut in pay. Angus was red hot and could sell any product that NCR had to offer and did so at an astonishing rate. Like himself, Angus too also had been known to not only sell vast amounts of the company's wares, but in spite of being married was quietly bedding virtually every operator he trained to use the equipment.
In an effort to divert Angus from engaging in a detailed dissertation of their mutual interest in sexual exploitations which he appeared eager to embark on, Guy turned to Haggis,
"As you've been living in South Africa for some time what's your opinion of the Apartheid Policy? Do the country's racial problems concern or have any affect on you and your wife?"
At this point Guy felt like the little Dutch Boy who had just removed his finger from the dike. Haggis raised his forefinger much like a teacher reprimanding his students and said,
"You Americans have a dreadful misconception of Southern Africa. Dr. Verwoerd who is called the Architect of Apartheid implemented the Apartheid policy when he was Minister of Native Affairs in the early 1950's. The separate development of the races which was described as a "policy of good neighborliness" became law requiring all black South Africans over 18 to carry a pass book which the locals called a *Dompass* or plainly a Dumb Pass. If that bloody block-head Smuts hadn't given it a name it wouldn't be condemned and labeled like it is today. Do you know that the government provides free medical and dental care to all the blacks while the whites have to pay for these services? The blacks in South Africa also enjoy the highest living standard in all of Africa, if it's as bad as they claim then why do the bloody Kaffirs continue to pour into the country

legally and illegally? It makes my blood boil when I see what's written and portrayed as a crime against humanity. Ask any Bantu on the street how his lot is and he'll tell you he's never had it so good. The bloody communists have developed a small, hard core group within the ANC that kill and maim innocent people with their terrorist attacks. Then the bleeding heart liberals immediately jump up and cry foul play saying that the deaths are justified in the fight for freedom. The African National Congress is run politically and militarily by blacks and white sympathizers who are trained and funded by Moscow. Both Oliver Tambo and his mate Joe Schlomo are nothing more than outright murderers. Schlomo was the head of the South African Communist Party but fled the country when the ANC was outlawed. Now, the two run their campaigns of terror from a base in Zambia and I might add with the blessing of Britain and the United States."

"Hey, hey calm down," Angus pleaded.

"Haggis you're acting like you've got a viper up your kilt!"

Guy looked at them both,

"No, please this is interesting. The things you have just told me are not what you find in articles in the main stream media like the San Francisco Examiner or the New York Times."

Haggis clearly annoyed responded,

"That's the problem. The worst failing is that the South African Government doesn't have an effective PR policy of disseminating true information that would help other people throughout the world fully understand what really is going on in the country. A generous retainer to Hill Knowlton or some other public relations outfit is what our Afrikaner brothers need and should invest in rather than all that wasted money they pay to belong to the United Nations."

Guy, duly impressed with Haggis' apparent convictions and assessment of the problem said,

"But Haggis, why are the South Africans so afraid of majority rule and….."

Haggis cut him off,

"That's a load of rubbish my friend, in Africa there is no majority rule in any country. White South Africans already know and the rest of the world only has to look north at countries like Uganda,

Nigeria, Rwanda or Ghana to see there's no democracy or majority rule. They're all only one party states with tribal factions in control. When the Europeans withdrew from these former colonies they left the local banks full of money, a trained civil service and strong economies with abundant natural resources. Following independence these countries immediately became corrupt one-party States with bankrupt economies whose populations were being slaughtered by inter-tribal factions. A good example is Kenya. Jomo Kenyatta, the leader of the treacherous Mau-Mau became the country's first leader after independence even though he was responsible for the deaths of thousands of whites and blacks. You can bet your last dollar that even the whites who lived through the uprisings will eventually be killed, lose their farms and be forced to leave. In other African countries like Uganda the mass deportation of Asians was carried out in some cases with less than twenty four hours notice. You see lad, these are just some of the injustices that rarely get in the press. Yet when some bloody Kaffir gets detained for a minor pass violation it's a major story. When the Voortrekkers moved north in their great trek there were no true indigenous natives or tribes. With the exception of Zululand all the blacks you now find in South Africa migrated from the North to find work in the prospering economy south of the Limpopo. Most people in the world are lead to believe that the White South African is trying to displace the blacks when in fact it's just the other way around."

Angus becoming noticeably annoyed broke in,

"C'mon Haggis we all know you want to preserve the status quo so you can carry on with your servants and a chauffeur to move you and the Mrs. around Jo'burg like the *Lairds of the Manor*."

"No, that's not the case at all you bloody fool, we know that some of the silly things have to be cleaned up. Having black and white toilets, separate seats in the park and pass laws that are outdated do need to be changed. These changes will come about in time, but should not make the whites second-class citizens which would surely happen under the ANC. If you've ever seen a photo of an African head-of-state in the papers take a look at who he has for body guards, without exception they're almost always whites. That's because of the tribal distrust that's evident across the entire continent. Just look at what Tom Mboya is doing as Kenya's Minister of Finance, a bright young lad educated at the London School of Economics, personable and doing a bang up job with his new country's treasury. One day he'll probably end up getting shot in cold blood by an opposing tribe because he wouldn't agree with some tribal chief in the Veld. Ridiculous! It will be such a waste, but that's what tribal factions can do. You know too, the governments and the people in West and East Africa would probably starve, but for the money their people send back from jobs in South Africa. Oppenheimer and his Anglo American Group do most of their trading north of us through front companies in Europe so the black governments won't have to acknowledge the fact they have active trade going on with companies in South Africa."

"C'mon Haggis, no more, no more politics,"

Angus demanded from his Scottish friend.

"I'll listen to no more of this bloody minded talk of Africa, black or white. Let's get down to some serious drinking and be happy we are all here in sunny California where the blasted Inland Revenue doesn't tax the booze to the point that it would be cheaper to drink petrol!"

Guy had two large rum and cokes which Angus vigorously condemned.

"How can you ruin good spirits with that bloody Coca Cola?"

Guy, never having been fond of hard liquor normally preferred wine, but if he had rum it was only with Coca Cola. He gently chided Angus that anyone who liked to drink warm beer should not be critical of what the Bacardi family recommended be taken with their rum.

"Let's eat," Haggis suggested, finishing the last of his Worthington E and setting the empty glass on the table. The threesome then adjourned to the dining room overlooking a placid Pacific Ocean. They had just finished their broiled lobster which was accompanied by an excellent Monterey Chablis as the waiter approached with the Irish coffees that Angus insisted they have as his guest.

"You know the best thing about Ireland is her Whisky" said

Angus who, after a number of pints of Worthington E followed by the wine had now become an expert on the Emerald Isles. Before leaving the table the waiter discretely handed Guy a message from the concierge, *Please call room 1102.* Excusing himself he made his way to the lobby.

"Hey, gorgeous what's up?" Guy said in low tones over the house phone.

"Nothing more than my fingers so far big boy, when are you coming up for some desert?" purred the seductive Sam.

"Soon sweetheart, go take a hot bath, turn on a dirty movie and slip between the sheets and think about me. I'll be there soon."

Guy returned to the table where Haggis and Angus had finished their Irish coffee and ordered a second round. "That's bloody good stuff even if it's diluted with coffee," observed Haggis.

"You know Guy someone like you could make a fortune in South Africa and while making all that money have a great time. You, like any connoisseur of the female species would fully appreciate the beauty of the Cape Province. The beauty of course being the bikini clad ladies on Clifton Beach. Authoritative sources have indicated that white South African women are without a doubt, the most beautiful women in the world including those found here in California, the South of France, or Marbella in Spain."

The more Haggis spoke the more interested Guy became in this distant land.

"Well it may be Okay for you, but I don't speak Afrikaans and don't know a soul in the country."

"You know me and you don't need to speak Afrikaans. Everything from the government is printed in English and Afrikaans. The language of the business community is English. The country badly needs specialists in all fields particularly computers and data processing. If you were interested I might even be able to have a job waiting for you the day you stepped off the plane."

Guy wondered to himself if this was the excess of alcohol speaking or if Haggis truly meant what he had just thrust upon Guy with such enthusiasm.

"Haggis, I've got another matter to attend to right now, but I'd like to hear more about South Africa tomorrow, could we meet

for breakfast, say 8:00?"
"You're on mate see you in the coffee shop at 8:00."
Haggis and Angus both grinned and blew him kisses as he left the table. The door marked 1102 was closed but unlocked. Upon entering the darkened room he could hear subdued groaning sounds coming from the television set, the only illumination was that produced by the X-rated film playing on the TV.
The nude body on the bed was still, lying face down, tightly clutching a pillow. Guy locked the door, slipped out of his clothes and turning off the TV slid silently next to the motionless form. Gently caressing the soft body and kissing her well rounded bottom his fingers began to explore the silky hair between her legs. Her moist vagina responded almost immediately as if she was experiencing a sexual fantasy in an imaginary state of consciousness. Rolling over on her back Guy's fingers and tongue continued their exploration causing her body to move gently in a pushing motion while her legs moved wider and wider apart. His tongue moved from between her legs up to her naval, gently kissing and caressing in its progress towards her firm round breasts. His extended tongue drew back and forth across her erect nipples which had grown hard with increased anxiety. As his hand gently massaged her breasts she reached between his legs and softy pulled at his penis which was now erect and standing firm in expectation. Their lips moist with anticipation met as if they both were one. Their mouths formed a gentle union with tongues moving and embracing as soft vines clinging with passion to one another.
Her breathing grew deep and strong as they rolled slowly back and forth with compassionate resolve. In a state of ecstasy her long nails were now piercing his back as if in fear her lover may fade from her grasp. She tenderly turned him on his back as her lips withdrew from his to begin a tender embrace of his neck, slowly moving down his body until she had him fully in her mouth. Gently stroking him her tongue moved slowly in eagerness as if consuming a mouth watering delicacy. Sam, now in a position on top of him in moist and longing expectation tenderly guided him deep inside her. Like a voodoo dancer in a frenzied trance she rose above him as her large breasts moved

with graceful rhythm. Simultaneously reaching the plateau, both trembled, her nails digging deeper into his back he moaning in ecstasy and her shouting, "Yes, yes, now, now!"

Two more times they came together in almost uncontrollable fury, each time with seemingly more warmth and greater emotion. Soon falling asleep in each others arms their smiles masked by the darkness, but each sharing a feeling of closeness and complete satisfaction. The illuminated clock on the TV indicated that it was now 4:15 a.m. Guy again took pleasure with his beautiful sleeping beauty that had awoken with his gentle caresses. Once more the plateau was reached before Guy dressed and returned to his room at 5:00 a.m.

Guy had set the alarm to wake him at 7:30 a.m. and groaned as he attempted to reach for the unpleasant screeching sound announcing that the appointed hour had arrived. He showered quickly and made his way to the coffee shop to meet Haggis and Angus.

"Morning your Grace." Angus said in a cheery tone.

Guy smiled, "Good morning gentlemen."

"And where did you spend the night my good fellow? We called your room last night to see if you'd join us for a night cap, but alas we found that Prince Charming was out somewhere. I hope it was good because you look bloody awful. I'd suggest that you not open your eyes too much as you may bleed to death!"

"Angus you're a real joker, I'm sorry I couldn't join you for a night cap. No, I wasn't in my room and whether *it* was good, bad or otherwise is none of your *bloody* business!"

After some orange juice and coffee the conversation turned once again to South Africa allowing Haggis to continue to expand on the positive virtues of life in Southern Africa.

On Friday morning, the day the conference was to close, Guy made arrangements to meet with Haggis the following week. In learning about the country Guy was interested in the opportunities that may be available if he made a move. Haggis was due to return to South Africa on a flight from San Francisco, but said he'd come down a day earlier from Seattle and could meet with Guy before returning to Johannesburg.

When the training conference ended Guy bid his farewells to

Haggis and Angus and while he was paying his bill met Sam in the lobby. He promised they would get together soon and suggested either he come to Los Angeles or she could spend a few days with him in the City. They kissed and with a gentle, but inconspicuous caress of her bottom, Guy left for the airport. Guy was satisfied that it had been a rewarding trip from both a personal and business standpoint. Little did he know his unexpected meeting with Ian "Haggis" Cowan would change his life forever.

Veronica was glad he was back. Their lovemaking on Friday's and Saturday's resumed interrupted only by walks in the Marina and afternoon tea at the St. Francis Yacht Club. Guy was preoccupied and Veronica kept inquiring as to what he was so deeply in thought about. Guy had South Africa on his mind and kept thinking about Haggis' observations of life there. It's crazy he thought, I've got everything going for me here, a good job with a future, a nice car and penthouse with probably the best view in the bay area, good friends both male and female, and of course the boat. As much as he tried to forget about South Africa it kept coming back into his thoughts.

On Saturday Guy again pressed Veronica to find out exactly who his mystery lover really was. Why wouldn't she tell him where she lived? Why all the secrecy? He became both annoyed and disturbed at her silence. Sunday morning, after a torrid Saturday night of love they were sitting in the solarium having coffee. Guy was pleading with Veronica and insisting she spend the day with him on the *Stiletto*,

"We can be at the Marina in Berkeley in an hour and we'll cruise up the delta, have a late lunch and be back by dark."

"I can't Guy. I've planned to spend the day with my mother. Sorry, but I just can't. Please bear with me. Soon, my time will be my own and we can be together all the time."

Veronica's voice had a sad tone, a tone he had not heard before. She kissed him gently and bid her farewell then slowly walked down the stairs to her car.

Guy looked at himself in the hallway mirror and spoke aloud, *Sorry my love but that's just not good enough. For months now we've been screwing our brains out and I don't even know where you live. Hmm, soon my time will be my own. What's that supposed to mean? I wonder what else you're not telling me.*

Guy picked up his car keys and looked out the window just as Veronica was getting into her car. Skipping every other one, he lurched down the steps at the same time pressing the remote that instructed Genie to open the garage door. At the turn of the ignition key the throaty engine of the Aston Martin roared and immediately came to life. As the Aston began to roll from its habitat he pressed the button to activate his car phone.

He could see Veronica's Buick in the distance just rounding the corner at the Safeway Supermarket. Much like the start of the race at Le Mans slow, fast, left, then right, the Aston Martin responded to Guy's every command without hesitation. Carefully keeping a safe distance between them he followed Veronica's Buick through the city streets towards Van Ness Avenue where it turned to join the southbound traffic of Highway 101.

Once out of San Francisco's fashionable Marina district the neighborhoods quickly altered from middle class down to almost poverty levels. The hunter and the hunted passed through the suburbs of Daly City and South San Francisco until Veronica reached the San Mateo turn off. After passing through South San Francisco the blue-collar class neighborhoods quickly changed to the rich and the super rich of Northern San Mateo County.

Guy knew San Mateo County well as his family and other relatives lived along the Peninsula in Burlingame and Redwood City. His grand and great-grandparents once had homes just south of San Mateo in Palo Alto. In days long passed the Young family had provided some of their land holdings to Leland Stanford for the expansion of his well known learning institution. Guy's grandfather once rented his garage to David Packard and his partner, Mr. Hewlett when they had come to him with a seemingly extraordinary idea about starting a company to build some sort of electronic instrumentation systems.

Guy's Cousin Beth, who was the oldest employee of San Mateo County, had often rubbed shoulders with the ruling classes and academia in her role as county librarian, while John W. his great-great grandfather after retiring as a General in the Army had become the Mayor of San Francisco and spent his weekends in the hills of San Mateo. Following his tenure as Mayor he then was appointed the U.S. Postmaster of San Francisco. It was said that during his weekends on the peninsula he developed and refined the first postal code system for San Francisco. His new postal delivery system in later years was called the Zip Code. As Guy drove along Highway 101 he thought of his family's many close ties with the Bay Area. By god, he thought, even Jim Young has been the Sheriff of Santa Clara County for maybe, what, twenty years.

After leaving the 101 Veronica turned and crossed the El Camino Real driving east towards the hills passing houses that increased in value with their elevated position on the hillside. Guy was only a few blocks behind her when she pulled into the drive of 1674 El Sueño Avenue. Pulling to the other side of the street a block away he shut off the engine. 1674 El Sueño was located in an upscale community and positioned nicely on a quiet street with a frontage of at least 1000'. The house was set back from the road about 500' with a large sweeping circular drive adorned with masses of flowers, sculptured shrubs and a large weeping willow situated amidst the manicured lawns. The magnificent house was a large Queen Anne masterpiece finished in burnished tans and trimmed in bronze. After Veronica shut off the engine a large Tudor oak door opened and a small Hispanic woman in a black uniform came out surrounded by four small children who rushed to the drivers' side of the car.

As Veronica got out of the car the three smaller ones were clinging to her while the small boy hung on the car door swinging with his legs up. Guy started to become uncomfortable and his stomach began to knot witnessing what appeared to be the apparent return of a mother to her children. *Hmm, no wonder she likes to screw so much, she's obviously a real producer with four kids! She said she was going to spend the day with her mother. If this was her mother's house she'd have to be much younger to have kids that age. Maybe a sister, hmmm, her mother is at her sister's house and she's come to collect her? What's the story? Strange..*, he said to himself.

After Veronica, the maid and the children had entered the house Guy sat quietly in his car trying to provide himself with some reasonable explanation. A few minutes later Veronica came out of the house alone and walked towards her car. Moments later the door of the house opened and the maid came out, after a brief conversation the maid returned to the house and Veronica got into her car and drove off. There was no time for Guy to drive away as Veronica was now coming directly towards where he was parked. He quickly leaned over in the passengers' seat hoping she wouldn't notice his car parked in the shade of another large weeping willow. Veronica was never taken with cars and had paid little attention to the Aston, something that had often annoyed him. Hopefully she wouldn't pay attention now. After the Buick had passed he sat up and turned the key in the ignition. Watching in the mirror he waited until the Buick had traveled well down the block then made a U turn and was again in pursuit. Obviously knowing the area she was using side streets and the back roads driving east through the suburbs of San Mateo. After crossing the El Camino Real she was heading in the direction of Highway 101 and the San Francisco Airport. When she reached 101 she crossed, passed the Hilton and then moved to the far right lane that leads to the airport's Arrivals area. At the curb in front of Pan American Airways she stopped the car. Guy stayed well back and in the heavy Sunday traffic couldn't be seen as he pulled against the curb in front of Japan Airlines. Guy, fully engrossed in his observations was surprised when he was tapped on the shoulder by a Police Officer.

"Sorry buddy, but this is only for picking up passengers, you can't park here."

The officer was very courteous, but firm, insisting that he move.

"Sorry officer, I'll be here only a minute. My friend forgot one of his bags and just went in to collect it. He walks with a cane so I wouldn't want him to wait. Could I stay for just a minute please," Guy said with a pleading voice.

"Okay, okay, but you better be gone when I come back," the officer said before continuing to walk down the line of cars.

"Thank God, if I would have to drive by her, it would be just my luck she'd see me."

At that moment, Guy noticed a tall man walking towards Veronica's Buick who was wearing a Pan American Airways uniform. The man carried an overnight case and a Pilot's standard issue black leather flight bag obviously containing his aircraft operations manuals. The large amounts of silver leaf on the bill of his hat and four silver stripes on the jacket arms indicated he was a long-haul Senior Flight Captain for Pan Am.

The Captain slid into the passenger seat of the Buick threw his bags into the back seat then kissed Veronica. They drove away with Guy following. Using the same route it appeared the Buick was returning to 1674 El Sueño. To avoid being seen he stayed well back as he was sure he knew where they were going. A short time later in the distance he saw the Buick enter the circular drive of 1674 El Sueño, Guy stopped, turned around and returned home.

"Robert Victor Morris and Veronica Katherine Morris-Gucci, 1674 El Sueño Avenue, San Mateo, California is shown on the registration for the Buick. The DMV registration records show they also own another car, a Ford Country Squire Station Wagon, is that all you need Guy?" said Chris Young of the California Highway Patrol in Sacramento.

"Yes, thanks Chris I appreciate the help. When the woman was reversing from a parking space at Sears she put a small scratch on the Aston. When she drove away she might not have realized she'd hit me and I didn't notice it till later. It's no big deal and I'm not going to do anything about it, just wanted to know who it was, off the record, of course." Guy said hanging up the phone.

Guy had called his cousin Chris, a lieutenant with the Highway Patrol in Sacramento saying he had a license plate number that he wanted checked out and just wanted to know who they were and where they lived. Chris told him that he could lose his job if it ever got out that he'd given out confidential records information, but was confident that Guy wouldn't abuse the privilege.

On Monday Guy met with Haggis and spent the day discussing the prospects and possibilities of Guy coming to Johannesburg. That night he and Haggis had dinner at the Rose and Thistle, an English Pub on Geary Street. Parting they agreed to keep in touch. From what he'd learned from Haggis and now knowing the truth about Veronica, he said to himself, *Look out South Africa, here I come.* From the balcony sipping his morning tea

Guy gazed out over the bay. The mist and fog provided a striking silhouette of the Golden Gate Bridge and a shrouded view of the hills of Marin County. He watched as a large ship passed Alcatraz before silently slipping beneath the Golden Gate Bridge effortlessly making its way on a westerly course towards the vast expanses of the Pacific. Guy mused at the thought that he too was a bit like that ship venturing forth on a long voyage.

While traveling to a foreign land would be easy, the challenge would be the logistics, advanced planning and the details he'd have to deal with. Resigning from his position at NCR, selling the car, the penthouse, the boat, and his furniture, telling the guys in the band, and then there was Veronica.

For the next few days Guy was unable to concentrate on his work. He devoted his time to a lined legal pad containing a list and Critical Path Analysis of the items he would have to deal with in the order of their importance. The first item on his list was to call the South African Embassy in Washington who promptly suggested he call the South African Consulate General in Los Angeles. No doubt as a result of his education, training and experience in computer systems with NCR the consular official said there would be no problem and immediately sent him the application forms required for persons wishing to relocate to the country. A few days later when the application forms for his residency arrived they seemed endless. For consideration of a residency application the Consulate required that he provide medical certificates, bank statements, credit reports supporting financial status, employment history, police clearance, and college transcripts, it went on and on.

The paperwork was never-ending; copies of this then a copy of something else, but fortunately the Consulate General's office was very helpful and assisted Guy in completing the required documentation for his application as an immigrant. Guy was elated when he was told that if his immigrant status was approved he would qualify for *Resettlement Assistance,* meaning they'd pay his airfare and the first two months in a residential hotel in Johannesburg. The checking and verification of his documents took a number of weeks to finalize, but in the meantime Guy told no one of his plans while continuing to communicate with Haggis in Johannesburg. Haggis sent him copies of the Johannesburg Star and the Rand Daily Mail along with a recent edition of Panorama, the South African equivalent of Life Magazine.

His phone bill, which had always made a large contribution to the profits of Pacific Telephone and Telegraph, grew to enormous proportions in view of his frequent calls to Haggis who had been sworn to secrecy. If Angus learned of his plans it might inadvertently get back to the company. His brief liaisons with Veronica continued, but were less frequent and with reduced intensity. At first he thought of telling Veronica that he knew of her hubby and the kiddies and that he was leaving, but the thought of prematurely throwing such a good screw to the wind just couldn't be justified.

On August 2nd the South African Consulate returned the documents confirming his approved immigrant status. The Consulate also advised him that as he qualified for Resettlement Assistance his passport should be sent to their office by registered mail. The following day Guy sent his passport and a week later it was returned containing an official residency stamp. Included with the documents and passport was a coupon for a one-way economy class ticket to Johannesburg and a voucher for two months in a residential hotel in Berea, a suburb of Johannesburg. He was ready to roll! Ads placed in the San Francisco Chronicle produced ten calls on the Aston Martin and twenty for the penthouse. The car went to the highest bidder, a lawyer in Sausalito who agreed to let him drive it until the end of the month. The penthouse was sold to a wheeler-dealer in real estate who lived on the peninsula in Atherton.

While not admitting it the wheeler-dealer clearly wanted the penthouse as a hideaway to enjoy frequent fornication encounters with a sexy mental dwarf who had accompanied him on all three occasions when he viewed the penthouse. Both liked the elegant décor and agreed to take all the furniture allowing Guy to make a clean break. When the time came for him to leave he could simply walk away without having to worry about selling individual pieces of furniture or the appliances. They would take possession on September 1st. Guy chuckled to himself after the closing knowing that his Queen Size water bed would continue to enjoy an active sex life when it became the lair and love nest for the new owner. The worst part of his departure preparations would be the sale of the *Stiletto*. The ocean racer had given him many hours of pleasure and was his way of releasing stress; it had become his psychological escape valve.

Unlike so many of his acquaintances he'd never had the need to see a psychoanalyst or a shrink. Some of his friends had regular appointments with a psychiatrist hoping the tell-all sessions would resolve their problems or at least help in dealing with the stresses of the fast lane. When he was stressed Guy found that a day or afternoon on the boat cruising at 60 MPH over the water was his outlet, his release to clear his mind and allow him to focus and resolve his own problems. He believed that his friends had probably spent more money to lounge on a shrink's couch and spill out their inter-most secrets than Guy had ever spent on the boat or its upkeep. Akin to losing a member of the family, Guy felt a tinge of sadness when a banker's son gave him the check as payment in full for the *Stiletto*.

Once his termination notice had been given to NCR, telling the band members he was leaving and then dealing with Veronica his departure preparations would be complete. The resignation to the company was addressed in a short letter that simply advised that he was going into business for himself as a program designer and unfortunately had to resign his position with effect from August 30th. His superior was surprised and dismayed at Guy's leaving, but after numerous attempts pleading for him to reconsider accepted that his star performer was leaving the cast. His resignation from NCR was reluctantly, but gracefully accepted. Guy was careful not to burn any bridges in case he might need the references that NCR could provide down the road.

His co-workers gave him a beautiful leaded crystal wine decanter with a card signed by all the staff. He waited until the second Friday in August to tell the band he was leaving and then the following day booked his flight via London to Johannesburg. Guy now had less than a week before departure day.

During one of their water bed sessions Veronica commented that he seemed preoccupied,

"Guy I don't know what's been on your mind, but something is bothering you, you're just not the same." Guy withdrew from her and rolled over on his back,

"I'm sorry, yes. I've had a great deal on my mind for the last few weeks and have been waiting for the right time to tell you. I've been offered a marvelous opportunity in Rio de Janeiro and have accepted the position. Once I get organized and get an apartment I want you to join me. Other than telling me you're single and that you're close to your mother, I really don't know much about you or your personal circumstances, but was sure you'd be excited about the move. I know that you have personal matters you'll have to attend to before you come so the timing is perfect. I've been anxious, but just waiting for the right time to let you know about the wonderful plans I have for us."

It was only a sham, but Guy had to convince her that she was being given this exciting opportunity to be with him on a thrilling adventure that included a new life in Brazil. Too bad she didn't know that he knew she was a married woman with four kids and domestic staff living in suburbia with an airline Captain who she had also been deceiving for at least a year. If she lived this secret life with him he wondered how many other men she may have been involved with before? Veronica may have found him to be preoccupied, but fortunately she hadn't detected any difference in his life style. The penthouse was the same because it had been discreetly sold intact and he still drove the same car while continuing to play the weekend gigs at Pedro's. She hadn't mentioned the boat probably because she'd never had any interest in the *Stiletto* having only been on the boat once. Guy did need a ride to the airport so why not get Veronica to drive him?

"Veronica, I'm leaving on the 31st and would really appreciate if you'd drive me to the airport. When I get to Rio and get an apartment I'll phone you and give you the address where I'll be living. It'll probably take me about a month, but once I'm settled in I'll send you a plane ticket so you can join me."

Her face showed the strain brought about by such a *matter of fact* proclamation by her lover. Her mind now in high gear, Veronica turned pale with fear. How could he call her? She couldn't give him her phone number as it would simply be too dangerous. If I gave him the phone number and Conchita answered the phone or worse yet, Robert it would be disastrous. Mulling the situation her mind was racing, it'll be hard to leave the children, but I'll do it. Guy knows nothing of my real life in San Mateo, maybe I should have told him? Rio! Yes, a new life with Guy in Brazil sounds exciting, I love him and I want to be with him. No more boring responsibilities, no more dreary women's clubs, no more hiding. No more having to slip away for secret rendezvous' while Robert was on a turnaround in either Paris or London and no more questions from that inquisitive little Mexican maid. Veronica contemplated her options then quickly sat up in bed,

"Guy, I don't quite know what to say. Yes, I can do it, but it will take me a bit of time to organize my affairs. When did you decide to do this? What about your job, the penthouse?"

"Veronica it's all taken care of. The penthouse is sold and I've resigned from NCR."

Guy felt relieved. His lover knew things were done, cast in stone and there would be no discussion because there was no turning back. "Guy, I've got to tell you something." Veronica then proceeded to bare her soul as she had done with her body many times before. She began telling him of her marriage, the kids, the house, where she lived, even down to her dislike of her mother-in-law. As she rambled on Guy was thinking that if ever an Academy Award was in order he should be considered for the way he thoughtfully and convincingly accepted her *True Confessions*. Unaware that he knew more about her than she realized Guy continued his performance acting surprised and astonished with her confessions of marital infidelity.

Veronica said she would indeed join him in Rio, but needed time to deal with her affairs. She would leave the children and her husband of fifteen years and simply walk away to a new life. From the beginning Veronica had deliberately and repeatedly deceived him. He would deceive her only once.

As Guy left the Montgomery Street branch of Bank of America he felt satisfied and secure that he had made the right decision in making the move. After closing his checking account at Wells Fargo he opened a new savings account with Bank of America depositing the $400,000.00 in proceeds he had received for the penthouse, the car and the boat. While getting established to cover his initial expenses in Johannesburg he bought $20,000.00 in travelers' checks. Once in the country he would open an account with a local bank that was a correspondent with Bank of America and transfer money from his savings account in San Francisco as needed. Haggis had warned Guy about the stringent and difficult exchange control regulations in South Africa and suggested he not bring all his money into the country, but only draw on his U.S. funds as required.

On the drive to the airport Veronica looked truly beautiful, she had her hair done and wore a tight fitting mini skirt that made Guy wish they had time to stop for some lovemaking along the way. As they drove she talked continuously until they reached the Varig Brazilian Airways curb-side check in. She stopped the car and after turning off the engine began to cry. Not wishing to endure an emotional scene at the airport,

"C'mon sweetheart not now there's no need for tears, we'll be together before you know it."

After removing his three large Samsonite cases and briefcase from the car Guy said,

"I'm not certain when I will call, but when I do, it'll be on one of the days and between the times you told me. If for some reason you don't answer, I'll hang up and call back. Take care of yourself, we'll be together soon."

As she pulled away from the curb Guy turned to the Sky Cap who had placed the bags on his cart and asked him to wait a moment. After Veronica's Buick had disappeared into the traffic he handed the Sky Cap a $10.00 bill.

"Sorry, wrong airline, let's go over to British Airways."

After changing planes in New York he arrived in London the following morning and happy that he'd upgraded to first class. The flight from JFK to Heathrow was pleasant in spite of having to deal with a guy sitting next to him who said his name was Charlie Barrett. During the flight as Barrett rapidly depleted the supply of Chivas Regal he became obnoxious and increasingly louder. Guy had never been fond of this distinctly local dialect that made most native New Yorkers like Charlie sound like cabbies from the Bronx.

The efficiency and courteous handling of arriving passengers at London's Heathrow by Her Majesty's Immigration was in sharp contrast to the grim, penetrating and expressionless stares of her Customs Officers.

After being told of the cab fare and with assurances that the Rembrandt Hotel was only a short ride from the airport the thought of struggling with three large cases between buses and airport terminals after an all night flight really didn't seem to be a good idea. He decided that the £15.00 cab ride was an easier option. When changing some dollars to sterling in the arrivals area the sweet little morsel at the Barclays Bank counter enlightened him on the somewhat mystical interpretation of Pounds, Shillings, Pence, and a Guinea. Guy smiled as he walked away deciding he'd figure out the funny-money later.

Arriving at the Rembrandt he found it was a lovely hotel located in the midst of fashionable Knightsbridge, close to some neat looking Pubs and situated directly across the road from the British Museum. During the drive to the hotel Guy found that the cabbie was from Hackney a borough in the east end of London. The cabbie told him that having been born in Hackney and being able to hear the sounds of Bow Bells made him a true cockney. Listening closely to decipher and understand exactly what the cockney cabbie was saying Guy thought of Michael Caine the respected and accomplished actor and another Londoner who after emerging from the depths of the Elephant and Castle had achieved towering acclaim in both the American and British motion picture industries. Depending on his role the eminent Caine could easily converse in cockney slang or communicate as a proper English gentleman. Even though Guy wanted to venture forth and see this great city he was worn out, but promised himself, like General Mac Arthur once said, *Someday I Shall Return!*

That night, exhausted from the flight he slept soundly. The following morning another cockney in another black cab deposited him at London's Heathrow airport with an hour to kill before the long haul to South Africa.

"Your attention please, BOAC announces the departure of its

flight 345 to Johannesburg with intermediate stops in Rome, Nairobi and Salisbury, Rhodesia. Those passengers requiring special assistance should proceed to Gate 33 for boarding. All other passengers please remain seated, Thank you."

Precise instructions delivered by a refined, but unseen voice from above.

The other passengers now congregating around the departure gate represented a multitude of countries and cultures of extreme and dramatic contrasts. Turbaned Sikhs carrying Sitars, Nigerians in their colorful robes and a gaggle of Asians were clustered together with small children who appeared like little mosaic dolls. Included in the group were their British masters properly attired in dark suits with stiff collars, some with bowlers and the ever present umbrella. Guy silently contemplated his future thinking, before I was just in the world, *but from here on - I'm of the world.* He laughed as a small grin swept across his face. A beautiful woman also waiting to board noticed the attentive grin from the handsome gentleman who appeared deeply engrossed in his thoughts.

The woman smiled and Guy, now feeling somewhat self conscious, blushed slightly and smiled back. Guy was later to learn that this beautiful creature was Rona Tannenbaum a confident and successful woman who had made her way to the top of her profession in South Africa. Making a few enemies in her precarious ascent to stardom she had unhappily forced herself to share casting couches with a few producers and directors until eventually she was introduced to Abe Silver. Abe had become a legend in the British film industry and in the process had made the Rank Studios what they were today. Fed up with the British weather and a disgusting labor government at 65 he immigrated to South Africa where he continued in the film industry with astonishing success.

During the filming of one of his block busters set in Mbabane, Swaziland he met Rona and they fell in love. They'd been married only a few months when Rona returned early from a shopping trip to find her beloved Abe in bed sodomizing a young starlet who, like many others was making her way to the *silver* screen through the bedrooms and casting couches of anyone promising stardom.

While she could have divorced her whoring husband and left with a considerable portion of his wealth she chose to accept Abe's offer of a small stipend and simply dissolve the marriage as quickly and as painlessly as possible. Considering Abe's clout and ability to negatively impact or even end her acting career her decision proved to be prudent. With his power and influence over the studios and their bosses he could easily have had her blacklisted.

In the divorce settlement she agreed to keep their penthouse overlooking the Point Yacht Club in the center of Durban, a large home in Rivonia and her Mercedes along with the payment of 5000.00 Rand per month for five years. Recognizing the potential problems with Abe and his considerable influence both in the Nationalist government and the South African film industry Rona had also thought about moving abroad. After successful and productive meetings with the Grade organization and Pinewood Studios she had seriously considered the possibilities in England. While there were opportunities to further her career abroad she dreaded the thought of leaving her beloved South Africa for the cold and dismal climate of the United Kingdom. Rona also had other interests that would prevent her from leaving the country.

With the announcement that all First Class passengers could board, Guy edged his way towards the jet way and after entering the plane the steward showed him to his seat, 3B. Guy always preferred an aisle seat so he wouldn't have to disturb other passengers on his sometime frequent trips to the lavatory while flying. After taking his seat he thought to himself *the gods are with me* when the beauty he had exchanged glances with in the lounge excused herself, as the steward directed her to seat 3A.

"Hi, I'm the American Ambassador of Good Will. Am I to enjoy the pleasure of such a magnificent traveling companion to Johannesburg? Will you be going all the way?" Guy said with a wide smile.

"Are all American Ambassadors so forward? We've haven't even met and you ask if I'm going all the way with you? Bit cheeky isn't it?"

Rona then bit her lip, thinking my God did I say that. She now realized that she probably shouldn't have had the three double Gin and Tonics in the lounge, but as flying always terrified her, a bit of booze always helped her relax. Oh what the hell, he's nice looking and we've definitely taken down any barriers.

Somewhat taken aback Guy responded,

"Cheeky? No, not really, we Yankee Doodles always take the direct approach. Cut away the chafe and get right down to the matter at hand. I think it's called diplomatic privilege with expedient resolve or something like that. And of course one might not be the first, but we should never forget that it's the second mouse that gets the cheese."

Following the brief exchange both settled down into their seats. Guy snapped on his seat belt while observing that his companion was having difficulty with hers. He leaned across looking at her and said,

"May I help? Those of us from the other side of the Pond are gentlemen as well as Knights in shining armor and always ready to assist a damsel in distress. Could be that my sole purpose in life is to be kind to others."

She smiled, "Hmm, sole purpose in life to be kind to others haven't heard that line before, but yes, please, I can't seem to get this ruddy thing to buckle up."

Guy pulled on her seat belt inserting the two ends as it snapped closed,

"There, you're set."

As he completed his task and leaning across the seat Guy's face was even with hers, their eyes met momentarily gazing at one another, until the steward interrupted, "May I get you a drink from the bar before we depart?"

"Yes please, what will you have Miss or is it Mrs.? Guy asked.

"It's Miss and I'd like a Tangeray and tonic."

"And I'll have a Rum and Coke," Guy said attempting to conceal his pleasure in finding that this witty, gracious and lovely creature may also be unattached.

———

As the airport exit doors to the street opened the brilliant sunlight bid a warm welcome as Guy Young made his official entrance to the Republic of South Africa. He then heard a voice from the crowd,

"Hey Yank need a lift?"

The accent was unmistakably Scottish and the smiling face that greeted him was his new found friend Ian Cowan.

"Hi Haggis sure do any idea where Berea is? I'll be staying at the Primrose Residential Hotel on Primrose Terrace in the fine city of Johannesburg," he replied with a wide grin, happy to be in South Africa after the long flight.

"Right mate, Berea is right next to Hillbrow where Maude and I live. It's only about 30 minutes from the airport."

The two then struggled as they forced Guy's luggage in the small trunk of the Mercedes 280 Sport conveniently parked outside the arrivals entrance. Haggis was obviously pleased with his little red beauty and liked to show it off much like a proud new father presenting his first born.

———

"She's back, came in today on the BOAC flight from London," the voice reported through the intercom on his desk. Hearing this Chris Van der Merve quickly stood and looking out his window reacted much like a hunter that had again sighted his prey. Van der Merve was a Chief Inspector with the South African Special Branch whose primary interest for the last 10 years had been focused on counter terrorism. He was a third generation Afrikaner who could trace his family roots back to the Voortrekkers. His father and his father before him had been farmers in the predominately Afrikaner Orange Free State.

While studying Political Science at the University of the Witwatersrand Van der Merve had recognized and accepted that blacks outnumbered the whites by five to one and their numerical superiority was increasing year by year. Today it was seven to one. He had decided on a career with the South African Police when two of his class mates were murdered by a faction of the African National Congress while returning from a holiday in Mozambique. Van der Merve had grown up on the family farm near Welkom a small town located half way between

Johannesburg, capital of the Transvaal and Bloemfontein the capital of the Orange Free State. Six families of blacks lived in quarters on the Van der Merve farm; all were employed by Chris's father and treated like extended members of the Van der Merve family. Chris could remember the many times his mother would be up into the early morning hours caring for a sick child or the times his father would be in Bloemfontein arguing with the local Magistrate attempting to get one of his workers released who, after consuming excessive quantities of Bantu Beer had been arrested for drunkenly conduct.

While the blacks and whites knew their specific places in this separated society Chris had been brought up to respect his black brothers and sisters. He often recalled when he and Ashanti, a black beauty and the young daughter of one of the resident families would slip into the barn for hot and heated sessions of secret fornication. Even though only 17 at the time, both were well versed in the government's policy of separate development knowing that if they had been caught severe punishment would have been inflicted by their parents. Adult copulation between the races meant jail. In spite of the prevailing rule of law and being a devout Afrikaner Chris also believed that there was a high degree of hypocrisy in Apartheid.

A sheepish grin always came across his face when he thought about the Dutch Reformed Minister who had been disgraced as the first person arrested in South Africa under the 1950 Immorality Act. The holier-than-thou preacher had bedded a black woman and got caught.

Ashanti was a work of art with fine features set on a tall slim body with large breasts that gave Chris great pleasure in fondling. She was bright too. When Chris moved to Johannesburg to attend university she had cried and wished him well while hoping they might see each other again. However, they both knew that APARTHEID would never allow them to be together. Chris had quietly mourned when he later learned that Ashanti had become involved with the underground movement in the Cape Province where she had been shot and killed during a terrorist raid the previous year. He hadn't learned of Ashanti's death until his mother called to tell him the sad news.

A short time later Chris met Julie Downing who was soon to become his wife. Julie of English extraction had immigrated to South Africa over the objections of her self- proclaimed blue-blooded parents. Major Peter Downing and his wife Fiona were large landowners who lived near East Grinstead, an upscale area south of London. Following Peter's retirement from the British Army's Royal Artillery they had taken to raising thoroughbred horses in the Sussex Downs. During his courtship of Julie, Chris had engaged in many heated arguments with the Downing's over South Africa's Apartheid policy which reinforced his opinion that the British were probably the biggest racists in the world. Downing was undeniably a bigot who loved reciting a favorite joke at his local pub, the Red Lion,

"When does a black gentleman become a WOG?" His response, "When he leaves the room."

The British Imperial and then Colonial Empires had allowed the wellborn English gentry to assume that they were the self proclaimed masters over the masses. After their African Colonies gained independence the English were confronted with thousands of Blacks and Asians who carried British Passports and now wished to live in the United Kingdom to take advantage of the country's cradle-to-the-grave welfare system. The Major and his snobbish wife felt that the Blacks and their Asian brothers could be tolerated as long as they were engaged in menial tasks such as running London Transport, collecting the trash or being employed as domestics, confined to living in the working class suburbs of London or the Midlands. The Downing's enthusiastically supported proposals by the Right Honorable Enoch Powell, MP who, in Parliament and speeches throughout the country proposed that the Blacks, Indians and Pakistanis be sent packing and repatriated to their native countries at British Taxpayers expense.

When Julie first told her parents that she was bringing a South African home for the weekend they almost wet their royal britches believing, because of her liberal views, their peaches and cream daughter had fallen in love with a black. While not totally convinced, the Downing's were somewhat relieved when they found their daughter's South African friend was actually white.

Julie had attended Roedean the prestigious girls' school in Britain. Later while pursuing a career in modeling in London she'd met the strapping 6'3" ruggedly handsome blonde blue eyed Afrikaner who at the time was on a law enforcement exchange with London's Metropolitan Police.

Holding the rank of Police Inspector while on an exchange assignment in London, Chris had been invited to a reception at the South African Embassy in Trafalgar Square to honor the visit of South Africa's newly appointed Foreign Minister. While looking forward to the reception and being able to enjoy the superb wines of the Cape Province he dreaded the mindless small talk that would always quickly lead to the country's politics. While mingling with the diverse crowd he smiled as he looked around the room thinking that even though the Springboks may have beaten all the rugby teams from Australia, Britain and the Commonwealth, the government of South Africa was still a strong and friendly ally of these countries and the United States. These same allies also knew that South Africa had sent its own men to die in every war that the United States and Britain had been involved in. Chris' own brother had lost his life in the Korean conflict.

We're not communists and we don't massacre the populations like they seem to do on a regular basis in West and East Africa, yet the bloody commies have turned the world against us while the Yanks and the Brits simply stand by and watch. *Bloody Hell! It's just not right,* he said in whispered tones to himself.

He first saw the beautiful Julie Downing standing next to the bar engaged in an animated conversation with an embassy commercial attaché. All the guests were given name tags to wear; her name tag displayed JULIE DOWNING. In true police fashion Chris discreetly checked her name against the guest list finding that Miss Downing had come to the reception as the guest of a rather boring little company director. The director represented British Ford who no doubt had been invited because of their extensive business interests in South Africa.

Always the police officer, Chris had been scanning the room scrutinizing the participants while observing the token blacks that had been included for the sake of public relations. The delegation from Malawi was off in one corner conversing with a small contingent of men suitably adorned in Brooks Brother's suits and polished penny loafer shoes. From their dress and short haircuts Chris concluded they were either the Canadians from down the street, or the Yanks from Grosvenor Square. The French Charge d' Affaires was in another corner with the Israelis most likely discussing a deal for the new Mirage fighter.

After leaving the Bar he spotted Julie standing alongside the diminutive Englishman from Ford. The little Englishman was ignoring his statuesque companion while directing his attention and interest to a short, balding, pudgy little man who kept waving his stubby arms in an effort to make some mute point. Clearly bored, her flashing eyes were also scanning the room much like a ship's radar seeking a target. When their eyes met both smiled and almost in embarrassment she looked down at her escort and began rolling her eyes while slowly shaking her head. Excusing herself from Ford she raised her glass taking a sip of the white Stellenbosch while moving towards a large window; the window overlooked the beautifully lit Trafalgar Square and Lord Nelson who in solitude stood guard atop his marble column. Chris made his way to the window and when standing next to her tilted his head slightly to the side whispering,

"This is boring. I know a raunchy little Pub not five minutes from here. Would you care to join me?"

Without turning she said, "I'll meet you downstairs at the door."

Following the brief encounter at the window she returned to her companion feigning of a headache and said she'd like to leave.

"Would you mind terribly to take a cab back to your flat? Knightsbridge is only a few minutes away, the Foreign Minister is returning to Pretoria in the morning and this is the only opportunity I'll have to speak with him," pleaded the little wimp from Ford.

Following a number of weekends with her parents and a passionate courtship during Chris' stay in the United Kingdom, Julie decided that she would accept Chris' invitation to visit South Africa and didn't return to England. During the ensuing six years Julie and Chris enjoyed a happy marriage and their happiness produced a little Chris Junior who arrived just over a year after their first meeting in London. Because of Chris's continued involvement with the Metropolitan Police the Van der Merve family came back to England for the duration of his assignments.

"Chris, line one, it's Julie." The shrill voice was that of his fellow South African, Inspector Jan Joubert also on temporary assignment in London.

"Hello Luv, caught any bad guys today?"

"No, it's too early my sweetie, you know the bad guys always sleep till noon and normally don't start their dirty deeds until after lunch. What's happening on the home front?" said Chris loosening his tie. "After you left for the office this morning Val called and asked us round tonight for some drinkee-poos, think you can get away a trifle early? Nanny can take little Chris out for a walk so we can fool around a bit before we go and if you'll promise to give me a few lashings with that 10" tongue, I'll sit on your face big guy."

Chris, visualizing the wide grin on Julie's face,

"How can I refuse an offer like that, I'll be home by 6:00."

Placing the phone back on its cradle then turning to Joubert,

"Okay mate, what's our Ms. Tannenbaum been up to in her travels? Did we get anything yet from J.B.?"

Joubert, shuffling through the papers on his desk looked up,

"Oh yes Chris, it's here somewhere give me a moment."

Jeremy Brown or J.B. was one of the first people Chris met after he reported for duty in London. J.B. was an agent with MI5, the British Security Service who had been on loan to the Metropolitan Police Special Branch as a liaison officer assigned to the A3 Section of the A Branch. The A3 Section dealt with foreign targets operating from bases in the United Kingdom. J.B.'s posting to A Branch had first been temporary then shortly thereafter during the tenure of Sir Roger Hollis, Director General of MI5 the assignment was made permanent.

Failing in his attempt to join the Secret Intelligence Service (SIS) colloquially known as MI6, Hollis subsequently joined MI5 where he was assigned to F Division, the section that dealt with threats from left-wing political groups specifically the

Communist Party of Great Britain. J.B. never liked Hollis or his Deputy Graham Mitchell and never fully trusted either of them as they were suspected of being Soviet Agents and key players in the Cambridge Spy Ring. Even though J.B. was *not-of-the-manor-born*, so to speak, Cambridge educated or a member of the *old boys' network* that held sway over this clandestine group, he was charismatic, well liked and had an enviable record of successes. His colleagues often referred to him as a Spy's-Spy.

Because of his high level security clearance he had authorization to access MI5 Registry Files kept at their headquarters on the ground floor of Leaconsfield House on Curzon Street in Mayfair. What J.B. wasn't able to glean from the Registry Files he could normally obtain over a pint at the Pig and Eye Club, the watering hole of the intelligence services. Through high level Memorandums of Understanding or MOU's the British, Australians, Canadians, and Americans had developed a common ground in their illegal activities involving destabilization programs and assassination conspiracies. They collectively shared a unilateral fear of Soviet penetration.

After Guy Burgess and David MacLean defected in 1951 the activities of the American and British intelligence services became even more focused on closer supervision and control of their agents. Chris could care less about the internal struggles between the CIA and their British counterparts; he was only interested in what affected South Africa. J.B. had become a valuable resource possessing a wealth of information on the KGB and Russian backed terrorist groups who centered their clandestine activities in liberal London. J.B. was truly a mole amongst moles. Generally most of his reports to Van der Merve didn't come through official channels, but were tendered unofficially.

"Here it is Chris," said Joubert.

The large brown envelope which was marked **On Her Majesty's Service–SECRET** contained a detailed report on Rona Tannenbaum's visit to London. The report began with the arrival of her flight in London and included her meetings and movements during the stay.

"Bloody bitch won't even use South African Airways when she

travels, probably knows we've got informants in the crew which is why she uses BOAC."

Van der Merve, obviously pleased,

"Joubert, have you read this? J.B. really out did himself with this bit of detective work."

"I haven't read the full report but glancing through it quickly see that she met with Abukutsa on two occasions, once when she arrived and then again the day before she left."

Kamba Abukutsa or Kamy as he was known to his friends is a native of Zululand and a friend and confidant of Oliver Tambo. Abukutsa had been recruited by Tambo's military chief Joe Schlomo to coordinate the ANC's liaison operations in London. Abukutsa had come to the attention of the British Intelligence Services when his name appeared in the Golitsin material that noted the Soviet's increasing interest in Simons Town, the joint British / South African Naval Base in the Cape.

MI5 knew that Joe Schlomo had received training in Moscow and before it was outlawed, was the head of the South African Communist Party. Aside from a few attacks on civilian targets in the Northern Transvaal his uncoordinated guerrilla forces had little success in their efforts of destabilization. Flora Solomon, a Russian émigré who had been close to Kim Philby was of interest to MI5 because she was a frequent dinner companion of Kamba Abukutsa. Because of its ongoing distrust of MI6, MI5 had intentionally displayed little interest in the Solomon / Abukutsa relationship to keep MI6 in the dark. MI5 dealt with intelligence involving espionage within the UK while MI6 focused on espionage and intelligence on an international level. As the meetings in London between Solomon and Abukutsa involved terrorist activities within South Africa MI6 is not in any way involved and has no business to meddle or interfere. Any involvement by MI6 could compromise a successful surveillance operation that has and is continuing to provide valuable intelligence on an ANC operation in South Africa and has nothing to do with the United Kingdom. While stroking his chin Chris scanned the file, then looked directly at Joubert,

"On Thursday she traveled on Central Line from Lancaster Gate to the Bank. At the Bank Station she then took the return Central

Line back to Lancaster Gate. At first this may appear strange, but maybe not so strange when the report say's she sat next to a KGB illegal on her return trip. The Watcher reported the two exchanged a few words before he gave her a copy of the Economist. Sorry Joubert let me translate. J.B. is using the Brits terminology, an illegal is an agent recruited by our Soviet friends and a Watcher is a person in our A4 Section that's assigned to follow diplomats and other baddies around the alleys, and in this case the Tubes of London."

Van der Merwe smiled at the puzzled look on Joubert's face. Joubert, shaking his head from side to side,

"Wow, J.B. sure has you educated in the workings of the Cloak and Dagger crowd."

———

On the drive from Jan Smuts airport into the city Guy and Haggis exchanged small talk. A first time visitor could only be impressed with this modern metropolis and the sprawling expanses of Johannesburg. The quiet, clean and well manicured residential suburbs on the outskirts of the city slowly disappeared in transformation from urban tranquility to the hustle and bustle of the inner city.

In true tour guide fashion Haggis suggested they take a short drive through the financial district and the center of town before going to Guy's residential hotel. The towering buildings of Market and Commissioner Street dwarfed the suited white bankers and brokers as they scurried to their deals while brown uniformed black messengers darted along the pavement to deliver stacks of brown envelopes. Guy laughed out loud when he saw a corpulent black woman with a roll of toilet paper prominently placed on the top of her head speaking with another woman who was seated on the steps of an impressive office building nursing a small child from her extended breast.

Driving northeast to the Hillbrow and Berea sections of this vast city they passed a small park when Guy noticed some printing on the back of the park bench *Nie Blankes*.

"What the devil does 'Nie Blankes' mean Haggis?"

"Well Guy you've just had your first taste of the Afrikaans

culture, welcome to APARTHEID," replied a smiling Haggis.
"It means if you're white you don't sit on that bench. *Nie Blankes* means No Whites; the bench is reserved for blacks only. The same thing goes for the loos or toilets to you Yanks. It'll be marked on the door whether the restroom is for whites or blacks. Always remember public conveniences are either for whites or for blacks, you never use anything that's designated for the blacks and they don't use the facilities for us. If you should walk into the wrong loo or sit on the wrong bench and a copper is around you could be arrested."

Guy remained silent during the short drive through Hillbrow engrossed in the multitude of people and beehive of activity. The restaurants were plentiful and represented cultures from every corner of the globe. Colorful signs recommended the delicacies of a large number of Indian, French, Italian, and Greek restaurants. Their signs identifying the diverse nationalities of their immigrant proprietors, reminiscent of the Mediterranean eating and drinking establishments of the Costa del Sol, the Riviera and the Greek Isles.

The little hotel on Primrose Terrace was tastefully painted in pleasing pastels and flowers and plants adorned its regal entrance indicating that in earlier times it may have once been a grand and palatial private home. Situated prominently on a hill, the hotel overlooked a section of the city that was part residential and part commercial. The manager and proprietress, a middle aged woman appeared from her clothing that she may have arrived on one of the Voortrekkers covered wagons from the Cape. Her graying hair was done up in a tight bun on the top of her head; wearing a long dress with a high collar and Mary Jane type flat shoes gave her the appearance of a wagon master's wife. Her words were spoken in English, but delivered in an authoritative heavy Afrikaans's accent that without question indicated she was in charge.

"We're pleased to have you with us Mr. Young. I have put all our rules and regulations together in an envelope for you. Your room is 125, down the corridor to the left. Breakfast is at 7:30 a.m. and dinner at 6:30 p.m. sharp. No cooking in the rooms and no music after 10:00 p.m., any questions?"

Turning she completed her instructions with, "Thank you, I'll see you just now."
Haggis smiled, "Welcome to the direct South African *matter of fact* approach."
Guy smiled, "Haggis what's this *I'll see you just now* bit?"
"Oh not to worry Guy, *just now* is an Afrikaans expression. It's a bit like when you yanks say, *see you later*, but in Afrikaans *just now* means the person may seen you again in two minutes or two years. You'll get used to it."
After helping Guy lug the bags to his room, Haggis turned to leave, then looking around the corner of the door,
"I'll fetch you at 8:00 and we'll treat you to your first dinner in the country. See you *just now,* mate," he said with a grin.
Guy looked around his new abode sizing up the limited storage space and the even more limited single bed. It took about an hour for him to organize his clothes and put his gear away as best as possible. He lifted the largest Samsonite case gently placing it on the bed. A slight nudge on the inner corners caused the false bottom of the case to snap open revealing last months issue of Playboy magazine and a small 12mm flare pistol with six rounds of phosphorus flares tightly wrapped in aluminum foil.
After placing his passport and bank book on top of the Playboy and flare gun in the false bottom he closed it placing the case on top of the wardrobe unit. He then put a strip of clear cellophane tape between the case and the back of the wardrobe so if someone got inquisitive and moved the case he'd know about it.
The concept of the residential hotel was created in South Africa to fill the need of the increasing number of immigrants coming into the country. This provided the country's new arrivals with a place to stay while they got jobs and found permanent accommodations. Residential hotels not only provided accommodation to new immigrants, but because of their low cost many times were favored by white South Africans coming from the rural areas of the country when they made visits to the cities. The friendships made in these usually small residential hotels or guest houses sometimes continued for many years after the parties moved on and in a number of cases developed into lasting relationships or marriage.

The Primrose had some thirty rooms for whites' only with accommodations for both male and female guests. The dinning room and a small bar that opened after dinner and on the weekends was situated overlooking a neat picture-perfect little garden. At a slow pace, a walk in the garden consisted of maybe three or four minutes over the white pebbles through dozens of little terracotta Gnomes placed strategically along the path. A fountain mounted in the center of a mosaic bird bath sprayed water to the delight of dozens of little multicolored birds that fluttered and played within the mist. Opposite the bird bath an aging black man was kneeling digging up the weeds, weeds that seemed more imaginary than real in this perfect setting. Dropping to one knee near the old man Guy said,

"Excuse me, my name is Guy Young, I've just moved in. Your garden is truly beautiful...." cutting Guy off, the old man, without stopping his work or looking up said,

"Thank you boss, I work very hard to keep it good, but Madam don't like us to talk with the people, she get mad and take it out on us."

"Sorry, I don't want to cause any trouble for you I just wanted to tell you how pretty your garden is." With that, Guy stood up and went inside.

"How's the room? I hope its satisfactory Mr. Young."

"Oh yes it's just fine," said Guy smiling to the manager who had dipped her head looking at him over the top of her Ben Franklin glasses. Returning to his room Guy slipped off his shoes, dropped to the bed and soon dozed off.

A door closing in the next room awakened him. Looking at his watch he saw it was 5:30. Cocktail time he thought to himself, as he stretched and looked out the window he could see the sun gently slipping over the horizon. With the exception of the single barman reading the afternoon edition of the Rand Daily Mail the bar was empty.

"Hello mate, what's your pleasure?"

The voice was unmistakably English. In short order Guy found the barman's name was George Dimbleby, a Yorkshireman who had immigrated to South Africa two years earlier after being discharged from the Royal Navy. George was a big fellow who clearly enjoyed being a barman along with having an eye for the ladies. Guy got a full run down on all the female guests at the Primrose and after hearing all the vital statistics, quickly decided that Beth Marans sounded like someone he'd like to meet.

According to George, Beth was from Cape Town and had recently moved to Johannesburg after being offered a promotion with the South African Broadcasting Corporation. George told him that she normally came into the bar around 6:00 p.m. At 6:10 Beth seated herself at the bar stool next to the stool that Guy had occupied for the last twenty or so minutes. Beth was indeed beautiful. Her long black hair framed a striking face with elegant features. She had large brown eyes and a bust that according to George, might if activated, be capable of breast feeding a hundred babies in one sitting.

She was quite small, probably only 5'1" and very delicate. They became immediate friends. Beth was like a sponge in her quest for knowledge about America quickly adding that she had never before met an American. It was curious he thought to himself, she's not only interested in what I'm saying, but in the way it's said. Guy had consumed a number of martinis that matched one to one against Beth's preferred Bombay gin over ice. After the third or fourth round of drinks Beth suggested they share a table at dinner. Had Guy not made arrangements with Haggis for the evening meal he would have quickly accepted. They parted agreeing to meet in the morning for breakfast.

———

"I glad to have you back missy," the black servant said opening the door for Rona.

"Thanks Oku, how have things been while I was away?"

"Okay, okay, no problem, Mister Abe came by to pick up a picture he say was his, Oh and just now a boss called, but I say you no come home yet. He say just tell you he call to buy car."

"Did the man say anything else?"

"No, he hang up quick."

"Thanks Oku," Rona replied kicking off her shoes entering the hallway.

"Oku, please run me a bath, I'm hot, tired and dirty."

Passing the table in the hallway Rona briefly glanced through the mail wondering how many the police had steamed open before they were delivered. Leaving a trail of clothes that were quickly picked up by Oku, Rona moved from the bedroom to the bathroom briefly standing before the full length mirror looking at herself. She rubbed her face then moving her hands around her back undid her bra and slipped off her panties. Her hands moved over her breasts gently rubbing her large nipples in a teasing fashion.

Thinking to herself, I liked that Yank and he seemed to like me, I wonder.... Her thoughts were interrupted by the ringing of the telephone.

"Sorry boss, no car to sell,"

Rona could hear Oku's voice as she spoke before hanging up the phone.

"Missy same boss call, want to know if you still have a car for sale, you not sellin' car are you?"

"No need to worry Oku, it must have been a wrong number, we haven't a car for sale."

Rona looking at the hallway clock showing 2:15 then in a low voice said, "Hmmm, 45 minutes. I've got to get moving to make it by 3:00."

Knowing that the Special Branch had tapped her phone when the ANC needed to arrange a meeting she would receive a coded call. A telephone call inquiring about an automobile or piece of furniture offered for sale indicated she should be in the library of the Witwatersrand University off Empire Street on the nearest odd hour. A call asking for a donation to a charity was for a meeting in the Historical Reference section of the Johannesburg Public Library at the corner of Market and Simmonds Streets on the nearest even hour. Rona looked at Oku, now swirling a bubble bath gel into the two-person sunken granite bathtub and attempting to mask her displeasure at having to forgo the bath for a journey into town,

"You know Oku, I'm going to skip the bath for now and go into town for a little shopping."

After slipping on her motorcycle leathers and stuffing a blonde wig inside the helmet which she always did to avoid any unwanted questions from Oku, she went to the garage. Rona made good time into town and after parking the bike entered the library at 2:50. She selected an empty table sitting down with her back against a book covered wall so she could observe the people and the movements in front and around her.

Placing a yellow legal pad on the table she began preparing a shopping list for the supermarket. After a few minutes and confident she hadn't been followed, she lifted her handbag from the floor to her left, set it momentarily on the table and then set it down on her right side. She couldn't see Charles, but knew that somewhere the ANC contact was watching and waiting for the appropriate all-clear signal. Had she not momentarily put the handbag on the table in front of her then to the floor on her right, but returned it to the left side Charles would have quietly departed.

The sequential movement of the handbag was the signal indicating an all-clear. If the handbag wasn't moved from her left to the table, then to her right this signaled she may have been followed or was being watched and the meeting was to be aborted. Moving somewhat like a goose slowly making its way to a pond, Charles waddled through the library. While not making eye contact he stood a few minutes at a bookcase near Rona studiously looking at the various book titles.

Charles, a small man no more than 5'5" was grossly overweight, totally bald and wore brown horn-rimmed spectacles with lenses that appeared to be at least an inch thick; he always wore the same gray double breasted suit, blue tie and carried a small leather case which made him look like a professor or a solicitor. Rona often thought that Charles appeared much like a caricature of Winston Churchill. Withdrawing a book from the shelf Charles sat down in a chair to Rona's left, placing his now open case on the floor between them. They said nothing for a few moments then without taking his eyes from the pages of his open book he spoke softly,

"I like the wig. Your short mahogany hair is beautiful, but being a blonde with long hair is a good cover. No one realizes that there's a famous star within their midst. Is London a go?"

Without looking up Rona continuing to pen her shopping list,

"The wig works. While my Special Branch followers would surely approve, at times like this it wouldn't be good to have my fans hovering about for an autograph. I saw the communiqué, but we can't meet in London, it's too hot. Everything has been arranged for the meeting to take place in Trieste. The plan is for them to stay in Ljubljana until they receive a call that our man has arrived at the Hotel Bristol. Both have rooms booked for the 30th. It's all here," she said, slipping a small brown envelope into his open leather case. They said nothing further. Before closing the book Charles placed a small envelope between the pages and discreetly slid his book to Rona. He then stood and departed through a crowd of Wits University students now congregating in the library. Rona put the envelope in her purse, closed the book and quickly left the library.

Later that night,

"Oh I really needed this," Rona thought to herself as she descended through the froth of bubbles filling the tub much like whipped cream crowning a massive cup of hot chocolate.

"Oku, Oku, please fetch me a bottle of the Roodeberg in the fridge," shouted the partially immersed Rona.

Sipping the cold Roodeberg brought back memories of the wine commercial she had starred in followed by a personal tour of the Roodeberg KWV cellars in Paarl in the Cape Province. Not only had she been paid handsomely for the commercial, but was complimented with two cases of the delicate wine for her efforts. Her thoughts were interrupted with the ringing of the telephone.

"Oku, please get that for me and tell me who it is."

Oku, in the adjoining bedroom,

"Yes this is her home, sorry boss I can't understand you, what? What? No, no, she home now. Guy? Guy? Guy what guy, who dat?" Oku was clearly having trouble understanding the American.

"Who is it Oku, shouted Rona."

"Just a minute boss... it's a boss man speakin' funny, he say he guy, but I dun understand him missy."

"Thanks Oku, I'll take it here." Picking up the bathroom phone, "Hi Guy, that was my maid Oku, she's never spoken with a Yank before and couldn't understand you. I'm pleased you called. I was planning to ring you in the morning. How are you settling in? Is the Primrose nice? "

"The hotel is great, the room's a bit small by American standards, but it'll do until I find something more suitable. You've been in my thoughts and I just had to call to say hello. If you haven't got anything planned how about lunch tomorrow? In the morning I'm going out with a Scottish friend to see some people about a job so if it's okay how about meeting, say 1:00?" Guy said with anticipation.

"Sure, that's a great idea I'd love to see you. Where will you be? I guess you'll be in town so let's meet at the Carlton Hotel, it's a nice hotel in the town center and easy to find."

Rona was pleased that her new found friend had called as he was someone she'd like to get to know better. She took a large swallow of the wine and slipped further down into the warm water. Possibly as a result of the wine or hearing Guy's voice or maybe both, Rona was aroused and slowly began to masturbate. It was a warm and comfortable feeling as she reached a climax gently laying her head back in a state of blissful contentment.

Guy hadn't fully appreciated how truly beautiful his new found companion really was until he saw her waiting for him in the lobby of the Carlton. Her sculptured body was accentuated within a stylish white leather mini skirt highlighted by a tight fitting halter top that was filled to capacity. She was nothing less than sensational. Following a wet kiss they moved hand in hand as they made their gracious entry into the dinning room while drawing the attention of other diners who paused to observe the dazzling film star and her handsome escort. First engaging in small talk about California then shifting to life in South Africa Rona expressed her sincere interest to help him with his search for a job.

"I can't say that I know anyone in the computer business, but I'll be pleased to do anything I can to help you."

Guy then told Rona that his morning had been interesting and encouraging.

"It seems that Haggis was right on the mark when he told me that with my experience I could virtually write my own ticket. After each of the job interviews which lasted less than 30 minutes I was

offered a position in sales. I met with the personnel managers of IBM, NCR and four smaller computer companies all of whom virtually pleaded for my expertise. IBM was generous in regards to compensation, but in spite of the money the thought of the bullshit I'd have to endure as a member of *Big Blue's* South African Family might be too much to endure. The idea of returning to the dreariness of dark suits topped off with a stupid hat in the warm environment of Southern Africa just isn't appealing. Now that I know what's available from the other company's and after considering the possibilities, I've decided to accept the offer from the German's at the Kienzle organization."
Rona smiled,
"Sounds like you've been busy. If you're sure that making the move to Kienzle is the best, hey go for it."
Before the interview in the company's offices in Braamfontein Guy had never heard of Kienzle Data Systems, but soon learned the background of the German company. The managing Director of Kienzle Gmbh had flown to Johannesburg to conduct interviews for the replacement of Hans Dieter Kirschner who had recently been transferred back to the Black Forest headquarters of the company after his promotion to the position of International Development Manager. The uninspiring interviews with NCR and IBM had been conducted by dreary little Englishmen who blandly read questions from a pre-printed script and were tedious, insipid and boring. The interview with the German's had been a different matter. Professor Doctor Heinrich Fredrik von Hannover who bore a striking resemblance to Rudolph Hess also appeared to share the same Nazi philosophy of Hess along with a number of the Führer's other followers who had been around during the period that Adolph was wreaking havoc on the civilized world.
Between 1936 and 1945 the *good* Doctor in addition to being a member of the Nationalist Socialist Party had become a celebrated research scientist with Kienzle. Having not been a member of the SS and with no direct or identifiable connections with the other nefarious German military factions he was able to avoid prosecution at the Nuremberg trials. After the war he rapidly rose through the ranks of the company to become its

Chairman. The Professor as he's known within the company was extremely proud of Kienzle's record of accomplishments which included the manufacture of timing devices for the V-2 rockets; which during the war caused continuing grief to thousands of civilians living in and around the cities of London, Manchester, Birmingham, and Liverpool.

The Professor had gloated over the fact that during the war Allied bombers weren't able to find the Kienzle factory which had been skillfully concealed in the dense hinterland of the Black Forest. Not knowing its location the Allies couldn't bomb it and stop its nasty business of producing components for the V-2. At least some of the Kienzle management was clearly egotistical and hateful holdovers from the Third Reich era, but they had made him a very good offer and they'd also be 8,000 miles away. During the interview Guy quickly concluded that while he didn't particularly like von Hannover and had some serious reservations with the company's history, the position and the money it paid just couldn't be ignored which is why he accepted the position as Kienzle's marketing director. As Rona spooned her last bit of Gazpacho, Guy downed another Cape Oyster while elucidating on his interview.

"Even though I really don't like the management, their offer was just too good to refuse. They'll provide me with a new Mercedes complete with a Chauffeur, an unlimited expense account, 30 days leave per year along with a comprehensive medical and dental program. In addition to a 3 year employment contract with an annual salary of 50,000.00 Rand I'll be paid monthly in U.S. Dollars by wire transfer to any bank of my choice anywhere in the world. With the exception of the first $25,000.00 of income which I'd have to declare to the IRS in the US, the rest of the package is free of taxes."

Rona gleamed with delight,

"That's great news! I was going to spring for lunch, but now that you're a man of means you get the lunch and I'll pop for the Champagne. Guy this is so exciting I'm truly pleased for you. I just know you'll do well."

With a childish grin Guy smiled acknowledging that he too was excited about the prospects.

———

The tall, well dressed man moved briskly down the crowded sidewalk of Jeppe Street while alternatively shifting his briefcase from one hand to the other. His dress and demeanor allowed him to easily blend into the mass of people, appearing as nothing more than just another banker or stockbroker off to a meeting over lunch. In fact he was neither, but a top ranking Mossad agent on his way to a private, prearranged meeting. The briefcase, along with a loaded 9mm automatic and silencer concealed in the false bottom contained coded documents of equal importance. Nathan Levine was the chief of Israeli Naval Intelligence based in Rome and the Mossad's principal operative in Europe. In addition to his work Levine was also a dedicated family man who even though having been in South Africa only three weeks constantly thought of his wife and family back in Italy. Under normal circumstances Nat would not have been involved in any missions or operations in Southern Africa. However, having established the initial surveillance and with knowledge of the ANC's European activities and the mysterious disappearance of Moshe Rosenberg, the Mossad's operative in South Africa the Memuneh had instructed him to visit Johannesburg.

The Mossad believed that the ANC in an effort to keep the organization in the spotlight and thriving was deceiving and paying little more that lip service to the Western Media. In spite of the ANC's propaganda on such issues as Individual Freedom, Human Rights, One Man One Vote along with other Anti-Apartheid Doctrines they were nothing more than a devious and dangerous Marxist organization. Since its inception the ANC had been backed and funded by other Communist groups, it maintained direct lines of communication with Moscow, Beijing, and Havana along with Israel's favorite twosome the PLO's Yasir Arafat and Libya's Muammar al-Qadaffi. Even though the ANC's figurehead Nelson Mandela had been imprisoned by the Pretoria Government the organization's present leaders, Oliver Tambo and Joe Schlomo, now based in Lusaka, Zambia, under the guise of freedom, continued to infect and deceive their followers with the myth of disingenuous communist doctrines.

Nat Levine was a handsome man with jet black hair streaked with gray and flashing green eyes that missed nothing. As he approached the large black ebony door of the renowned Spargi's Restaurant it swung open with a greeting from a tuxedoed Maitre d' who tendered in crisp and cultured public school English,

"Good Day Sir, may I help you?"

"Yes please, I'm lunching with Ms. Jeydi."

"Oh yes, please follow me sir, Ms. Jeydi is awaiting your arrival," offered the smiling maitre d' as he led Nat to a small booth in the corner of the room. Spargi's, a well known eatery located near the centre of Johannesburg's financial district was a favorite haunt of the City's elite. The restaurant was favored by Gold Barons, Bankers, insurance moguls, and QC's who rubbed elbows and mingled with the movers and shakers of the film industry and the entrepreneurs of this city of gold.

Vicki Jeydi was born in Miami, Florida to Jewish parents and held both American and Israeli passports. After graduating from Florida State University she traveled to Israel to work on a Kibbutz and decided to stay. Concerned with Israel's ongoing security troubles and the threat posed by the country's aggressive Arab neighbors she enlisted and received an officer's commission in the IDF. Recognizing her unique qualities and potential she was selected to receive specialized military training as a covert agent. As a result of her commitment and skills she quickly rose to the rank of major and was assigned to the AMAN's top-secret cell, Unit 131 reporting to Colonel Binyamin Gibli, the chief of Israel's military intelligence.

Later while on a temporary assignment with the Mossad, a civilian service that does not use military ranks she worked undercover as a graphic designer in London under the code name Katherine DuPont. After developing an intimate relationship with the Palestinian Mustapha Ihram she successfully infiltrated the PLO's military arm in London. Through her involvement with Ihram Vicki was able to gain information which foiled the attempt by the terrorists to murder six members of the Knesset while on a trade mission to the United Kingdom. Known as Operation Ashdod its success had supported and strengthened the

Israeli prime minister's view that the Mossad should be expanded and provide increased opportunities for women agents in the Israeli Intelligence Services.

Vicki Jeydi soon became a valuable asset who at 37 was not only beautiful, but had proven herself to be a clever, cunning and industrious street-smart operative. Through her assignment with the AMAN she had worked closely with SHIN BET, the domestic intelligence service before being permanently transferred to the Mossad.

Reuven Zaslanski who had shortened his name to Zaskani was known by the name Reuven Shiloah and was the first Director of the Mossad, a post he held before moving to a senior position at the Israeli Embassy in Washington. The Mossad, being a relatively small and close-knit service Shiloah had met Vicki and encouraged her to accept an offer as part of her intelligence training to come to the United States. Following her arrival in the U.S. she enrolled in a political science course at Washington College in Chestertown, Maryland, a short drive from the Israeli Embassy in Washington, DC. During her studies and tenure in Chestertown she was in regular contact with Shiloah who considered her an invaluable asset to the Israeli intelligence community. In addition to speaking with an American accent which provided a good cover, she was conversant in five languages which included a fluency in Greek, Arabic and Russian.

"Shalom," she responded in a low tone, rising to her feet in traditional military fashion. As they both sat down she asked,

"What's up?" Before either said another word she placed a copy of Moby Dick on the table between them. While the book appeared normal the inside pages had been cut away providing a hollow space 4" square and 1" deep. The space within the pages of the book contained a Shiloah Scrambler; a multi-directional audio-jammer conceived and named for its creator, Reuven Shiloah. The ingenious device had the capabilities to desensitize any eavesdropping microphone and scramble conversations or even whispers. In all public meetings between agents the Mossad ordered the use of the Shiloah Scrambler as mandatory. Its lightweight and small size allowed it to be effective in a pocket when standing operatives conversed or placed in inconspicuous items such as a handbag or book positioned between the parties as long as they were no more than 3' apart.

Nat, first scanning the room then began speaking in a low voice, "Moshe's last report provided several of the details of the ANC's plan to eliminate Verwoerd and said that he was getting close, but would keep digging. From the chatter picked up on the wire taps the hit is scheduled to take place on September 3rd. So far the shooter has only been referred to as JADE. Once he's able to identify who JADE is, he said he'd include it in his next report. That was last month, since then we've heard nothing. It's all here on the tape. After you listen to it follow the normal procedure of disposal."

Vicki smiled knowing that after gleaning the contents of the tape it would be destroyed when she dropped it in a glass of household bleach. Vicki first met Nat when he had been assigned as a liaison officer in the Israeli Defense Ministry when Operation Susannah, known as the Lavon Affair caused the collapse of the 1954 covert sabotage campaign in Egypt. Pinhas Lavon, the Defense Minister lost his job as a result of the mission's failure and resulting scandal. The political fallout had been headlined in the highly censored Israeli press as *Esek Bish,* in Hebrew עסק‘ מלוכלך or literally *Dirty Business.*

Vicki, only in her twenties at the time of the Lavon Affair had only recently completed her initial intelligence training, but during the training had drawn the attention and developed a close friendship with Colonel Binyamin Gibli, the present head of the AMAN. The AMAN was later lead by Meir Amit who was now the director of the Mossad.

"Moshe hasn't made contact for over a month which is a bit strange. Exactly what's in the works is still unknown. We don't know the identity of JADE, what's being planned and when it's coming down is still a blank. Special Branch reports indicate that Rona Tannenbaum met the two targets in London. From the wire tap they confirmed that the meeting they've been talking about was changed and now has been scheduled in Trieste."

Vicki smiled,

"Special Branch told me that our little sexpot has apparently picked up a new friend. She wasn't seen with him in the U.K., but the two sat together on the flight from Heathrow. It got their attention because when they arrived in Jo'burg they left the plane separately acting as if they didn't know each other. Tannenbaum was questioned by Customs and her hand luggage was searched, but nothing of interest was found. Even though they didn't talk to one another at the airport, as we speak they're having lunch together at the Carlton."

Quickly glancing around the room Nat's inquiring eyes carefully noted each face then looking at Vicki,

"What's his name and what do we know about him? Could he be JADE?"

"He's an American. Special Branch says his name is Guy Young and apparently he has just immigrated to South Africa from California. Langley checked him out but neither the CIA nor the FBI having anything on him and INTERPOL says he's clean. No criminal record, no subversive memberships and there's no flag burning or anti-government activities in their files. There may be something that the FBI missed or overlooked, but so far there's nothing to tie him in with the ANC or the PLO. The FBI got a report from a lawyer who was a part-time musician who worked with him in San Francisco. The lawyer said the only thing he knows was something concerning a disgruntled lover he dumped in California. He was a manager for an American computer company, drove an Aston Martin, lived in San Francisco's Marina District, and always paid his bills on time. Everything else on the guy comes up blank, for whatever reason it appears he may have just decided to leave the U.S. After his application for immigration was approved through the South African Consulate in Los Angeles he flew to Johannesburg after an overnight stay in London. At the moment he seems to be clean, but we'll continue to make inquiries. The FBI ran his social security and passport numbers and found that he graduated from San Jose State College then worked for IBM and NCR. The Young's were apparently early pioneers having arrived in California in the 1840's. The earliest relation was a retired army General whose family members and their descendants were big in politics and another was a cattle baron, the City of San Francisco has a street named in their honor. On the weekends he played drums with a jazz band at a small bar in San Francisco, he only smokes a pipe and there isn't anything to indicate a problem with drugs or alcohol. He's straight and clearly likes the company of women. His hobbies are limited to racing high performance hydroplanes and flying ultra light aircraft. There's not much to go on, but I think it'd be wise to keep an eye on him, just in case he's a sleeper."

Looking up from the menu while nodding his head, Nat acknowledged the information. Now enjoying their Spinach Salads, Nat, while wiping a small crouton from his lower lip asked,

"I wonder what it is these bastards are up to. Could it be they've thrown us off and that there's something more than what we think we know? We've obtained the basics of their plans, but we're still not sure who all the players are. I'd sure like to know what's coming down in Trieste and the real purpose for the meeting. If the assassination of the Prime Minister is successful and results in chaos do you think that maybe they're planning an armed insurrection from north of the Limpopo?"

Vicki shook her head,

"Nat I just don't think the ANC leadership is that stupid. They've got around 6,000 of their followers in training camps in Zambia, but know that the South African Air Force and the Army would quickly annihilate any rag tag guerilla force that would try to cross the northern borders. From our human intelligence sources the plan to assassinate the PM as we know it appears to have been finalized, at the moment we just need to identify the shooter and where it's going to happen. The April 9th attempt in 1960 to kill the prime minister was before we really got involved and there hasn't been any evidence to tie the shooter in with the ANC. The shooter, David Pratt, was simply an Anti-Apartheid farmer who managed to get two shots off which fortunately didn't kill him. Verwoerd quickly recovered, but we need to be damn sure we've covered everything to make certain the next attempt on his life isn't successful either. With what we've got and a little luck I think we should be able to prevent the assassination before they even try it."

Taking a small note book from her purse Vicki began reading the coded Hebrew text.

"On Saturday morning the 3rd of September Verwoerd will meet with the Prime Minister of Lesotho, Chief Leabua Johnathon before he makes an important policy statement at the parliamentary session on Tuesday the 6th concerning the resettlement of the Bantu Nationals and a new economic program. On the 3rd following his meeting with Leabua Johnathon he's arranged to have lunch with the French Ambassador at 1:00. After lunch he's scheduled to leave Pretoria at 2:30, his car and two police escorts will proceed south on the Botha Highway to Verwoerdburg and Irene passing through the suburbs of Jo'berg. The party will make a brief stop at the home of Jimmy Kruger, his old political ally and then proceed to Vanderbijlpark by way of Vereeniging. The Prime Minister will visit the home of his friend and another political ally, Paul Miller, the Managing Director of Thomas Baldwin Steel in time for tea. After tea he's scheduled to arrive at his home around 6:00. The only time he's ever alone is when he takes his evening stroll near his home along the Vaal River's Golden Mile. He always leaves his home around 6:30 and returns to the main house by 7:30 when he and his wife Betsie have dinner. If our information is correct the hit has got to take place on the 3rd sometime between 6:30 and 7:30 during his evening stroll. As you know our sources in London and Rome believe that an Italian will be brought in for the job. The ANC communiqués we've intercepted refer to an operation called HAR. We're not sure why it's called HAR and maybe a bit simplistic, but could it be Hit and Run? So far no one in the ANC has used a name other than HAR and they only refer to the shooter as JADE. Somehow a boat is involved, but we don't know how or why they'd use a boat. The Verwoerd home is on the Vaal River so it's possible that the shooter may make the hit from a boat, but we shouldn't overlook the road that runs alongside the riverbank on the opposite side. Special Branch can put a helicopter up and have an unmarked boat patrolling the area, but as it's a Saturday there will be a lot of other boats on the river in addition to the cars of families picnicking along the riverbank. In any case, unless we can get a positive ID on JADE the Special Branch's air and marine units wouldn't know who or what they'd be looking for. If JADE is a professional as we believe, he or she would surely use a silencer with a scope. Along this stretch of the Vaal it's less than 200m wide, with a sniper rifle fitted with a scope the shooter wouldn't have to be close to get a shot off. From what we've picked up from the phone taps it seems that after the hit JADE will leave the country by air which would have to be on a flight from Jan Smuts Airport. There are only a few international flights leaving the country in the evening and I doubt they'd use the BOAC flight to London, but if the shooter, who we only know as JADE is an Italian and kills Verwoerd it would be logical that their escape could be on the evening Alitalia flight to Rome. But not knowing if the shooter is a man or a woman and without a positive ID or any actionable intelligence we wouldn't be able to hold any of the flights or individual passengers. We've got a pretty good idea of what's coming down and we think it'll be on September 3rd, but there are still a number of blanks that have to be filled in if we're going to prevent the ANC from killing Verwoerd. We've also got the problem of not knowing whether JADE is in hiding somewhere in Jo'burg or maybe hasn't been brought in yet. Even though we haven't identified the shooter, Avi feels the profile fits Giovanni Loggia. Loggia is a professional killer who is believed to be the assassin who killed Rafael Trujillo, the dictator of the Dominican Republic in 1961. He was in Santo Domingo at the time, but quietly disappeared after Trujillo was shot. The Interpol Bureau in Rome has him on their Red Notices, but Loggia hasn't been seen. Even if they found Loggia there's no hard evidence to hold him and they can't pick him up if they can't find him. Loggia was reportedly last seen in Genoa two months ago when he met with Marco Vinci, an elusive arms dealer who's also on Interpol's surveillance list. After their meeting in Genoa, both Loggia and Vinci dropped out of sight. The South African Special Branch checked all the arrivals over the last 90 days, but didn't find anyone entering the country that even remotely fitted Loggia's description."

Rubbing his eyes Nat looked up at the ceiling,

"I just can't put my finger on it, but I hope we haven't become too complacent and missed something important. Why did

Tannenbaum suddenly go to London? Why do so many damn people know about the meeting in Trieste? Could the Trieste meeting simply have been a deliberate diversion to throw us off to chase smoke and mirrors? And now with only a few weeks to go we have a somewhat non-descript Yank coming on the scene? Have the plans been changed? Could we have overlooked that maybe this Yank is the shooter and he's purposely keeping a low profile? When Kennedy was president he wanted to have Cuba's Castro assassinated under a program dubbed Executive Action. In code it was known as ZR/RIFLE under the direction of the CIA. The primary mission of ZR/RIFLE was political assassination which along with eliminating Fidel included Patrice Lumumba of the Congo and Trujillo in the Dominican Republic. It's possible that maybe our ANC friends picked up some ideas from ZR/RIFLE which they're using now. Vicki, I'm more that a bit concerned. We're running out of time. We must keep digging and identify JADE. In case the ANC has a sympathizer in their office let's have Special Branch leave some files on HAR on the Chief Inspector's desk when he leaves for the day. The files should just have some generic information so in case they have an informant, maybe a cleaner or someone even higher up the phone taps will reveal any increased traffic. If they've got someone on the inside we need to know."

Nat wiped his mouth, dropping the napkin on the remains of his salad. He stood then slowly turned to walk away,

"Thanks for the lunch, call me tomorrow."

On the drive back to his modest flat in Hillbrow Nat kept repeating to himself the complexities of a kaleidoscope that surrounded a seemingly well planned assassination; a killing that he had the responsibility to prevent. Dr. Hendrik Verwoerd, the Prime Minister of South Africa may be called the Architect of Apartheid, but he was also an ally and a good friend of the State of Israel. Nat dreaded the thought of submitting his interim report on what was known simply as Operation Ashkelon knowing he didn't have all the pieces to the puzzle. If the ANC succeeded in killing Verwoerd it would be bad for the State of Israel and even worse for him. A failed mission would unquestionably bring about an immediate end to his career with the Mossad.

His boss Meir Amit, Director of the Mossad not unlike his predecessor Isser Harel had become the Memuneh believing that HUMINT or human intelligence was important while placing increased emphasis on technological advancements and computer sciences. Amit was fanatical when it came to achieving successful results; he saw the defeat of Israel's enemies through his agent's dedication, enthusiasm and technological superiority that could only be achieved with initiative, cunning, determination, and aggressiveness. Their continued support of terrorist organizations such as the ANC and the PLO was allowing China and Russia to expand their influence in Southern Africa. The destabilization of governments backed by the West and the elimination of friendly heads of state was carefully planned and executed solely to broaden the interests of Beijing and Moscow.

The Israeli's knew that with PLO support the ANC had clandestine training camps in Zambia with China supplying arms and munitions while the Russians provided money along with military advisors and influence to assure the support of the Black African Countries to the north. At the same time the Portuguese in Angola and Mozambique were facing Marxist organizations cloaked under banners of independence, the most dangerous being the FRELIMO movement in Northern Mozambique. Most White South Africans felt secure knowing that the Portuguese dependencies surrounding their borders were dominated by whites which allowed Pretoria to covertly assist these strongholds to retain power. Even with the Portuguese in control militarily, the South African government knew the communists were actively engaged in funneling Marxist ideologies and the tools of destruction to the FRELIMO rebels.

———

Rona and Guy's lunch at the Carlton was a memorable experience which continued until after 3:30 p.m. After finishing a second bottle of a vintage Dom Perignon Rona's suggestion of coffee at her home brought a broad smile to Guy's tan face. Rona said her housemaid Oku had the afternoon off which would allow them to be alone in her spacious modern split level home.

"Guy let's go for a swim. Give me a moment to change. I'll go slip out of these clothes and meet you at the pool."

"That sounds like a great idea, but I don't have a swim suit." Smiling provocatively as she turned leaving the room,

"There's no one here but us so don't worry."

After removing his clothes Guy approached the heated swimming pool and with his toes tested the water temperature. Considering it was still winter in the southern hemisphere the agreeable 80° radiated by the water was more than inviting for skinny-dipping. Surfacing after a dive he could see the now nude Rona approaching the pool with a silver tray containing a bottle of wine and two glasses.

"May I tempt my Yankee friend with a bit of chardonnay from our famous Roodeberg vineyards in the Cape? Wiping the wet hair from his face and smiling,

"Yes please my gracious mermaid that would be great." After filling two glasses which she set on the side of the pool along with the bottle, Rona gently slid into the pool and embraced Guy. Gently pulling her naked body close he began stroking her hair while kissing her neck moving upwards to her wet lips. She slowly raised her legs until they were tightly locked around his waist. With their lips in loving embrace their tongues began a deep and passionate exploration. Guy tenderly massaged her vagina before dropping below the surface to continue the treatment with his tongue. In a state of accelerated ecstasy rapidly reaching a climax Rona screamed,

"Oh my God, yes, yes."

Gasping for air as Guy rose to the surface,

"You know it might be wise for us to move to the shallow end of the pool so we don't drown."

In the shallow part of the pool Guy spread his arms along the edge of the pool allowing his body to float on the surface. Gently stroking his extended penis the excited mermaid took him into her mouth moving as if she was softly mouthing a large banana. After a number of minutes of their sensuous foreplay and to prevent a premature eruption of Mount Vesuvius Guy rolled Rona onto her back while penetrating her most precious of orifices. Vesuvius enjoyed multiple eruptions each time with the maiden acknowledging her satisfaction.

"Guy you're fantastic! Let's finish the wine, take a shower and continue playing in my bedroom."

"Sounds good to me my fair maiden, let's do it."

The cool jazz of Johnnie Dankworth and Cleo Lane emanating from the bedside radio provided a serene ambiance while the remaining wine was consumed. They continued pleasing each other in the shower with each alternatively on their knees, first with the maiden mouthing Guy's hardened male extremity followed by an extended tongue gently massaging the maiden's most private of parts. After each had dried the other they slipped between the sheets. As they kissed Rona spread her legs as Guy moved to a position of penetration when the phone rang.

"Bloody hell who could be calling now?"

It was a few minutes after 5:00, in reaching for the bedside phone it fell to the floor. Picking up the receiver she heard a voice say,

"Sorry to bother you I'm calling on behalf of OXFAM we'd like to know if you'd be willing to make a contribution to our charity."

A worried look crossed Rona's face,

"Yes I'd be pleased to. I'll take care of it right away."

A call asking for a donation to a charity was a signal for an ANC even-hour meeting in the Historical Reference section of the Johannesburg Public Library at 6:00.

"Guy I'm sorry, but I'll have to cut off our play-time for the moment. I've got an important meeting in town."

Guy, surprised at her decision,

"Do you have to go right away, can't it wait?"

"Sorry, but something has come up that I have to deal with. When I get done I'll call you."

After Guy left, Rona quickly dressed in her black riding leathers, grabbed a brown wig and helmet then proceeded to the lower level of the house and the garage which faced a large park. Walking around her Mercedes she mounted a black BMW R69S motorcycle and secured the helmet's strap under her chin. As the motorcycle's engine roared to life she activated the remote and the garage door began to open. Ducking under the partially opened door she pressed the remote again and the door began to close. 20 minutes later a lady motorcyclist with long brown hair placed her helmet on the floor and sat down across the table from Charles in the Historical Reference section of the Johannesburg Public Library.

In low tones,

"Hello Charles, I wasn't expecting a call what's up?"

"I'm glad I caught you at home and pleased that you were able to come so quickly. There's a bit of a problem. We don't know exactly how much they might know, but our sources say that efforts are being increased to identify JADE and make the connection between the SABRA and the meeting in Trieste. We're not sure how much Special Branch knows about HAR or if it's been compromised. In addition to trying to identify JADE, they're looking for an Italian named L-o-g-g-i-a. They also have an interest in an American by the name of Guy Young who apparently just arrived in the country."

Frowning Rona looked at Charles,

"Loggia? I wonder where this came from. I don't know anyone by this name? Guy Young I know. He's an American who I met on the flight from London. Other than spending some time with me since we arrived I don't understand why they'd have an interest in him. He's been to my home for drinks and knows I'm an actress and do commercials, but doesn't know anything else about me."

Charles, first glancing around the room,

"I'm worried that our friends may be getting too close. Last night while she was cleaning the Special Branch office in Jo'berg our Maggie found a confidential file marked HAR that had been left on superintendent's den Drijver's desk. Before she could open and read it she heard someone in the hall and quickly returned to her cleaning duties. This is too coincidental as den Drijver's too smart to do something like this. I think the file was purposely left on his desk to see if we might have someone on the inside. It's also possible that our friends may have developed a source within the SABRA to provide them with information. In case of a possible penetration we need to be extremely careful. We're getting too close to HAR to have it compromised. I think it's unwise for us to continue our library meetings."

Placing a slip of paper between the pages of a book Charles then slid it across the table to Rona and in hushed tones,

"The first number is a public telephone at the Shell petrol station near your home. The second number is a public telephone on Jeppe Street near the courthouse. If we need to talk I'll call you at your home from the public phone on Jeppe Street to inquire if you're interested in a subscription to The Johannesburg Star. You'll respond that you already have a subscription and hang up. In one hour after I call, you go to the Shell station and call me at the number on Jeppe Street."

"Okay, in view of the tap on my phone this is a good idea, but will clearly disappoint Special Branch who can't listen in to conversations on public phones. Charles, I agree that we need to be careful, but the only people who know the identity of JADE other than you are Kamy and Abu Alouf. I'm sure they may have their suspicions, but if Special Branch had anything solid on those involved with the SABRA the identity of the *Raven* or anything at all on HAR it would have been shut down. We'd have been arrested and put on the boat to Robben Island. I know they tapped my phone, but Special Branch doesn't hear anything of importance. When I leave home all they see is a helmeted rider on a motorcycle leaving the garage. No doubt they've checked the BMW's number plate and know it's registered in my name, so they may think it's me, but because you can't see the rider it could also be a man. In any case the guys sitting down the street in the same black Ford doing the surveillance gave up trying to follow a bike in traffic. When I come to meet you or travel to the Brinkman farm for my shooting practice I always vary my routes and make sure no one follows me. When I leave home in the Mercedes I'm always followed by the black Ford, but the only information Special Branch may learn is who does my hair and where I buy my clothes and groceries. I understand your concern, but don't worry."

Rising from the table Charles smiled faintly,

"We'll talk soon, in the meantime stay safe."

At home after the garage door had closed she removed the helmet and after changing clothes in her bedroom dialed the number of the Primrose,

"May I speak with Mr. Young please?"

"Sorry, Mr. Young isn't in his room. He left a few minutes ago, but said he'd be back in an hour or so in case anyone called."

"Thanks, please tell him that his new friend called. I'll call later."

"Sure no problem, do you wish to leave your name or phone number?"

"No, he'll know who it is."

From downstairs Oku called out,

"Missy you be here for dinner?"

"Yes Oku, I'll be here. I've got no plans, but you needn't stay. I'll fix something for myself when I get hungry."

"Okay missy, if there's nothing else I see you in the morning."

After Oku had left the house Rona removed one of the full width storage drawers concealed below the mattress frame of her bed. Setting the large drawer on the bed she removed a layer of various night gowns and lingerie. Beneath the lingerie was a black canvas bag 50" long, 12" wide tied neatly at the top with a Nylon cord. The bag contained a Walther P38 9mm semi-automatic pistol, 12 cartridges and a Russian SVD Dragunov sniper rifle fitted with a PSO-1 telescopic sight and 12 rounds of 7.62mm cartridges. While not knowing the identity of the buyer or exactly what the target was in his meeting in Genoa Marco Vinci had recommended the recently released SVD for its accuracy in the range of 1,300m. With a length of 48.2" weighing less than 10lbs and with deadly killing power Vinci believed that the SVD would provide the perfect solution for what ever the buyer had in mind. After receiving his payment from a third party Vinci, through a Mafia contact with Alitalia air cargo then arranged for the disassembled Dragunov and P38 to be delivered to a farm with an address in Doornfontein. Placing the Dragunov against her shoulder Rona pointed the weapon at the reflection in her full length mirror then quietly said,

"Bang you're dead."

Temporarily mesmerized in thought she was startled by the ringing of the telephone,

"Hey gorgeous sorry I missed your call. I just stepped out to pick up some pipe tobacco and to meet Haggis at the Fox & Fiddler for a pint. When can I see you again?"

Having been told by Charles that Guy was now in their sights and being watched by Special Branch, who she knew would be listening, decided it was best to cool the relationship at least for the time being,

"I'm going to be busy doing some commercials for the Roodeberg people in the Western Cape so I'll be away for awhile. When I get back I'll call you."

"How long will you be away?"

"I'm not sure maybe a couple of weeks, but as soon as I get back I'll call you."

Guy, somewhat remorseful,

"I'm going to miss you, but I guess business is business so I'll be patient."

The 1st of September 1966 was a beautiful, clear day in Johannesburg. Being a Thursday Oku would first visit the market to do the week's shopping before coming to work and starting her daily chores. As the killing of Dr. Verwoerd was only two days away Rona decided that a final reconnaissance of the access road along the Vaal was necessary to make sure nothing had changed that could compromise or adversely affect the HAR.

After slipping into her motorcycle leathers she proceeded to the garage and put on her brown wig and helmet before pressing the remote to open the garage door. Rona enjoyed riding the BMW. The motorcycle provided her the freedom to avoid or go around the road works and sometimes horrendous traffic congestion that plagued the city. The bike also gave her the ability to quickly reach the open roads of the countryside.

After passing Heidelberg she had an urgent need to stop and have a pee. Finding a petrol station she parked the bike and carefully removed her helmet so as to not to disturb the wig. She could have left the helmet on, but with a full helmet that covered her head she appeared to be a man who could either be black or white. In attracting unnecessary attention she might be challenged by a local Afrikaner who saw a helmeted motorcyclist enter a restroom reserved for white women only so with her wig in place and appearing as a female she used the women's rest room. Removing the leathers so she could sit on the toilet she laughed thinking how easy it was for a man to relieve himself when a women had to drop everything to perform the same function. The rest room stop was uneventful and no one saw her enter or leave.

A short time later after reaching the approach road to the Vaal Dam she turned entering the unpaved road that ran parallel to the river bank. After traveling 9.8 km down the road in the distance she could see the home of Dr. Verwoerd on the opposite bank. Continuing slowly along the road she came to a cluster of bushes set beneath two trees where she briefly stopped. Quietly thinking *hmmm, the width of the river is 200m, when Verwoerd walks along the river bank 800m in either direction from his home I'll have a clear shot. The bushes will provide cover for the motorcycle laid on its side and the tree trunk can be used to support the rifle. This is perfect.*

––––––

"Hello missy. I dun shopping and cleaned the hall closet. You have a good ride today?"

"Yes, thanks Oku, it was such a beautiful day I thought a little ride in the country would be refreshing. We're there any calls?"

"No missy no call, you want me to make you a bath?"

"Yes, that would be nice."

In the bedroom Rona returned the weapons to the drawer then removed a leather pouch that contained 20,000.00 U.S. dollars, her South African passport, airline ticket and her new Italian passport and driver's license. The blonde woman pictured on the Italian passport photo page was Rona Tannenbaum the *Raven* A.K.A JADE who, while living in Italy would be known as Anna Bono. If everything went as planned she would disappear until the dust had settled then reappear as mysteriously as she had disappeared. Returning the pouch to its hiding place she decided it was time for a bath. Partially submerged in the tub she lit two vanilla scented candles and gazing around her glass and marble bathroom thought how much she would miss the luxury and elegance she had become so accustomed to. Aside from Abe her life had been good. She would miss the excitement of her budding career and her beloved South Africa, but would look forward to the day after the ANC had taken control of the government when she could return. She hadn't seen the villa located on the outskirts of Perugia, but had been assured that it was charming and radiated the elegance typically found in the 17th century estates of Italy's Umbria region.

The Villa, her safe-house, had been graciously provided by an Italian Communist Party Official for her use during the year that she was to disappear. She would also be provided with an Alfa Romeo coupe, a live-in maid and a gardener come-handyman to look after the pool and grounds. The arrangements for the villa and her forged Italian passport and driver's license having been finalized and provided during the meeting in Trieste had been passed to her by the KGB agent during their brief encounter on the tube in London. The identity of JADE had been successfully concealed along with the HAR mission; the only matter left remaining was for her to kill the prime minister. When this task had been completed she would leave the BMW in the parking lot at the airport and following a brief nod to Charles watching nearby would check-in and board the Alitalia flight to Rome. Drying herself as she entered the bedroom in a silk dressing gown,

"Oku, Oku, please come?"

"Yes missy, what you need?"

"Oku, on Saturday I'm leaving on a trip and not sure how long I'll be gone. Inside this envelope is 5,000.00 Rand which includes 2,100.00 Rand to cover your wages for the next year. While I'm away I want you to come to work everyday just like you do now to look after the house. I've made arrangements with Mr. Berger, the bank manager that during my absence he is to pay the monthly phone and water and electricity utility bills by direct debit from my account at Barclays. After you take out your wages please use the remaining 2,900.00 Rand to pay any other incidental bills that may come to the house in my absence."

"Where you go Missy? Why you gone for so long? What I tell people who ask for you?"

"If anyone asks just tell them I'm away working. There's no need to say anything else."

Oku clearly didn't understand what was happening and for her own safety didn't need to know anything more. Oku with the envelope in hand left assuring her that she'd look after everything, but hoped she'd be back soon. After she was alone Rona removed a leather shoulder bag from the closet; inside the bag she carefully placed underwear, a black pants suit, one pair of Gucci shoes, some assorted cosmetics, and the leather pouch containing her airline ticket, two passports, Italian driver's license, and the cash.

The 3rd of September was a crisp and cloudless day. She hadn't slept well, frequently waking and looking at the ceiling with thoughts of pulling the trigger, the escape and the adjustment of living in Italy. After finishing her morning tea and croissant she took a shower then proceeded to purge and cleanse her personal files of any incriminating documents. After burning anything that might be of interest to the authorities and flushing the ashes down the toilet she decided to take a last swim in the pool. Lying motionless on an inflatable pad she began slowly paddling around the warm water of the pool while wistfully looking at the clear blue sky. Her mind reflectively recalling thoughts of her bitterness towards the apartheid government, the disappointment in her marriage to Abe, her career, her beautiful South Africa, and wondered whether her new American friend would still be here when she returned. The day dragged on then realizing it was almost 4:00 she began thinking,

I need to be on the riverbank across from the Verwoerd house no later than 6:15. If I'm a few minutes early I can hide in the bushes. I'll need about an hour to reach the Vaal so I must leave no later than 5:00.

Setting the bag containing the SVD Dragunov and the P38 on the bed she untied the knot placing both guns on the bed. After loading 10 rounds in the detachable box magazine she returned the SVD to the bag. Loading 8 rounds into the single-stack magazine Rona placed the P38 in the shoulder holster then slipped into her riding leathers before proceeding to the garage. Snapping the gun bag to the frame of the motorcycle, she strapped the overnight bag to her back and put on her blonde wig and helmet. Sitting in the park across the street from the garage Inspector Joubert watched as the garage door opened then spoke into his radio,

"Batman, Robin, Sky-King, this is Mother Goose the target is moving."

"Batman, Robin, copy? Sky-King do you copy?"

"Batman here, we copy."

"Sky-King, that's affirmative."

At that moment Batman and Robin, two Special Branch officers on unmarked Suzuki motorcycles positioned at the Shell service station started their engines and waited for the BMW to pass. Sky-King, a Special Branch helicopter completed its pre-flight as the main rotor spun into action and slowly lifted off the pad at police headquarters. Waiting until the BMW passed Batman and Robin followed and while maintaining a safe distance kept the BMW in view. Batman on the black Suzuki first stayed closer to the target while Robin on the red Suzuki fell back, each then alternating in case she might expect being followed. On the outskirts of the city Sky-King picked up the surveillance from 2,000'. From the homing device Special Branch, unbeknownst to Rona, had placed on the inside of the rear fender of the BMW Sky-King was quickly able to establish a visual of the motorcycle as it made its way out of the city.

Before reaching the access road along the Vaal River the black and red Suzuki motorcycles both dropped back leaving the overhead surveillance to Sky-King, the eyes-in-the-sky. The helicopter having descended to an altitude of 1,000' was 2 miles behind and downwind which prevented it from being seen or heard by the helmeted BMW rider.

"Mother Goose, Mother Goose, this is Sky-King. The target has reached ground zero."

Approaching the bushes she laid the BMW on its side and removing the sniper rifle from its case placed it between the limbs of the tree while adjusting the scope.

"Sky-King, Sky-King, this is Mother Goose, execute."

Not knowing she had been followed and unaware of the helicopter Rona assumed she was safe in the cover provided by the tree and bushes which prevented her from being seen from across the river. Startled by the loud noise and wash of the rotor blades as it swooped directly above her head she looked up as the bullets from the Uzi ripped through her body. Momentarily stunned by the excruciating pain the sniper rifle fell from her grasp. Dropping first to one knee then falling on her back blood gushed from her mouth. JADE was dead.

"Mother Goose, Mother Goose, this is Sky-King. Target eliminated. Mission accomplished, we're returning to base."

"Well done Sky-King, Mother Goose out."

A short time later Batman and Robin accompanied by two Special Branch officers in an unmarked police van placed the motionless body of Rona Tannenbaum in a black body bag then, after loading the BMW in the van left the scene. Charles, waiting patiently at the airport became concerned when Alitalia announced the departure of its flight to Rome, but Rona had failed to appear. Finding a pay phone he called her home, Oku answered.

"Hello is the lady of the house in? I'm calling to inquire about a subscription to the Johannesburg Star."

"I sorry boss, but the lady no here she be gone for a while so we need no newspaper."

Charles now seriously concerned didn't respond and hung up. Rona clearly hadn't made it to the airport because he would have seen her. Her maid said she was gone which was the plan, but where was she? He decided to wait until later that night to watch the news to see if there was any report of the death of Dr. Verwoerd. On Sunday Charles scoured the Sunday papers and listened to the South African Broadcasting Corporation, but the SABC radio news had nothing about the prime minister other than his meeting with Chief Leabua Johnathon and their joint communiqué.

On Monday there were still no news reports about Verwoerd or about Rona Tannenbaum. A perplexed Charles was more than concerned, but there was nothing he could do except wait and hope that Rona would contact him. By Tuesday, September 6th Rona still had not contacted him. Charles was surprised and puzzled when he read in the newspapers that Dr. Verwoerd was clearly alive and scheduled to make an important policy statement at the parliamentary session that afternoon, September 6th at 2:15 p.m.

On September 6th Dr. Verwoerd entered the House of Assembly, then after taking his seat, Dimitri Tsafendas, a parliamentary messenger standing nearby took a large knife from under his vest and stabbed the Prime Minister four times in the chest. After restraining Tsafendas a group of medical doctors who were Members of Parliament rushed to assist while giving Verwoerd the kiss-of-life. Verwoerd was rushed to Groote Schuur Hospital, but was pronounced dead on arrival.

"Nat, this is Vicki, have you heard what happened this afternoon in Cape Town? Verwoerd was murdered!"

Noticeably shaken Levine gasped,

"Who did it? I thought by eliminating JADE the threat on his life had been removed. Looks like the ANC have been cleverly misleading us. While they had us chasing Tannenbaum around Johannesburg who we now know was JADE, it looks like the assassination was actually planned to be carried out in Cape Town right under our noses. Vicki, do you know any more about what happened?"

"It was a parliamentary messenger by the name of Dimitri Tsafendas. Apparently he waited until Verwoerd entered the chamber then walked up to him and took a knife from under his jacket and stabbed him four times. The police said that other Member's of Parliament tried to give him the kiss-of-life before he was taken to the Groote Schuur hospital; but when Verwoerd reached the hospital he was pronounced dead on arrival. Special Branch doesn't have anything on Tsafendas, but think he must have been a hired killer. That's about all I know at the moment."

Nat responded,

"I'll follow up with Pretoria, but you keep on it too. I guess we really screwed up. Vicki, please keep digging to see if Tsafendas had any ties to Tannenbaum, the ANC or the SABRA people. With Verwoerd dead there's nothing more for me to do here. I think its best that I head to Tel Aviv and get busy with some damage control with Meir. He'll need to work on an explanation for the prime minister and our failure with Operation Ashkelon. Keep me posted."

With that Nat Levine hung up the phone.

"Joubert this is Vicki, have you learned anything more? Tomorrow Nat's flying to Tel Aviv to report to Meir Amit, but has asked me to keep tabs on what's happening. Have you got anything more on the killer and his political connections?"

"Hello Vicki, except what we've pulled from the records there's still not much on Tsafendas. His mother was from Mozambique and he had dark skin, but wasn't classified as a colored. His workmates said he was having a relationship with a colored woman and because sexual relations between people of different races are illegal he'd applied for reclassification as a colored. It could just be an ANC cover-up, but Tsafendas told our officers that he wasn't interested in politics and had no political connections. So far it appears that he was a loner that fancied Bantu Beer which he drank a lot of. His workmates apparently didn't know him well but always thought he was a bit crazy. Our people are making inquiries with the lads from the attorney general's office to see what else they can find. I'll call you if anything else develops."

"Thanks Joubert, by the way what's happening with the body?"

"Tannenbaum was alone when she was taken out and there were no witnesses. Our boys removed the serial numbers on the BMW and took her body and the motorcycle to the Veld on the air force base outside of Pretoria. They buried her and the bike along with 20kgs of caustic soda so in a few days she'll dissolve and disappear forever. We had one of the office secretary's call her home and the maid said she would be away working and wasn't expected back for some time. The maid saying that she's away works for us. Because of her popularity we're sure that sooner or later her fans will start asking questions and wondering where she is, but eventually her disappearance will simply remain a mystery. We've kept the Russian SVD sniper rifle and the P38 she was carrying to see if we can determine where the weapons came from and how she got them into the country. I'll keep you posted."

Days and then weeks passed with more and more questions about the whereabouts of Rona Tannenbaum. The studio bosses, her agent and the newspapers frequently called, but each time Oku told the same story that she was away working and wouldn't return for some time. The studio knew they hadn't sent her away on an assignment and her agent was puzzled that she would accept work without the agency knowing, particularly as she was under contract.

"Oku this is Guy Young. I haven't heard anything from Rona in a long time and would very much like to get in touch. Before she left all she said was that she'd be away working for a time doing some commercials. I know she may have told you not to tell anyone how to reach her, but I'm really concerned."

"Sorry boss, I don't know where she at. She tells me she gone for maybe a long time."

"Alright Oku, I'm at the Primrose Terrace you have the number so please call me if you hear from her."

"Okay boss, but you no worry her okay and back soon."

After the assassination of Prime Minister Verwoerd on September 6th Guy's life changed. Special Branch officers visited his office over and over again repeatedly asking the same questions. What was his connection to Rona Tannenbaum, was he or his friends' members of the ANC, what his views on the government's Apartheid Policy were, and what his real purpose for coming to South Africa was. Each time he repeatedly answered that Rona Tannenbaum was a friend, he and as far as he knew none of his friends were members of the ANC. He told the officers that while he didn't necessarily agree with Apartheid he wasn't having any type of relationship with a black or colored person, unless that is they believed that Rona Tannenbaum wasn't a white. Guy was constantly harassed by Special Branch who then began pressuring people in his office wanting to know who he called, who his friends were, and what blacks or coloreds he was associating with.

Being unable to identify any subversive connections the surveillance and Special Branch interest eventually dwindled. However, in December the question of his associations with blacks or coloreds resurfaced as a result of an invitation from Guy's chauffer Bernard. Even though Guy's relationship with Bernard was always kept on a professional level he had learned a great deal from him about the life of a Zulu and the Bantu living under the Apartheid regime. Bernard, a Zulu having had the benefit of an education at a missionary school was well-spoken and to some extent worldly. From his interest in reading the magazines Guy regularly gave him and conversations while driving him around Bernard soon expanded his knowledge of San Francisco, wine from the Napa Valley and Hollywood's motion pictures. Bernard was fascinated with his job working for an American from California and frequently asked about America. He often spoke about his 10 children who he believed he had had with 3 or 4 women which he frequently referred to as his wives. Bernard lived in Soweto, the infamous black township of Johannesburg, a few weeks before Christmas the invitation came.

"Boss I'd like for you to come to my home and have Christmas dinner with my family. It would be an honor for us to have you at our home."

"Bernard that would be great, I'd love to come, but you'll have to give me directions to your house." Bernard penned a map on a sheet of paper handing it to Guy while pointing out the streets leading to street number 15 and his home at house number 28.

"Okay boss, you'll have no problem finding my house, but you must get a pass so you can enter Soweto. The passes are issued by the Police, but as it might take a few days you should apply for the pass right away."

"If I'm just coming to dinner why do I need a pass?"

"Boss that's the law, if you enter Soweto or any Black Township without a pass you could be arrested, they are very strict about this."

Guy subsequently visited police headquarters to get a pass assuming it would be a routine matter. Not being overjoyed at having to visit police headquarters he nevertheless put on a happy face and after completing the application entered the office of the inspector.

"Good morning, my name is Guy Young. I'd like to get a pass to have dinner with my chauffeur who lives in Soweto."

A jolly green giant in a uniform reminiscent of an overweight SS storm trooper demanded,

"Sit down. What's the purpose of the visit?"

"I work for the Kienzle Organization in Braamfontein. My

chauffeur Bernard, who also works for Kienzle, has invited me to his home for Christmas dinner. I plan to go to his home about 4 in the afternoon and leave about 8pm."

Handing the application back across the desk,

"You can't be in the township after dark as it's too dangerous."

Returning the application to the green giant's desk,

"Well in that case I'll go at 2 and leave by 6 so I'll be out before it gets dark."

"Why are you so determined to visit Soweto? Are you a journalist?

Guy, thinking to himself *O-Boy* here we go again with the, *are you a journalist* bit.

"No, I'm not a journalist. I work with computers the only thing I write is computer programs. Why is it such a big deal to obtain a simple pass just to have dinner with a co-worker? When I first arrived in South Africa I lived at the Primrose Terrace Residential Hotel, but subsequently leased a penthouse. I wanted my chauffeur to visit my home, but he said this wouldn't be possible. So he invited me to his home for Christmas and told me that I needed a Pass."

"If your Bernard lives in Soweto under our laws he's not a co-worker he's a Black. Whites have no business socializing with Blacks or being in a Black Township."

"Hang-on a minute, I just want to have dinner with a friend, you make it sound like we're plotting an overthrow of the government. This is really silly."

Guy quickly realized that his casual remark of overthrowing the government hadn't been very smart. The green giant was not amused.

"Your application is denied. Please close the door as you leave."

Back home Guy was infuriated and perplexed by the attitude demonstrated by the brainless green giant. He mixed himself a double vodka martini and dropped on the settee. The following day he spoke with Bernard.

"Yesterday I went to the police station and completed the application for a pass to visit you for Christmas dinner, but it was denied. If they think that denying me a pass is going to stop me from having Christmas dinner with a friend they're badly mistaken. I've got the map of how to reach your house and if I don't get lost I'll be there around 2:00 pm, but I've got to leave before dark."

"Boss that's not a good idea, if you get caught you could be thrown in jail and they might even deport you. The police have patrols roaming through Soweto and many people are paid by the police to be informants. If the police didn't see you there's a good possibility that one of their informants would see the Mercedes being driven by a white man and immediately report you to the police. I'd really like you to come, but without a pass it would be too dangerous. As you've filled out the application for the pass they have your name, a copy of your residency card and the make and license number of the car. Also if they caught you in my house they might arrest me as well."

"Bernard this is really crazy. Two friends are prevented from having dinner together just because one is white and the other is black."

"Boss I know it sounds crazy to an American, but that's the law in South Africa. Apartheid is focused on separating the races which means no contact."

The second week of December Guy left the office early telling Bernard to leave the car in the garage as he'd be walking home. From the office he made his way to Woolworths, in the toy department he bought 10 fluffy stuffed animals and an assortment of candies. After purchasing a bottle of perfume for Bernard's wife and a wind breaker jacket for Bernard he asked for the presents to be gift wrapped and delivered to his home. Law or not, no one was going to tell him who he could or couldn't see on Christmas Eve. On December 24th he loaded the gifts into the car and set out for Soweto. Following the written instructions he easily found Bernard's house. Parking the car in front he was enthusiastically greeted by Bernard and his extended family.

"Boss what are you doing here? You should not have come because your pass was denied."

"Bernard I'm not staying, but Santa Claus told me to deliver these gifts."

Bernard's cluster of excited children began taking the gifts into the house as a crowd quickly formed around the car.

"Boss thank you very much, you are very kind, but please don't stay as the police may come."

"Yes, I know okay, I'll leave now."

Driving away Guy looked in the rear view mirror to see all the children and Bernard standing in the street waving a farewell. Before reaching the entrance to the township the sirens and flashing lights of a police Land Rover signaled him to stop. With guns drawn the police officers positioned themselves on each side of the Mercedes.

Looking down the barrel of a pistol pointed at Guy one of the green giants demanded,

"What are you doing in Soweto? Show me your pass?

"Oh sorry, I don't have a pass. I just dropped off some presents to a friend and I'm leaving now."

"Shut off the engine and give me your driver's license and papers." Taking his driver's license and the car's registration papers the green giant returned to his vehicle. A few minutes later he returned.

"Mr. Young you applied for a visitors pass to Soweto and it was refused. You have entered the township illegally and therefore I'm placing you under arrest."

The Mercedes was towed to a police compound and Guy was taken to a grubby little police station in the Land Rover where he was finger printed, photographed and questioned by a senior green giant.

"Mr. Young you're a foreigner who's been given permission to live in our country. With foreign residency status you are required to abide by our laws. If you do not abide by our laws you will be deported. While you may have liberal laws in your United States our races are not allowed to mix and anyone who violates the law will be punished."

After completing his brief, but forceful lecture on Apartheid the senior green giant instructed one of his minions to drive Guy to the holding compound where he paid the towing charge and was allowed to leave in the Mercedes.

After the Christmas holidays Guy was pleased to learn that his appearance in Soweto hadn't been reported until after he had left Bernard's house. The police questioned Bernard and his wife, but hadn't arrested or fined them. After the Soweto incident Guy was followed and frequently summoned to police headquarters where he was repeatedly questioned about his connection with Rona Tannenbaum and the outlawed African National Congress.

"I don't know exactly what you want, but Rona Tannenbaum was only a nice lady that I met on a flight from London. It was only later that I learned she was a famous movie star. I've been to her home, but we never discussed her private life. I haven't spoken with her or seen her since sometime in late August and as far as I know she had no political leanings one way or the other. If she did she never mentioned it to me. She told me that she was going away on an assignment and would be gone for sometime. I've called her home a couple of times and her maid tells me the same thing that she's away on an assignment and won't be back for some time. The only thing I know about the ANC is what I read in The Johannesburg Star. Sorry, but that's all I know."

After a number of months of being hassled by the authorities Guy decided that life under Apartheid and living in a police state wasn't exactly what he had in mind for peace and tranquility. Even though he was making and saving a lot of money everyday life wasn't the best and he decided to leave. He began selling off his furniture, gave a termination notice for the lease on the penthouse then told Haggis he was leaving. The Kienzle Organization reluctantly accepted his resignation and he bid his farewells to the people in the office.

"But lad, why are you leaving? You've made a real niche for yourself at Kienzle and making a pot full of money while bedding every lovely lady you've come to meet."

"Haggis I just can't get used to or accept the hard-line black and white policies of Apartheid. At Christmas when I wanted to have dinner with Bernard and his family I went through hell applying for a pass to visit Soweto only to find it was refused. Okay, so I didn't have a stupid pass, but I only wanted to deliver a few gifts to a good friend and his family and was arrested. Then there's the Rona angle. She and I had become intimate friends, but then strangely without a word she mysteriously drops out of sight. I have no idea what she may or may not have been involved in, but in one of my frequent interrogations the police told me she was the head of the SABRA Faction, a Jewish anti-government terrorist group that's involved with the ANC. I told the coppers I'd never heard of anything called SABRA and that Rona never mentioned or said anything about such an organization. I've been questioned, hassled and harassed by the cops who I believe have tapped my phone and now follow me everywhere I go. Seems like they think I'm some sort of a cloaked terrorist or revolutionary. I've been offered a job in London and accepted it. Hopefully I'll have my affairs tidied up so I can fly out around the 15th. I'm looking at some flats in Knightsbridge and Kensington and once I know where I'll be living I'll send you the address."

On the 8th of March Guy Young left South Africa to begin a new life in the United Kingdom. The South African newspapers continually ran stories about the strange disappearance of the glamorous movie star Rona Tannenbaum adding that she's never been found – dead or alive. The Star quoted Jan ter Meer head of South Africa's Special Branch who reported that the police agencies had conducted an extensive missing persons search, but had been unable to locate her. Then later the police authorities began circulating unconfirmed reports that Ms. Tannenbaum had been seen in Israel. These clearly bogus reports implied that she had left South Africa as a result of her fading career brought about by her divorce from the movie mogul Abe Silverman.

Guy knew this was untrue and was disinformation dispersed by the Special Branch to deceive her friends and fans in an attempt to hide whatever actually had happened. Because of their relationship Guy was confident if Rona was living in Israel or anywhere else in the world she would have contacted him, sooner or later. The Special Branch had told him about the SABRA and the connection between Rona and the organization, but he always doubted if it was true. Dimitri Tsafendas who killed the Prime Minister was never connected to the ANC and was able to escape the death penalty on the grounds of insanity saying a large worm in his stomach had told him to kill Dr. Verwoerd.

Hit & Run

As a result of the growth and expansion of yacht ownership in the United States a marine finance group known as Blue Sky Credit or BSC evolved and emerged as a key player. Under the guidance and imaginative leadership of its president, John (Jack) Dunn, BSC grew and flourished, ultimately becoming an industry leader. Based in New Jersey, BSC offered creative financing programs to major yacht dealerships, yacht brokers, yacht management companies, and affluent private individuals.

Eddie O'Brien, a Nautical Surveyor based on the Caribbean Island of Puerto Rico, provided technical support and expertise to a wide range of clients including marine underwriters, banks and admiralty lawyers in the U.S. and the United Kingdom. BSC had engaged O'Brien on a number of occasions and was pleased with his work. With an increasing book of business BSC soon found that in addition to their in-house counsel and lawyers retained in other parts of the country they also needed a qualified nautical expert on their team to act as an independent consultant. To satisfy this need Jack retained O'Brien as a maritime expert to assist BSC's lawyers with litigation support throughout the country.

Frequently engaged as BSC's maritime expert O'Brien testified in yacht valuation cases in Federal District Courts in New York, Texas, California and Florida. As a result of his litigation expertise and a number of successful verdicts he developed a close professional and personal relationship with BSC's lawyers and the company's head office staff. During a meeting at BSC's New Jersey offices regarding a case coming to trial in Houston, Jack told O'Brien of a possible problem involving a high value 65' Hatteras sport fisherman in which BSC had originated and approved the loan which was subsequently funded by the Argus Financial Group.

BSC enjoyed a commercial relationship with Argus where in cases of yacht values over $1m BSC would deal with the initial applications and approvals then sell the loans to Argus for funding. Upon their acceptance of the loan Argus would pay BSC 1 or 2 percentage points as the loan originator. This particular loan for a $1.5m Hatteras had originated from BSC's Miami office. Following the initial review Miami then sent the documents to BSC's headquarters in New Jersey for processing. BSC in accordance with their normal procedures after approving the loan passed the documentation to Argus who funded the loan. During the first year the payments were received as agreed, but then the yacht's owner, Mr. Pedro Cantara Vasquez abruptly stopped making his monthly payments. Even when the loan became three months in arrears Argus viewed the situation as little more than a collection problem. When their efforts to reach Vasquez by telephone and registered mail failed the Argus collections manager contacted Pier 66 where the *Costa Brava* was kept, but was told that neither Vasquez nor the yacht was in the marina. As Argus was named as a co-insured on the insurance policy the collections manager contacted the insurer and was told there was no insurance coverage in place as the Policy had been cancelled for non-payment of the premium. With the yacht missing and no insurance coverage Argus realized they may have a problem and needed help. After consulting with Jack his suggestion was that Argus should contact BSC's maritime expert Eddie O'Brien.

Following a lengthy telephone conversation O'Brien accepted the assignment to first locate and hopefully recover the missing vessel. To insure O'Brien had the pertinent information Argus sent a copy of their file on Vasquez to O'Brien by Federal Express, but unfortunately the loan file and police report contained few details. The information only confirmed that the Hatteras had disappeared from her berth at Pier 66 Marina in Ft. Lauderdale sometime during a two month period after Vasquez had died. According to the file when Mrs. Vasquez found that the *Costa Brava* was missing it was only then, maybe two months after it was gone, that she reported the theft to the police and then contacted the insurance broker. The insurance broker told her that the Policy had been cancelled three months earlier because the renewal forms hadn't been returned and the premium had not been paid. Following the cancellation of the Policy the insurance company said they had, as required, properly notified Argus as a co-insured and the loss payee shown on the Policy. Argus disputed that they had been notified of the cancellation alleging they hadn't been made aware of the cancellation until after they found that the vessel was missing.

As Argus was named as the loss payee on the Policy a Notice of Cancellation should have been sent by certified or registered mail with a return delivery receipt. However, the insurance company was unable to produce a copy of the return receipt or any other documentation proving that the Notice had been sent by certified or registered mail. Alleging that they had not been properly notified of the cancellation Argus filed a claim for $1.5m the insured value of the *Costa Brava*. As litigation loomed on the horizon lawyers for Argus cautioned that a lawsuit would be time consuming, lengthy, costly, and then may be unfavorable depending on the Court's view and opinion of coverage. While the lawyers believed that Argus may have a reasonable argument until such time as the court rendered its decision they wouldn't be entitled to any proceeds under the Policy. In view of the yachts high value the lawyers agreed with the decision for Argus to instruct O'Brien and take whatever steps necessary to locate and hopefully get the Hatteras back.

In reviewing the Vasquez file O'Brien found that there was another person who had an interest in the missing yacht and this person wasn't exactly a *white-hat*. One of the principal players involved with the Hatteras and a *silent* business partner of the late Pedro Vasquez was Don Francisco Marquez who lives in Mérida on Mexico's Yucatan peninsula. Marquez was known as *el Jefe* of the *Los Zetas* Drug Cartel a *black-hat* and definitely not a nice guy. The word-on-the-street was that no one ever had a problem with Don Francisco because if a problem arose Marquez would simply have the problem killed. Without any doubt he was a dangerous character, but did have one endearing characteristic, he liked big boats. O'Brien found that Don Francisco loved fishing and frequently was a guest on the *Costa Brava* when he was able to visit Miami using a forged passport or on other occasions when the late Pedro took the yacht to Mexico. As Don Francisco had grown very fond of the *Costa Brava* and even though only speculation, O'Brien theorized that Don Francisco may have decided that as Pedro was no longer of this world he would no longer need his yacht.

Before interviewing the wife of the late Pedro Vasquez, O'Brien visited Pier 66 in Fort Lauderdale where the yacht had been kept. At this point it wasn't clear if Don Francisco Marquez was involved or had anything to do with the theft, but if he was O'Brien reasoned that the yacht could now be in Mexican territorial waters. O'Brien learned through trusted sources that to protect and sustain his illicit business activities Don Francisco had a number of politicians, the military, federal, and most of the local law enforcement authorities on his payroll.

If Don Francisco was involved because of his political clout he'd want to keep the *Costa Brava* in Mexico and as far away from the U.S as possible. He was smart enough to know the yacht couldn't be taken to Mexico's Pacific coast because of the potential problems of seizure when passing through the Panama Canal. Veracruz and Tampico were commercial ports that could accommodate a yacht of this size, but would be inconvenient for someone living in Mérida. Through a process of elimination O'Brien evaluated each of the marinas and yacht harbors on Mexico's Caribbean coast that could accommodate a yacht of this size and provide convenient access for someone who lived in Mérida. O'Brien focused on Progresso, Cozumel and Cancun.

————

At the height of his career as a successful and creditworthy businessman Argus Financial had loaned Pedro Vasquez the money to purchase the 65' Hatteras *Costa Brava,* but were extremely unhappy when they found that their security on the loan was missing, especially when the yacht was uninsured. Pedro Vasquez, a Colombian national had been issued a Green Card by the U.S. Immigration and Naturalization Service and been a resident of Miami for 10 years. In happier days he owned a thriving business importing cut flowers from Ecuador and Colombia. The late Pedro apparently sold a lot of flowers which allowed him to acquire an exquisite penthouse on Brickell Avenue, a couple of Mercedes for him and his wife along with a number of other toys which included the *Costa Brava*. In recent years the U.S. Customs Service and the Drug Enforcement Agency had kept Pedro and his thriving business under surveillance because of strong suspicions that somewhere concealed amongst the imported flowers or in the shipping containers there was also a large quantity of cocaine. As all containers entering the Port of Miami are not inspected it's obvious that Customs picked the wrong containers to inspect because they were never successful in finding the drugs.

Pedro's wife, Juanita Beltran de Vasquez was a beautiful and graceful woman in her mid forties who without a doubt enjoyed the elegant lifestyle of the United States in contrast to her previous existence as a struggling model in Bogotá. Contrary to her late husband's love of boats she was always sea sick, hated the sea, the *Costa Brava*, and boating in general, unless of course, the boat might be the Carnival cruise ship *Fantasy*.

The Vasquez penthouse on Brickell Avenue was truly magnificent. The walls were adorned with numerous original paintings and bronze sculptures by the eminent Spanish-Puerto Rican artist Angel Botello, often referred to as the Caribbean Gauguin.

"Good morning Mrs. Vasquez, my name is Edward O'Brien I've been asked by Argus Financial to look into the disappearance of the *Costa Brava*, thank you for your taking the time to see me. I'd appreciate your help in learning what transpired in the days just before and after the unfortunate passing of your husband Pedro and when you first learned that the *Costa Brava* was missing?"

The relaxed widow seemed anxious to speak,

"You know, unless Pedro insisted I rarely went to the boat because I would get sea sick even just sitting on the boat in the marina. I've never liked the boat. To the best of my recollection I hadn't been to the marina for a number of months before Pedro died. I don't remember exactly, but think it may have been a month or two after poor Pedro went to heaven when Carlos called me. Carlos works at the marina and because he is also from Columbia we became friends. Carlos said that when he returned from his holiday he noticed that the *Costa Brava* wasn't in its slip. He hadn't thought much about it because he thought that Pedro was probably fishing in the Bahamas or maybe had gone to Cancun. After another few weeks had passed and the *Costa Brava* still had not returned Carlos called to ask if I knew where it was. As Pedro had passed I telephoned the police to report that our boat was missing and went to the police station to fill out a report. I then called Felipe, the insurance agent. Felipe was very nice, but told me that our insurance policies on the boat, cars and our home hadn't been renewed. I asked him why and he told me because the premiums hadn't been paid. Then the loan people started pestering me with phone calls and registered letters with demands for delinquent loan payments and for a copy of the insurance policy. My lawyer said as Pedro is dead I shouldn't make any payments to Argus as the boat was their problem not mine. If it may help I'll give you some photographs of the boat. I'm sorry, but there's really nothing more I can tell you."

Later in the day O'Brien visited the marina office at Pier 66 and met with the manager, Charlie Taylor,

"Eddie O'Brien, that name's familiar. Didn't you do a survey here on an Azimut a few months back?"

"Sure did. You have a good memory. Please call me Eddie."

"Eddie, it's not our normal practice to keep records of the individual vessel movements of our regular customers. Even if the vessel is relinquishing its berth and leaving Pier 66 permanently I wouldn't necessarily be concerned as long as all the dockage fees had been paid and were up to date. Let me have a look at the record for the *Costa Brava*, I see here that for the last number of months the dockage charges had always been paid automatically and charged to the owner's American Express card. Hmm, this is a bit strange, look at this, the last payment we received wasn't on the card, but was paid in cash. There's no name on the receipt and whoever it was paid three months dockage in advance."

Passing the marina's copy of the receipt to O'Brien he saw it had no name on it, but confirmed the payment had been made in cash.

"Charlie would you mind if I spoke with the person in charge of marina security and have a look at the security work logs to see who was on duty when the boat was first reported missing?"

"Sure, that's no problem. Irma Waterville, she's the lady that was in my office when you came in, her office is next door. I'll call her and tell her its okay for you to have a look at her records."

"Hi Irma, my name is Eddie O'Brien and......"

Before he could barely get the words *Costa Brava* out of his mouth, Irma, a sleazy bottle-blonde red-neck dressed in a black Mickey Mouse look-a-like uniform, blurted out,

"I don't want y'all talking to my guards they don't know *nutin'* about the boat and didn't *saw* it leave."

O'Brien asked, "Who are *they*?"

With obvious sarcasm,

"*They* Mr. O'Brien are *my* marina security guards. I dun already talk to 'em and no one saw the boat leave. No one said the *Costa Brava* missing, dockage been paid, we got no interest in'er."

"I'm sorry Irma, but I need to have a look at the security work logs."

Clearly unhappy Irma gave the security logs to O'Brien. The security logs indicated that Irma and two other guards worked nights and three others did the day shift and swing. Having spoken with Charlie O'Brien knew that when a boat leaves there isn't a formal record kept unless the vessel may be one that's behind on their dockage fees, but this would be unusual as this up-scale marina rarely had deadbeats to contend with. Once outside the building and out of Irma's view one of the security guards whose name tag indicated his name was Peter pulled O'Brien aside saying he had some information that he might be interested in. Peter suggested they meet after his shift ended at Chuck's Steak House. Chuck's, a restaurant favored by the yachting crowd is also located on 17th Street in Ft. Lauderdale about a mile west of Pier 66. From a first impression it appeared that Peter was a savvy, street wise type who clearly was of the opinion that he deserved much more recognition than he received as a low paid security guard. At 10:30 p.m. O'Brien left his rental car in the parking lot at Chuck's and entered the steak house. After sliding into the booth Peter's first question was,

"How much is the reward for getting the boat back?"

"Back from where, do you know where the boat is? My client hasn't authorized me to offer any reward, but if you've got any solid information that may be helpful which leads to the recovery of the Hatteras, I'd be prepared to personally pay you for any specific information that may be useful. If we can recover the boat there would be a reward and you'd get the money."

"How do I know I can trust you?

"You don't. Peter, my only interest is the return of the *Costa Brava*. If you help me, I'll help you."

"Okay, but you must promise me that my involvement will be kept secret and the reward must be in cash."

O'Brien agreed, "Tell me what you know and I'll tell you what its worth."

Eagerly Peter began,

"About a week after Pedro Vasquez died I saw this guy Marquez sitting with Irma in a green Jaguar in the owners' parking lot just before her shift started. One of the other guys I work with said he was a nasty character and was involved with drugs. I don't know if Irma may be dealing for him, but thought it was a bit strange because I had never seen the Mexican with Irma before and didn't think they even knew each other. I knew the Mexican and Vasquez were friends because I'd seen him a few times before when they went out fishing, but he wasn't one of our regular customers and he didn't have a boat at Pier 66. I didn't give their meeting too much thought until a couple of days later when I was working inside one of the storage sheds I saw Marquez and Irma together again in the parking lot, but this time Marquez gave Irma a large brown envelope. I was inside the shed about 100' away so they couldn't see me, but when Irma opened the envelope I saw her pull out a bundle of money. A few days after that I saw Irma with Marquez a third time, but by this time the *Costa Brava* wasn't in her slip. When I told Irma that the Hatteras was gone, she told me that if I knew what was good for me, I'd better keep my mouth shut."

"Peter I'm not exactly sure what Irma's meeting with Marquez may have to do with the Hatteras, but from what you've told me I think its worth following up in case there might be a connection. As a gesture of good faith here's $500.00. If I'm able to establish a connection between Irma and Marquez and I can locate the Hatteras I'll give you another $1,500.00. No guarantees and I can't say how much it would be, but if we get the Hatteras back and she's undamaged I'm sure my clients would agree to pay you a generous reward."

"Okay, that's a deal, let's shake on it, but if you come back to Pier 66 for any reason you mustn't speak to me. Irma's a real bitch and would fire me if she knew I was talking with you. I live in Dania this is my home address and telephone number. If I come across anything else I'll call you and let you know."

Three days later Peter called.

"I've got a friend who works on the fuel dock who gave me some information that may be of interest. My friend told me that on the Tuesday, the 23rd of September the *Costa Brava* left Pier 66 after topping off her fuel tanks, there were three very nervous Mexican guys on board. My friend, a Cuban, knew they were Mexican from their accent and when they paid for the fuel in cash they also had some Mexican Pesos mixed in with the U.S. Dollars. Is this of any use? Maybe the *Costa Brava* is in Mexico? If I pick up anything more I'll let you know." Peter hung up the phone.

Clearly this was very important information. Marquez was a Mexican, with the dock attendant confirming that when the *Costa Brava* left Pier 66 it had a Mexican crew on board definitely pointed to Mexico. The fuel tanks on a Hatteras 65' hold a total of 1,800 gallons and with full tanks there would be more than enough fuel for the Hatteras to reach the Marina Hemmingway or Varadero on Cuba's north coast. O'Brien reasoned that after topping up the tanks in Cuba the *Coast Brava* could then easily make it to any one of the Mexican ports on the Yucatan. Whether it would go to Progresso in the northern Yucatan, Cancun or Isla de Cozumel was open to speculation. With trusted and reliable contacts in Havana and others in Mexico O'Brien asked his contacts to check the marinas and let him know if there were any recent arrivals of 65' Hatteras sport fisherman. The inquiries proved negative, but with frequent flights from Miami O'Brien decided that Cancun with her many marinas would be a good place for him to start looking.

A bustling tourist development located on Mexico's Caribbean coast, Cancun consists of a cluster of international luxury hotels with white sand beaches and a number of marinas, charter boats, great restaurants, and even better cantinas. After identifying the players O'Brien realized that matching wits with the Mexican *black-hats* would at best be challenging, but he just may get lucky and find the *Costa Brava*. He'd have to be careful because if he did find it and his identity or motives were inadvertently exposed he could easily be fed to the sharks off Isla Mujeres.

As Vasquez and Marquez had many times gone fishing in Cancun O'Brien might just get lucky, if the boat wasn't there he'd then move on to the other Mexican ports where the Hatteras could be. Arriving in Cancun on the afternoon American Airlines flight, O'Brien rented a Volkswagen Beetle from Avis and checked-in at the Hotel Fiesta Americana before venturing down to Friday's for a Cuba Libré. Cancun in the Mexican State of Quintana Roo is a narrow peninsula with a large protected lagoon on one side and the Caribbean Sea on the other. Because of the depth of the water most of the larger boats are moored in marinas on the Caribbean side along the Boulevard Kukulcàn. Equipped with a miniature camera, digital recorder and three bottles of Evian mineral water O'Brien headed south on Blvd. Kukulcàn checking out a number of different yacht harbors before reaching a small marina situated behind a tourist watering hole called Carlos & Charlie's.

Passing the restaurant O'Brien found the marina had an inner dock for small boats and an outer dock positioned in deeper water for the larger sport fishing yachts. Passing the row of small boats on the inner dock he then made his way to the outer dock. In the first slip along on the outer dock O'Brien saw a 65' Hatteras flying a Mexican flag, there was no name on the transom or on her port or starboard bows. Slowly passing the Hatteras O'Brien moved further along the dock stopping briefly at the stern of a 1970's vintage Bertram 31' to admire the classic beauty.

With the Hatteras at a 45° angle to his left O'Brien could see that the forward hatches were closed, the sliding door from the cockpit to the main saloon was shut and the air conditioning pumps either weren't working or the a/c wasn't turned on. There was no wind and it was a warm 90 degrees. Considering there was no a/c running and the cockpit door and all the other hatches were closed it was a pretty good bet that no one was on board.

Returning to the stern of the Hatteras moored a few feet from the dock and while casually looking over the boat O'Brien took a number of photographs with the miniature camera held covertly in the palm of his hand. Squinting he tried to read the Hull Identification Number (HIN) imbedded on the starboard side of the transom that was about 5' from the dock. Squinting he tried to convince himself with 20/20 vision he should be able to read the 6mm characters of the Hull Identification Number, but only HAT, the first three digits of the manufacturer's identification code was clear. The remaining nine numbers of the HIN simply weren't readable, but fortunately were still there.

At five in the afternoon the docks were empty with the exception of a young lad who was concentrating on varnish work on a boat at the far end of the dock and a half dozen people in the restaurant chatting over a Corona the local cerveza. O'Brien knew that the only way he was going to confirm the HIN was to get on the dive platform. Thinking to himself, *I wonder if I could jump the few feet to the dive platform, take a rubbing of the HIN and be back on the dock before anyone was the wiser? The people in the restaurant appeared to be disinterested tourists, but what if they weren't and were locals who had their boats in the marina or a restaurant worker or waitress saw me jumping on the boat? Hmmm....*

O'Brien's mind was in overdrive. He was sure it was, but unless he could get a clear rubbing of the HIN there was no way he could positively determine if this Hatteras was in fact the *Costa Brava*. If it was the *Costa Brava* and he were to get caught going on board without permission or fall into the water attracting unwanted attention to what he was doing or even worse get arrested, it would be - game over. If this were to happen his cover would be blown, the boat would probably disappear again and they might never get her back. He'd only have one chance and pondering his options decided to wait and returned to his Beetle rented earlier in the day. Further down Blvd. Kukulcàn he parked in front of the Cancun Marine Club and drank a bottle of the Evian mineral water; deep in thought he watched a glorious sun as it descended over the horizon.

An hour later he returned to Carlos & Charlie's parking between a swarm of other Beetles whose occupants had no doubt gathered for the happy hour. From the safety of his Beetle he watched for any activity on the Hatteras. A little after seven the restaurant began to fill, but there was still no one on the Hatteras. In the fading light he compared the photos he had been given by Mrs. Vasquez with the Hatteras found on the outer dock. The gold Lee Outriggers were the same as in the Vasquez photos, the ships bell mounted on the port side of the cockpit matched, as did the life raft secured on the foredeck fitted with a blue cover positioned next to a deck crane on the port side. The gear on the unnamed Hatteras matched the photos of the *Costa Brava*.

Casually strolling into Carlos & Charlie's O'Brien ordered a Coke. The waitress, a Canadian, was friendly and asked if he liked Cancun? Responding that he was a little bored with the beach and wanted to go fishing he inquired if any of the boats in the marina might be available for charter. The waitress said she knew that the *Pescador* the 31'Bertam which he had admired earlier was available for charter. She said the big boat at the end of the dock had only recently arrived in the marina and wasn't sure, but thought they might be doing half or full day charters. He finished his Coke and returning to the Beetle he reviewed his notes and the obvious similarities of the *Costa Brava* with the Cancun Hatteras.

Just after 8:00 p.m. a red Volkswagen station-wagon pulled in and parked next to the restaurant. The two male occupants got out and went to the Hatteras. The two stayed on board for about an hour before closing the boat and entering the restaurant, by the greeting they received from one of the waitresses both appeared to be regular customers. An hour later the two drove away with O'Brien following at a safe distance behind them. He followed the red VW station wagon until it left the peninsula and drove towards the old city located on the mainland. Back at the Fiesta Americana he thought about the dimly lit dock at Carlos & Charlie's, a dimly lit dock that would hide the Hatteras from any prying eyes in the restaurant.

Returning to Carlos & Charlie's Dock a bit after ten, O'Brien checked to see if the red VW station-wagon was in the parking lot. He then looked around the bar to see if the two Mexicans might have returned by other means before slowly meandering down to the Hatteras. The restaurant was busy with customers laughing, eating and drinking. No lights were shown on any of the moored boats on either the inner or outer docks and no one was out walking on either of the docks, they were empty. Being obscured in the shadows with no lights on the docks those inside the restaurant could see little more than an outline of the boats moored on the outer dock. With a few sheets of paper torn from his notepad and a soft pencil O'Brien leapt on to the dive platform of the Hatteras and in a few seconds had taken a rubbing of the HIN from the transom. Back in his Beetle he compared the HIN from the *Costa Brava* to the one from the Cancun Hatteras – they matched – he'd found the *Costa Brava*.

O'Brien thought to himself, okay you've found it, *now how do you get it back?* From the phone in his room at the hotel O'Brien called Marty Devine his contact at Argus. It was well after midnight when Marty picked up the phone at his home in Morristown, New Jersey. Over the scratchy and poor phone line, "Marty, Marty, this is Eddie O'Brien. I'm sorry to call you so late, but wanted to give you some good news. I've found the *Costa Brava*; she's in Cancun, Mexico."

"Wow, that's great! Please never worry about the hour when you've got news, especially good news. You can call me anytime. Who has the boat? Is anyone on board? What condition is it in? God I've got a million of questions. Have you notified the police? Will the police help us detain the boat? I guess the most important question is can you get it back to Florida? Hello, hello, Eddie, Eddie still there?"

"Yeah I'm still here, sorry the phone line is so bad."

"Marty the boat appears to be in good condition, I didn't see any damage. The name has been removed from the transom, but I know for sure that she's the *Costa Brava* because I took a rubbing of the HIN and it matches. At the moment I don't know exactly who was involved in taking her, but I think it's probably a guy named Francisco Marquez. I won't go into all the details over the phone, but Marquez is involved with some nasty business in Mexico and definitely not a Mr. Nice Guy. If it is Marquez he'll have the police and the Captain of the Port on his payroll so I can't get the authorities or the police involved as it could be bad for my health, if you know what I mean. There are two Mexicans on board who appear to be crew. They haven't seen me and the people in the marina don't think I'm anything more than a tourist. The boat's moored in a marina on the outer side of the lagoon so there's direct access to the Caribbean. I've got an idea for a plan that if you agree I believe will work. I've got to find out is how much fuel is in her tanks and if the engines are okay. If there aren't any problems and there's enough fuel and I'm able to get a delivery crew on board I think we could snatch the boat and go, let's just call it a *Hit and Run*. Because of the people we're dealing with we'd have to be certain that whatever we do is carried out with military precision or else we'd have a real problem, or even worse, dead."

"Eddie of course we want the *Costa Brava* back, but I want to make it very clear Argus can't and won't condone any illegal activities. Once you know what you want to do, how you'll do it and how much it'll cost, call me. I must emphasize the call me, no faxes or anything in writing. Please keep in mind that while we want the boat back we want it back in one piece so what ever you plan it has to be without any damage to the yacht. I repeat Argus will not condone any illegal activities. Before you do anything I'll need to know exactly what you have in mind to recover her, how much it will cost and if it can be recovered without exposing her to any danger."

"Marty I'm almost certain that the Hatteras was stolen from Florida by Francisco Marquez. Marquez is a drug lord who has a nasty record of killing people who get in his way and both the Federal Policia Judicial and the local cops are on his payroll. I'm sure he's not going to just hand over the Hatteras and wave us good bye as we drive it home.

I've got an idea, but need to put a few pieces together to make sure we get it right. I'd do my best to protect the boat and minimize the dangers, but I can't give you an iron-clad guarantee there wouldn't be any damage to the boat or danger to the crew."

"Eddie, please don't forget Argus is a public company and therefore we couldn't get involved or put our name to anything that's illegal. The loan is in default and if we can't get the boat back we know we're facing a substantial loss, but we could face an even greater loss from the adverse publicity from the fallout if your recovery plan failed and became an international incident. Before you do anything please provide me with the full details of what you've got in mind. If you think it will work I'd then discuss it with our legal people. If the lawyers don't have any objections I'd probably verbally suggest that you do it, but remember, if it doesn't work you're on your own. I'll deny any knowledge of what you do or didn't do. Is that clear?"

"Okay Marty, no problem, I'll go to work and as soon as I put the pieces together, I'll get back to you. Time is of the essence so we'll need act quickly. She could be moved or Marquez could get clever and remove the HIN, engine and serial numbers of the electronics making a positive ID impossible. If they remove all her identification numbers she could be flagged and registered in another country and you'd never get her back."

O'Brien worked into the night putting together the details of the *Hit and Run* which he believed was clearly a job for *the Clan*. If the plan was to work successfully it had to be carried out with military precision. After completing the plan the following afternoon O'Brien called New York to present his proposal.

"Hi Marty, please listen carefully to what I have to say."

For 20 minutes Marty listened intently while O'Brien explained precisely what he had in mind to successfully pull-off the *Hit and Run* to recover and remove the *Costa Brava* from Cancun.

"Marty, that's it in a nutshell. I'm confident it'll work. If it sounds plausible talk it over with your legal beagles, if they don't object call me and give me the green light. If you don't like it the only alternative would be to write off the loan. Because of the players involved I don't think there are any other options. In any case, I need to know right away. The crew I have in mind for the job, if I can recruit them, are South African friends that for now we'll call *the Clan*. I first met them after they sailed from Cape Town and now live on their boats in Sint Maarten in the Dutch Caribbean; with their experience they'd be perfect for the crew. All we need is three people."

"Eddie are you sure you can rely on this Clan?"

"Definitely, the three are a husband and wife and a single guy, all are reliable and experienced sailors. I've used them in the past on let's say, sensitive assignments."

"If you're happy with them Eddie that's fine with me as long as they can be relied on to keep quiet about what they might be doing. What's this going to cost?"

"Including paying *the Clan*, my fees, the travel expenses and fuel and dockage costs I believe we could put everything together for about $30,000.00. The only possible danger is if the Mexican Navy attempts to stop the Hatteras before it leaves Mexican territorial waters. However, I'm confident with the element of surprise any problems with the Navy can be avoided because by the time they can mobilize and get underway the Hatteras will be long gone. Marquez is chartering the Hatteras for half and full day charters which gives us easy access to get on board. Just like a normal customer we'll charter the boat to go fishing. The only difference being that we just won't return it."

"What about the crew? When it leaves on the charter it'll have the captain and mate on board. You didn't tell me what happens to their crew when you don't return the boat to Cancun? You can't bring two undocumented Mexican aliens into the United States. When the boat makes its stop and clears in with two unhappy Mexicans the Belize authorities are going to have a lot of questions. Especially when the Mexicans start screaming that the boat was stolen from Cancun."

"Marty please don't ask and don't worry about the crew. They won't be brought into the U.S. or Belize and they won't be harmed. Let's leave it at that."

"Okay Eddie, I'm still a bit in the dark, but if the Mexican crew isn't harmed and won't be taken to Belize or the U.S. seems like your plan might work. Because Argus doesn't know exactly what you're doing and we haven't approved anything in writing the lawyers think it's worth a try. Once you confirm it's on, I'll wire the funds to your Bank of America account in Miami. The wire will simply show the payment as fees, no specifics. Don't forget, even though we'll provide the funding, if for any reason it fails Argus will deny any knowledge of what you did. Agreed?"

"No problem Marty, as soon as I speak with *the Clan* and confirm they're on board, I'll let you know it's on. You can then wire the money. In the meantime please FedEx certified copies of the U.S. Coast Guard documentation and the loan agreement to me in Puerto Rico."

In the meantime O'Brien's contacts in Mérida and Cancun further confirmed that Marquez was indeed a very bad guy who had all the Federal and Local authorities in Quintana Roo 'in his pocket'. If the Mexican law enforcement authorities somehow became aware of the plan they would clearly attempt to thwart the recovery of the *Costa Brava* and if Marquez had any inkling about what was coming down he'd promptly have both the interior and transom Hull Identification Numbers removed to prevent any legal identification of the Hatteras. If Argus was to get the *Costa Brava* back it could only be accomplished through a successful *Hit & Run*. O'Brien flew out of Cancun the next day and returned to Puerto Rico. The following day FedEx delivered the vessel's documentation papers and $30,000.00 was deposited in O'Brien's bank account.

He kept reminding himself that the removal of the *Costa Brava* had to be well planned, quickly executed and above all, where no one would get hurt – or killed. *The Clan* was perfect for the job; the three of them could pull it off while appearing like tourists simply chartering one of the many boats available for fishing. The woman would drive the Hatteras while the men took care of the two Mexican crewmen. The Mexican Navy has a base at Isla Mujeres and a gaggle of run-down patrol boats providing coastal surveillance between Cabo Catouche and Punto Allen. Further to the north they also had an old ex-US Coast Guard Island Class Cutter stationed in the Port of Progresso which was normally out-of-service for repairs. Not known for doing anything in a hurry O'Brien was confident that by the time the Mexican Navy eventually got underway the Hatteras would be long gone.

During the time that O'Brien lived on the island of Sint Maarten in the Netherlands Antilles he had made a number of friends, some legitimate and respectable and others, well scallywags. Having spent a number of years in Durban and Cape Town he was particularly drawn to the South African sailors who had made this Dutch island their home. They were generally experienced, big, trustworthy specimens of mankind who possessed a special knowledge of the sea; they also enjoyed a cold beer equally with making money.

An hour after arriving in Philipsburg O'Brien met with *the Clan*, telling them that the plan was to take a 65' Hatteras from Cancun and deliver it to Belize, but emphasizing that if the *Hit and Run* failed they'd probably end up in a Mexican jail. *The Clan* included Pieter, his wife Fran and Jacob, Fran's brother. After listening to O'Brien's scheme they agreed to carry out the recovery of the *Costa Brava* and for their efforts each would receive $5,000.00. O'Brien then explained the details,

"I'm going to buy a 9' inflatable boat from Wal-Mart in Fajardo and from the local marine store a chart of the Yucatan peninsula south to the Guatemalan border. Fran, from Wathey Travel you need to purchase three round-trip tickets from Sint Maarten to San Juan. The outbound must be on Saturday morning on the American flight with the return any day two weeks later. The return portion isn't important because you won't be using it so pick any day that's available. I've booked your round trip from San Juan to Mexico City with COPA and made your hotel reservations through Bird Travel. On Saturday I'll wait for you outside customs at San Juan airport. The American flight arrives at 11:15 a.m. so you should be through immigration and customs by 11:45 a.m. We'll then drive to the Denny's Coffee Shop in Isla Verde where I'll give you $1,000.00 in cash the hotel confirmation and three business class tickets for the COPA afternoon flight from San Juan to Mexico City that makes an intermediate stop in Panama. The COPA tickets are round trip to avoid any possible problems with the Mexican immigration authorities because they don't like travelers who arrive with only one-way tickets. You'll just play the role of tourists on their way to a holiday in Cancun. In any case when the time comes for you to leave Mexico it won't be by plane. I want you to buy three large sports bags that you can carry on the plane; they need to a reasonable size for your gear, but be sure they'll fit in the overhead compartments. Don't get any bag that's too big and can't be carried on board. The COPA flight from Panama is scheduled to arrive in Mexico City at 10:57 p.m., and their flights are usually on time. I've made reservations for two rooms at the

Mexico City Marriott Airport hotel. One for Pieter and Fran de Meier and the other for Jacob Edstrom, your real names are used because you'll need your passports for the flights and the hotel will ask you for passport identification. You can walk from the airport in Mexico City to the Marriott over a walk-way near the international arrivals area. If the plane is on time and allowing a few minutes for immigration and customs you should be in your rooms by 11:45 p.m. Here are your tickets for the morning Mexicana flight to Cancun. Once you get to Cancun take a taxi to the Hilton. Here's a copy of the hotel reservation. It's really important that no one in Sint Maarten knows where or why you're going away for a few days. Tell whoever you get to look after your boats while your gone that you're going to visit friends someplace; and don't make any phone calls from the hotel room's phone in Mexico City or Cancun. I'll call you when I get to Cancun."

Arriving in Cancun on Monday afternoon O'Brien checked into the Fiesta Americana Hotel and from a pay phone in the lobby called the Hilton.

"Hey Fran, did you guys have a good trip?"

"Hi Eddie, yep the trip was great, first time I've flown business class and decided this is the only way to fly. How about you?

"Yeah it was great, no problems. I whizzed through customs and they didn't see the inflatable boat or the other stuff in my bag. Mexican customs is a bit like a casino with Green and Red lights. You press a button and if you get a red light they look in your bags. I got a Green light so I was a winner and they waved me through. So far the *Hit and Run* seems to be on a winning streak beginning with my Green Light role of the dice! Fran, this afternoon I'd like the three of you to take a taxi to Carlos & Charlie's on Blvd. Kukulcàn, the cabbie will know the where its at. Our Hatteras is tied up in the first slip on the outer dock and there should be two Mexicans on board. If they're not there wait in the bar until they come back and make arrangements to charter the Hatteras for a full day of fishing on Wednesday. Give them a deposit of $400.00 and tell them you'll pay the balance on Wednesday. If they ask where you're staying, but only if they ask, tell them you're staying with friends at the Condominium

Vista Real no. 12. They won't know it, but I checked it and Vista Real no. 12 is an empty unit. After you book the charter take a taxi to the Calinda Hotel, next to the Calinda is a small bar called La Bodega. It's a popular tourist watering hole and normally busy, but has some secluded booths in the back so we can talk without drawing any unnecessary attention. This will give us a chance to go over any final details before 'show time.' If you guys get to La Bodega before I arrive just wait for me. I'm planning to first visit Carlos & Charlie's to book a half-day charter on the Hatteras for Tuesday afternoon. On Tuesday I'll see what fuel is on board and make sure everything works. See you guys later."

The name that O'Brien used for the charter was Thomas A. Chance, a tourist from San Francisco who paid his $550.00 half-day charter fee in cash. When the crew asked where O'Brien was staying in Cancun he replied,

"I'm at the Condominium Dos Marinas staying with a friend who owns one of the condos."

In case they asked, O'Brien had visited Dos Marinas earlier in the day and was ready with the number of an empty unit, but they didn't ask which one. After paying the charter fee Mr. Chance got his receipt and left. Later in La Bodega when Fran asked why O'Brien had used the name he told her that T.A. Chance seemed appropriate considering he was clearly *Taking-A-Chance*.

From his visit with Mrs. Vasquez O'Brien knew that the *Costa Brava's* Caterpillar engines had been serviced just before Vasquez died at which time she'd been hauled, anti-fouled and her shaft cutlass bearings had been replaced so he was confident that the Hatteras would be seaworthy for her next trip. O'Brien had also obtained an inventory list of what was on the vessel before Marquez had stolen her, but needed to check to see during the charter what equipment was working and most importantly, what fuel was on board. The *Costa Brava* had left Florida with a good compliment of electronics including 72NM radar, SSB and VHF radios, two video depth sounders, EPIRB, and a Robertson auto-pilot, all of which was hopefully still working.

Unsure of what nautical charts were on board before leaving

Puerto Rico O'Brien purchased a copy of the Reed's Nautical Almanac for the Caribbean and a chart of the Yucatan coast. If there weren't any charts onboard *the Clan* could us the charts O'Brien brought along.

———

Thomas Chance's charter of the Hatteras on Tuesday was uneventful; the Mexican crew was pleasant and accommodating. While on the flying bridge after departing Carlos & Charlie's O'Brien was able to confirm that both engines and the main Kohler generator were running efficiently. The engine tachometers and synchronizers indicated the engines to be humming along at 2200 RPM; with a clean bottom the Hatteras was soon making just over 30 knots towards the fishing grounds. The propellers and shafts were turning smoothly with no vibration. All the electronics were functioning and the radar set at a range of 16 nautical miles told the crew they had a clear path ahead. The Captain was operating the boat from the flying bridge station while the crewman was busy in the cockpit setting up the fishing gear and preparing the bait.

The Sailor 25w VHF radio was not turned on. O'Brien casually asked if the radio worked at which time the helmsman turned it on quickly adjusting the ear piercing squelch control. He then turned the radio off saying that they rarely turned it on because of the constant and boring chatter. O'Brien was pleased to hear this. If the VHF radio was on the Mexican Navy's Doppler radar could pick up a signal and show the vessel's position. If the Mexican's didn't normally use the VHF radio Wednesday's charter with the radio turned off would be considered normal. Normal in the event the Navy was monitoring with their radar looking for a signal. The fuel gauges showed that the 1,800 gallon tanks were 3/4 full indicating there was at least 1,350 gallons on board. Of the 445 gallons of fresh water the vessel carried the water gauge indicated at least half was on board.

About five miles out O'Brien got into the fishing chair and played the role of a novice angler for about an hour catching a few small Dorado before complaining of seasickness and asking that they return to the harbor. Having been paid for a half day, which was non-refundable, the Mexicans had no problem returning the seasick *gringo* to the marina. After leaving the Hatteras O'Brien quickly drove to La Bodega and found *The Clan* sitting in a secluded booth. He briefed them on the day's events reporting the fuel and water levels, condition of the engines and generator, oil and transmission pressures, and the electronics. The only thing O'Brien didn't know was exactly how much if any, extra lube oil was on board.

"When we returned to Carlos & Charlie's Dock the engine room door from the cockpit was open. I saw two five gallon containers of Texaco URSA engine oil, but I have no idea how much oil is in the containers. While we were underway at around 2200 RPM the gauges on the bridge showed the correct oil pressure and she wasn't smoking so I don't think you'll need to add any oil or use what may be left in the containers. Let's go over what's happening on Wednesday. At 8:00 a.m. you check out of the Calinda and pay the hotel bill in cash. You'll take a taxi to Carlos & Charlie's each carrying the soft sports bags that you brought with you. Jacob, your bag will hold the tightly wrapped Wal-Mart children's two-person inflatable boat, both rolls of Duct Tape and the Zip-Loc bags. Fran, you carry the 12 MREs (meals-ready-to-eat) which I obtained from the U.S. Navy Base in Puerto Rico. Pieter, you carry the charts of the Yucatan coast and the Reeds Nautical Almanac along with any snacks you want to munch on. After you pack the items cover the contents with your clothing. A few minutes after you pull away from the dock Fran and Jacob should go up on the flying bridge and engage the helmsman in conversation. Pieter, you remain in the cockpit with the other crewman. Once the Hatteras is about five or six miles offshore, Jacob, you give a nod to Pieter at which time you each grab the diminutive Mexicans forcing them to the deck. While Jacob is holding the Captain on the bridge, Fran, you position the throttles to idle at about 900 RPM and place the transmissions in neutral then with his hands behind his back wrap the Captain's wrists with the Duct-Tape then move to the cockpit and do the same with the crewman that's being held by Pieter. With the element of surprise and acting simultaneously I'm sure the Mexican crew can be overcome quickly and without any injuries. Once the helmsman has been taken from the bridge to the cockpit both Mexicans are to have their ankles securely wrapped in duct tape in addition to a single wrap around their mouths and eyes. It is important that you move quickly to prevent the crew from grabbing one of the fillet knives in the cockpit or the flare gun that's secured in a locker on the bridge. Please remember that once the Mexican's are overcome and securely wrapped you should not speak, but only communicate by hand signals. Any questions so far?"

Fran shook her head. Jacob asked,

"Where exactly are the fillet knives kept?"

"There may be others, but I saw three in the port side drawer of the wet bar in the cockpit. After the Mexican crew has been securely, let's say wrapped, Pieter, you inflate the rubber boat and place it in the water. Take the Mexicans to the dive platform and gently put them in the rubber boat back-to-back. They'll be blindfolded with their arms and legs bound with the Duct-Tape so I don't think they'll struggle much because they won't want to fall in the water. You need to be careful when you put them in so as to keep as much water as possible out of the little boat. After the two are in the inflatable boat make one pass of the Duct-Tape around their shoulders as this will keep them together and back to back. The Duct-Tape will eventually loosen, but at least temporarily it will keep them from moving for fear they'd both end up in the water and maybe drown. Put the flare gun and six flares from the Hatteras in a Zip-Loc bag and four bottles of drinking water between them in the center of the boat. Both of the Mexican's speak and understand English so the only time anything is to be said is after they are placed in the rubber boat. Fran, you tell them in English that they should be careful and not move around because as well as drinking water there's a cocked flare gun placed between them that could go off. If they capsize the boat they will lose the flare gun and may become shark bait. Pieter, before you cast them off be sure to spin the little boat to disorientate the occupants. When the Hatteras moves away, being disorientated the Mexicans will only be able to guess what direction it may have taken. They will most likely opt for the closest landfall which would be a northeasterly course towards the Cuban coast. Problem is you're going to Belize"

"Eddie, do you think it's wise to cock the flare gun? Suppose it went off after they were in the inflatable?"

"No Fran the flare gun won't be cocked, but they won't know it and it might stop them from moving around until you're long gone. After you've set the Mexicans adrift, Pieter you take the helm and put the Hatteras on a southeasterly course. Fran, you and Jacob make a thorough inspection of the boat's vital systems to ensure everything's working. You need to check the bilges for excessive water and make sure all the pumps are working. Jacob, you should have a quick look through the engine room and check the Racor fuel filters, belts, stuffing boxes, shafts, seals, through-hull valves, hoses, and connections. Fran, you start in the forward cabin and moving aft literally tear the boat apart. You need to make a complete and thorough inspection of the interior, checking carefully for drugs and firearms if you find any they should be thrown overboard. Anything else that can't be identified or looks suspicious is to be wrapped with duct tape, secured with fishing hooks and weights and thrown overboard. I think it's a pretty good bet that the Mexicans in their little boat will eventually be spotted by other vessels transiting the area as the north setting current pushes them inshore towards Puerto Juarez. In any case it shouldn't take the Mexicans much time to splash some water and eventually loosen the duct tape without capsizing the little boat. We can be sure that as soon as their hands are free they'll start firing the flares. Our little Mexican friends might be a bit uncomfortable for a couple of hours, but will have a great story to tell the senoritas back in Cancun. Once you've moved to a point about a mile or two from where you dropped the Mexicans, Pieter, turn on the boat's VHF radio, switch to channel 71 and in your best Spanish transmit two words, *ADIOS AMIGO*. I'll be monitoring channel 71 on my hand-held VHF, when I hear *ADIOS AMIGO* I'll answer *SI SENOR*. After we exchange the radio transmissions we turn the radios off. This is important to avoid possible detection by the Doppler radar on any Mexican naval patrol boat that might be looking for you and pick up your position from the radio transmission. Maybe a couple of hours out you might momentarily turn on the radio to see if there's any chatter about the Hatteras, but then keep the radio off until you've entered the territorial waters of Belize."

―――――

On Wednesday, a few minutes after 10:00 a.m. *ADIOS AMIGO* and *SI SENOR* radio transmissions were exchanged indicating that the Hatteras was underway. Two hours out Pieter turned on the radio to check if there might be any chatter about their dirty deed as they fled the scene. There wasn't. Once well offshore and outside of Mexican jurisdiction with her U.S. documentation on board the *Costa Brava* if necessary could use her radio, but with any luck this wouldn't be necessary.

In the planning of the *Hit and Run* the closest safe-refuge was Belize City some 250 nautical miles to the southwest of Cancun. Running at about 2,200 RPM the *Costa Brava* would do about 33 knots; O'Brien calculated that she should be able to complete the passage in just over 7.5 hours. When O'Brien chartered the *Costa Brava* on Tuesday he found that she had about 1,350 gallons of fuel on board which with a 10% reserve would provide at least 1,215 gallons of useable fuel. If O'Brien's calculations were correct and depending on the sea state the engines at 2,200 RPM would burn between 92.4 and 99.0 gallons per hour. Assuming a worst case scenario burning 99.0 gallons per hour, still only 742.5 gallons of fuel would be needed, so there was plenty of fuel. It was unlikely, but in case lube oil had to be added to the main engines O'Brien hoped that the five gallon pails he'd seen in the engine room were full. He also hoped the fuel was clean, but if not, that there were spare fuel filters on board.

With the Hatteras on its way O'Brien checked out of his hotel and headed for the airport. He caught an Aero México flight to Mexico City that connected with a flight to San Pedro Sula in Honduras followed by a short hop to Belize City. At dusk O'Brien arrived at the airport outside Belize City and took a cab to the Radisson Fort George Hotel & Marina. Even though O'Brien knew it was much too early he still looked out over the Caribbean Sea in anxious anticipation hoping to see the lights of the *Costa Brava* approaching in the distance.

The next morning O'Brien walked to the marina to arrange a berth for the Hatteras and for the vessel's arrival and clearance with the Port Authorities. Just before noon he saw that his ship was coming in. Having arrived off Caye Caulker in the early morning hours and even though he had the Reed's Almanac to use as a pilot, Pieter wisely decided to wait until dawn before weaving through the dangerous outer reefs and making his entrance to Belize City. After securing the Hatteras in the marina and clearing in, O'Brien invited *the Clan* to lunch. The MREs had kept them going on the trip down, but Pieter, Fran and Jacob were ready for a real meal. Over lunch they recounted the last 24 hours which they said had been fairly uneventful. Pieter said that the two Mexicans virtually wet their pants when they were pounced on and made no attempt to resist. No doubt a wise decision considering the 250lb muscular builds of the two former rugby Springboks.

Fran had added a personal touch when she told the Mexicans that if she saw them move too soon she'd turn around and run over them with the Hatteras. That hadn't been in the Plan, but then she thought - what the hell! *The Clan* confirmed that the Mexicans sat frozen for as long as they could see them with binoculars. About two hours out they lost the port engine due to a clogged filter, but were able to change the filter and restart the engine about 10 minutes later. They continued at around 2,000 RPM for most of the voyage and said the seas were calm which provided for a pleasant trip. The *Hit and Run* had been carefully planned and executed with great professionalism thanks to *the Clan*. Other than the two Mexicans set adrift who may suffer continuing nightmares, no one was hurt or injured. After securing the Hatteras and enjoying a good night's sleep O'Brien accompanied *the Clan* to the airport where they boarded the morning American Airlines flight from Belize City to Miami with a connection to Sint Maarten.

With the help of the marina manager in Belize City O'Brien arranged a caretaker for the Hatteras and paid two months dockage. He then called Marty in New York to report that the plan had been effectively completed and their *loan asset* was safe and sound at the Radisson Marina in Belize City.

Argus was delighted that she had been successfully recovered and was being looked after by a responsible gentleman with whom O'Brien would check with on a regular basis. Marty worked out an arrangement with the widow for Argus to take possession of the boat so it could be insured and eventually sold. Mrs. Vasquez was pleased as she never really wanted the *Costa Brava* in the first place. Working with Argus' lawyers in New York O'Brien met with an interested party who subsequently purchased the boat to use in a charter fishing business in the Cayman Islands. After deducting the recovery costs Mrs. Vasquez received a payment representing her late husband's equity in the boat. Argus recovered the outstanding balance of its loan plus the accrued interest. The Cayman Islands Corporation that purchased the Hatteras changed her name and re-flagged the boat on the Cayman Registry. On her trip from Belize City to George Town in the Cayman Islands the newly renamed and re-flagged Hatteras did **not** pass through Cancun.

Lost and Found

It was a warm and bright summer day as Ronnie Fox set his afternoon tea on the patio table and began reading the San Juan Star to see what had been happening in the world when the phone rang.

"Good afternoon Ronnie, Mark Davies here. No doubt you're probably enjoying the sunshine while I'm here looking out over Fenchurch Street that's been drenched with bloody rain for the last week. The reason I'm calling is about a loss that I'm a bit concerned with, particularly because the Hull Policy has an agreed value of $1.2 million. The *Yankee* is a 27m 30 year old steel ketch. I'm not certain if there are any let's say, irregularities with the loss, but to be on the safe side I'd like you to have a look. Could be there's nothing wrong, but I just want to make sure that everything is on the up and up, if you know what I mean."

"Hey Mark nice to hear from you and yes, the sun is shining my condolences for your weather. Sorry to hear about the loss, what's the story?"

"During her passage from the Far East to Florida the *Yankee* reportedly flooded and sank somewhere south of Acapulco, Mexico. The notice of loss we received said that she went down 5 days ago when she was about six miles offshore. I'm the lead on the Slip along with a number of other underwriters, but we're all a bit concerned with a claim of this magnitude. The owner of the yacht and our assured is an American who lives in Singapore, he only recently purchased her and planned to sail her to Fort Lauderdale where he'd sell her at a profit. We have a survey and appraisal valuation from a Lloyd's Surveyor in Hong Kong. The surveyor gave her a clean bill of health and completed a Trip Survey that OK'd her for the voyage so everything appears to be genuine. My concern is why she sank and if she might be salvaged. When we hang up the phone I'll fax you the file and I'd appreciate if you could deal with the matter with some urgency."

"Sure Mark, I'll load up the fax machine with paper and get on it right away."

The 20 page fax from Mark contained a copy of the Master's Statement, the survey carried out by the Lloyd's Surveyor and the photo pages of the passports of the American crew who were on board. The next day having received the documents Ronnie was on board the Mexicana Airlines flight to Acapulco through Mexico City accompanied by his son Josh.

"Gee dad that was a great flight, it sure was nice of your friend Luis to upgrade us to First Class."

"It's always nice to have friends in high places. Luis is Mexicana's Station Manager in San Juan and being a frequent traveler he generally upgrades me if there's space upfront. First or Business Class does make flying a bit nicer especially with the perks you get. Let's grab our bags and pick up the rental car."

Josh had been to Acapulco before, but always was fascinated by the scenery and the classic architecture on the drive from the airport. As they drove down from the mountains Josh was excited with the view of Acapulco Bay as the road wove its way past large haciendas and the famous 'Jackie O' disco set precariously on the hillside. In reaching the Costera Miguel Aléman, Acapulco's main street bordering the bay, Josh pointed,

"Hey dad, there's the Hilton, is that where we're staying?"

"Yep, that's it. We'll check-in and leave our bags in the room and then go see Maria at the yacht club."

"Buenos días María. Ha sido algún tiempo que nos hemos visto, espero que usted y su familia han estado bien. Sabes algo acerca del yate *Yankee?* Yate o si pudo haber estado en el club de yates recientemente."

"Hola Ronnie. Gracias, yo y mi familia hemos estado muy bien, disfrutando de la temporada de verano. Veo que tienes a tu hijo Josh con usted, él es realmente un gran chico. Si prefieres hablar en Inglés yo preferiría Inglés para que pueda mejorar mi ingles."

After the initial greetings had been exchanged in Spanish Maria, so she could improve her language skills preferred to speak in

English.

"The *Yankee* was here a couple of weeks ago, but after she left I learned that she had sunk somewhere around Puerto Angel. Let me have a look. Yes, the *Yankee* was here for three days and was tied up on the outer pier. From the note here in the file seems she sank about a week ago. Puerto Angel is on the Gulf of Tehuantepec which is about 500 miles south of here and just north of the border with Guatemala. As you know Ronnie, this part of the coastline is known for its violent storms, but I haven't heard of any bad weather."

"Thanks Maria. I received word of the sinking from the underwriters and the reason Josh and I came to Acapulco is to try and find any of the crew. Do you know if any of them are still around?"

"When the *Yankee* was here there were four people on board. I really don't know if any of the crew is still here except maybe Willie. I haven't seen the Captain or the two ladies, but Willie's been back to the Club a number of times looking for work. He told Ernesto that he was a licensed chief engineer and was looking for a job as a mechanic or really anything else he could find. He said that the yacht's owner hadn't paid him and he was getting low on money. Wait a moment and I'll check with Ernesto, the dock manager to see what he knows."

Speaking in Spanish on the speaker, "Ernesto, this is Maria. I have someone with me who would like to talk to Willie. No, Willie, Willie, remember he was the gringo who was on the *Yankee*. Have you seen him recently?"

Ernesto did remember him,

"Yes, Willie was at the Club yesterday. I told him that I didn't have any work for him and most of our members have permanent crew to look after their yachts, but that he should keep checking with me in case anything comes up. He said he was staying in a small *pensión* near the Club and would check back in a couple of days. I told him when he came back to either speak to me or to you in the office, anything else Maria?"

"No, eso es todo. Gracias Ernesto."

The prestigious Acapulco Yacht Club is located on a peninsula southwest of the main city on the southern side of the bay in a mostly upscale residential neighborhood. There are no McDonald's or skyscrapers only the occasional Jaguar or Mercedes that may be seen vigilantly intermingling with pedestrians and bicycles on the narrow lanes set amongst the tile roofed villas. The Villas all adorned with emerald swimming pools were protected by high walls ruffled with bougainvillea carefully arranged amid flowery lanes and the gently sloping hillsides that descend to the peninsula's white sand beaches. Carefully secluded amongst this cornucopia of beauty are a few cheap guest houses, bodegas and cantinas that cater to the servants of their masters. With the passport photograph of Willie Low obtained from the underwriting file, Josh and Ronnie began their search of the areas pensións and cantinas in an effort to locate him. Josh, always with a sense of humor decided that their search should be dubbed the L.O.W.

"L.O.W? Low, that's his last name. I don't understand."

"I know, I know, but I'm not referring to his last name. Dad, just think about it for a minute. L.O.W. is for Look-Out-Willie. Look out Willie because here we come."

"Okay, funny, funny."

Operation L.O.W. began around the Barrio Cobadonga near the Plaza de Toros then progressed to Barrio de Tambuco which was closer to the Yacht Club. After visiting 8 or 9 establishments they entered the Cantina Cortez on Avenida Bugambilias. Sitting at the bar Ronnie and Josh saw Willie nursing a warm Corona. Smiling Josh whispered to Ronnie, "L.O.W."

On two stools next to Willie, father and son sat down ordering two cokes and some *tapas* in Spanish then began speaking in English much like the millions of other North American tourists who visit Mexico each year. After ordering another beer and obviously starved for English conversation Willie turned to the cantina's new arrivals and inquired,

"Hey are you guys Americans or Canadians?"

"We're Americans, what about you?"

Pleased to find fellow countrymen Willie smiled,

"Yeah, I'm an American too, from Seattle. Where are you guys from, tourists?"

"I'm Ronnie and this is my son Josh. We live in Puerto Rico. We

just arrived and now doing the tourist bit. Are you a tourist too?
What's your name?"
Extending his hand,
"Nice to meet you, my name's Willie Low. Nope, I'm not a
tourist. I've been in Mexico for a couple of weeks, but trying to
get back to Seattle because I'm running out of money."
"Sounds interesting, you're in Mexico, but you're not a tourist
and you're running out of money, then why are you here?"
"Oh we just sank a boat and I'm waiting to be paid by the
owner." Hoping that Josh had maintained his composure Ronnie
turned to find him listening intently, but smiling at Willie's
revelations. Clearly surprised at Willie's candor with total
strangers Ronnie continued the conversation,
"But why would you sink a boat?"
Calmly he responded,
"To collect the insurance money, this American Guy who lives in
Singapore buys this old hulk for a few thousand dollars and takes
it to Hong Kong where he cleans it up a bit. Then he pays a few
bucks to a surveyor who puts a value on the thing for a million
bucks so he can insure it. I'm working as a Chief Engineer when
my employer goes bust and I find myself stuck in Hong Kong,
low on money and looking for a job. The surveyor he's got on the
payroll tells the American I'm looking for work. He tells me what
he wants to do and if I'll do it and keep my mouth shut, he'll hire
me. His surveyor buddy also organizes a Captain, who along his
girl friend and her friend agree to cooperate and off we go. The
plan is to sail the boat to a remote location along Mexico's West
Coast where the crew can scuttle her and safely get ashore.
George the Captain knows the area well and decides that the
desolate coast off Puerto Angel would be perfect. Its simple we
pull the plug, row ashore, have a short vacation and the owner
collects a million bucks. After he gets the insurance money he
gives the surveyor his 10% cut, pays each of us $25,000.00 and
buys us our plane tickets back to Seattle while he walks away
with maybe $800,000.00 that's tax free."
Feeling he was on a roll with the talkative fraudster Ronnie went
on to ask,
"Willie I don't know much about boats, but tell me, how do you

make a boat sink?"

Willie casually replied,

"She had two big Detroit diesel engines that suck up a lot of seawater for cooling it's easy, you close the sea cocks, cut the rubber cooling lines and then open the sea cocks again and the boat sinks. With the amount of seawater coming in I thought she'd probably go down in maybe an hour, but hadn't figured on the air pockets inside the hull. The fuel and water tanks which we had not topped up in Acapulco, so we could keep the money, were almost empty so the air inside helped keep her afloat. Because of the air in the tanks I had to cut the fuel and water intake lines so the tanks would fill with seawater. Fortunately the sea was calm so while we waited and watched as she sank we inflated the life-raft just in case anyone saw us from an airplane or from the shore it would look real."

"Did any one get hurt?"

"No, we didn't even get our feet wet until the dinghy hit the beach and we had to walk ashore. The Captain was really smart because he told the insurance company that we were six miles offshore when she went down where the water depth is over 3,000 feet. At this depth the Captain knew the insurance company wouldn't be able to salvage her. If she couldn't be salvaged they'd never find out why she sank. They couldn't even look for the *Yankee* because they wouldn't know where to look. Truth of the matter is that it was flat calm and we were only about a quarter mile from the shore. After we piled our gear into the Boston Whaler it took us only a few minutes to reach the beach. Because we wouldn't need the Whaler any more we sold it and the motor to a fisherman and split the money."

"*Yankee,* was that the name of the boat you sank?"

"Yep, the *Yankee* is on the bottom, it'll make a great new home for the fish!"

During the conversation Ronnie was recording all the information on his pen recorder while making mental notes. This was important considering that the Captain had lied in the Sworn Notice of Loss which had indicated that the yacht was 6 miles from the coast when it sank. In preparation of his Thesis for a masters' degree in criminal justice, Ronnie had become familiar with a pattern of criminal behavior sometimes referred to as *arrogant divulgence*. After engaging in a criminal act and not getting caught, perpetrators had a tendency, almost an eagerness to brag about their crime to unknown and seemingly disinterested parties. Arsonists are known to enjoy watching a building they had set ablaze while murderers will deviously attend the funerals of their victims. Willie, in a display of *arrogant divulgence* was clearly pleased with himself and what he believed had been the perfect crime in the successful sinking of the *Yankee*.

"Ronnie if you're really interested let me have your address in Puerto Rico and when I get back to Seattle I'll send you some of the photographs I took when we sank her. It took quite sometime for her to go down so I've got a bunch of great photos. I'd like to see them too, but the damned insurance company hasn't paid the owner so he hasn't paid me. The others had money to fly home, but I have to wait until the owner gets paid so he can send my money to the Western Union office in town."

Smiling in agreement, Ronnie politely responded,

"Bloody insurance companies will cancel your policy in the blink of an eye if you don't pay your premium, but the moment you have a claim and you want your money they sit on it. Willie, I'd really like to see your photos. I've got a suggestion. There's a KISS One Hour Photo Shop on the main drag near the Hilton if you'll let me have the film I'll get it processed and we can meet later. I'll pick you up and we can have dinner at Diego's where we can wash down the fajitas with some of their great Margaritas while we look at the pictures."

"Ronnie that would be fantastic, I'd really like to see the photos and didn't like the thought of having to wait until I got back to Seattle."

After driving him to the small *pensión* where he was staying Willie gave Ronnie three rolls of 36 exposure 35 mm film. Knowing that he'd only have them once as he'd have to return the negatives Ronnie ordered multiple sets of 8x10, 5x7 and 4x6 color prints at a cost of $1,500.00. After paying the bill and having been such a good customer the photo lab's manager thanked Ronnie giving him three disposable underwater cameras and asking that he please come back again.

Later that evening at Diego's Cantina Ronnie gave Willie one set of prints and the negatives. Over dinner Willie described the subjects in the photos while carefully explaining the details of each one. By means of the photographs he'd taken before, during and after the sinking Willie never realized that he was providing the photographic evidence of the fraud to the insurance company's investigator.

"Here's a shot of the life-raft after it was inflated. This one is the Captain taking his last pee over the rail before she sank and this is all of us going ashore in the Whaler. The Captain was a stickler for details so he planned to scuttle the *Yankee* just off Zipolité beach where there's a hippie commune called Shambhala. We were only there a few days before taking a bus back to Acapulco. Apparently some gal from LA set up Shambhala a few years ago with her Mexican boyfriend. It's like a nudist colony with lots of marijuana and free love if you know what I mean. It's a neat place with some cool broads. Oh, this one is Gayle and Barbara holding a bottle of Tequila dancing under a beach shack at Shambhala, they were celebrating the end of the trip."

"Willie I thought you said that there were only four people on board the *Yankee*, you, the Captain and the two ladies."

Pointing at one of the photos Ronnie said,

"Look, in this photo there are four people, did you take the photo with a delayed shutter release or did someone else take the picture?"

Willie smiled,

"During the crossing and after we left Acapulco there was only the four of us onboard when the pictures were taken, Bob the Captain, Gayle his girlfriend and Barb, Gayle's friend. When we left San Diego we had five people on board because that's where we picked up Alicia."

"Alicia? Who's Alicia and what's in all the boxes stacked on the aft deck and alongside the wheelhouse?"

"I didn't know it at the time, but Bob had made a deal with a guy named Pepe. After we left San Diego Bob told me that Pepe was a biggie in the Sonora drug cartel and wanted to get his girlfriend Alicia out of the U.S. He also asked Bob to buy a bunch of gear in San Diego, hide Alicia on the boat and bring her and the gear to Acapulco. It was only after we left San Diego that we saw Alicia. Bob told us that she'd been arrested on narcotics charges and was out on bail. Bob said that for $10,000.00 he'd agreed with Pepe to hide and bring Alicia and the high tech gear to Acapulco, Bob said he'd split the ten grand with us so we'd each get $2,500. One of Pepe's lieutenants picked up Alicia and the equipment the night we arrived at the Acapulco Yacht Club. When we left Acapulco there were only the four of us onboard. I'm pretty sure that Bob didn't tell the owner about his side deal with Pepe, because all he was interested in was for us to sail the *Yankee* south where he said, *she would be sunk and sold to the insurance company.*"

Having entered San Diego with four persons on board and departing with five, especially when the fifth is a fugitive, Willie clearly wasn't aware that falsifying the yacht's immigration documentation was a federal offence.

In addition to pictures of Alicia a close examination of the 8x10 photo enlargements showed a number of boxes stowed on the aft deck. From their external markings the boxes were from Katzenberg Marine in San Diego and contained Doppler radars, high tech electronic, and other radio/navigation equipment. Equipment of this type requires special permits before it can be exported. With a fugitive on board the hi-tech equipment had obviously not been cleared by U.S. Customs before the *Yankee* left San Diego. Along with the recording of Willie's revelations and $1,500.00 in photographs Ronnie and Josh returned to Puerto Rico. The return trip to San Juan sadly was in coach because Ronnie knew no one in Mexicana Airlines management in Mexico City. The following day by Federal Express Ronnie sent his report and one set of the photographs to the London insurers.

"Well done Ronnie. The report and photographs are astonishing. It's incredible what you uncovered in only a few days. Keep it up and you might find yourself labeled the *Legend of Lime Street.* As Willie told you that the *Yankee* is close to the beach do you think we should consider engaging a salvage crew to bring her up? If you believe she might be salvaged we'd hold off issuing the denial of the claim. The owner doesn't know that we know, but I'm damn sure that once the claim is denied he'll instruct an attorney to file a lawsuit. If we get involved in litigation we of course have Willies photos and if admissible the recording of Willie's statement that she was intentionally scuttled by the crew; scuttling by the crew is not an insured peril of the sea. Thanks to you we've clearly got the evidence to support a denial. However, to be prudent in case of litigation it would be a good idea to have photos of the engine cooling water intake hoses that had been cut and those of the fuel and water tanks. What's your opinion on raising her? As she's lying close inshore and you could locate her, could she be salvaged? What do you think?"

"Mark I really think that the cost of salvaging the vessel would be prohibitive. The closest salvage companies who could do a job of this size are located in Panama and Southern California. Also, I think you should consider that the *Yankee* was grossly overvalued. Even before she was scuttled she'd have been worth no more than $100,000, maybe $125,000. The cost to mobilize a salvage crew would be expensive. Whoever did the job would need at least two tugs and a crane barge and the costs would probably be somewhere around $200,000, maybe more. Because of the vessel's God awful location I'm sure no salvage company would be willing to accept the job under a Lloyd's Open Form of No-Cure-No Pay. The Gulf of Tehuantepec is known for its frequent storms that develop and blow in from the wide expanses of the Pacific Ocean. If a storm developed during the salvage effort it would seriously cripple or maybe close down the operation. The closest harbor is Puerto Escondido which is located a couple of hours to the north and it's not really much of a harbor. I don't think that raising the *Yankee* is viable, but there is another option that you may want to consider. I've done some trajectory calculations using Willie's photos. Taking the height of the mast in relation to the height of the dunes along the coast line I was able to determine the distance that the vessel was from the shore when she broke the surface. From these calculations I believe she's sitting on the bottom probably no more than 1.25 miles from the beach. Along this stretch of the coastline the water depth progressively gets deeper ranging from a few hundred feet to depths of over 3,000 feet three miles from the beach. From the trajectory calculations I think the *Yankee* is probably lying in about 180 feet of water. From the photos we know she sank in a calm sea and there was no wind. The current is about 3 knots and sets on a northeasterly flow. A number of the pictures show she had her main sail and Jib up when she sank. With the main sail and Jib up when she went down she'd settle on the bottom and would be visible on a high-definition Side Scan Sonar. In a depth of 180 feet and considering the set and drift of the current I think we'd find her somewhere in a grid of about 1 square mile. At this depth the divers, at least two would be needed, would have no more than about 15 minutes bottom time. After we locate the *Yankee* with the sonar she'd be marked with a surface buoy anchored to the wreck. The divers would focus primarily on the engine room and could make an easy descent to the wreck by pulling themselves down using the buoyed anchor line. Once on the wreck they'd go directly to the engine room and take a number of photos of the cut lines. The bottom surface in this area is sand and because she's got a full keel she wouldn't remain upright, but will be found lying on either on her port or starboard topsides. If the assured sues to get paid he may attempt to argue that the *Yankee's* hull impacted something which caused her to sink. To prove this wasn't the case the divers would take a few photos of the hull to prove she hadn't hit a partially submerged container or anything else. Photos of the cut cooling hoses and the fuel and water intake hoses, and the undamaged hull would prove a scuttling by the crew and eliminate any assertion she sank as a result of hitting something."

After listening intently Mark said,

"Ronnie as you're a certified SCUBA diver how about getting wet for me? You've met Willie who gave you the photos he took and in case the matter goes to litigation we'd need you to testify as an expert, could you dive on the *Yankee* and take the photographs?"

"Sure that's not a problem the only thing I'd ask is your approval to engage two divers to accompany me to do the dive. One would go down with me while the other diver would remain on the surface in the dive-boat to handle the lines. The area is very remote and I wouldn't want to rely on a local fisherman to get us up in case we had a problem. Also, there are no decompression

chambers or hospitals in the area in case we got into difficulties."
Mark was obviously pleased,
"If we go ahead how soon you could organize things and do the dive?"
"Once you gave me instructions to proceed I'd contact two guys that I've worked with in the past. Both are trained in hard-hat and SCUBA and are totally reliable, they live in Morgan City which is close to New Orleans. The only hang-up might be if they're committed to other jobs, but even if they're presently working they owe me for some favors so I might be able to entice them away. I'm sure they'd have no problem in taking a break from inspecting dirty pipe lines in the Gulf for a job that involves a quick dive on a yacht in the warm waters off the coast of Mexico. It's been 6 or 7 months since I last worked with them on a dive we did together in the Bahamas, but their fees at the time was $1,000.00 per day plus expenses. To get them onboard I'd offer them $1,200.00 a day plus expenses. If you decide to go ahead I'd suggest you budget for say three days and include the expenses for the air fares, hotel and rental of the dive gear in Acapulco which in total I believe should be around $9,500.00. Because of the depth they may suggest we use re-breathers which they could rent in New Orleans and bring with them."
"Ronnie this sounds like a viable option. As long as you're comfortable with doing the dive and believe it can be done safely let's go ahead. Check if and how soon your mates would be available. I'm lunching with the other underwriters at the Marine Club tomorrow. Unless they have any objections I'll confirm everything before noon your time."
"Mark every experienced diver always considers safety first. A dive can be dangerous whether you're down one atmosphere or in this case five. This dive will be dangerous not only because of the depth, but because at least one of the divers must go through the main saloon to get to the engine room to photograph the cut hoses. On deck a sail boat has standing rigging that has to be navigated in addition to the loose running rigging that will be waving freely in the underwater current. With this multitude of lines a diver needs to be extremely diligent. If his breathing lines or dive tank where to become fouled on deck or worse yet while

he's inside the hull and the other diver couldn't free him before their bottom time or air ran out he's dead. Bottom time is a major element of safety and it isn't actually how long you're on the bottom, but measured from the time you enter the water until you get back to the surface. The reason I would first buoy and mark the wreck is to save time in descending and returning to the surface. At about 180 feet, getting to the wreck then slowly ascending to avoid the nitrogen effect or the Bends would at best take 12 minutes. This would give you no more than 2 or 3 minutes to take the photos and get out. The area is known to be heavily infested with sharks because the local fishermen drag their catches behind their small boats when returning to Puerto Angel which bloodies the water. We also must consider that there are no decompression chambers or hospitals in case of the Bends or other injuries."

———

"Hey Bubba, what's been happening in the bayous? It's been a while since we shared that plate of Cajun crayfish at the Fish House in Morgan City. I hope you've been busy and well."

"God Damn it's good to hear from you Ronnie, what have you been up to? Are you still playing around with those big yachts on that enchanted island of Puerto Rico? How's Josh? I guess if you've been training him as a surveyor he's probably about ready to take over your business."

"Josh is great and having a ball traveling with me especially when I can get him out of school for a few days. We got creative and made a deal with the Headmaster; because my practice takes me to some out-of-the-way places he gets the approval to miss classes, but only if when he goes back to school he presents a written paper and gives a short presentation on his observations of the country we visited. Because Josh is fluent in Spanish he made a bang-up written and verbal presentation about our last visit to Panama. He really wowed them. We've just returned from a short trip to Mexico and he's working on his presentation to give to his class next week. The visit to Mexico is why I'm calling you. I've got a case where a large yacht was scuttled near Puerto Angel which is just south of Acapulco. She's lying on a sandy bottom about a mile offshore. I figure she's in about 180 feet of water. To sink her, the yacht's Chief Engineer cut the salt water intake lines on both engines. I need to photograph the cut lines to support the underwriters who are planning to deny the claim because of the intentional scuttling. As the area is a bit remote I want to have divers with me that I can count on and of course the only divers I would really rely on would be my friends the Cajun bubbleheads, Jeff Majon and Joe Boudreau. Jeff, I don't know if you and Joe are busy, but I'd sure like you guys to come along. I've told the underwriters that you'd be paid $1,200.00 a day plus expenses. Mark Davies, the Underwriter, is calling me tomorrow, but in the meantime I wanted to check to see if you and Joe might enjoy a holiday in Mexico."

"Joe and I just completed a pipeline inspection for Chevron so you might say we're between jobs. If the Mexican thing is anything like the Bahamas it'd be great to tag along. When would it happen?"

"I'm supposed to get the green light tomorrow so probably sometime next week. I know we could rent the normal SCUBA gear in Acapulco, but if you think we should use re-breathers, which I don't think would be available in Acapulco you could rent three sets and bring them with you. As soon as I get the go ahead from London I'll call you. Once everything's confirmed I'll arrange your flights from New Orleans and send you the pre-paid tickets. We'll need sonar to locate the wreck, but because it's not exactly legal to bring a Side Scan Sonar unit into Mexico, I'll bring mine in my hand luggage. Please check with Joe to make sure he's onboard. I'll call you to confirm everything tomorrow."

"I'll ask Joe, but I don't think we'll need rebreathers. We'll only be down once and it'd be a pain in the ass to lug three sets with us all the way to Mexico. We'll talk tomorrow. Y'all take care."

———

"Sorry Josh, but I won't be able to take you with me on the trip back to Mexico. London has asked for some photographs of the yacht and if it's a go I'll leave on Tuesday and should be back either Sunday or Monday. Jeff and Joe are coming along for backup. I've arranged for you to stay with Poncho and Lucy while I'm gone so you won't miss school. Tell the Headmaster that I'll be back to attend the PTA meeting a week from Friday and I won't miss your basketball game on Saturday."

"Are you going to see Willie while your there? Maybe he'll have some more pictures for you HA-HA-HA."

"No. I won't be seeing Willie. I'll only be looking for the yacht with Jeff and Joe. I don't think there's much more he could say anyway. If there's anything you want me to bring you from Mexico let me know."

———

The flight back to Mexico City was uneventful and pleasurable especially as Ronnie's seat was 3D in First Class. The trip was even better after passing through Mexican Customs and his bag containing the Side Scan Sonar wasn't opened. Arriving at the airport in Acapulco he proceeded to the Hertz counter to collect a rental car.

"No, no, no, I don't want a Volkswagen. I have two large friends that will be with me and a VW is too small. I'll need the car for a week so please let me have a mid-size four-door."

"I'm sorry Mr. Fox, but the only car that's available now is the VW Beetle. We'll have a mid-size four-door later today which we can deliver to your hotel if that's alright."

"Okay, let's do the paperwork and I'll take a taxi to the Hilton. About what time will you deliver the car?"

"We have a four-door being returned today at 2 p.m. We'll clean the car and have a driver bring it to you no later than 3:30. We can't do the paperwork now, but the driver will bring the rental contract with him when he delivers the car. As you are a Gold Club member I have all the information I need so you'll only need to check the car for damages and sign the contract. I do apologize for the inconvenience, but most of our customers prefer the Beetle."

"Thanks, normally a Beetle would be fine, but this time I'll be carrying two big bulls and a Beetle can't carry *dos toros grande*."

"Welcome back to the Hilton Mr. Fox, it's nice to see you. As a member of the Hilton Honors Program I've upgraded your room

to the concierge level. I see you'll be staying with us for five days." Looking at his name tag,
"Thank you Senor Lopez, yes, I'll be enjoying your hospitality until Monday. I have two colleagues who will be joining me. The names are Majon and Boudreau, they too will be checking out on Monday. I made the booking with my American Express Platinum Card. If it's possible I'd really be grateful if you'd upgrade their rooms to the concierge level."
"No problem Mr. Fox, I'll put them in rooms near yours on the concierge level. Is there anything else I can help you with?" "No, thank you."

––––––––––

Mingling amongst tour operators and taxi drivers hustling for fares Ronnie positioned himself in front of the crowd congregating in the airports arrival area holding a sign he'd printed in bold letters, 'CAJUN BUBBLEHEADS.' When saw them he shouted,
"Joe, Jeff, over here, over here!"
Pushing their trolley towards him Jeff and Joe both waved in acknowledgement.
"Hey Ronnie, nice sign, at least you used bubblehead and not airhead! Considering the sign I think you should buy us a drink, maybe two."
"There's nothing wrong with the sign because you're both bayou Cajuns and bubbleheads, but in any case I'll at least buy the first couple of rounds. How was the trip?"
"No problem, except when Joe found that he'd left his passport at home. If he would have gone back to the car, taken it out of the parking lot, driven home and then back to the airport we'd have missed the flight. Instead he took a $70 taxi ride, asked the cab to wait while he picked up his passport and got back to the airport so he could check in. Then he got trapped in security by some brain-dead TSA gal who probably was a hooker in an earlier life. I guess because his boots set off some alarm the stupid TSA broad insisted they keep scanning his Tony Lama's. I waited for him at the gate. We boarded just as they closed the flight. It was tight, but we made it."
On the drive to the hotel the trio exchanged small talk,

reminisced about the Bahamas and caught up with each others activities.

"Your rooms are ready. You can check-in and drop your bags; I'll wait for you at the poolside bar."

A few minutes later Jeff and Joe entered the bar. Jeff was in his traditional Levi's while Joe was wearing a flowered Hawaiian shirt, bright red shorts and his Tony Lama alligator skin cowboy boots. As they approached, Ronnie, observing how he was attired smiled,

"Hey Joe, you're really colorful, but cowboy boots? What do you want to drink the regular Wild Turkey over ice?"

"Make it a double."

"Jeff, you want the same?"

"No, I want one of those fancy ones, what's it called, a Mai Tai?" After the drinks arrived Ronnie briefed his friends on the background of the *Yankee* and exactly what they had to do. Both were flabbergasted at hearing the story and amazed that Willie would tell his story and provide incriminating photographs to a complete stranger.

"I've rented three sets of SCUBA gear from a dive shop run by a Frenchman who the NAUI say's has the best reputation in Acapulco. He's also provided new aluminum tanks that will give us the maximum 3000psi. The buoyancy vests are also new. It's about a six hour drive to Puerto Angel so we'll plan to leave tomorrow morning around 0600. There's only one small hotel in Puerto Angel where we'll stay. Once we arrive we'll leave our gear at the hotel and go down to the harbor and get a fisherman to take us out to where I think the *Yankee* is sitting on the bottom. The high resolution Side Scan Sonar will help us locate the wreck; once we find her the Garmin hand-held GPS will give us an exact position when we return for the dive. From what I've put together from the trajectory calculations the coordinates will be very close to 15"39' 27.06" N – 96"30' 50.72" W. Yesterday in Acapulco I bought 300' of light line and tagged the line every 30' from 150' onward to show depths along with a 10lb Danforth anchor and a yellow flagged buoy to snag the wreck that we'll use to pull ourselves down to the hull. If everything goes as planned we should have the wreck marked and be back at the

hotel before lunch. I'll give the fisherman $50.00 to take us out to locate her and then another $50.00 the following morning for the dive. There's no inclement weather in the forecast for the next 7 days and the sea is generally calm before noon. In the afternoon the seas build, but the waves are still only between 1.5' to 2.5'. If we leave the harbor at 0600 we should be able to do the dive, get the photographs and be back by 1000 or 1100 hours. One of you will remain in the boat with the fisherman to keep us alongside the marker buoy and to help with the lines. You can decide who's to stay in the boat and who's going down with me. The road between Acapulco and Puerto Angel is really shitty, some of its paved, but most parts are gravel. There's no lighting, few small villages in between and the police told me that sometimes bandits will try and stop passing cars. Even though we should be done and packed up in the early afternoon I don't think it would be wise to try and return to Acapulco the same day. We'll just take it easy and leave early the next morning so we'll be back before it gets dark. Our flights don't leave until Monday so we'll have a couple of days to chill-out in Acapulco. Did I miss anything?"
Jeff looked at Joe, who nodded in agreement,
"Nope, sounds like you've got everything covered. The only question I've got is how long will it take the guy in London to pay us?"
"Everything's been approved, so the moment I get back I'll request the payment. I could pay you, but prefer to have London pay you direct. This way the payment isn't shown on my bank statement and I don't have to worry about the IRS hitting me for taxable income. I'll have the Underwriter either mail you a check or if you'll give me your bank information he can wire the funds. Just let me know what you prefer."
Joe looked at Jeff and simultaneously they said, "Wire."

———

By 0615 the intrepid trio was on the road south to Puerto Angel. Other than a few stops to relieve themselves and three or four Mexican army check-points the trip was uneventful. They arrived in Puerto Angel just before 1300 starving for food. The hotel's restaurant wasn't exactly a Michelin five-star experience, but did offer an assortment of chicken dishes and sea food, the house specialties being calamari and sword fish. Joe opted for the swordfish, but didn't understand the sauce which was said to contain *ajo*. Ronnie explained that *ajo* is garlic and in Latin America the seasoning of choice which is generously applied to many foods and sauces. Joe decided on the swordfish with the *ajo* sauce. He enjoyed the tasty experience, but reeked of garlic for the next four days.

That afternoon the three proceeded to the harbor and found Pedro a local fisherman. As $100.00 in US currency was more than he normally made in a month Pedro, who surprisingly spoke reasonably good English, enthusiastically offered the use of his boat that was fitted with a 100hp Yamaha outboard for the two days it would be needed. For such a generous payment if Ronnie had asked, Pedro probably would have enthusiastically thrown in his two daughters, wife or other members of his extended family. The seas were calm as the small fishing boat proceeded out of the harbor before turning to a northwesterly course with Ronnie giving directions.

"Pedro please turn the boat a bit more to the left. We're heading for a spot about a mile or so off playa Zipolité. Good, thanks, just hold this course for a few minutes."

While the small boat made its way across the serene surface of this part of the Pacific Ocean Jeff and Joe connected the Danforth anchor and marker buoy to each end of the mooring line. Ronnie began fitting the sonar transponder to the bottom of the fiberglass hull with putty. Once the transponder was in place he activated the sonar unit and turned on his GPS. After 3 or 4 minutes the GPS unit had found five satellites targeting their position on the screen.

"Okay Pedro, please put the engine in neutral."

Ronnie now had a full screen picture of the barren, flat sandy ocean floor.

"Pedro this is a GPS unit that from a satellite tells us where we are. I'd like you to hold the GPS and slowly motor the boat in the direction of this arrow that's shown on top. Please maintain this speed and move forward slowly until I tell you to stop."

Pedro having never before seen a GPS or a Side Scan Sonar

didn't really understand, but was fascinated, particularly in being able to see the ocean floor. Carefully holding the GPS Pedro proceeded precisely on course. The peace and tranquility was shattered when Ronnie shouted,

"There she is, there she is!! We found her. Look, she's laying on her port side and the main and jib is still up just as the photos showed when they sank her. Jeff, please write the GPS position on the notepad. Amazing, it's only a few degrees off from where I thought she'd be. According to the Sonar she's sitting in 198' of water. Joe, start playing out the buoy line. Pedro, please continue slowly moving the boat forward until I tell you to stop. Okay, okay, now turn the boat around so we're heading against the current. Right now we're about 100' upwind of her. Joe, feed the buoy line out to the 180' marker so the anchor will be about 15' or 20' feet from the bottom. Pedro, see here this is the boat we've been looking for, I want you to keep us in a straight line so the anchor that Joe is dropping snags the boat, Ok?" Moments later Joe shouted, "Ronnie, Ronnie, I've hooked her."

"Okay Joe, pull on the line to make sure it's snagged something solid and won't pull loose or fall off. When it's hooked yank on the line to set it."

Pulling on the line Joe called out,

"I'm pulling and it's secure."

"Great, let the remaining line play out and hang on to the buoy. Pedro, please put the engine in neutral and let the boat drift. Joe, hold on to the buoy to be sure it snags and holds our boat. If we don't hold then we know it's pulled loose from the wreck."

It seemed like an eternity, but in fact only a few minutes as Pedro's boat slowly turned and drifted with the current until the buoy line became taut. The *Yankee* had been snagged.

"Well done Joe that was a nice bit of anchoring. When we get back to the harbor the drinks are on me."

"Hey Ronnie that was a piece of cake! If the dive tomorrow is as easy as what we did today like they say in our neck of the woods, *we'll be choppin' in the tall cotton.*"

That night after a substantial quantity of *cerveza frio* the threesome feasted on calamari and swordfish with extra portions of roasted *ajo*. The following morning over breakfast they collectively decided that there should be a suitable reward for their efforts when they returned to Acapulco, all agreed they would celebrate their success with a visit to Jackie O's disco.

The following morning after loading the tanks and dive gear into Pedro's boat, Ronnie turned on the GPS. At 0700 hours Pedro fired up the Yamaha and they left the harbor under a blue sky and calm seas. A short time later arriving at the marker buoy they were surprised to find at least 10 of Pedro's fellow fishermen engaged in line fishing and harpooning large swordfish. Even more surprising and alarming was that amongst the fishermen and swordfish were an incalculable number of large sharks wildly thrashing in a display of frenzied feeding in the blood filled water. With disbelief they watched as almost immediately after the fishermen had secured a line to their catch for its tow back to Puerto Angel the sharks were eating the swordfish in most cases leaving only the tail that remained tied to the fishing boats.

Looking at Jeff and Joe Ronnie said,

"Shit, I can't believe this. There's absolutely no way we can get in the water with this many sharks in a feeding frenzy and devouring anything that moves or doesn't move. For the Love of God, this is unreal."

Stunned by the sight Ronnie, Jeff and Joe looked at each other not believing what they were witnessing. Pedro on the other hand was neither fazed nor surprised, but realizing the gringos were upset,

"Amigo you know this is very common. When a big school of swordfish come close to the shore many, many, sharks appear. Sharks very hungry eat *muy rapido*. Because our boats not big can't put big fish in little boat so must tow to get them to *puerto*. Lots of times we catch many fish, but only a few get to Puerto Angel in one piece."

"Thanks Pedro that's nice to know. I'm sorry to learn that you guy's can't get your catch back to port in one piece, but because I want to get back in one piece there's no way in hell we're going to get in the water with a bunch of hungry sharks. Damn, Damn, Damn..."

The screen of the Sonar displayed a good picture of the *Yankee* which was only partially clouded by the bloodied water near the surface. Ronnie then got an idea.

"Under these conditions it's clearly too dangerous to dive on the *Yankee*. If a shark mistook one of us for a swordfish and decided to have us for lunch there are no medical facilities even if we were to survive an attack. I've got an idea that may work. Diving to take photographs of the cut hoses with so much blood in the water is out of the question, but suppose I take a number of photographs of the boat that's displayed on the Sonar screen. I'll get a lawyer to prepare an affidavit for you and Jeff to sign; under oath you guys affirm that on this day and time and at these GPS coordinates you both saw the *Yankee* on the bottom and witnessed the photographs taken of the wreck from the Sonar screen. We clearly aren't going to do the dive, but Underwriters would at least have the Sonar photos to support the photos from Willie confirming that she sank as Willie said. What do you think?"

"I agree neither Joe nor I are going swimming in the middle of a bunch of hungry sharks for any amount of money. The photos of the Sonar screen and our affidavits are the only option."

With that Ronnie took a number of high definition color photographs of the Sonar screen and of the shark infested bloody water on the surface above the *Yankee* then cut the line holding the marker buoy and asked Pedro to take them back to Puerto Angel. They didn't eat swordfish that night for dinner, but when they returned to Acapulco they did visit Jackie O's. On Sunday Jeff and Joe returned to New Orleans and Ronnie flew to Puerto Rico.

————

"Hey dad, how was Mexico. Did you find the boat?"

"Yeah we found her, but couldn't do the dive because of a bunch of hungry sharks. I've got some photos being processed that I'm sure you'll be interested in."

"Hungry sharks, what do you mean by that?"

"Well it's a long story, but in a nutshell after finding the boat on the first day we planned to dive on her the next. When we go out to do the dive there's a bunch of local fishermen in the area bringing in swordfish that the sharks decided to eat before the fishermen could get them back to Puerto Angel. The water got bloodied from the feeding frenzy so we couldn't dive. Anyway, when I get the photos back you'll see what I mean."

———

"Mark, Ronnie here, I'm back."
"Ronnie, I've been anxiously waiting to hear from you. How was the trip to Mexico, successful?"
"Well sort of, I chartered a small fishing boat out of Puerto Angel and we found the *Yankee* off Zipolité beach exactly where she was supposed to be and buoyed her in preparation of diving on her the following morning. When we arrived at the buoy the next day we found a number of fishing boats that were pulling in swordfish from a large school. Unfortunately the swordfish had attracted a huge number of sharks that were eating most of the swordfish before the fishermen could tow them away. Because of the sharks frenzied feeding the water became bloodied with many of the sharks attacking each other. It was just too dangerous and no way that we could dive or even enter the water. While we might have had problems during the dive I hadn't figured on having a problem with sharks. As I mentioned to you earlier if any of us got hurt there are no medical facilities in the area. Using the hand-held GPS unit and the Side Scan Sonar we easily found the wreck on the bottom and had a good picture of her resting on her port side on the sandy bottom. The next day when we were confronted with the shark problem the Sonar display gave us a good picture in spite of the bloody water, but because we couldn't dive on her I decided to take color photographs of the *Yankee* from the Sonar screen just to prove she was there. Willie's photos have a number of shots of her undamaged bow and the starboard side as she slowly sank with the main sail and Jib still flying. Because she sank on an even keel its unlikely that the port hull was damaged because she sank in an upright position. If there were damages to the port side she would have listed to port as she went down. If you agree I'll send the Sonar photos showing the bloodied water and the wreck on the bottom to Cochran & Forsberg the admiralty lawyers in New Orleans. Ben Cochran can prepare affidavits for Majon and Boudreau to

confirm the photos and what they saw then have them sign the affidavits under oath. Once the affidavits are signed I'll ask Ben to FedEx them to you. It's disappointing that we couldn't get to the hull to photograph the cut intake lines, but it was just too dangerous. I've asked Majon and Boudreau to send me their bank details so you can wire their fees direct to them. As I advanced their plane tickets and paid the hotel I'll include the expenses incurred along with my invoice. You can settle this in the normal manner. I also have a suggestion that may allow you to avoid litigation if the denial is challenged by the assured. The Captain and crew illegally transported a fugitive who had been indicted for narcotics trafficking. In transporting the fugitive and hiding her on the *Yankee* the ships crew manifest was falsified. The Ship's immigration departure form is a sworn document submitted under oath by the Captain. The Captain declared there were four persons on board, but vessel departed San Diego with five instead of the declared four. Submitting a falsified departure form is a federal violation. They also acted for a Mexican drug lord in the transportation and export of navigation and electronic equipment that requires customs clearance so the Captain obviously didn't advise US Customs. All this is documented. My suggestion would be for me to fly to San Diego and meet with the U.S. Attorney and make a *deal.* If he'd agree to issue indictments and prosecute the owner and the crew I'd provide him with a copy of Willie's recorded statement and the photos showing not only the fugitive, but also the equipment from Katzenberg Marine in San Diego with markings that identify what's in the boxes. I think that if the assured and his co-conspirators were under federal indictment they might think twice about challenging the denial of the claim."

Mark was silent, but listening intently as Ronnie relayed the events in Mexico and his suggestion of involving the US authorities.

"Do you really think that the U.S. Attorney would be interested in pressing charges against the *Yankee's* owner and her crew?"

"Without a doubt, the yacht has an American owner and was registered in Wilmington, Delaware so she flew an American flag. The vessel's master and crew were all Americans from

Seattle, Washington. As the boat and the crew are all American this clearly gives the U.S. authorities jurisdiction. I'm sure that the U.S. Attorney in San Diego would love to nail anyone who was involved with aiding and abetting a fugitive to avoid prosecution; particularly a fugitive from their jurisdiction who had been charged and indicted for drug trafficking and was out on bail. The Feds would also charge the ship's master who they can prove has committed a felony by submitting a fraudulent vessel departure form. In addition to conspiracy they also can hit him for the illegal exportation of high tech marine electronics that was to be used by boats owned by a drug lord to evade detection by the Coast Guard and U.S. Customs. It's a nice little package all of which happened in the backyard of the U.S. Attorney in San Diego. I think he'd jump at the chance to bust these clowns."

"Okay, then go ahead this is a good idea. Is there anything you need from me?" Ronnie replied;

"No, I've got the underwriting file that has everything including the photo pages of the crew's passports. Other than notifying the other government agencies I don't think the Feds will go after the American owner because he's living outside the United States and would surely deny any knowledge of what the crew did to escape prosecution. I also doubt the U.S. government would want to get involved with the hassle and expense of his extradition."

———

"Good morning, my name is Ronnie Fox. I'm an investigator for a syndicate of Lloyd's Underwriters in London. I'd like to speak with Mr. Samson; I have a matter that may be of interest to the U.S. Attorney's office."

"I'm sorry Mr. Fox, but Mr. Samson is in Washington and won't be returning until next week. What exactly is the matter you wish to discuss?"

"I don't feel the details would be appropriate to discuss over the phone as it involves the transport of a fugitive to avoid prosecution who was in your jurisdiction and the illegal export of marine electronics for a Mexican drug cartel."

"Just a moment please."

After a few moments,

"I think you should speak with Ms. Jennifer Gonzalez, who is the assistant U.S. Attorney. I'll transfer your call."

"Good morning Mr. Fox, my name is Jennifer Gonzalez, how can I help you?"

With Ms. Gonzalez listening intently, Ronnie detailed the saga of the *Yankee*.

"I'm tied up this morning, but could you come by this afternoon around 4 p.m.?"

"Unfortunately Ms. Gonzalez I wouldn't be able to see you this afternoon because I'm based in Puerto Rico, but if you are available I could be in your office on Thursday."

"Puerto Rico, I'm sorry, I thought you were calling locally. Hold on a second and let me have a look at my diary. I'm in court on Thursday morning, but how about anytime after lunch, say 2:30 p.m.? My office is in the Federal Building, 4th floor Room 1231."

"2:30 would be fine."

Two days later Ronnie was on the afternoon American Airlines flight to Miami. That night he had dinner at the Outback Restaurant in Fort Lauderdale with Alan Adara, an old friend who was a respected yacht broker. The following day he caught the American flight to Los Angeles where he picked up a rental car from Hertz, drove to San Diego and checked into the Hilton near Mission Bay. Meeting Ms. Jennifer Gonzalez was a pleasurable experience. She was not only a stunningly beautiful brunette, but was extremely smart and charming with a captivating sense of humor. Eagerly consuming the extensive and documented evidence of the illegalities that would confirm a successful prosecution on multiple charges, she graciously thanked Ronnie for coming forward with information which she described as tantalizing.

"If I needed you in court would you be willing to testify?"

"No. Ms. Gonzalez, may I call you Jennifer?"

"Oh, yes please."

"Jennifer, here's the deal. You've got the transcript of Willie's statement. You have over a hundred photographs that Willie took. The photos include a picture of the fugitive, Alicia and the boxes of gear purchased from Katzenberg Marine. My practice takes me to Mexico, Panama and many other places in Latin America where many times by necessity I need to work with some pretty unsavory characters. If my name or picture where to appear with any connection or relationship with law enforcement it could let's say, be injurious to my health. I'd be pleased to work with you to fill in any gaps or assist in any way possible, but my involvement must remain confidential. This includes people in your office who should be limited to a 'need-to-know-basis'."

"It would really be beneficial if you'd agree to testify or even be deposed."

"Sorry, not interested."

"Okay, your point is well taken, I understand. I'm sure that Bob Samson would like to speak with you, when are you returning to Puerto Rico?"

"Tomorrow morning. When Mr. Samson gets back he can call me, but you've got everything I've got. There are some people in London who have an interest in the *Yankee*; can I tell them that your office will be proceeding with the filing of charges?"

"You've got interested people in London? What's their interest?"

"They are the Underwriters that insured the yacht for her trip to Fort Lauderdale. Their only interest is from the insurance standpoint. They instructed me to investigate the loss and from what I discovered will probably deny the claim. They've got no interest in the crews smuggling escapades, only the hull insurance."

"You can advise the folks in London that the U.S. Attorney's office will review what you've provided and will proceed. Right now I can't tell you exactly what charges will be brought, but clearly they all will be considered felonies."

Pleased with his meeting in San Diego, Ronnie returned to Puerto Rico and sent a full report to the underwriters who subsequently denied the claim.

The American owner retained counsel, but upon learning that the Captain and crew had been arrested and charged under the relevant federal statutes he withdrew the claim. After a few phone calls from San Diego to expand and clarify subjects shown in the photos Ronnie heard nothing further until six months later when he received a fax from Jennifer Gonzalez.

'Subject: William Low arrested by Federal Agents upon arrival at Seattle's SEATAC airport, charged with Conspiracy he was taken into custody. Following transfer to San Diego Low was denied bail as a flight risk and was incarcerated awaiting trial. During interrogation when confronted with the facts he agreed to cooperate and turn states evidence in return for immunity. Captain and crew of the vessel were subsequently indicted and convicted on all charges and subsequently sentenced to 8 years and 5 years respectively. In one of my meetings with Low I asked how the authorities might have obtained copies of the photographs that were introduced as evidence in the case. He said that he had met an American tourist who was traveling with his son who, because he had no money, kindly offered to have his photographs processed so he could see them. Mr. Low believes that when the employees of the photo lab saw the pictures they notified the Mexican Federal Policia Judicial who then contacted the U.S. authorities because the yacht flew an American flag.' The fax ended with, *Thanks. Nice job by an informant who will remain anonymous ...*

FRENCH TOAST

"Good morning Eddie, Jan te Koop here, its midday in Amsterdam, but knowing you get up with the chickens I knew it would be a good time to catch you. I've got a problem."

"Good morning Jan, nice to hear from you sorry to hear you've got a problem, but as you know I always welcome your problems with enthusiasm, what's up?"

"Sometime in the last couple of weeks an Irwin 52' sailboat disappeared from her mooring in Simpson Bay Lagoon off Marina Royale on the French side of Sint Maarten. The German owners who live on the boat are normally onboard, but had returned to Munich to spend Christmas with their families. During their absence they asked Dieter and Imgard Krokat, their friends in Grand Case to occasionally drive by and keep an eye on the boat while they were away. A week later when their friends went to have a look, the Irwin wasn't there. They checked with the harbormaster and the police on both the Dutch and French side of the island, but they knew nothing about the yacht. A Mr. Brown whose job it is to open the bridge on the Dutch side said he had no recollection of the Irwin leaving. It's possible that with the number of boats that pass through the channel he wouldn't necessarily remember a particular boat. However, the lagoon is land-locked and boats can only get to the open sea by going through the channel on the Dutch side when the bridge is open so clearly it didn't just blow away."

"Jan do you have any photographs of the boat? I'll also need a copy of your underwriting file. This will give me the hull identification number along with specific information about color schemes and personal items that the owner may have installed that I can use for identification if she can be found. ID stuff is important because Irwin's in the Caribbean are about as common as bicycles in Holland."

"Good idea Eddie, I plan to speak with the owners today and will let them know you're on the case. I'll fax you everything I have either later this afternoon or tomorrow morning. And by the way how's the Old Amsterdamer holding up?"

"It's almost gone. I'll be in touch."

The Underwriter and his wife Gretchen knew of Eddie Ryan's fondness for a particular mature Dutch cheese called Old Amsterdamer and had a good laugh when they learned of his experience on his last visit to Holland. After reaching Amsterdam's Schiphol airport he purchased a wheel of Old Amsterdamer in a duty-free shop, but then found it wouldn't fit into his carry-on luggage. Fortunately an understanding restaurant manager cut the wheel in four sections and wrapping the smaller pieces in tinfoil allowed him to squeeze it inside his bag. Amsterdam's Schiphol or Barajas in Madrid were always Ryan's favorite airports to and from Europe because of the excellent flight connections from San Juan. From experience he found the airlines that serve these airports were also a bit more relaxed when it came to carry-on bags, especially those passengers who might carry large wheels of cheese.

Later in the day Ryan received a ten page fax containing a photo and the particulars of the missing yacht. Extracting the significant details Ryan added the photo and details of the yacht to a Stolen Boat Circular which he faxed to a number of marinas and port authorities in the Caribbean and the Bahamas. The following morning he was on a plane to Sint Maarten and after clearing immigration picked up a rental car from his long-time friend Amin Khan owner of Paradise Car Rental. As he started to leave the parking area of the Princess Juliana airport he heard,

"Hey, Eddie baby, Eddie baby."

The voice was unmistakably that of his good friend Ernie Gracetti a former New Yorker who a few years earlier had mysteriously transplanted himself on this Dutch Caribbean island. Because of his happy-go-lucky and good-natured personality complimented by a seemingly endless supply of cash Ernie had gained the reputation as a high-roller who loved to party and soon became one of the islands more eligible bachelors. After a few drinks Ernie would occasionally reminisce about his background, but generally was reluctant to talk about how he had quietly abandoned New York and ended up in Sint Maarten.

Along with a pit-bull named Killer and a caged parrot called Bernie he lived comfortably on his yacht moored in the Simpson Bay Lagoon. Out of respect for his privacy Ryan never pressed him as to whether his hasty relocation had been to escape from some perceived problem with the Mob or he just wanted to enjoy an early retirement at 40.

While he was working in New York Ernie had been in the trucking business with other members of his extended family. Once after consuming a number of vodka martinis he briefly told Ryan of an uncle who was a Capo in the Gambino crime organization, but never mentioned whether Uncle Guido was also interested in trucking. Ryan never asked for further details. Ernie was simply a good looking Italian guy with a great personality who oozed with charm. Everybody who knew him liked him.

Generous to a fault Ernie was always the first to buy a round of drinks at his favorite Italian eatery appropriately named *Good Fellas*. After helping him successfully resolve an insurance claim the previous year Ryan and Gracetti became close friends.

"Hey guy, what brings you to the Friendly Island and how's Josh? Does he use the sonic toothbrush I put him on to?" Then in the same breath, "Let's have lunch."

Ryan didn't have to ask where. They drove to the Simpson Bay Marina. Over lunch and confirming that his son was happy and enjoying his new high-tech toothbrush the duo caught up on the local happenings.

"Ernie I'd like you to put the word out about a yacht that's been reported missing, if you hear anything *on-the-street* I'd appreciate if you'd let me know. Of course there's a 10% reward that the underwriters will be happy to pay for information that leads to a successful recovery."

Ryan gave Ernie a dozen of the Stolen Yacht Notices which he said he'd distribute around the island especially the watering holes frequented by the boating crowd. Ryan then drove to the French side of the island where he spoke with the owner's friends who had been responsible for watching the boat.

"Mr. Krokat my name is Eddie Ryan....." Interrupting, "Please call me Dieter."

"Okay, Dieter I'm here on behalf of the underwriters who insure the *Elle;* the underwriter said that you were looking after her while the owners were in Munich for the Christmas holidays. I understand when you found that the *Elle* wasn't on her mooring you called the owners to tell them that their boat was missing and then reported her disappearance to the Gendarmes, did you do anything else? I'd appreciate if you'd fill me in on the background."

"Mr. Ryan," interrupting, "Dieter, please call me Eddie."

"Okay Eddie. We had lunch with Gerhard and Elle on Friday the 22nd at Le Petite Chef at Marina Royale in Marigot. After lunch we all took their dinghy to the *Elle* and Gerhard showed me where the bilge pumps were to confirm that they were working and said the batteries would automatically be kept charged by solar panels. He said they'd leave the dinghy chained and locked on the marina's inner dock so we could get onboard. The *Elle* was moored by two anchors just outside the Marina Royale so it could easily be seen from the dock. Gerhard said every now and then we should take a look at her when we were in the marina to make sure the anchors were holding and everything was okay. He asked that we go onboard maybe once a week to open the hatches to air her out. On Saturday the 23rd my wife and I drove Gerhard and Elle to the Princess Juliana airport and had coffee after they checked in. Gerhard gave me the keys to the boat and the dingy and the phone number of his son in Munich and said they'd be back in a month. A week after they left we went to Le Petite Chef for lunch and planned to check on the *Elle*, but found she was gone. I called Gerhard to tell him that the *Elle* was missing then filed a report with the Gendarmes in Marigot. I feel bad that she's been stolen, but don't know what else I could have done. There's really nothing more I can tell you."

"Thanks Dieter. I understand your feelings. If you didn't have anything to do with the disappearance you've got nothing to worry about."

Dieter, clearly upset,

"What do you mean, *if I didn't have anything to do with the disappearance?* Do you think or are you implying that I was in some way involved?"

"Dieter you were looking after the *Elle* in the owner's absence and had keys to the boat. I don't know you and apologize if you may feel offended, but in the course of investigating the theft everyone involved and all the possibilities have to be considered."

"Gerhard and Elle are our friends and I can assure you that I was not involved in any way."

From his demeanor Ryan had a gut feeling that Dieter wasn't involved, but as he had access to the *Elle* was a possible suspect.

"I do appreciate your help and assistance. My main objective and focus is to find the *Elle*. Here's my card with my phone and fax numbers in case you might hear something please free to call me. Thanks for taking the time to see me."

Ryan left reasonably confident that Dieter may not know anything more than what he had told the owners, but at the moment couldn't be excluded. After leaving some of the stolen yacht notices at the bars surrounding the Marina Royale in Marigot, Ryan caught the evening flight back to San Juan. A week later after watching the CBS evening news to find what was going on in the world the phone rang.

"Is this Eddie Ryan?"

"Yes, this is Eddie Ryan, who is this?"

"Right now my name is not important. What is important is what I have to tell you, please just listen. I understand that you are offering a reward for the Irwin sailboat that was taken from French Saint Martin earlier this month. I didn't take the boat, but I know who did. What's even more important is that I know where the boat is right now. If I tell you were the boat is, will you pay me the reward money?"

"Wow, that's a lot in one breath. Let me get this straight, you weren't involved in the theft of the boat, but you know who was and where it's at and if you tell me where the boat is you want a reward for the information, right? Sorry my man, but that sounds like a scam, I'm not interested, thanks for calling."

"Wait, wait don't hang up. I know it may sound a bit funny, but it's true. The boat was stolen to order."

"Stolen to order, what the hell does that mean?"

"Last month I was visiting my girlfriend who lives in Martinique. One night we had gone out to dinner and met these two guys who were in the bar at La Belle Époque, a restaurant on Route de Rothschild in Fort de France. After a few bottles of wine they got a bit tipsy and started talking and told us that they had hitched a ride on a sailboat that had recently arrived in Martinique and dropped them off in the marina at Trois Islet. They said they didn't clear in with the authorities because they had French passports and were planning to leave for Saint Martin as soon as they could get a ride. I asked them why they were going to Saint Martin and one of the guys said they were going to pick up a sailboat."

Ryan's curiosity now aroused asked,

"How did you get into a conversation with them in the first place and why would they tell you this, what's your name?"

"Forget about my name, it's not important. I have a pony tail and was dressed like a yachtie; you know shorts, loose shirt, open sandals, those sorts of things. They were drinking at the next table and had been eyeing my girlfriend when the big guy who appeared to be in charge introduced himself as Emilio. He looked over and asked me if I had a boat in Fort de France. I told him I had a 46' ketch named the *Evasion* which I lived on in Marigot at the Marina Royale in Saint Martin. Emilio then asked if he and his friend could join us and we began talking about boats, marinas, you know just general boat stuff. After ordering another bottle of wine he said that he was looking for someone who might be interested to work for about ten days or so as crew. Emilio said the pay would be good, but everything had to be kept quite; if we were interested he said the two of us could earn $1,500.00 and our return tickets from Cartagena. I was intrigued at the *keeping quiet bit* and asked why this was necessary. Emilio then told me that he worked for a guy who was with the U.S. government in Bogotá. After drinking more wine Emilio told us that when he first met the American he said he was a commercial attaché then later told us that the attaché bit was only a cover because he actually worked with another agency in the embassy. Emilio said he had worked for the American before and never had a problem. Previously when the boats he wanted were delivered to Cartagena the guy paid him in cash. After the last delivery Emilio said they were celebrating and both had had too much to drink, because the guy had told him he was a commercial attaché at the U.S. Embassy, but was paying him to steal boats he was curious about what the guy really did. It was then that the American told him that the agency he worked for was the CIA. As they'd been drinking Emilio didn't know if this was true or just bullshit. Emilio said he really didn't care who he worked for as long as the guy paid him when he delivered the boats. From time to time Emilio said the American would contact him and tell him that he wanted this or that boat and where to find it. Last year he said they had taken a 46'Bertram sport-fisherman from the Virgin Islands, but usually the boats they picked up were newer sailboats. In this case Emilio said he was told exactly what boat was to be *picked-up* and exactly where it was; all the boats the guy wanted were always somewhere in the Caribbean. Emilio told me that he had *delivered* three boats this year and everything went fine, no problems and he made good money."

Even though the callers' story seemed a bit bizarre Ryan was paying close attention at what he had to say. Ryan then asked,

"Did Emilio tell you what would happen if he got caught taking the boat? Would the American help him….?"

Before Ryan could finish the question the caller cut him off,

"Look I don't know the whole story, but Emilio told me it had to be done quietly because if they got caught while taking a boat they'd be on their own, but once they were in Venezuelan or Colombian waters everything's covered. He also said there would be no problem with the U.S. Coast Guard because the American had access to confidential information through the embassy in Bogotá. He'd know when and where the Coast Guard cutters would be on drug interdiction patrols so these areas had to be avoided. The guy said that even though the owners may report the theft to their insurance companies and the local cops, he knew that missing boats generally don't receive any attention until long after they're gone. Because of intensive surveillance Emilio said they would always avoid going near Cuba and would stay away from the Yucatan channel. Knowing this Emilio said they would never go west or use the shorter route across the Caribbean, but would go east and stay well offshore into the Atlantic before taking a southerly heading. When they were south of Grenada they would turn to a south westerly course and hug the Venezuelan and Colombian coastline to avoid detection."

"Why didn't you and your girlfriend take the offer?"

"Didi, my girlfriend didn't believe their story and thought they were slimy characters. I don't how flush they were, but didn't seem to be worried about their next meal or drink. They bought us dinner and paid for four or five bottles of wine. Didi declined their offer outright, I told them I'd think about it and maybe see them in Saint Martin."

"Then what happened, did you see them again?"

"I flew back to Saint Martin. About a week later I hear someone rattling the anchor that's tied to my stern rail, its Emilio shouting, Hervé, Hervé, we've arrived."

"So your Christian name is Hervé."

"Yeah, yeah, okay, anyway Emilio and his mate Francisco come aboard my boat. After sitting down in the cockpit Emilio got right to the point and wanted to know if I had thought about his offer? He said the boat that he was going to take was at anchor in the lagoon near the marina. He said there's no one on board so he wants to organize a crew right away and leave as soon as possible. He said that normally he and Francisco could handle things by themselves, but because of the size of the boat they'd need to go at least 100 miles due east into the Atlantic before turning to a southerly course so he wanted four people on board to cover the watches. Emilio knew the bridge on the Dutch side opened once in the morning and then again at 4:00 p.m. He wanted to be able to leave when the bridge opened in the afternoon so he could be well offshore before anyone realized the boat was gone and maybe even be in Colombia ahead of anyone being the wiser."

"Is the boat still in Colombia?"

"Yeah, I guess I shouldn't have said that."

"Never mind, go on."

"Emilio said the American always contacted him through a friend who owns Le Bar in Gustavia on St. Bart's. When Emilio spoke with him the guy said he wanted the Irwin in St. Martin to give to a heavy weight in Bogotá because it was the type of yacht the

Colombian wanted. He said the boat flew a Dutch flag, but was owned by a German. Emilio said there hadn't been anyone on the yacht for the last few days because all the hatches were closed. He said the owners were probably away for the holidays and why he needed to move quickly. Emilio said that all the boats they picked up were always taken to a small marina along Colombia's Caribbean coast where they'd change the name, remove the hull identification numbers then repaint the trim and the boot stripe a different color because then they'd simply disappear. Emilio told me that one time he was curious about who this guy really was so he called the American Embassy in Bogotá, but he wasn't there. The telephone operator only said that he was an attaché in the commercial section."

"Hervé did Emilio tell you the name of the American in Bogotá?"

"No, he never told me his name."

"That's quite a story, but now that I know the background and where the boat is why do I need you?"

"You need me because I know where Emilio is in Cartagena. It's pretty clear that he obviously got his crew who may still be on the boat. One call from me to Emilio at the Cartagena Yacht Club would see the boat disappear again and then you'd never find it. Even if you did find the boat with the hull numbers gone you couldn't make a positive ID. With no hull identification and considering the clout of the American guy who had the boat stolen in the first place the Colombian authorities would laugh if you tried to recover it and don't forget the boat is registered in Holland not the US."

Pondering a response,

"Okay, I agree the information may be helpful, but the Underwriters would never agree to pay you a 10% reward because you had knowledge of the crime before it was committed. Of course you could also be charged with aiding and abetting which is a criminal act for not reporting what you knew to the French Gendarmerie or the Dutch Police."

The silence was deafening.

"You can't do that!"

"You really don't think so? I wouldn't push your luck. You my friend Hervé, owner of the yacht *Evasion* docked at the Marina

Royale in Marigot who has been a party to grand theft could end up losing your boat in addition to spending a few years in the slammer as a guest of the French Republic."

Ryan thought that Hervé had hung up the phone, but during the silence must have quickly realized he might be in deep trouble. Ryan knew it would be better to keep Hervé talking and even more important to keep him listening.

"Look Hervé you made a big mistake in not reporting what was coming down to the authorities which would have prevented the theft in the first place. Now you are trying to illegally profit from something that should have been reported before it ever happened, naughty, naughty, Hervé. Having said that, maybe I can help you, but the 10% is out of the question. In every case any reward that's paid is based only on the recovered value of the yacht and only after its safe return to the rightful owner. Any damage or theft of the gear or personal effects that was on the boat is deducted to come up with a recovered value on which the 10% is based. But under the law as you aided and abetted in the commission of a crime you're a co-conspirator and clearly not entitled to any reward. However, if your information is reliable and we recover the yacht I would be willing to suggest that Underwriters pay you a flat sum of $2,000.00."

Obviously annoyed, Hervé shot back,

"That's crazy, I give you information that leads to the recovery of a yacht worth $250,000.00 and you give me a pittance of $2,000.00."

"Sorry Hervé, that's the deal. Take it or leave it. I'll give you 24 hours to think about it and let me know what you decide. If I don't hear back from you by this time tomorrow I'll start moving."

Ryan hung up the phone and poured himself a glass of a very nice Cabernet Sauvignon. Ten minutes later the phone rang,

"This is Hervé I'll accept your offer."

"Okay Hervé call me tomorrow before noon. In the meantime I'll see if the Underwriters agree."

The following day at 0530 Atlantic Standard Time Ryan called the Underwriter in Holland to give him the news and ask his approval for the $2,000.00 payment to Hervé – if they got the boat back. At 1100 Hervé called.

"Hervé I've spoken with the Underwriter who isn't particularly happy with paying ransom to someone who was involved and was in a position to prevent the theft, but because he wants the boat back he's agreed to pay you $2,000.00, but there are conditions. You must agree to fully cooperate; if we get the boat back and can prosecute the thieves you will agree to testify at their trial. Also, I'd like you to come to Cartagena with me to identify Emilio?"

"That's crazy, these are bad people. If Emilio sees me in Cartagena and finds I'm involved in any way with your efforts to recover the Irwin I'm sure he'd kill me. You tricked me into giving you all the information and now you want me to risk my life for a measly $2,000.00. I don't think so."

"Hervé I didn't trick you into anything you're the one who voluntarily provided the details of the players and where the boat is. I can understand why you wouldn't want to go to Cartagena, but if you give me some additional information I might be able to avoid you having to do this. To start I'll need a full description of Emilio and Francisco. Write down everything you know about them. I want to know if they smoke and if so, what brand of cigarettes are they right or left handed, any distinguishing marks, tattoos or scars, the color and length of their hair, the color of their eyes, and a description of the type of clothes they were wearing when you were with them in Fort de France and later when they were on your boat. You must include everything and I do mean everything that you and Didi observed in the time you spent with them. At this stage of the game I'm not sure where or how Emilio, Francisco or anyone else who is involved could be brought to justice, but if we go to trial your testimony cannot be waived. The prosecution probably wouldn't be in Colombia because of jurisdictional issues. If they were arrested in either Marigot or Philipsburg you'd have to agree to cooperate fully with the Dutch and French authorities and that's it."

"Okay I don't like it, but I'll agree. Didi's a pretty good artist so I'll get her to do some pencil sketches of both of them and fax everything to you at the number on the Stolen Boat Sheet."

Ryan wanted a bit more,

"How about the crew Emilio hired, do you know who they are and what they look like?"

"No, I never saw who he finally got, but they'd probably be locals. I'll ask around and see what I can find out."

"Okay please get me the sketches and everything you can remember about Emilio and Francisco and do it now. Time is of the essence because if they start altering the boats appearance and removing the hull numbers it will make my job even harder. Remember, no boat, no $2,000.00."

Ryan didn't feel it was necessary to tell Hervé that even if the hull identification numbers were removed he still might be able to identify the boat by matching the serial numbers from the engine, transmission and the electronics that he had from the survey in the underwriting file. However, matching the serial numbers could only be done if Ryan was able to get on board. Hervé and his artistic girlfriend Didi didn't waste any time. As soon as the details and the sketches arrived Ryan was on a COPA flight to Cartagena through Panama. With the exception of being a quagmire of crime, corruption and drug-trafficking, Cartagena is a beautiful walled colonial city reminiscent of old Spain. In an effort to blend-in Ryan avoided the glitzy tourist hotels and stayed at a small inn used by businessmen located in what was described as a 'safe section' of the city. After checking in Ryan took a taxi to the Cartagena Yacht Club to see if he could find Emilio, Francisco or maybe even the Irwin. After a Coke at the bar (the kind you drink not put up your nose) Ryan had a taxi drive him along the coastal road just outside of the city where Hervé said he might find the *Elle*.

After driving around for an hour or so he found an Irwin 52' tied up to a small dock along the breakwater of a narrow channel to the west of Cartagena. Using binoculars from a safe distance Ryan saw that the hatches were closed which in the sub-tropical heat meant it was a pretty good bet that no one was on board. He could see that the vessel's sheer stripes along her topsides were a brownish tan color and there was no name or hailing port shown on her stern. The stolen Irwin had blue sheer stripes and the name *Elle* and hailing port of *Curacao* painted on the transom. Even though the name on the transom had been removed and the color of the sheer stripes was different the yacht had specific and personalized deck gear that was unique to the *Elle.*

Pondering momentarily, okay, the name and hailing port have been removed but the deck gear is a perfect match, this has to be the *Elle.* He wondered if he could somehow see the hull number on the transom, assuming it was still there. Moving closer to the Irwin his confidence increased further when he saw the custom stainless steel dive platform that had been designed and installed by the owner along with a small royal blue and yellow telltale with the letter *E.* The telltale which had been sewn by the owner's wife was tied to the upper mizzen port backstay. Now confident that the *E* was confirmation that this was the *Elle,* Ryan returned to the Cartagena Yacht Club and took a seat at the end of the bar which was rapidly filling with the yachting crowd preparing to avail themselves of the Happy Hour.

"G'day mate welcome to the Cartagena Yacht Club. My name's Pete, I've got my boat here, you on a boat?"

"No just a landlubber doing the tourist bit."

"Well Yank let me buy you a real beer, Katie love, give us two of those cold Fosters."

"Katie's my lady who works at the bar during the week to earn a few pesos so we can eat. I'm a generous bloke so I let her have the weekends off so she can keep our boat clean."

Pete, even though clearly a bit chauvinistic was an outgoing and friendly Aussie who, apparently craving for a bit of male companionship especially to a new arrival, was always anxious to tell his sea-going stories which probably had been told many times before.

"Ten years ago I decided to do a walk-about. I did the single-handed bit and sailed from Sydney to the Marquesas. After a quick stop at Santa Maria in the Galapagos I set a course for Panama. Dropped the hook off Balboa for a couple of days, but got fed up with the rocking and rolling from the wake of the crew launches going back and forth to the ships anchored offshore. After getting through the Canal I tied up for a couple of weeks at the Panama Yacht Club in Colon before setting a course for Bonaire figuring when I arrived I'd start a diving business. A few days out of Colon off the Colombian coast I got caught in a westerly and the bloody mast came down. I was able to jury rig a small sail and make it to Cartagena, been here ever since. Had a few local ladies to keep me company then a while back I met Katie. She was down on her luck after having a fight with her bloke who kicked her off his boat. She had no money to get back to London so I gave her a job doing some varnish work on my boat and well, the rest is history."

"That's an interesting story. How big was your boat?"

"32 foot from stem to stern, a great sea boat. I ended up selling her to a Brit who replaced the mast and rigging and sailed away. I never heard from him again. You know there are a lot of stories like mine around here. See the couple at the table under the Heineken sign? One night they say they hit a floating container offshore, patched the hole and made it to Cartagena. They had no insurance so they got the boat hauled at the Manzanillo Marina and have been here over a year trying to fix her up with money they make doing minor repairs and other odd jobs. The blond guy at the end of the bar is a Swede who's been around for about six months. He has the 65' Swan tied up on the outer dock and obviously has a few bucks. He got himself hooked on the cheap drugs and doesn't seem to have any intention of leaving. The two burly long haired guys sitting over there in the corner wearing the St. Maarten T-shirts are French, they arrived a couple weeks ago and from their obnoxious attitude both are clearly pissed-off at the world. During the day they sit in the bar sucking on a few beers then at night find a boat with nobody on board and sleep in the cockpit. I don't know what their story is, but it's not exactly Alice in Wonderland."

Ryan thinking to himself, hmm, French, St. Maarten T-shirts and been here a couple of weeks. Even though the faxed drawings weren't the best and Didi clearly wasn't the artist that Hervé had made her out to be, there was a resemblance. I wonder if they're Emilio and Francisco.

"Well mate, enjoy your visit, I've got to go on a walk-about to do some shopping. By the way the restaurant here has the best seafood in Cartagena and it's cheap."

After Pete left Ryan took his Fosters and walked over to the two Frenchman.

"Excuse me, I see you're wearing St Maarten T-shirts, do you live on St. Maarten?"

With a heavy and distinctly French accent, but clearly not interested in small talk the larger of the two looked up and mumbled,

"Lived at Oyster Pond for awhile…"

Feeling lucky and hoping for a response Ryan answered,

"Anywhere near Captain Oliver's?"

The mention of Captain Oliver's, a small marina on the French side of the island located at Oyster Pond sparked an immediate interest.

"You know Captain Oliver's?"

"Oh sure, I lived on the Dutch side a few years back and had a small catamaran that I sailed out of Captain Oliver's Marina, I'll never forget that terrible entrance on the windward side. Can I buy you a beer?"

"Sure, sit down."

Waving at the British barmaid,

"Katie may we have three beers please."

Becoming more relaxed in finding that Ryan knew the island the two Frenchmen were pleased to have someone to talk to especially a fellow sailor. With the back of his hand wiping some beer that had dribbled from the side of his mouth the larger of the two asked,

"When were you last on the island?"

"I haven't been back for a couple of years. How long have you been in Cartagena?"

"A couple of weeks, we delivered a boat."

"So what are you doing now, just playing the tourist bit?"

"No, we want to get out of here, but haven't been paid for the delivery or given our return air tickets home."

Hmm, return air tickets? Wondering where they were returning to Ryan asked,

"Where's your home?"

Taking a large swig of beer the one who Ryan believed was Francisco said, "St. Bart's."

"Well I guess while your waiting you can sit back relax and enjoy the scenery."

"We're not relaxing. After we got here that son-of-a-bitch we did the job for left and told us he was going to Bogotá to get our money. We've not seen him since. If he's not back by the weekend we plan to take the matter into our own hands."

"Is his boat still here?"

"Yeah it's tied up just out of town, but the bastard won't let us stay on the boat while he's not here. We're down to our last few dollars and forced to sleep on boats where the owners are gone because we can't afford a hotel."

Asking Katie for another round and feigning a genuine concern,

"You know if you don't get paid and the boats still here you could file a lien and a seaman's claim with the authorities for your wages, it's done all the time."

"Well it's not quite that simple the guy who hired us doesn't own the boat, but I can't get into it because it's too complicated."

Bingo! These were the ones who stole the *Elle* from Saint Martin and now enraged because their attaché paymaster hadn't come across with the money they'd been promised. Before Ryan got up to leave he had to restrain himself as he really wanted to say, but didn't, *Sorry guys, I guess there's just no honor amongst thieves.*

The two thugs weren't pleased in being made to wait, especially considering they were running out of money and had no place to stay. Ryan thought it was strange that they weren't allowed to at least sleep on the Irwin while waiting for their money. This seemed like a really stupid move on the part of their American paymaster.

Ryan then wondered how much they had been promised for stealing the Irwin. Under these unusual circumstances he pondered whether it might be an opportunity to get creative and attempt a potentially dangerous scheme to double cross Emilio's paymaster. That night in his hotel Ryan weighed his options. Emilio and Francisco were broke and stuck in Cartagena with no place to sleep and no way to get back to St. Bart's. Ryan knew it would be risky, but suppose he were to tell Emilio who he really was and that he was in Colombia to recover the Irwin. Suppose he were to offer them $5,000 each for the safe return of the *Elle* to Saint Martin and no problems with the police? Lay it on the table and level with the two and take the chance that they weren't getting more from the attaché, which he didn't believe would be the case. While they might get upset and rearrange his physical features or even worse disfigure him permanently, they'd have little to gain.

Emilio and Francisco weren't stupid and being thoroughly pissed-off might see Ryan's proposal as a means to get even with the other American. In addition to cutting their losses they might even make a profit. If they did agree to take the Irwin back to St. Martin Ryan would need to have the Irwin's owners withdraw the theft report with the French Gendarmes in Marigot so they wouldn't be arrested when they returned. Before this was done Ryan had to convince the two that the proposal offered a quick way to get them out of their current predicament. If they agreed to the deal Ryan also decided to try and add the condition that they get out of the boat stealing business. To guarantee their part of bargain and avoid prosecution he'd insist the pair give him copies of the photo pages of their passports. He would say this was ostensibly for the Gendarmes to use in clearing the Irwin and its crew back into St. Martin.

Because of the time differences and being a weekend Ryan might not be able to reach the Underwriter to get approval for his plan however, considering a hull value of $250,000.00 he felt confident that the Underwriter wouldn't object to a double-cross to get the boat back for maybe another $10,000. Ryan also considered what other options Emilio and Francisco really had. Even if they had been promised more money to steal the Irwin they had received nothing, the pair were actually out of pocket. In addition to not receiving anything, Emilio would have had to pay the extra delivery crew out of his own money. Ryan reasoned it was worth a try.

The next day was a warm and clear Saturday morning. After breakfast Ryan went to the Market in the town's square and bought some T-shirts for Josh and a leather case for himself, then stopped at a small cantina to have coffee and Arepas. Even though not exactly recommended for a proper diet, he loved Arepas the tasty South American biscuit made from flour and fried in lard that probably contained somewhere around 10,000 calories. A doctor friend once told him that even one Arepa has enough cholesterol to bring down a Sumo Wrestler.

After leaving the cantina and before returning to the Yacht Club to present Emilio with his proposal Ryan decided to have another look at the Irwin. As the cab rounded the corner passing a small cluster of shacks on the waters edge he could see clouds of smoke rising in the windless sky near where the boat had been moored. The area from where Ryan had previously seen the Irwin was now jammed with people. He told the cab driver to wait and quickly hoofed it around a fire truck and through the crowd who were watching a boat that was burning about 300' from the shore. The boat had been cast off from the dock and was now ablaze in the center of the channel. Once the hull's highly flammable resin had ignited the Irwin became totally engulfed in flames and had burned almost to the water line. The main mast had fallen forward and appeared like a battering ram lying over what was left of the bow. The mizzen mast lay sideways partially in the water with the lower half caught in the charred remains of the boat.

As Ryan approached a dismayed looking man, obviously a tourist from his clothing and holding some fishing tackle turned towards him saying,

"You know if the boat had been left alongside the bulkhead the fire service might have been able to extinguish the flames. Who ever threw off her lines probably didn't realize that the current would move the boat downwind to the center of the channel beyond the reach of the firemen's water hoses."

"Yeah the guy who cast her off probably wasn't a sailor and didn't realize what he was doing."

In the distance standing by a small fence in an empty lot further down the channel Ryan saw the two Frenchmen standing with their arms crossed and for the first time both had smiles on their faces. The next morning Ryan was on the COPA flight to Panama on his way back to Puerto Rico. After breaking the news to the Underwriter in Holland Ryan called the Marina Royale in St. Martin and left a message for the master of the *Evasion* to call him. A short time later Hervé called, "Eddie, how did everything go did you find the boat?"

"Yep, I found the boat, but things didn't turn out as hoped."

"What happened? Did you find the crew? Did you find Emilio? Did he find out who you were?"

"Calm down Hervé. I never met up with the crew, but I did find Emilio and Francisco, they never knew who I was or why I was in Cartagena. They thought I was just a tourist. Over a beer Emilio told me that after they had arrived in Cartagena he had paid off the delivery crew and bought them return tickets to Sint Maarten. Emilio paid everything out of his own money because he expected to be paid by the American who had left for Bogotá. Emilio and Francisco waited patiently for two weeks, but never received their money. On Saturday, because they hadn't been paid they torched the Irwin."

"What! They burnt the boat?"

"Sorry Hervé, there's nothing left."

"Are you still going to pay me for helping you?"

"Pay you for what, the remains of a burnt boat in Cartagena? Next time before you get involved in the nasty business of stealing boats you should call me first. Good-bye Hervé."

CUBA LIBRÉ

After high value yacht was stolen from a charter fleet located in Dutch Sint Maarten the charter company carried out an exhaustive air search, but couldn't find her. Underwriters in London contacted Andy Jones for his assistance. After receiving a faxed copy of the underwriting file, Jones a marine surveyor based in Puerto Rico flew to Sint Maarten. In Phillipsburg he met with Martin Brevet, manager of Sun Charters to gather information surrounding the disappearance of the yacht.

"Hi Martin sorry to hear about the loss of one of your boats, what exactly happened?"

"Hey Andy nice to see you, last Thursday the *Victory,* a 70' cat returned from a charter and because at the time our dock was full the skipper anchored her off Bobby's Marina. She wasn't booked for another charter until the following Friday so we decided to leave her on the hook until we had space to bring her alongside for cleaning and provisioning. When I left the office on Saturday afternoon about 1700 I saw everything was okay and she was still at anchor. Sunday morning about 0900 her skipper called me at home and asked if I'd moved her because she wasn't were he'd left her. As I hadn't moved her and she wasn't anywhere in the harbor it became apparent that she had been stolen. I called Eppy who runs an air charter service out of Princess Juliana and asked if he could take me up right away to do a search. We searched a wide area; north to Sombrero, east to Barbuda and Antigua, then south to Guadeloupe before looking around Saint Croix, but we couldn't find her."

"If you saw her at 1700 on Saturday and the skipper saw that she was gone at 0900 Sunday there's a window of about 14 or 15 hours when she could have been taken. She's fast so she could have been somewhere outside the area you covered and maybe on her way to Central or South America or even north to the Turks and Caicos Islands. I'll send some stolen boat flyers to the various ports and law enforcement agencies to see if anyone has seen her. The *Victory* is insured for $500,000.00 so with a 10% reward offered for her return I'm confident something should eventually surface. In the meantime please let me have a copy of her registration documents. I'd also like you to get me a copy of the Dutch police report with copies translated to English and Spanish. If you might hear anything please let me know."

A week after the stolen boat flyers had been distributed Andy received a phone call. The caller asked, "Is this Andy Jones?"

"Yes. Who is this?"

"My name is Didier. I'm calling about the *Victory*. I saw your stolen boat poster and the $50,000.00 in reward money you're offering."

"Didier thanks for calling, what do you know about the boat?"

"I know where she is can I receive the reward money?"

Andy's interest perked,

"Of course if the *Victory* is returned you'd be entitled to 10% of her recovered value. The payment is less the cost of any damages to the gear and equipment that's on the boat at the time we get her back. The full reward is only paid if the boat is returned in the same condition it was before it was stolen."

"If I tell you where the boat is, you must pay me the $50,000.00 reward first. The boat is in the same condition as it was when it was stolen."

"Sorry Didier that's not the way it works. How do you know this is the boat I'm looking for? Did you steal the boat?"

"No, no, no, I didn't steal the boat. I have a friend who's seen the *Victory* and says it's in the same condition as when it was taken from Bobby's Marina on September 13th."

"Hang on. You say you didn't steal the boat, but you know it was taken on September 13th and that it disappeared from Bobby's Marina which was not on the stolen boat flyer. The flyer only said it was taken from Sint Maarten. If you didn't steal the boat you wouldn't know when and where it was taken from or have any way of knowing it's in the same condition now as it was when it was stolen. Sorry Didier, but what you're feeding me is a bunch of crap. You want me to pay you $50,000.00 for nothing more than a fairy tale. Sorry, but I'm not interested."

"Look, if you want the boat back I want to be paid the reward. If this can be agreed I can even take you to the boat."

"Like I said, I'm not interested. Before any money changes hands I'll need verifiable confirmation that the boat you're talking about is the catamaran *Victory*. That's it - period."

"Wait a minute I've got an idea. My friend who first told me about the boat saw the *Victory* and took pictures of her. I have the pictures of her sitting at anchor. Why don't we meet and I'll show you the pictures that will convince you that she's the *Victory*."

"Hang on you first told me that your friend saw the *Victory* now you're saying he took pictures?"

"Yes, I have a number of pictures of her at anchor that I could show you. Let's meet."

"Where are you in Sint Maarten?"

"No, I'm not in Sint Maarten, I'm in Fort Lauderdale."

"Fort Lauderdale!"

"Yes, Fort Lauderdale. Could we meet tomorrow or the day after? If you could come we can meet at the Denny's Coffee Shop at the corner of 17th Street Causeway and Federal, say, 3:00 p.m."

"Okay, I'll be there tomorrow. How will I know you?"

"I've seen your picture in the newspaper so I'll know you. 3:00 p.m."

Andy took the morning American Airlines flight to Miami, picked up a rental car and drove to Fort Lauderdale. At 2:30 p.m. he entered Denny's and ordered coffee. At 2:55 p.m. a long haired unshaven 20's something guy and his girlfriend dressed like an aspiring gypsy entered the coffee shop and walked to where Andy was sitting.

"Andy, I'm Didier, this is Claudette."

"Didier, Claudette, nice to meet you. What've you got?"

Laying the photographs on the table Didier proudly said,

"You see there is no denying that this is the Cat that was stolen from in front of Bobby's Marina in Sint Maarten on September 13th."

"The photos are only of the port side so the name on the transom or cross beam can't be seen. It appears to be a similar custom Cat and type as the *Victory,* but there are dozens of yachts of this type in the Caribbean so it may or may not be the one I'm interested in. I see from the photos that the hatches are open. Is someone living on the yacht?"

Didier snapped back,

"No, no, my friend secured the vessel to be sure it was safe, but didn't go onboard. The port fuel tank is a quarter full and there's half in the starboard tank other than a bad solenoid switch and minor problem with starting the port engine the boats fine and everything's intact."

"So what you're saying is that your friend stole the *Victory* and was able to steal her without ever actually being onboard and then he was able to open the hatches from the outside of the vessel. C'mon Didier, give me a break you must think I'm pretty stupid if you think I'm going to believe that bullshit."

In pressing the point that the hatches were open in the photograph, Didier became unnerved and then admitted that he had been on board.

"Okay, I was on the boat, but that's all I'm going to say. When my friend first told me about the boat I went to see it and took the photos while it was at anchor. This is the *Victory*, if you want it back, I want the reward."

The photographs of the vessel were important, but what was even more noteworthy was what was around the yacht, the topography, sea state, trees, and the buildings details that provided a picture of the surrounding area. The photographs showed a West Indian type building situated near water that was light blue and therefore shallow. The low coastline displayed scrub and small pines protruding from a sandy, coral ringed beach indicating the photos of the stolen vessel may have been taken in the lower Bahamas, somewhere in the Turks and Caicos or possibly along the South Coast of Cuba.

As Grand Turk and Provo had been thoroughly searched in the last month, Andy focused on the Bahamas Out Islands and Cuba. From nautical charts of the area and Cuban tourism material his attention was drawn to the southern cays in the Gulf of Batabano on Cuba's southern coast. The topography was similar to the photos and there was a small yacht harbor at Cayo Largo del Sur, but most important, Cayo Largo had an airport which allowed the thief or thieves a way to leave. Changing tactics under the guise of sincerity Andy said that even though he would still need to make a positive ID to be certain that this was the vessel he'd agree to make arrangements for the payment of an advance of the reward to Didier. Upon hearing this he became relaxed and exhibited a broad smile. Andy suggested that the reward funds be placed in escrow with a bank or attorney. Once the escrow payment was finalized they could together travel to the yacht to confirm its present condition and organize its return after which the reward would be released to Didier. This bothered Didier.

"Because of where she's located you as an American might have a problem if you want to see her because of travel restrictions. I don't want to get into this right now, but maybe I can get you a picture of her transom that shows her name. In he meantime here's the name and phone number of an attorney where you can send the money."

Travel restrictions could only mean one place, Cuba. As Didier had specific knowledge of exactly how much fuel was on board, earlier problems with the port engine and other particulars which could only be known to the thief, Andy was confident that Didier had stolen the boat and now knew for sure it was in Cuba at or near Cayo Largo. However, to keep Didier off-balance and continue the guise Andy kept pressing him to reveal its location.

He then decided to offer Didier an opportunity to steal a bit more. The possible location of the boat was narrowed question by question about fuel, water and provisioning availability. Deciding to flatter Didier he said that as he was obviously a very skilled and knowledgeable sailor asked if he would be willing for an appropriate fee to return the yacht to its rightful owners in Sint Maarten. Didier readily agreed asking how much would he be paid for the delivery.

"That will depend on how many days it'll take you to sail from where ever the vessel is now back to Sint Maarten?"

Didier quickly responded,

"Probably around eight days. It'll take a little more time because we'd be beating, with headwinds to Philipsburg."

Unwittingly Didier carelessly added,

"Actually the last time I did the trip with following seas and running before the wind from Sint Maarten, it only took six days."

Knowing that the sailing time from Sint Maarten to Cayo Largo del Sur would be approximately six days Andy ended the meeting by telling Didier he would make arrangements for the payment of the money to the attorney he'd selected in Fort Lauderdale. Didier was told that the arrangements for the payment of the reward might take a week to ten days so he should be patient. Once the lawyer had confirmed to Didier that he'd received the escrow payment they would meet to arrange for the delivery. Andy then drove Didier and Claudette back to a seedy motel located on Federal in Fort Lauderdale. During the meeting Andy had documented the conversation on his pen recorder while discreetly taking a number of photos of the pair with a shirt pocket camera.

Now convinced that the *Victory* was in Cayo Largo Andy had no intention of paying Didier anything, but had to stall while convincing him that he would be receiving a sizeable reward in addition to the delivery fee. Even though somewhat remote, Cayo Largo del Sur has an airport with daily flights to Havana so anyone leaving a yacht would have a means of departure. The distance between Sint Maarten and Cayo Largo del Sur is approximately 1,300 nautical miles, six days sailing time. When Andy offered him expenses and $200.00 per day for the delivery in addition to the reward Didier eagerly accepted. Andy then called his friend and contact in Havana, Andre Deville. Deville a French National lived in Havana and was the shipping agent for a number of European firms that exported goods to the island. After previously helping Deville resolve a theft claim of significant proportions he and Andy had become close friends.

"Bonjour Andre, this is Andy in Puerto Rico. How are you my friend?"

"Buenos Dias Andy. Yes I am fine and everything is good. How are you and your son?"

"We're both fine, Josh is doing well with his studies and I'm busy with my work which is why I'm calling. Recently a large catamaran was stolen from Sun Charters in Sint Maarten. I think that she may have been stolen by a Frenchman and his girl friend and believe she's now in Cayo Largo del Sur. It's only a small harbor, but any chance you might know someone there?"

"Cayo Largo, sure I know it. The resort has become a tourist hotspot because of its pristine beaches, good diving, fabulous hotel, and it's also got an airport. Varadero and Hemmingway are still popular with the Europeans, but Cayo Largo is gaining popularity as the premier of upscale resorts in Cuba. The tourism department pushes and promotes it because the development is partly owned by Fidel and Raul who quietly get a cut of the income. The harbor is very small so there are no facilities for ships, so anything I send has to go by air. I think a Cuban Coastguard Officer that I knew when he was in Havana may now be in Cayo Largo. He's coming up for retirement and heard that he was made Port Captain at Cayo Largo during the interim. I'll call el jefe at the headquarters of the Autoridad Portuaria, call me back in 20 minutes. I'd call you, but sometimes it takes me an hour to get a line to make an international call."

Andy waited 30 minutes.

"Hi Andre, any luck?"

"Yes. Pedro Delgado, the Coastguard Officer I know is now in charge of the harbor at Cayo Largo. Have you got a picture of the boat you're looking for? If you do fax it to me and I'll ask if it's there."

"I do have a number of photos of the boat, but it might not be a good idea to send him the pictures in case he's in cahoots with the people who stole it. What I'd prefer is for you to call him and tell him you have some French friends who may be visiting Cayo Largo. Ask him if a big white catamaran with blue sail covers is anchored in the harbor. How soon can you call him? I'm really anxious to know if it's there."

"As soon as I put the phone down I'll make the call. Call me back."

"Great!"

Andy made himself some coffee and 15 minutes later called.

"Andre please give me some good news."

"The catamaran is there. Pedro said it arrived and checked in about a week ago, but my French friends Didier and Claudette aren't on the boat. They only stayed for two days and then flew to

Havana. Pedro said that Didier gave him $300.00 and asked him to look after the boat until they got back. Pedro's a stickler for government procedures so he would have taken a copy of the photo pages of their passports and made a record in the Port's Inbound Log with the details of the boat's stores and its date of arrival. Andy, please tell me exactly who *my friends* Didier and Claudette are?"

"Andre your friends stole the catamaran from Sint Maarten. Because of its remote location where the U.S. Coast Guard has no jurisdiction they picked Cayo Largo to hide the boat. I really appreciate your help. I'll be coming to Havana and staying overnight at the Hotel Nacional, then flying to Cayo Largo. My flight from Cancun is scheduled to arrive at Jose Marti on Wednesday at 1440 hours. I'll take a cab from the airport and will be at the hotel around 1530 hours. If it's convenient let's plan to meet at 1630 in the garden bar, over a Cuba Libré for me and Dubonnet and Soda for you I'll fill you in. I'm booked to fly to Cayo Largo on Thursday and would appreciate if you'd tell Pedro that another friend, me, will be coming by to see him about 1130."

"Andy, it'll be great to see you on Wednesday. I'll let Pedro know you'll be stopping by on Thursday."

Because of travel restrictions Andy, using a travel agent in Santo Domingo arranged a flight to Cancun, Mexico for Monday with connecting service on Wednesday to Havana on Cubaña Airlines. As Americans are technically not permitted to fly to Cuba the travel agent in Santo Domingo would also arrange his flights between Cancun and Havana, but he'd collect the Cubaña tickets from a travel agent in Cancun.

As the Cubaña flight from Cancun to Havana only operated on Wednesdays and Saturdays it provided a good opportunity for him to visit an old friend who was the manager of the Cancun office of a Florida based shipping line. His friend Captain Alan Lucia met him at the airport and after collecting his Cubaña tickets from Viajes Internacionales de Cancun they reminisced about their long friendship over a number of margaritas at Maria's Cantina. Alan had an interesting and colorful background; having a Mexican mother and American father he'd lived in Acapulco and attended university in Mexico then went to sea before distinguishing himself as one of Mexico's early matadors. He later turned to the sea where he became an internationally respected and acclaimed yachtsman. They first met and had became close friends many years ago when Alan was the manager of a large Marina and Yacht Harbor in Fajardo, located on Puerto Rico's Eastern Coast.

————

Andy was pleased when Cubaña's Russian built Ilyushin 62 eventually landed at Havana's Jose Marti Airport being of the opinion that the aging aircraft could easily fall apart at any time he was glad it was a short flight. With only a carry-on he proceeded to Cuban Immigration presenting his passport with a small sheet of blank white paper that had been placed between the pages. The immigration officer stamped the sheet of paper indicating his entry; the opposite side of the sheet would later bear the stamp of his departure from Cuba. Upon his return to Cancun the stamped white paper would be thrown away so his passport would have no record of a visit to Cuba. The drive from the Jose Marti airport was interesting. The first thing an arriving visitor sees outside the airport is a large white-washed wall painted with a massive picture of Ché Guevara adorned with the words *Socialismo o Muerte*. Andy thought to himself, hmm, Socialism or Death, not really much of a choice.

Entering the Hotel Nacional was like taking a trip back in time. The hotel lobby was adorned with a collection of ferns and potted plants placed strategically amongst colorful ceramic Spanish tiles. The peaceful ambiance was reminiscent of a bygone era where one might expect that at any moment Humphrey Bogart, Peter Lorre or Sidney Greenstreet would silently emerge from the shadows.

His room was pleasant providing a magnificent view over the broad esplanade of the Malecon and Caribbean beyond. Only moments after he entered the room the door opened,

"Señor welcome to the Nacional, my name is Sylvia, I am your maid. If you need anything please let me know. If you have any laundry that needs to be cleaned please don't have it done by the hotel. If you let me have your laundry I can wash it and have it back in your room early the next morning and it will only cost you half of what the hotel will charge."

"Thanks Sylvia, but I won't have any laundry because I'm only here for a few days."

A short time later while sitting at a table in the garden bar,

"Andre, Andre, over here, over here."

"Hey Andy, it's great to see you. Where's your son?"

"He's back in Puerto Rico. Because it's a bit of a hassle for American's to come to Cuba, over his strenuous objections I had to leave him home with friends."

"Please tell him I said hello. Everything is set up for you to see Pedro tomorrow. The Cayo Largo resort is a fabulous place I know you'll enjoy your visit. To bad you're only going to be there for the day."

"I really appreciate the introduction to Pedro. I want to see and take a few pictures of the catamaran and get a copy Pedro's log that shows when Didier and Claudette cleared in with the boat. I'd also like to find out if I can unofficially enlist Pedro's help in getting the boat out of Cuba."

"Pedro's a great guy who did me a lot of favors when he was a Coastguard inspector in Havana. He's only got a few more months to go before he retires so I'm sure he'd be amenable to helping you for some Yankee dollars."

After a number of drinks and relating the story of the *Victory*, the two parted and Andy prepared for his visit to Cayo Largo. Shortly after passing the picture of Ché and his less than subtle message of Socialism or Death Andy entered the departure lounge of Jose Marti Airport just as the flight to Cayo Largo was being called.

"Cubaña vuelo 518 para Cayo Largo del Sur està listo para embarcar. Todos los pasajeros por favor acceden por la puerta 4A, Gracias."

Walking across the tarmac he saw an aircraft in the distance, but thought to himself this surely couldn't be the one to Cayo Largo, but it was. Passengers were boarding by means of a loading ramp that had been lowered from the back of the plane. The plane, an aging Russian built Ilyushin 76 military transport aircraft had been converted for passenger service. Along with a throng of tourists and Cubans, Andy proceeded up the loading ramp. He was then directed to seat 17C by a somewhat scruffy flight attendant who was smoking a small cigar. Sitting next to Andy in 17D was an elderly lady who too was smoking a slightly larger cigar. The smoke from her cigar floated in a dark cloud filling the air to the dismay of another passenger sitting in seat 16D, who turned and looking over the seat forcefully complained. The passenger in 16D best described as a young American or Canadian ivy-league college student began shouting his displeasure in English. Speaking no English, the student's demand was simply ignored by the Cuban senior citizen who obviously only spoke Spanish.

After the ramp was closed the grubby female flight attendant still puffing away on her cigar told the agitated ivy-leaguer in 16D, in English, to shut up, adding please to her demand. She then proceeded up the aisle to see who or who hadn't fastened their seat belts. A procedure no doubt to insure that if the plane crashed or caught fire, the bodies would remain in their seats for the ease of removal. As the Ilyushin engaged in a shake, rattle and roll along the taxiway in preparation for takeoff Andy looked out the window. What he saw was a bit troubling. Alongside the taxiway and airport perimeter were at least a dozen or so Ilyushin 62s, Yak 42s and Antonov 24s squeezed together or stacked one on top of another much like a junkyard. Some were missing wings, others had no engines and several were without landing gear. All had been cannibalized for parts. Since the collapse of the Soviet Union the supply of spare parts for Cuban aircraft first diminished then disappeared entirely. To keep their small fleet in the air Cubaña were cannibalizing grounded planes and stripping them for parts to keep the others flying. Hoping that his short flight to and from Cayo Largo would be uneventful he said a silent prayer asking God for forgiveness for his sins, whatever they may have been.

———

An hour later as the Ilyushin creaked to a stop in Cayo Largo Andy unbuckled his seat belt while quietly thanking God for deliverance. The package tour he had arranged for his visit to the island included transportation to the marina and the resort were they would be provided with lunch and entertainment. After reaching the marina he looked at the anchorage and saw a white 70' catamaran with blue sail covers. He'd found the *Victory*. He chuckled to himself murmuring, 'I guess I can really say that *Victory* is in sight.'

Andy then proceeded to the office of Comandante Pedro Delgado.

"Buenos dias Comandante, mi nombre es Andy Jones, soy amigo de Andrés. Estoy interesado en el catamaràn que està anclado en el Puerto."

"Es un placer conocerte Señor Jones, bienvenido a Cayo Largo. Por favor, yo hablo un poco de Inglés y me gustaria aprender a hablar màs, podemos hablar en Inglés?"

In the exchange of greetings the Comandante explained to Andy that he'd appreciate it if they could speak in English because it would allow him to improve his skills with the language.

Andy smiled, "English would be fine as it's probably a lot better than my Spanish."

"Thank you Mr. Jones....."

Before the Comandante could finish the sentence Andy interrupted,

"Please my first name is Andy, there's no need for the mister."

"Okay Andy and please call me Pedro. What is it that I can help you with?"

Across the desk Andy pushed copies of the *Victory's* registration papers and the theft report from the Dutch police with the Spanish translation.

"Pedro the catamaran was stolen on September 13th from Sint Maarten in the Netherlands Antilles. There may be others involved, but I know for sure that Mr. Didier Colbert and a woman by the name of Claudette Levant sailed the catamaran from Sint Maarten to Cayo Largo. The police report and the boat's registration papers will provide you with confirmation that the theft took place. Didier contacted me and said he knew where the catamaran was and wanted me to pay him the reward that the boat's insurance company offered for its return. I met with Didier and Claudia and from the information they provided I narrowed my search to Cayo Largo." Listening intently Pedro said, "Coño, when they cleared in I thought they were such nice people. They seemed just like the other cruising yachts that occasionally visit Cayo Largo while sailing in the Caribbean. They were here a couple of days when the man told me that they had to go away on some sort of business, he asked if I'd being willing to keep an eye on the catamaran until they returned in about a month. He said he'd pay me $300.00 and as 300 Yankee dollars is a lot of money I agreed. Under Cuban law the particulars and a copy of the passports of the crew of all private yachts must be entered in the Port Captain's Log. If it will help, I can let you see the Log entry for the catamaran."

"Yes please, I'd very much like to see the entry and would appreciate if you could let me have a photocopy of the entry and of their passports. Could we go out to the catamaran so I can have a look around?"

"Of course you may go on board. There's no need for me to accompany you. Use my rowing boat that's tied up to the dock. While you go on board I'll make the photocopies. The catamaran is open and here are the engine keys."

Only 200 yards away Andy boarded the *Victory*. A number of the deck hatches had been opened slightly for ventilation and the sliding door to the main saloon was unlocked. The port and starboard hulls accommodating the cabins and heads were clean and showed no damage. The galley situated in the starboard hull was also clean. There were a few unopened liter bottles of Evian sparkling water, but no food. Before starting the engines Andy opened the sea cocks for the salt water cooling. The fuel gauges indicated that the 125 liter tanks were about half full. The starboard engine started without a problem and following a couple of blows to the solenoid the port engine sprang to life. After a brief look at the sails and inside the storage lockers and cabinets he returned to Pedro's office.

"Andy here are the copies of the Log entry and their passports. What will you do now?"

"Pedro I need your help. The fuel tanks are about half full and the sails are okay, but there are no provisions on the boat and I'll need to organize a delivery crew to sail her to George Town. It's only about 162 nautical miles, but we need to put enough food and drinking water on board for a crew of three to get to the Cayman's. Once she's in George Town she can be provisioned for the voyage back to Sint Maarten. With your contacts I'd appreciate if you'd arrange to quietly provision the boat with say 40 liters of drinking water, 5 kilos of rice and beans, a quantity of tortillas or bread, some instant coffee, and any canned foods you can get a hold of. It's going to take me a few days to put everything together so you'd have time to organize the provisions. Didier won't be coming back, but you'll still have to keep an eye on the catamaran. For your help I'll pay you $3,000.00 in cash. I only have $1,000.00 with me which I'll give you right now. I'll get the remaining $2,000.00 to Andre as soon as I get back to Puerto Rico and will have him fly to Cayo Largo to give it to you. Will this be okay?" Pedro exhibiting a broad smile,

"I'm going to retire from the Guardacostas in a few months time and my pension is very small, $3,000.00 would be fantastic. You can count on me. I must however be very careful because if Havana were to find out what I was doing I would surely lose my job and probably be thrown in jail. You must not use the telephone or fax to contact me. Please, only communicate with me through Andre. If need be you call him and then he can call me. How soon will you give the $2,000.00 to Andre? If you can give him the money early next week there's no need for him to come to Cayo Largo. On Thursday and Friday I'll be in Havana for a meeting at the Autoridad Portuaria and can meet Andre on either day in the afternoon."

"Thanks, that's fine Pedro. I'm flying back to Puerto Rico through Cancun on Saturday, on Monday I'll transfer the $2,000.00 to Andre's bank in Fort de France. He may not have the funds right away, but he knows me and has American money that he uses for his shipping business so he can give you the money when you're in Havana. Once I have the crew organized I'll call Andre to give him their names and the date of their arrival in Cayo Largo. If you can start organizing the provisions and put them onboard we should plan for the crew to be here on

Thursday morning, two weeks from today, they'd sail the same day as soon as it gets dark. After you close the office and leave I think that the boat should weigh anchor. If anyone happens to see the catamaran sail away they can't expect you to stop her if you're not here."

"That sounds fine with me. I have a friend in the resort's hotel that can get me the provisions and put them onboard. I'll pay him and say that Didier gave me the money for the provisions because when he returns they plan to sail away. When he finds the boat gone he'll believe Didier left and think nothing more about it because he's been paid. I close the Port Office at 1730 hours and it starts getting dark soon after. No one has ever looked at my Log book, but if anyone should ask, which I'm certain would never happen, I'll just say that Didier put a lot of food on board and left at night without checking out because the office was closed."

"Pedro it's been a real pleasure meeting you and I very much appreciate everything you've done and will be doing to help. Inside this envelope is $1,000.00. I'll call Andre tonight and tell him that I'll send the additional money to his BNP account in Fort de France so he'll be able to give you the other $2,000.00 when you guys meet next week. I'll get the delivery crew organized and Andre can confirm everything with you for two weeks from today. If there's any problem on your end tell Andre and he can call me. It's now time for me to get on the bus back to the airport. Muchas gracias amigo - hasta lluego."

––––––

As the Ilyushin bounced down the runway at Jose Marti then screeched to a stop Andy crossed himself while quietly saying a couple of Hail Mary's as the ramp opened. Outside the airport terminal he was besieged by an enthusiastic group of taxi drivers all eager for a fare. Andy selected Armando because he was the only one who wasn't overly aggressive. Armando, the proud owner of a 1959 Chevrolet sedan that was clearly showing the wear of taxi service carefully maneuvered his relic out of the airport through the throng of the other aging automobiles of a pre-Castro Cuba. A short time after leaving the airport and a dutiful wave as the taxi passed Ché and his sobering message displayed on the wall they entered a narrow lane meticulously adorned with manicured shrubs and trees that served as the Hotel Nacional's entrance. Andy went immediately to his room and called Andre.

"Andre, Andy here. I just got back from Cayo Largo. Thanks to you I had a great meeting with Pedro and he's agreed to help me get the boat out of Cuba. I'm going to pay him $3,000.00 for his efforts, but as I only had $1,000.00 in cash with me, I need your help again. I'll be back in Puerto Rico over the weekend and on Monday I'm going to wire $2,500.00 to your BNP Paribas account in Fort de France. Pedro's coming to Havana next week for meetings with the Port Authority on Thursday and Friday and I'd appreciate it if you'd give him the $2,000.00 I still owe him. The other $500.00 is for your helping me. I'm going to work on putting together a delivery crew who will travel to Havana in two weeks. They'll arrive on Wednesday then on Thursday take the flight to Cayo Largo. Once I confirm the crew I'll call you with their names so you can call Pedro to let him know who will be coming to take the boat. In the meantime he'll provision the boat with enough food and water for her to make it to Grand Cayman. The delivery crew will arrive about midday on Thursday and as soon as it's dark will weigh anchor and get underway. Pedro's asked me not to call him because the government always listens to incoming overseas calls so we'll do everything through you. When I call you I won't say anything except the names of the crew."

"Wow! You've really been busy. No problem with the money, I'll call Pedro and arrange to meet him either on Thursday or Friday and as soon as I know the names of the crew I'll call to let him know. Hey, you don't have to send the additional $500.00. You've done a lot of favors for me over the years and I'm pleased to help."

"If you don't want the $500.00 then give it to your lovely wife. Next time she's in Fort de France she can go shopping or if you're in San Juan you can take me out to dinner. I'd suggest we have a drink tonight, but I'm really bushed. It's been a stressful day. Right now I'm going to call and see what flights may be available for me to leave Havana tomorrow. The Cubaña flights to Cancun only operate on Saturdays, but I might try for one through Kingston or Santo Domingo. Love to the Mrs. we'll talk soon. Ciao."

———

As he had a prepaid ticket from Cancun he couldn't change his Saturday return. On Sunday morning Andy called Martin at Sun Charters in Sint Maarten.

"Hi Martin, I've got good news. I found the *Victory* at a small harbor on an island off Cuba's southern coast. I enlisted the help of the local Port captain by the name of Pedro Delgado who's agreed to help us. The boat's in good condition and there's plenty of fuel. I ran the engines and other than that minor starting problem with the port engine, both are running fine. In any case the crew will only need the engines when leaving Cayo Largo, which is where she's at now. It's about 162 nautical miles and a straight shot to George Town. When they reach George Town they should anchor off Seven Mile beach which is an open anchorage so they won't need the engines. In Cayman they'll need to provision for the trip back to Sint Maarten. Please send me the names of the crew so I can let Pedro in Cayo Largo know who will collect the boat. Just in case the guy who stole the *Victory* has any friends on Sint Maarten you or the delivery crew shouldn't say anything about what's coming down. There are daily flights from Havana to Cayo Largo. Because the crew won't be Americans they can fly from Princess Juliana to Santo Domingo then direct to Havana. It's important that they be in Havana on Wednesday so they can take the Thursday flight to Cayo Largo. Once they arrive they should go to the Port Captain's office and he'll take them to the boat which is anchored close to his office. During the afternoon the crew can check out the boat and once it's dark sail to the Cayman's. They should take a small amount of cash to cover their incidental expenses and one night at the hotel in Havana, a couple of hundred dollars should be enough. You need to wire whatever you feel appropriate for the provisioning to the Barclays Bank in George Town so the funds will be available after they arrive. How soon can you get me the names of the crew?"

"Andy that's fantastic news. I think I'll get Bob Gray, a Brit to skipper her, but I'll have to see who he wants to take along as crew. The crew will either be British or South African. I can give you their names later today. Great work, I'm happy to know there's no damage to her."

That afternoon Martin called with the names of the British crew. Andy called Andre to give him the names and confirmed that $2,500.00 had been deposited into his account at BNP Paribas in Fort de France. Early the next morning Andre called.

"Bonjour Andy, I called Pedro and gave him the names of the crew and he confirmed that the provisions will be put on the boat on Tuesday or Wednesday. He'll look for Captain Gray a week from Thursday."

———

"Martin, Bob here. Just wanted to let you know we're in Havana and staying at the Havana Libré. In the morning we're booked on the flight to Cayo Largo."

"Thanks Bob. Andy called and the Port Captain, Pedro Delgado is expecting you. The boat has been provisioned so you can leave as soon as it gets dark. Call me when you get to Cayman. I've wired $1,000.00 to Barclays in George Town so it'll be available when you get there, it's in your name so take your passport with you when you go to pick it up. Andy suggested that when you get to Grand Cayman you should anchor off Seven Mile Beach. I've booked rooms for the three of you at the Holiday Inn which is also on Seven Mile Beach. The supermarket is in town so you'll need to grab a cab to do your shopping. Andy also said there's a great Tex-Mex restaurant near the hotel called the Lone Star where they have British beer on tap and thought you might like to check it out. Have a safe trip."

The next day Bob and his crew arrived in Cayo Largo and went to the Port Captain's office.

"Comandante Delgado, my name is Bob Gray; I'm the skipper of the *Victory*. We'd like to go on board to check things over before preparing to sail after dark."

"Mr. Gray it's a pleasure to meet you. The provisions have been put on board and everything's stacked in the main saloon. The dinghy is on the dock outside so you can go to the boat now. Oh, there's something else. There will be two other persons who will be leaving with you and will get off the boat in Grand Cayman."

"What! I wasn't told of any passengers coming on the trip I don't......." Pedro interrupted him.

"There's nothing to worry about. I'm the Port Captain and will insure your departure is without incident. The two persons will be on board after 1730 hours when the Port Office closes, but before 1800 hours. As soon as it's dark you can weigh anchor and get underway."

Hearing this, Bob the delivery skipper felt a little better.

"If you say everything is alright then that's fine with me. I just want to be able to leave without any problems."

"Don't worry; I assure you there won't be any problems."

At 1700 hours Mrs. Juanita Delgado, wife of Pedro Delgado entered the Port Office carrying two small suitcases. Pedro tidied up his desk putting some selected papers in one of the suitcases along with his and Juanita's Cuban passports. At 1730 he paused, looked around and walked to the door. On the wall behind his desk was a large framed picture of Comandante Fidel Castro, before closing and locking the door he turned briefly and said,

"Adiós Comandante y Buena suerte."

After helping Juanita into the dinghy he then handed her the suitcases before getting in himself. As he pushed the dinghy away from the dock he looked around and found the dock and beach was empty. Upon reaching the catamaran he grabbed hold of a cleat on the port hull and called out,

"Mr. Gray, Mr. Gray, your passengers are here."

Peering from the cockpit Bob Gray somewhat startled looked down at the dinghy.

"Comandante, I don't understand?"

"Mr. Gray, this is my wife Juanita. We are leaving Cuba and coming with you as far as George Town. I will explain everything when we get on board. Please take the bags. After we get out pull the dinghy around and tie it to the port topsides so it can't be seen from the shore."

After they all were sitting in the main saloon patiently as the sun disappeared on the horizon Pedro began,

"I have been in the service of the Guardacostas for 20 years and rose to the rank of Capitàn de Navio. In Cuba we have two types of pesos; one is the convertible peso which is on a par with the U.S. dollar and worth 25 times more that the national Peso. All government employees are paid in National Pesos. I'm only 51 and will retire in less than 3 months and my pension will be paid in National Pesos which is almost nothing. Thanks to Andy and his French friend I've now got enough dollars to allow us to leave Cuba and travel to the United States. Neither of us has any family still living in Cuba because our parents are dead and my sister and her family left Cuba in an escape boat and took our son Rafael with them. They now all live in Miami. Rafa went to university and became a successful lawyer. We've always dreamed of getting out of Cuba and going to America, when Andy helped me earn the money and I learned that the catamaran was going to the Cayman Islands we decided that this was our chance and I immediately contacted Rafa. Because I am a senior Cuban Naval Officer Rafa contacted the U.S. authorities who said they would classify us as defectors and we'd be allowed to enter under the asylum program. When Rafa received our U.S. government immigration papers he sent them by courier to the Government of the Cayman Islands which will allow us to enter the Cayman's without any problems with their immigration authorities. After we arrive Rafa will send our prepaid tickets on Cayman Airways from George Town to Miami. Because I want to find a job he's set up an interview for me with a shipping company that has business in Latin America. The shipping company needs someone with my experience in port operations who speaks both Spanish and English. Until we get our own home we'll live with Rafa. Well, that's the story of your passengers."

Bob and the crew all smiled and brought their hands together with high-fives.

"I'm really pleased for you both and even more pleased that we're in a position to help you achieve your dream. It was unfortunate that the *Victory* was stolen, but thanks to you and Andy we got her back and will be leaving Cuba with two very happy passengers."

As darkness fell the *Victory* motored out of the harbor while the crew raised the sails and set a course due south for the Cayman Islands. It will never be known if it could be seen from the shore, but a happy ex-Cuban Coastguard Officer hugging his wife while standing on the foredeck raised his hand and gave a thumbs-up.

When the *Victory* arrived in Sint Maarten Andy inspected the catamaran and confirmed that she was undamaged. Later he met with the Dutch police and the Gendarmerie Maritime in Marigot at which time Andy provided them with the photo pages of Didier's and Claudette's passport and a copy of the Cuban government's official log of the stolen catamaran's entry to Cayo Largo. Didier never called Andy again.

Langley, Virginia
Headquarters of the CIA
The Worlds Most Dangerous Terrorist Organization

To insure the unimpeded flow of Venezuelan oil to the United States and to protect and conceal *The Company's* clandestine involvement with regime change, assassinations and narcotics trafficking from Colombia through Venezuela it is necessary to install a puppet government in the Miraflores Palace in Caracas.

They determine that this new government should be lead by a charismatic socialist revolutionary and former paratroop commander who the *The Company* believes will follow Washington's agenda. The Central Intelligence Agency with the assistance of the US Coast Guard embarks on a clandestine mission to destabilize the democratically elected government and install Hugo Chàvez as the President of Venezuela.

After assuming control of the government, Chàvez double-crosses the CIA and begins to actively support the anti-American policies of Fidel Castro, the late Muammar al-Qaddafi and the late Saddam Hussein.
Hugo Rafael Chàvez Frias
remains the President of the Bolivarian Republic of Venezuela.

The Reverend of Caracas

Mark Kelly, a naval architect and professional engineer had gained international recognition as a result of his patented invention of an innovative marine propulsion system designed for naval assault craft, coastguard and other marine law enforcement vessels. His interest in law enforcement came about after graduating from the U.S. Army's Military Police Academy; following his Army service Kelly was transferred to a law enforcement unit of the U.S. Air Force before moving to the Coast Guard. Rising to the grade of Commander in the U.S. Coast Guard Reserve, he served as an intelligence officer in the Coast Guard's 7th District Greater Antilles Section in San Juan, Puerto Rico. In recognition of his support of U.S. maritime interests Kelly was elected and served as vice-president of the Puerto Rico Council of the Navy League of the United States headquartered at the Roosevelt Roads Naval Base in Ceiba. Kelly lived with his young nephew Mike Evans in a garden apartment at Castillo del Mar also located in Ceiba and 5 minutes from the Naval Base.

———

Following her graduation from Stanford University Mark's Sister Jennifer moved to London to pursue a career in journalism. First working a number years for the City's tabloids she was subsequently hired by The Sunday Times of London where her assignments as a journalist took her to a number of conflict zones and wars in the Middle East, Africa and Asia. Her griping and captivating stories of war and genocide drew the attention of the paper's management who soon elevated her to the position of senior foreign correspondent. While in Guatemala working on a story about the genocide and mass murder being carried out by the country's army under the direction of an agency of the United States government she met the dashing Michael (Mick) Evans. Mick, a Brit of Irish ancestry was a Major in the British Army's Special Air Service, the SAS. After completing jungle warfare training with the SAS in Belize he rose rapidly in the officer corps. Following tours at SAS headquarters and the Ministry of Defense in Whitehall Mick was assigned to duty serving as the military liaison officer at the British Embassy in Guatemala City. In spite of their demanding work schedules the courtship intensified and blossomed. The handsome SAS officer and the beautiful American journalist soon found themselves madly in love. Their passionate liaisons continued after both returned to London. A few months later they married, bought a small cottage in Berkshire and soon after were blessed with the arrival of their first child Michael Evans, Junior. With young Mike being cared for by a live-in nanny Mick and Jennifer were able to pursue their careers through daily commutes to the City by British Rail from Maidenhead to Paddington. Aside from Jennifer's never-ending demand to meet deadlines and occasional assignments abroad they enjoyed an enviable togetherness and two or three times a week were able to relax with friends in the ambiance of their local Pub, The Bell & Dragon in nearby Cookham. On occasion to relieve Jennifer from having to prepare the Sunday Roast, they'd treat themselves to a meal at the Complete Angler in Marlow.

As members of the SAS had been assigned to deal with the Northern Irish Troubles and were also involved with the Falklands War, Jennifer was always thankful that Mick hadn't been called. Everything was normal for the happy transatlantic family until the fall of 1985 when Mick returned home and told Jennifer that he'd have to be away for awhile. He said he'd received orders and been assigned as an advisor to a special operations command operating abroad. Because of SAS security regulations he was unable to provide any details, but simply said that the mission involved the flow of narcotics in the Golden Triangle in Asia and through the Cartels in South America. Jennifer was distraught. Knowing he couldn't say exactly where or what he'd be doing she didn't press for details, but prayed for his safety. Her prayers were in vain when three months later she was advised by the Ministry of Defense that her husband had been killed in the line of duty. His body was being returned from Bogotá and was scheduled to arrive at RAF Brize Norton the following week.

After the funeral the Commanding Officer of the SAS presented young Mike with his father's beret adorned with the SAS badge inscribed 'Who Dares Wins'. He told Mike that his father was a brave man who died in the service of his country and would never be forgotten. From that day forward Mike always carried his father's badge with him while both struggled with their loss. Jennifer was a good mother, but recognized it was important for her to be strong in comforting and helping her son overcome their terrible tragedy. As the sole provider she also understood that it was important for her to move on with her career; then the Gulf War broke out. Her editor asked if she would like to cover the hostilities for the Times. Knowing that she wouldn't accept being separated from her son for an extended period her editor assured her that it appeared that the war wouldn't last long and she'd probably only be away for a week or two. Jennifer accepted the assignment and left for Kuwait three days later.

The following week when entering Baghdad embedded with a British Brigade Jennifer was killed by mortar fire. Mick's parents were the first to know and sent Mark a cable advising him of his sister's untimely death. Mike's elderly grandparents lived in Glasgow and said he was with them at their home. In memory of their only son they wanted to keep him, but simply weren't able to care for him. They asked if it would be possible for Mike to live with Mark. He replied of course. With an American mother and an English father Mike had both American and British nationality and both passports. The following week Mark flew to Gatwick then on to Glasgow and returned with Mike. Quickly mastering Spanish Mike easily adapted to his new home and school on the island of Puerto Rico. As time passed and even though knowing that Mark was his uncle, Mike soon began referring to Mark as his Dad.

———

It was a clear and cloudless fall day with Puerto Rico being cooled by light breezes from the southeast; the Atlantic to the north and Caribbean Sea to the east were blessed with calm and virtually flat seas. Enjoying his morning coffee on the balcony while gazing out over the Caribbean Mark thought of his boat Ms. PIGI, imagining that she would be gently tugging at her mooring lines anxiously anticipating the 80 MPH run to the British Virgin Islands. The custom built Magnum offshore racer with her high-powered engine would effortlessly cover the 70 miles from Puerto Rico to Village Cay in Road Town, Tortola in just over an hour allowing ample time for the Happy Hour at the Pub on Wickham's Cay.

The incessant ringing of the phone shattered the peaceful serenity which unbeknownst at the time would dramatically change his life - forever. The planned visit to the British Virgin Islands would have to be postponed.

"Mark, Desmond here. Good morning my friend, I do hope you're well. How would you like a bit of a get-away in beautiful South America? I've got a bit of a problem. At the moment I'm not sure of all the facts, but have a few notes that Liz jotted down during a phone call she took this morning while I was in a meeting at Lloyd's. Unfortunately the phone line wasn't the best so Liz only got the basics of the loss; the assured told her that he and his crew were uninjured after his yacht had gone aground on the Venezuelan island of Los Testigos and that they were now in Caracas. Under the Policy we've got the hull and machinery covered for $400,000.00 with a deductible of 2%. Needless to say I need someone I can rely on to get on the claim as soon as possible and as you're my man in the Caribbean can you get on it?"

Desmond or Dizzy as he was affectionately known in and around Lime Street where many of the marine underwriting syndicates are located in the City of London was an Underwriter who also dealt with claims when he was the Lead on the Underwriting Slip.

Dizzy's secretary, Liz O'Brien was a fiery Irish lady with long black hair and piercing blue eyes set on a dazzling body that could stop traffic. With a weakness for Paddy's Irish Whisky it's possible she may not have been hired for her typing, short-hand or office skills, but her bubbling personality made her a pleasure to work with. Liz and Mark had become friends in part because of their shared Irish ancestry. Even though she was from Ireland while Mark had been born in California, Liz in her classic Irish brogue always enjoyed pointing out that if it were not for Whisky the Irish would rule the world. Mark had first met this stunning female on one of his visits to London when Dizzy had invited him to lunch at the Marine Club, a lunch that included Liz.

At the time the Marine Club located a basketball court away from Lloyd's was the center of the universe for marine underwriters, brokers or anyone else who had the inclination or need to mingle shoulder-to-shoulder with the patricians of the insurance world. While his colleagues in the Market considered Dizzy to be a lucky chap, he often had to contend with the snide comments rendered by his peers about his less than competent, but beautiful and well endowed assistant. The pin-stripe and bowler hat brigade at Lloyd's was known to frequently mutter that her bountiful bosoms if activated, might be sufficient to feed the entire company of Her Majesty's aircraft carrier Ark Royal. As a result of Dizzy's wealthy family, a public school education at Kings College in Cambridge where his curriculum was limited to rudimentary subjects, but his prominence as an acclaimed bowler on the cricket squad had unquestionably opened the doors to a number of opportunities in the City. Dizzy's admirable connections ultimately lead to his gaining a favored position in the London insurance market.

Being at ease in the good-natured whirl of the City Dizzy took advantage of every opportunity to socialize especially when entertaining his American colleagues at lunch which always included his stunning assistant. When Liz walked through the Club which always was packed at lunchtime, it was akin to biblical times when Moses parted the waters of the Red Sea.

Before the world was blessed or cursed with the emergence of e-mail and the Web, depending on your point of view, Mark's instructions and communications with underwriters in the United Kingdom and Europe were generally received by means of facsimile or FedEx couriers. Receiving a personal telephone call from Dizzy was a clear indication that the loss in Venezuela was of considerable importance. Even though Dizzy said he had limited information he was hoping that the catamaran *Sundowner* might be salvaged.

"Mark I'll fax you what we've got on the loss and the policy information. During the phone conversation the owner told Liz that he and his sole crewman had been taken off the *Sundowner* by the Venezuelan military and flown by helicopter to Caracas. He said that they'd be staying at the Tamanaco Hotel in Caracas until they could return to Miami. Because the yacht was documented in the United States the owner reported the incident to the American Embassy where he spoke with the U.S. Coast Guard Attaché, a Lieutenant Commander by the name of James McBride."

Clearly concerned with the loss, Dizzy wanted Mark to get to Caracas immediately to assess the situation. A short time later the fax machine began churning out the details from London. After reading the documents from Dizzy, Mark called McBride in Caracas. At first the Coast Guard Officer seemed a bit cold in his demeanor, but slowly warmed as he relayed the story confirming that the Sundowner had indeed been stranded on the island of Los Testigos and shortly thereafter had broken up in the pounding surf.

"I think I should tell you Mr. Kelly that with the exception of a Venezuelan Navy radar installation which monitors Venezuela's eastern sea approaches, Los Testigos is uninhabited. It's surrounded by reefs and only accessible by helicopter and the right of entry requires approval from the military authorities. As there's nothing left of the boat the owner, Rob Johnson and Bill Miller, his crew, should be able to provide you with everything you might need. If you feel that you must visit the island I can obtain the necessary approvals, but only if it's really necessary."

The conversation with McBride ended with their agreement to meet at the Embassy upon Mark's arrival in Venezuela. 24 hours later Mark was on the flight to Caracas. It was a beautiful sunny day as the American Airlines flight from San Juan made a wide turn and paralleled the Venezuelan coast in her final easterly approach to Caracas' Aeropuerto Internacional Maiquetia Simón

Bolivar. From his window seat he could see the imposing buildings of the Venezuelan Naval Academy prominently situated on the hillside with a commanding view of the industrial area overlooking the port of La Guaira. Above and behind the Academy were the cloud shrouded mountains that separated the sea from the capital city of Caracas. Mark had been to Venezuela a number of times previously to deal with casualties and always enjoyed his visits, becoming fond of the country and her warm hearted people.

After making his way through the maze of immigration and customs formalities, Mark was descended upon by a swarm of enthusiastic taxi drivers. Each assuring him of the best rate for the traffic congested journey into the city while offering their solemn assurances that they would quickly deliver him to the steps of the U.S. Embassy in the center of Caracas.

Pedro, an aging driver who had an equally aged Chevrolet sedan appeared to need the fare more than the other aggressive hustlers. After agreeing to a flat $18.00 for the trip, Pedro grabbed Mark's bag while forcibly pulling him through the throng of people congregating around the arrivals area. After leaving the airport a visitor's first exposure to Venezuela on the drive to the Caracas metropolitan area is of barren hills and carbon monoxide filled tunnels that penetrate the high mountains from the coast to the inland city. Depending upon the congestion and degree of bumper-to-bumper confusion the 19 miles from the airport to Caracas can take anywhere from 40 minutes to 2 hours. During the drive the visitor is soon exposed to the expanse of hillside dwellings known locally as *Ranchos* that clutter and cling to the mountains between the coast and the capital. Literally thousands of Venezuela's poor, estimated at 80% of the population, are crammed into makeshift houses perched precariously on the open hillsides one on top of another with no running water or sanitation facilities. Electricity is cleverly and illegally tapped from the power lines that pass through the area.

The low price of gasoline and diesel fuel is evidenced by the hundreds of cars and trucks that appear like ants at a picnic and further confirmed by the massive traffic jams that must be tolerated when entering the city. Having successfully endured the one hour drive from the airport to the U.S. Embassy Mark was pleased to see the *Stars & Stripes* flying from a fortress type building just off one of the downtown boulevards in Central Caracas. A cluster of buildings surrounded by high fences and roving surveillance cameras made up the Embassy complex. One building situated to the left obviously housed the visa section as evidenced by a long line of people waiting their turn. Patient souls all waiting for interviews that hopefully would lead to successful immigration status and their legal entry into the United States. To the right of the main complex was a large multi-storied building partially shielded from the public eye. The building, protected by a high steel fence and a series of checkpoints housed the Diplomatic Mission where the military attaché sections were ensconced. This bastion of American power and influence was shrouded and topped with multiple antennas and aerials. Radio antennas and satellite dishes of the US Army, Navy, Air Force, Coast Guard, FBI, and CIA, along with a host of other secret spy types; all operating clandestinely to keep a covert eye on Venezuela from behind cannon proof glass and reinforced concrete.

After clearing the external security check points Mark found himself inside a bullet proof enclosure explaining to a Marine guard that the purpose of his visit was to see the U.S. Coast Guard Attaché, Lieutenant Commander James McBride. The interrogation and identity check was conducted by a Marine who identified himself as Lance Corporal Billy Larrabee from Little Rock, Arkansas. Successfully passing security, Larrabee then made a phone call advising McBride that a Mark Kelly was waiting downstairs to see him. In a slow southern drawl Larrabee looked at Mark saying,

"I see from your driver's license y'all are from Puerto Rico. I know Puerto Rico. I was stationed at Rosy Roads before I received orders to report for Embassy duty in Venezuela. I really liked the place especially *them* pretty ladies and the cheap rum. I've only been in Venezuela for a couple of weeks, but it sure beats the hell out of wading through the water after being pushed out of a landing craft and crawling around the sand on Vieques Island."

After relating his views of Rosy Roads the congenial corporal escorted Mark to the 4th deck and introduced him to McBride. While the other services, Army, Air Force and Navy had Captains or full Colonels as their attachés Mark was surprised to find that McBride was of such a junior grade. As a Lieutenant Commander McBride had only achieved the minimum rank that permitted him to be posted as an attaché, but clearly had friends in high places or a mentor somewhere in the government who had been instrumental in his appointment to prestigious embassy duty. McBride's' uniform was crisp and well tailored, but displayed few military ribbons awarded for Coast Guard missions and accomplishments. Motioning to a chair for Mark to sit, his shifty eyes darted round the room seemingly uncomfortable with direct eye contact.

"Good Morning Commander, I'm Mark Kelly the naval architect assigned to the *Sundowner* case. You'll recall we spoke on the phone about the U.S. flag catamaran that stranded at Los Testigos and the possibility of meeting up with the master and crew before they returned to the States."

Leaning back in his chair to gain access to a file drawer in his desk McBride withdrew a folder placing it in front of him,

"Of course I remember our conversation. As there wasn't any need for them to remain in Caracas Mr. Johnson and his mate Mr. Miller were able to catch an earlier flight to Miami and left yesterday. I've taken their notarized statements and made a copy for you."

After a few minutes reviewing the statements and looking at a number of photos taken by the Venezuelan Coastguard Mark realized that a visit to Los Testigos wouldn't be necessary as the yacht had been destroyed in the grounding. The only remaining part of the catamaran was a small piece of her transom showing a portion of the vessel's name *Sundown...* The notarized statements that McBride had taken were complete and contained the details of the *Sundowner's* last few minutes as a whole boat.

The statements indicated the vessel's last plotted position, date, time, speed, and the other normal boiler-plate navigational details. Both statements confirmed that the cause of the stranding had been because Bill Miller, who was at the helm at 0200 hours on the morning of the stranding didn't actually know the vessel's true position. Miller, being off course by some 2 nautical miles caused the *Sundowner* to go aground on the out-lying reef at Los Testigos Island. Miller said that they had attempted to back-off the reef with the main engines and then tried to kedge the vessel free using her anchors, but their efforts were unsuccessful in the heavy seas. It appeared the owner had made an effort to save the vessel after the stranding and to mitigate the damages, but she'd broken up in the surf. There obviously wasn't anything left of the vessel to inspect. As the loss was a result of a navigational error, unless other evidence to the contrary surfaced a claim of total loss would be covered under the hull and machinery policy. Getting up from his chair McBride slowly meandered around his desk while momentary glancing at a photograph of President Bush on the office wall,

"You know in my speaking with the two they appeared to be genuine. Miller was clearly embarrassed in not paying attention to the course they'd set from St. George's, Grenada to Margarita, but after hitting the reef realized there wasn't anything more he could do but get ashore. My reading of the two based on a number of years in the Coast Guard which was on board everything from a Point Class up to a Medium Endurance Cutter is that there wasn't anything suspicious in the loss of the catamaran. The Venezuelan Coastguard on Los Testigos reported that they searched the shoreline and the remains of the wreckage for drugs or other contraband, but didn't find anything. I had our LEGAT, the Legal Attaché who's the FBI guy here at the Embassy run them through EPIC, the El Paso Intelligence Center and their Local and State law enforcement agencies and the reports came back clean. Both the owner and his crewman apparently were pillars of the community - no problems with narcotics, no records and no warrants." Returning to his desk McBride turned and with a smirk said,

"The only item in the owner's background check that might lead me to question his honesty and integrity was a note that he was a personal friend of George Bush, but as George Herbert Walker Bush is my Commander-in-Chief, I'll leave it at that."

Mark stood up preparing to leave when McBride held up his hand asking if he might have a few minutes to discuss another subject. Returning his chair Mark said, "Fire away."

"Yesterday when I was preparing the Situation Report about the *Sundowner* I called Washington and mentioned that you were coming to investigate the loss, I found that you've got quite a reputation with the Flags at headquarters. I spoke with Admiral Dicker who told me that you're a Commander in the Coast Guard Reserve working in the intelligence section. Dicker said that for a number of years you've also been actively involved with the British Coastguard and the U.S. Coast Guard Auxiliary. He said you'd been instrumental in developing dependable sources that's resulted in a reliable and trustworthy *intelligence* pipeline for the Coast Guard and a number of other foreign law enforcement agencies in the Caribbean and Latin America."

With obvious satisfaction Mark smiled and replied,

"You're quite thorough. That's right, I've been in the Reserves for the last 15 years and because of the nature of my work as a naval architect and marine investigator have on occasion had the need to cooperate and assist international law enforcement which in turn has shall we say, opened some doors for the U.S. Coast Guard. Why do you ask?"

McBride stood and again briefly gazing at the picture of Bush said,

"The Venezuelan Navy and Coastguard could really use your skills and expertise in their organizational and management development. They're one of our biggest suppliers of oil and if we can assist and strengthen their military establishments they might become an even stronger ally and a better friend of the U.S."

Turning in his chair for direct eye contact with McBride,

"But what's this got to do with me?"

"You've got a proven record in intelligence gathering. In addition to founding, organizing and then training the Coast Guard Auxiliary units in the U.S. Virgin Islands you were instrumental in the creation of search and rescue units in the British, French and Dutch Caribbean islands. You then followed through with some top-notch liaison with the various governments to obtain their cooperation and support for the United States. I understand that in 1983 the Dutch government even made a recommendation to the U.S. State Department that you be appointed the Honorary Consul of the United States for the Dutch Caribbean islands of St. Maarten, Saba and St. Eustatius. There's no question that what you've done has proven to be an unquestionable benefit to the United States and particularly to the Coast Guard. Would you be willing to consider a similar mission for the U.S. Coast Guard in Venezuela?"

"That's a big order Commander. The work I've done in the past has been supported by some pretty influential people and I couldn't have accomplished anything without their support. Derek Ancona a retired British Royal Navy Commander and the Chief of Her Majesty's Coastguard in London helped me in by-passing and cutting the red-tape so I could get the training materials needed for the British Dependencies. Admiral Ben Stabile who at the time was Vice Commandant of the U.S. Coast Guard and Capt. Bruce Beran who later was promoted to Admiral and became Pacific Maritime Commander were my mentors with the Coast Guard training efforts in the Caribbean. When we were getting started Ben told me to prepare a *wish-list* of what I needed which allowed me to by-pass the normal bureaucracy. Bruce was the motivation behind the Antillean Sea Rescue Unit in Sint Maarten. After the Unit was formed he and his wife Connie actually came to Sint Maarten for the commencement ceremonies, which was a first for the Coast Guard. After the ball got rolling it required countless hours of preparation and coordination with the various governments to get everyone reading from the same page. What you're asking me to do would be quite a task with even greater responsibility considering a country the size of Venezuela. If I were to agree to accept the mission what help would you be willing to provide?"

Pondering his reply McBride said,

"Whatever you need we'll get it for you. Please think about it and if you've got the time I'd like you to meet Nicholas Toschenko. Toschenko is a Captain in the Venezuelan Coastguard who regularly bugs me to death about getting the U.S. Coast Guard to help in providing training and support. He's also a close friend of Rear Admiral Jose Antonio Blanes, the Commandant of the

Venezuelan Coastguard. Toschenko is an interesting character, he was born in Venezuela, but his grand-father was an officer in the Czar's army. His family later moved to Bulgaria where his father, who trained as an engineer, became an officer in the Red Army. After World War II the family immigrated to Venezuela. Toschenko also has, let's say, a side job as an advisor to MARAVEN, a subsidiary of PDVSA, the Venezuelan National Oil Company. I think the best way to describe Nicholas is that he's a mover and shaker and well connected. He's very close to the Commandant and through some distant family ties is also related to a number of the Navy's Admirals. Toschenko is trying to develop a Venezuelan Coastguard Reserve and Auxiliary force based on what the U.S. Coast Guard has with one exception; the fledgling Venezuelan Coast Guard Auxiliary is actually a Para-military arm of the regular Coastguard which is a branch of the Navy. Like our Auxiliary the officer corps and enlisted ranks are made up of volunteers, but the Venezuelan Auxiliary has a high level of law enforcement authority. The Venezuelan Navy want the Reserves and Auxiliary trained so they can be brought into play to suppress possible civil unrest or even a coup d'état. If you'd be willing to accept the mission it would provide the U.S. Government with a reliable source of intelligence from someone who's on the *inside* and with direct access to the military establishment. The connection would be good for us and the Venezuelan Navy. As the Coast Guard Attaché along with the support of another interested agency at the Embassy, we're in a position to provide whatever assistance you might need. Here's Toschenko's contact information, you'll be able to reach him at one of theses three phone numbers. The first number is his direct line. Think about it and let's keep in touch."

Out of curiosity to see exactly what Captain Toschenko had in mind after leaving the embassy and checking in at the Euro Building Hotel, Mark called the first number on the list.

"Commander it's kind of you to call. McBride told me that you were in town and would be telling you of our needs. I was hoping to hear from you. I'm in my office at MARAVEN, in Chuao which is only 5 minutes from your hotel. Would it be possible to meet so we might speak?"

His accent was thick and heavy confirming McBride's comments that Captain Toschenko's origins were that of a White Russian family from the former Soviet Union.

"McBride and I spoke briefly about the Coastguard and how I might be able to assist you. What you're doing for the naval forces is quite commendable. I'm here on other business and thought I'd have to go to Los Testigos today or tomorrow, but now find I won't have to go after all. Where exactly is your office located?"

Hoping that Mark wouldn't change his mind, Toschenko quickly responded,

"Please come to the front door of the Euro Building hotel, I'll send a car and driver to collect you in 10 minutes."

"Okay, I'll look for your driver."

The meeting in Toschenko's office began at 1500 hours and ended shortly after 1900. Toschenko began with a long dissertation of the background and history of the Navy and Coastguard while frequently referring to a number of charts spread across his desk. The charts showed where Navy and Coastguard bases were positioned along the Venezuelan coast with a description of patrol vessels and the personnel who manned them. The charts also indicated the number of Navy and Coastguard officers and sailors that were deployed at each naval station. Toschenko said the flow of narcotics from Colombia was steadily increasing because the Coastguard's interdiction efforts were ineffective, in part because they were being compromised as a result of corrupt members of the Venezuelan military who were receiving payments from the drug cartels. Toschenko believed that because of government corruption and certain rebellious army officers there was the possibility of civil unrest or even a coup d'état. Toschenko said it was important that the Navy and the Coastguard be ready to defend the country if necessary.

After the lengthy meeting the two naval officers enjoyed an excellent dinner at La Estancia, an outstanding Argentinean restaurant in Chacao in central Caracas. Over dinner Toschenko told Mark that even though the democratically elected government was said to be corrupt and was institutionally dysfunctional he had sworn to uphold the law and had unwavering support of the Constitution. In addition to being a technical advisor to the national oil company he was also a Coastguard Officer who was committed to protecting the country's sea lanes against all aggressors which placed him in the forefront of the war on drugs.

In September 1991 at the request of the U.S. Coast Guard Attaché and under the direction of Headquarters in Washington, Mark agreed and accepted the assignment for the mission to assist in the training of the Venezuelan Coastguard. Two weeks after their initial meeting Toschenko called,

"Good morning Commander this is Nicholas Toschenko. I hope that you are well. I'm looking forward to your return to Caracas, how soon can you come?"

"Hello Nicholas it's nice of you to call. I've been busy working on some ideas for you to consider regarding the training. I've put together a general outline and proposal of what I believe would work as a model for the Venezuelan reorganization and training initiative. I'll finish the drafts this week and if it's convenient I'll plan to return to Caracas on Wednesday the 12th. I've booked the American flight from San Juan, but have it on hold until I could confirm it with you. My flight is scheduled to arrive at 1340 hours, is this okay with you?"

"Yes, Wednesday the 12th is fine. I've spoken with the Commandant and he's anxious to meet with you as soon as possible. I'll pick you up at Maiquetia and wait for you outside Aduanas. It's only a ten minute drive from Maiquetia to Coastguard Headquarters in La Guaira."

———

On Wednesday the 12th American Airlines upgraded Mark to Business Class which made the short flight even nicer. Outside the arrivals hall Mark found Toschenko waiting for him in his Class 'A' uniform. He welcomed Mark with a traditional Russian bear hug which promptly bent the frames of Mark's Ray Ban sun glasses hanging from a light cord around his neck.

"Commander it's wonderful to see you again. I've made arrangements for us to meet with the Commandant and he's looking forward to meeting you. Admiral Jose Antonio Blanes is

a pure navy type who works by the book and won't tolerate any loose ends. He has a passion for excellence. Even though he's an Admiral, he wants his people to work with him not just for him."
While walking towards his car in the airport parking lot Toschenko continued talking,
"The Venezuelan Coastguard is new, as I told you it was only created a short time ago as a branch of the Navy and that's why we need help. Jose Antonio has virtually transformed the Comando de Guardacostas from a somewhat non-descript branch of the Armada into a well disciplined and proud sea service. Together we're trying to create a Coastguard Reserve and Auxiliary Command modeled after those in Britain and the United States. Your help will make the difference in making our dreams come true for Venezuela. Last year I was able to attend the U.S. Coast Guard training facility in Yorktown, Virginia and brought back some good ideas. From what I've seen the British Coastguard is a bit different to what we might need in Venezuela, but maybe a combination of the British and the U.S. Coast Guard Reserve and Auxiliary would be good for us. What do you think?"
Mark smiled, looking at Toschenko's crisp white uniform with its glistening gold shoulder boards and other appointments felt ever so humble.
"Nicholas I believe our first objective should be to determine exactly what the Admiral wants as to the precise purpose and mission of his reserve and auxiliary forces. Based on what I've learned from you, McBride and my experiences elsewhere, I've put together a draft proposal for the Admiral's consideration. As I see it the first step would be the implementation of the organizational and management structure. This would include the different command levels and the operational groups responsible for boarding's related to interdiction, search and rescue, vessel inspection, aids to navigation, training, and so on. I have also included a critical path analysis of the training programs with a proposed time frame for the accomplishment of each of the tasks. It's important that each step we take and before we take it, should be approved by the Admiral or the Coastguard's Executive Officer."

Toschenko, briefly glancing at the outline with a quizzical look on his face said, "Vessel inspection, what's that?"

"The vessel inspection program is focused on the assessment of fire fighting and other safety and life saving equipment that must be onboard ships and yachts to comply with their Flag State Regulations. Shipmaster's and the crews regularly undergo these compliance inspections by Port State Control and Coastguards so they never give them much thought. Vessel inspections are also a guise for Coastguard personnel to board yachts and ships to see if they might be engaged in trafficking narcotics or transporting illegal aliens. During these inspections a trained Coastguard inspector always observes and notes the demeanor of the crew while looking for altered structures including compartments or areas that show they may have been recently welded or modified. Inspectors also consider the cargo, the ship's manifest and where the vessel has been or where it's going; if the inspector has any doubts, the ship or yacht should be detained for a more detailed inspection which may include the use of sniffer dogs."

Taking a binder from his briefcase and leafing through the pages while Toschenko drove, Mark told him about the various training subjects, including maintenance logs, fire extinguishers, life jackets, and flares.

"We'll go over all the requirements in more detail later. From what you've told me most of the officers read and speak at least a little English, but the procedures should be translated into Spanish for the non-commissioned officers and sailors who don't."

As Toschenko's Mitsubishi Trooper turned into the Coastguard base at La Guaira the gate opened as the duty officer came to attention and saluted smartly, an acknowledgment that was promptly returned by Toschenko. The headquarters building was painted in the blue and gray colors of the Guardacostas; on the top of the building the National flag of Venezuela and the Comando de Guardacostas fluttered in the fresh easterly breeze. The Admiral's office was located on the third deck. As they approached the Admiral's yeoman rose from his desk and snapped to attention rendering a crisp salute.

"Gentlemen please come this way the Admiral is expecting you.

May I bring you refreshments, coffee or a cold drink?"
Mark replied,
"Some of your excellent Venezuelan coffee would be just fine, black please."
"And you Captain Toschenko?"
"Coffee will be fine."
Rear Admiral Jose Antonio Blanes, Commandant of the Venezuelan Coastguard was a handsome, lean and self assured officer who had the bearing and demeanor of one accustomed to being in charge. His smartly tailored white uniform was complimented by shoulder-boards decorated with the gold embellishments of those of flag rank. The Admiral had neatly groomed hair showing a touch of gray and a tanned face, he smiled as they entered his office.
"Nicholas it's a pleasure to see you again, how is your wife and daughter? And your son Nicholas is he progressing with his studies at the Naval Academy?"
"Thank you for asking Admiral, the family is well and Nicholas Junior is still struggling with the intricacies of celestial navigation. Admiral, please allow me to introduce Commander Mark Kelly, an officer of the U.S. Coast Guard in Puerto Rico. Commander Kelly is the gentleman that the U.S. Coast Guard Attaché Jim McBride spoke with you about."
The Admiral smiled and extending his hand said,
"Welcome to the headquarters of the Venezuelan Coastguard, it is an honor to have you here. After learning of your work for the U.S. Coast Guard in the Caribbean, I have been looking forward to your visit."
After shaking hands the three sat down.
"Sir, it is I who is honored to have been asked to participate in helping the Navy with their endeavors in the organization and training of the Coastguard's Reserve and Auxiliary forces. I understand that you are personally acquainted with our Commandant, Admiral J. W. Kime and therefore will be well informed of the benefits that a strong reserve and auxiliary can provide to the regular forces. In the United States the number of reservists and auxiliary actually outnumber the regular Coast Guard. Without the assistance of the Reserve and Auxiliary the

U.S. Coast Guard could not fully perform or carryout their increasing number of missions."

The Admiral stood and walking to the window overlooking a row of ex-U.S. Coast Guard Cutters donated by Washington, turned and said,

"Yes, I have spoken with your Commandant as well as with Admiral Paul Wilding, the Atlantic Maritime Commander both are impressed with your work in Latin America and the Caribbean. From your experience and professional training in the maritime field and with the leadership and organizational skills that you've demonstrated within the U.S. Coast Guard, I hope that with Captain Toschenko's enthusiasm and support, you can do the same for my command."

The Admiral, radiant with enthusiasm carefully detailed his ideas of the programs that he wanted to introduce and adapt for the Venezuelan Coastguard and her Reserve and Auxiliary forces. He clearly had done his homework as many of the programs mirrored those of the U.S. Coast Guard. Mark handed the Admiral a letter of introduction and the Proposal which he'd prepared in anticipation of the meeting suggesting the organizational and command structure of the Venezuelan Coastguard Auxiliary and Reserve forces. The Proposal included a synopsis and general overview of the program including a Critical Path Analysis and timetable detailing how the mission could be accomplished within a given time frame. In expressing his pleasure and appreciation of the proposal the Admiral was ecstatic,

"Commander this is outstanding."

The Admiral then summoned his yeoman asking that he call Capitán de Fragata Bravo Mayo and request that he come to his office. As a Capitán de Fragata, the equivalent rank of a U.S. Coast Guard Commander, Bravo Mayo was the Coastguard's Executive Officer who reported directly to the Admiral and was responsible for day-to-day operations.

"Capitán please allow me to introduce Commander Mark Kelly from the U.S. Coast Guard Greater Antilles Section in Puerto Rico. Mr. Kelly will be working with us at headquarters in the development of our Reserve and Auxiliary forces to enhance the effectiveness of our regular forces. I would like you to work out the details of implementation with Nicholas and Commander Kelly and keep me informed. Commander Kelly will work with my full authority and is to have the full cooperation of all members of the Comando de Guardacostas."

Mark returned to Venezuela two weeks later during which time he and Toschenko communicated frequently by phone and fax. To kick off the training programs Toschenko had made arrangements for Mark to speak at the next joint dinner meeting of the ANDM, the *Asociación Nacional Marinos Deportivos*. The meeting would also be attended by members of the Coastguard Auxiliary Group Picua. The Picua group while headquartered in Caracas had their operational facilities in the port city of Carenero, a two hour drive to the east. The meeting was attended by twenty auxiliaries from the Grupo Picua and another fifteen men and women who were officers from other Commands of the regular Coastguard. The ANMD was a maritime organization made up of individuals and companies whose support and goal was to make available and provide basic educational programs to the recreational boating public of Venezuela. The Venezuelan Coastguard Auxiliary and the ANMD had parallel and overlapping objectives which provided both organizations with a blended membership.

The meeting began with a short welcome speech by the ANMD's President Edwin Neufeld, who then turned the podium over to Toschenko. While Toschenko was speaking Neufeld whispered that Mark should know that in addition to his responsibilities with the Coastguard, Nicholas was also the ANMD's National Operations Director. Toschenko was eloquent in his dissertation elaborating on the progress made over the last year while emphasizing the need for a strong and well trained Auxiliary. Toschenko then introduced Mark.

"My friends and distinguished colleagues I am pleased to introduce Commander Mark Kelly, an Officer of the United States Coast Guard in Puerto Rico. Commander Kelly has offered to help us bring our dreams of a professional, well trained Coastguard Reserve and Auxiliary to reality. Mr. Kelly and I have met with Contralmirante Jose Antonio Blanes who has ordered the full cooperation and support of the Guardacostas and the Armada."

Mark stood and raising his right hand to his forehead saluted the group then turning slightly, saluted Toschenko. Obviously pleased, Toschenko smiled and started clapping the group stood and followed Toschenko's lead with enthusiastic applause. After two hours of intense questions, answers and a continual flow of La Selecta, the premier Venezuelan rum, the pressures of a motivated and enthusiastic audience began to take its toll. Arriving back at the Euro Building hotel Toschenko pressed for them to have a night-cap, Mark politely declined opting instead for a cappuccino.

———

Upon Mark's return to Puerto Rico in addition to keeping up with the demands of his marine practice, he continued drafting the text of a short test and preparing the format for the various subjects that would be covered in the Venezuelan Coastguard's training manual. Nelly Ortiz, Mark's dependable and ever reliable secretary who, in spite of her other responsibilities worked tirelessly to translate the test and other materials from English into Spanish. With both hoping that the fractured Puerto Rican Spanish would reasonably resemble the Spanish spoken and written in Venezuela. Toschenko and Mark were of the same mind that before starting with the training in Venezuela they should first determine the level of knowledge and skills of their students. It would be foolish to start classes at the 6th grade level when the students may be ready for post graduate work. As the program progressed Admiral Blanes and Capitán Bravo Mayo continued to provide Kelly with advice and assistance with technical matters relating to course subjects or compliance with existing governmental and naval regulations. Both overwhelming supported the mission. The support was first evidenced when the Admiral authorized the use of the Escuela de Guardacostas, the Coastguard School located at headquarters in La Guaira for the Auxiliary and Reserve training classes.

As the training cycles expanded increasing numbers of officers, petty officers and sailors of the regular Venezuelan Coastguard were included in the classes. The initial training classes began in La Guaira but soon progressed to other naval installations throughout the country in Maracaibo, Punto Fijo, Puerto Cabello, Puerto la Cruz, and Isla Margarita. The first tests administered in La Guaira and later at other facilities revealed a sound level of knowledge and comprehension of basic nautical skills while exposing an overwhelming eagerness and enthusiasm to learn. The passion to learn and the thirst for knowledge demonstrated by the pupils would best be defined as *total commitment*.

———

Even though temporarily relieved of his duties as a U.S. Coast Guard Reserve Intelligence Officer, Mark still had to earn a living practicing as a naval architect so his visits to Venezuela were scheduled every two weeks and limited to five days. Arriving on a midday flight from San Juan he would be met by Toschenko who would drive him to either La Guaira or other locations where training would immediately commence and many times ending after midnight. At 0600 hours the following morning Toschenko or a navy car and driver would collect Mark from his hotel and take him to Higuerote where, at the Carenero Yacht Club, on-the-water-training would commence.

On the 5th of December 1991 in recognition of the successful training efforts, the Board of Directors of the ANMD presented Mark with a Diploma of Excellence for his collaboration and educational support of the Venezuelan Maritime Services. During the second week of January 1992 Mark found himself busy training the Coastguard in Maracaibo, located in the eastern region of Venezuela. The heavily guarded Coastguard Base on Lake Maracaibo protected this important region due to the oil terminals located on the eastern shore of the lake. Coastguard protection of Lake Maracaibo and the Gulf of Venezuela was crucial because of the increase in narcotics trafficking that was known to pass through the area. The sectors to the west and north of Maracaibo were also important military regions because of the penetration of rebels loyal to Colombia's National Liberation Army (ELN) and the Revolutionary Armed Forces of Colombia, known by its Spanish acronym FARC. Because of its remoteness and open border, the ELN and FARC regularly used the area around San Antonio and Castilletes on the Guajira Peninsula for the over-ground movement of arms and the delivery of large consignments of drugs from Colombia to the coast. From Castilletes the drugs would then be delivered by go-fasts to the ABC islands or to ships waiting offshore.

———

Following a crew briefing, two unmarked Coastguard patrol vessels departed the Maracaibo Naval Base in calm seas under a cloudless sky. The first vessel a 38' Scarab Interceptor powered by twin 1,000 hp engines, identified as Charlie Golf Tango was under the command of Captain Toschenko with a crew of three. The second vessel a 42' Fountain Lightning, with twin 1,100 hp engines, identified as Charlie Golf Zulu was under the command of Commander Mark Kelly, it also had a crew of three. CG Tango was to proceed offshore to the eastern perimeter of Lake Maracaibo while CG Zulu would engage in surveillance of the western shoreline. Both vessels were equipped with radar scanners and the crews carried side arms. Once in position CG Tango and CG Zulu would patrol and conduct surveillance northward around the Gulf of Venezuela and rendezvous at the naval facility at Las Piedras. Twenty minutes after departure Charlie Golf Tango made the first VHF radio call.
"Guardia Nacional Golfo de Venezuela ésta es Guardacostas CG Tango ¿copia?
"Guardia Nacional Golfo de Venezuela this is Coastguard CG Tango do you copy?"
"CG Zulu this is CG Tango, do you copy?"
"CG Tango that's affirmative." Toschenko then radioed,
"We have a go-fast 4 miles at 11 o'clock. Radar track indicates a course for Aruba. A Guardia Nacional vessel appears to be shadowing, but does not respond to our calls; will stop and board go-fast for inspection, request CG Zulu stand-by for back-up."
"CG Tango that's affirmative, CG Zulu standing by."
Now on a plane and running at full speed CG Tango was quickly closing on the go-fast. When CG Tango was about one mile from the go-fast the Guardia Nacional patrol boat then took a position

between CG Tango and the go-fast then in English, radioed,
"CG Tango this is Guardia Nacional Maritima Mike Echo
Foxtrot, you are to stand down. The vessel of interest is
proceeding with our permission. You are ordered not to interfere.
Please confirm." As the Guardia Nacional patrol boat had a
canon on her foredeck and the crew was armed with automatic
weapons the Coastguard was obviously out gunned so standing
down was clearly a good idea.
"Mike Echo Foxtrot affirmative."
"CG Zulu did you copy?"
"CG Tango affirmative"
"CG Tango will abort, returning to base."
After the vessels had been secured and the crews released Kelly
and Toschenko met in the officer's mess.
"What the hell was that all about? The go-fast definitely had
something on board they shouldn't have been carrying, but when
we attempt to board them the Guardia Nacional tells us to get
lost. Nicholas, please tell me what kind of bull-shit is this?"
"Mark, this is a problem that we've been faced with for some
time. Naval Intelligence knows that there are a number of
National Guard Officers that are involved with narcotics
trafficking and we've just met one of them. These same Guardia
Nacional characters are also suspected of selling arms to the
Colombian rebels. The head of the Naval Intelligence Section is
Admiral José Dante, who is my second cousin. Last summer my
family and I were at his home for a barbecue and we were talking
like you American's say, *off-the-record*. My cousin told me that
the corruption in the Guardia Nacional especially their Unidad
Maritima, is getting worse because so much money is changing
hands. He knows that payoffs are being made to the senior
officers in Caracas and to the commanding officers of maritime
commands throughout the entire country. He learned that Ernesto
Lopez, the CO of Detachment 76 of the Guardia Nacional Unidad
Maritima in Isla Margarita recently purchased an expensive
condominium in Porlamar and along with a $400,000.00 mansion
in Caracas he also bought a new Mercedes. Because Lopez
couldn't possibly do this on the salary of a Teniente Coronel
Dante had Lopez put under surveillance; from the Colonel's

travel records he learned that early last year Lopez began visiting Caracas every Friday and meets with an American diplomat at the Golf Club. As Margarita is a major drug transshipment point seizures were pretty regular before Lopez and the American started meeting, but after their meetings the seizures abruptly stopped. My cousin had one of his staff call the Embassy, but the switchboard operator only said that the American was a commercial attaché. Dante's sure that the attaché line is only a cover for his side business of transporting drugs. This seems to fit and why we have to be careful because the Commanding General of the Guardia Nacional in Caracas is attempting to take away our law enforcement responsibilities and keep the Guardacostas out of drug interdiction."

Clearly bewildered Mark looked at Toschenko,

"If the Guardia Nacional is in the business of narcotics trafficking with the support of the U.S. government it really doesn't make much sense for us to continue the training. We go out, get ready to nail a trafficker, but then have to stand down because the Guardia Nacional is protecting them. Nicholas we're wasting our time. It's common knowledge that for at least the last 10 years Guardia Nacional General Ramon Guillen Davila has been on the CIA's payroll and storing drugs in a warehouse built and owned by the CIA for shipments to the U.S, but what you're telling me now is that the entire Guardia Nacional is on the payroll. This is crazy."

"Mark I understand your frustration, but we've got to keep at it. Every time it happens we must make a report to the Commandant so he can follow up with the Minister of Defense. I think if we press on and keep doing our job the situation may hopefully change."

Disillusioned, Mark decided that the Guardia Nacional's involvement in narcotics-trafficking and efforts to curtail the drug interdiction program needed to be addressed with his superiors in a face-to-face meeting. The meeting was scheduled for the morning of February 4th 1992 at naval headquarters located in the San Bernardino section of Caracas. If the Guardia Nacional problem could be resolved Mark was confident that the interdiction program could be effectively expanded and continued throughout 1992 and beyond. But then on February 4th there was a problem.

The meeting at Naval Headquarters abruptly ended when tanks and ground forces under the command of Lieutenant Colonel Hugo Chàvez attacked the Miraflores Palace in an attempted coup focused on the overthrow of the government of Carlos Andres Perez. In addition to Chàvez, who orchestrated the coup, the other principals involved in the plot were Lieutenant Colonels Francisco Arias Cardenas, Joel Acosta Chirinos, Jesus Urdaneta Hernandez, and Jesus Ortiz Contreras. Following his surrender Lieutenant-Colonel Hugo Chàvez spoke on Venezuela's National TV, his words translated from Spanish read: *"First and foremost, I would like to say good morning to the People of Venezuela. This Bolivarian message is directed to the valiant soldiers of the Parachute Regiment of Aragua and the Armored Brigade of Valencia. Comrades at arms, regrettably for now our objectives and goals in the Capital City were not accomplished, that is to say, we here in Caracas were not able to take power. All of you did very well, but it is now time to reflect as there will be new situations because our country must head towards a better destiny. So hear my words, hear Commandant Chàvez who gives this message, please reflect and lay down your arms because now our planned objectives on a national level are impossible to accomplish. Comrades at Arms listen to my message of solidarity. I appreciate your loyalty, I appreciate your bravery and courage; and I, before the country and before all of you assume the responsibility of this military Bolivarian movement."*

The bloody coup was unsuccessful, but immediately gave Chàvez folk hero status with the country's poor.

On March 5th Mark returned to Caracas to resume the meeting that had ended prematurely in February. While acknowledging the problems with the Guardia Nacional the Admirals could not provide a positive resolution, but said the matter would be studied by the Minister of Defense and his advisors. In spite of being unable to resolve the Guardia Nacional problem Mark was pleased when Admiral Blanes told him he had been awarded a permanent commission as a Captain in the Venezuelan Navy and Coastguard Command.

In addition to the officers commission he was to become the Senior Policy Advisor to the Commandant - Coastguard Command of the Venezuelan Navy. Knowing that U.S. Citizens aren't permitted to become members of a foreign military, Mark called Admiral Dicker at U.S. Coast Guard Headquarters and was surprised when Dicker told him that *Washington* had no objections and had willingly approved of his officers' commission in Venezuela's Naval Forces.

———

After accepting the commission from Admiral Blanes and receiving his personal congratulations Mark went to the Coastguard's Office of Personnel Registration where he was given a medical examination, had a blood sample taken to determine blood type and was photographed and fingerprinted. He then received his new military ID card identifying him as an officer in the ARMADA DE VENEZUELA. Returning to the third deck he took the opportunity to give Admiral Blanes a copy of the newly completed Coastguard Reserve and Auxiliary training manual he'd brought from Puerto Rico. Copies of the Auxiliary manual were reproduced by the Navy and within two weeks had been distributed to all Coastguard Commands throughout Venezuela. Also in March Mark was surprised when Rear Admiral Robert E. Kramek then Commander of the U.S. Coast Guard's Seventh District in Miami, who later became Commandant of the U.S. Coast Guard, sent Mark a Certificate of Appreciation *For his continuing support of Coast Guard Programs and Missions.*
Mark found that Admiral Blanes had another surprise in store for him when on June 12th 1992 the Commandant awarded Captain Mark Kelly the *HONOR AL MERITO - Order of Naval Merit - First Class* for his services to the Venezuelan Navy and Coastguard. In his acceptance speech, not normally being at a loss for words, Mark struggled for the appropriate terminology to adequately express his appreciation and gratitude. Mere words seemed inadequate for this immeasurable honor that the Minister of Defense and the Commandant had bestowed upon him during the formal presentation ceremony. Because the award had been

given to an American citizen the event was covered by the national press and Venezuela's television networks. The intensive media coverage was because the *Order of Naval Merit* is normally only awarded to Venezuelan citizens who are serving members of the armed forces. When Jim McBride who had not been invited to the formal ceremonies at Navy Headquarters learned of the citation he phoned Mark that evening at his hotel.

"Mark congratulations on receiving the *HONOR AL MERITO*, you know the commendation is on a par with our Navy Cross. I don't think anyone outside of the Venezuelan military has ever received the medal." Then in the same breath McBride said,

"I'd like to ask a favor. Next time you're with the Admiral maybe you could suggest he might consider me for the decoration. I know you've got a lot of pull with the Venezuelan Flags and if I were to be awarded the medal it would really look good in my personnel records."

Being a bit surprised and flattered by the request,

"Jim that's a big order, I don't know what the Admiral's reaction might be, but I'll mention it if the opportunity presents itself."

The following month Mark was invited to a cocktail party at McBride's home in Caracas, the guest list included the Commandant, a gaggle of Admirals and Generals who commanded the Army, Navy, Air Force, and National Guard, and a sprinkling of government ministers. Mark, waiting patiently until Blanes had consumed his usual two drinks, knowing that during public functions the Admiral never consumed more than two scotch and waters and believing at the time that he was a friend, casually asked if Jim McBride had ever been considered for the Order of Naval Merit? The Admiral smiled and gently placing his arm on Mark's shoulder said,

"Captain, this Citation is only awarded to exceptional sailors and marines who have clearly demonstrated a service to the navy, service that is above and beyond the call of duty. Because of your dedication and effort you were commissioned as an officer in my command and earned the Citation. When the time comes that McBride spends more, or at least the same amount of time helping the Venezuelan Coastguard as he does playing tennis, I might consider it. The same goes for John Hill. When Captain

Hill, the U.S. Navy Attaché spends less time with our Navy's junior officers on the golf course and more time dealing with our procurement requests, he too may be considered."

Oops, realizing that he'd struck a sensitive nerve Mark knew it was best to drop the subject and let McBride do his own bidding. The Admiral then went further,

"You know this isn't only a Navy problem, General Martinez, who commands the Venezuelan Air Force tells me he has the same problem with the U.S. Air Force. At least three times a week Colonel Graham, the Air Force Attaché is determined to tee off by 1000 hours then immediately after the game he's at the bar. He apparently has a high capacity with low tolerance. I understand that last Wednesday he was so inebriated that his aide had to virtually drag the Colonel to his car."

Mark was to later learn from Toschenko that the Admiral wasn't the only person who wasn't overly impressed with Jim McBride and the assistance that he was supposed to be providing to the Venezuelan Coastguard. Over lunch one day in Carenero when his name came up Toschenko referred to McBride as a *Pippisote,* an unflattering Venezuelan comparison of a man to the male sex organ.

––––––

The following week Renaldo Perez, Commander of the Coastguard's Auxiliary and Reserve forces on Margarita Island contacted Mark to see when he would be available to provide basic training for a number of new members of their auxiliary unit.

"Mark I'd be very grateful if you could schedule us for the training and please bring Mike with you. My daughter Jeanette would like very much to see him again. If you can bring him along he'd have someone to keep him company and entertained while we were involved with the training. We also have plenty of room so during the visit you're more than welcome to stay in one of our guest rooms."

In civilian life Renaldo, after gradating from college in the United States qualified as a Certified Public Accountant and had built a successful practice after returning to Venezuela. Renaldo lived on Margarita Island with his wife Eva and their two children, Jeanette who was 16 and Hector age 14. Their home was a large magnificent penthouse near the Hilton Hotel overlooking the Caribbean. Mike, having met Jeanette and Hector on a previous visit was more than anxious to accompany Mark. While Mike liked playing video games with Hector he was more inclined to spend time with Jeanette, a tall blonde and beautiful young lady. Jeanette with her parent's permission, even though only 16 regularly appeared in television commercials and modeling assignments for cosmetics and bathing suit advertisements. Renaldo said that during their visit Jeanette was having a piano recital and would like Mike to attend.

Packing for the trip included Mark's uniforms, swim suits and Mike's dark blue blazer and tan trousers for the recital. The training mission proved very successful while Mike had a great time at Jeannette's piano recital and even more fun when they later went to the beach. While both were clearly prejudiced, Renaldo and Mark agreed that his beautiful daughter on the arm of a tall well mannered young gentleman from Puerto Rico was quite impressive. After the recital Mike always insisted that he come along on subsequent training missions to Margarita. Because of Jeanette's limited English, Mike told Mark he would always be grateful that he'd insisted he learn Spanish.

———

The visit to Margarita and later to Caracas had been successful and a happy time except for the untimely death of Fermin Yanez and Maria Alonso. Fermin was an active member of the ANMD and a powerhouse in the government hierarchy in Caracas, because of their mutual interests they had become good friends. In addition to his Coastguard responsibilities Fermin was a successful businessman and a creative soul who owned most of the motion picture theaters in Venezuela. During Mark's visits to Caracas they would frequently enjoy dinner together at La Estancia, his favorite restaurant. La Estancia was also the preferred eatery of Venezuela's film directors, producers, actors, and the studios financial backers. While dining, fans and regular customers were able to mingle shoulder to shoulder with the upper crust of Venezuelan society. The diminutive entrepreneur while small in stature; he was only 5'4" and probably weighed no more than 120 pounds when soaking wet, was an intellectual giant. In addition to Coastguard matters he and Mark would often discuss the country's growing political problems and government corruption that was increasing at an alarming rate. Through Fermin's introduction Mark met the glamorous Venezuelan actress Maria Alonso.

As a result of her popularity their passionate and amorous relationship soon became the subject of the gossip columns in Venezuela's national newspaper El Universal. The affair tragically ended when she was murdered along with two of her friends in an attempted car jacking near Plaza Bolivar.

The following month Fermin Yanez died. Along with over a hundred of his friends, business colleagues and fellow coastguards Mark sadly bid him farewell at his funeral in Caracas. Within two months Mark had tragically lost two people that were close to him. He would miss their wisdom, their laughter and their precious friendship.

Mark continued with the training exercises in different parts of the country, but was becoming disillusioned knowing the involvement of the U.S. government and their payments to the Guardia Nacional Unidad Maritima to facilitate the CIA's drug business.

———

On October 1st 1993 Mark attended the regular monthly meeting of the Eastern Puerto Rico Council of the Navy League of the United States held at the Officers Club at Naval Station Roosevelt Roads in Ceiba, Puerto Rico. During the meeting Mark was surprised to learn and flattered when Hector Nieves, the Council President presented him with an engraved wall plaque that was inscribed,

A Special tribute to a Distinguished U.S. Merchant Marine
For his numerous contributions to our Nation and The Navy League of
the United States.

The Officer's Club at Rosy Roads is positioned high on a hill overlooking the Caribbean Sea in an area of the Base known as Bundy. Across from the "O" Club, the Bachelors Officer Quarters or BOQ's provide accommodation to visiting or retired personnel and active duty military officers and pilots. The pilots are either temporarily based at Rosy or from the air-wing components of the various carrier groups who are involved in live-fire training exercises off the coast of the Puerto Rican island of Vieques or engaged in target practice involving drones near St. Croix in the U.S. Virgin Islands.

The large circular bar situated in the center of the Club was generally surrounded by VC-8 helicopter and F-16 pilots unwinding from the day's operational exercises or others reminiscing about their sorties over Iraq during the Gulf War. Many were still dressed in their colorful emblem emblazoned jump-suits, while others relaxed in shorts and island style flowered shirts. Local civilian members of the Navy League were always properly attired in long trousers, shirt and tie or open Guayabera shirts.

Mark's attention was roused when he noticed a scruffy individual lurking in a corner of the Club wearing a poorly tailored suit. The man clearly didn't fit. The man's narrowed eyes kept darting around the room, when Mark looked at him he'd quickly look away. He was alone and didn't speak to anyone, his peculiar behavior made Mark curious as to who he was and why he was in the Club, especially as he appeared to be watching him. As the Director of Military Liaison for the Navy League, Mark had been joined at his table by two navy lieutenants, one the aide to the Base Commander, the other the Commanding Officer of the Sea Cadets unit. The Lieutenants and Mark were engrossed in conversation concerning an award ceremony for the Sea Cadets that would be hosted by the Base Commander. Being attentive to the Lieutenants and focused on the planning of the program Mark lost sight of the man who didn't fit. Towards the end of the meeting and having moved surreptitiously around the room the man approached from behind startling Mark when he put his hand on his shoulder and said,

"Commander may I speak with you privately for a moment."

The two Lieutenants graciously excused themselves and the man sat down.

"My name is Joseph Vela I'm an Attaché and Second Secretary in the Commercial Section at the American Embassy in Caracas. The Embassy has been observing your work with the Venezuelan Navy and is impressed with what you have accomplished. Your efforts have had a very positive effect not only on the diplomatic front, but also in improving the relations between the military establishments of Venezuela and the United States. I have something I'd like to discuss with you, but I don't think that now would be the appropriate time. Would it be possible to meet tomorrow, say for dinner? What I have to discuss with you is very important and crucial to your Venezuelan Mission and to the affairs of the United States."

"Sorry Mr. Vela, I must say I'm curious at what you need to discuss, but unfortunately I'm leaving early tomorrow morning to deal with a case for British underwriters in Panama and won't be returning until next week."

Obviously perturbed in finding that Mark would be away, Vela frowned,

"Okay then when will you be back in Venezuela?"

"I've a meeting scheduled at Naval Headquarters in Caracas in two weeks."

With a curt, "I'll be in touch,"

Vela then vanished amidst the throng of naval officers filling the Club.

Towards the end of October Mark returned to Venezuela to meet with Capitán Bravo Mayo regarding a presentation he was scheduled to give at the Naval War College which would be attended by the Minister of Defense, Generals commanding the Army and Guardia Nacional and Admirals of the Navy. The presentation proved to be a success and through a number of personal introductions gave Mark direct access to a number of key Government Ministers and Venezuela's military hierarchy. Following the reception Mark returned to the Euro Building hotel and found a white envelope that had been slid under the door of his room. The envelope was addressed to Commander Kelly. The return address printed in bold type on the upper left corner indicated the sender to be the Venezuelan-American Chamber of

Commerce – Caracas; the hand-written and unsigned message stated, *I will be in Puerto Rico on November 5, 1993 and would like to meet you at the Navy League meeting to finalize our arrangements.* Mark pondered the message, asking himself, *what arrangements?*

———

At the Navy League meeting on November 5th Mark was busy discussing the budget with Council President Nieves when Vela approached and taping him on the shoulder said,
"Commander it looks like you're still busy, would it be possible for us to meet tomorrow night for dinner? I'd like very much to discuss our mutual interests in Venezuela."
"Sure Mr. Vela tomorrow would be fine. Tonight I am pretty much tied up with Navy League business. Shall we say, 1930 hours here in the 'O' Club?"
At 1925 hours Mark entered the 'O' Club. Vela in the same rumpled suit who a month earlier had introduced himself as a Second Secretary in the Commercial Section of the American Embassy in Caracas was sitting at a corner table picking at a bowl of peanuts.
"Hello Commander I'm pleased to see you, how was the trip to Panama?"
"The trip was successful. I got your note when I was in Caracas. After mentioning *our mutual interests in Venezuela*, I've been looking forward to meeting with you again, but curious as to the *arrangements* you made reference to in your note."
With a mouthful of nuts as pooled saliva drooled from the corner of his mouth Vela began to speak,
"You know our ambassador has been closely monitoring your activities in Venezuela and is impressed with the promotions and the accolades that you've been awarded by the Minister of Defense for what you've done for the Venezuelan Navy and Coastguard. What you've accomplished has been a great service to the United States and has been very positive in fostering our good relations with the Venezuelan government."
Pleased with this apparent praise and that his efforts had not gone unnoticed by the U.S. Embassy, Mark became even more

curious. Then Vela spoke,

"We are particularly interested in learning more about the military, especially the country's naval forces and would like to enlist your help. The Ambassador has spoken a number of times with McBride and Jim's replacement, Commander Gary Soy and both agree that you're the guy who really knows what's going on."

Considering that Vela had contacted him and the introduction had come through the Coast Guard Attaché and the Ambassador, it appeared that whatever *they* needed must be official in nature. Vela, chewing on another handful of nuts he'd crammed into his mouth coughed, then continued speaking,

"As we're both on the same team I want to level with you. I'm not really a commercial attaché I'm the Station Chief of the Central Intelligence Agency assigned to the embassy in Caracas. I use the cover as an Attaché and Second Secretary in the Commercial Section of the Embassy for obvious reasons, reasons I'm sure you understand. Because Venezuela is a major supplier of our oil Washington feels it's essential that we keep a close eye on what's happening in the country to insure that there's no disruption, shall we say, in the *pipeline*. Since the impeachment of Carlos Andres Perez there's been a growing dissatisfaction with the current administration and the problems brought about by the FARC guerillas that are moving freely back and forth across Venezuela's porous border with Colombia."

First glancing at the buffet table Vela said, "Let's get something to eat, dinners on me."

Moving from serving dish to serving dish Vela piled large quantities of food on his plate. To prevent it from falling to the floor he began eating with his fingers while returning to the table. Considering Vela's gluttonous attack on the buffet table it appeared that he may not have eaten for many days. After sitting down he stuffed a handful of prawns into his mouth causing the cocktail sauce to drip onto the red gingham table cloth. Wiping his mouth while still chewing,

"You know you're really lucky to be able to live so close to Rosy Roads and have this great food at such a low price. Good restaurants in Caracas are really expensive."

Gasping for a breath of air between bites Vela continued,

"Please tell me a bit more about what you're doing in Venezuela."

Taking a sip of his iced tea Mark explained,

"After each visit I prepare a detailed report of the training, which includes a list of who attended, where the training took place and the subjects covered. The report is sent to the Commandant of the Venezuelan Coastguard with a copy to Admiral Dicker in Washington. Dicker and I assume others at Headquarters review the reports which as well as providing the details of the training exercises also includes the specifics about staff meetings with the Venezuelan Coastguard and Admirals at the Comandancia de la Armada in Caracas, and at the Naval War College at Mamo. I've brought along some photos and the press clippings of the mission that you might like to see."

On the edge of the table beyond the range of Vela's drip zone Mark opened a large red binder and began leafing through the pages. The binder contained numerous photographs and a document file on the Venezuelan Initiative. Listening intently Vela repeatedly questioned Mark on the persons in the photos and when and where they had been taken. Now gnawing on a large cut of roast beef Vela then acknowledged that he too had seen the reports.

"Mr. Vela I'm curious, if you've seen my reports sent to Washington I don't see any problem in providing you with additional briefings, especially if you're working with the U.S. Coast Guard, but why the duplication?"

Almost choking on the large piece of beef he had unceremoniously stuffed into his mouth, "No, no, no, you've missed the point. First off, I want you to understand that anything and I mean *anything* that we discuss now or in the future must be kept strictly confidential. Anything that we talk about goes no further. Is that understood?"

"It all sounds a bit sinister, but okay."

Vela continued,

"The Venezuelan military is of interest to us because, along with other operations in the area, we also have a big investment in let's say, the import-export business. Not all, but many CIA operations in Latin America are financed by means of the financial return we get through counter-intelligence operations working with the drug cartels in Colombia. Obviously these activities have to be kept quiet because if anything got out it would quickly become fodder for the politicians who would try and shut us down. We have a number of key military people in the country who are on our payroll and turn a blind-eye to our movement of drugs from Colombia through Venezuela to the markets in the United States and Europe. As a result of your training of the Coastguard, it looks like Blanes is planning to go head-to-head with the Guardia Nacional and the Unidad Maritima which would cause some serious problems with the boats we have moving along the coast. Because of the nature of the business we've got enough problems to contend with and don't need any additional aggravation from the Coastguard. We also have concerns about some of the politicians who run the government. To keep a lid on things it's important that we have detailed *information* and keep close tabs on the *players,* namely who's with us and specifically on those who may oppose us in the event of a regime change. The CIA must insure that the country is run by a president and politicians that will follow our agenda and play ball, not by clowns who may have their own ideas. During the 1970's there were a number of regime changes that we orchestrated in Latin America, but the real *biggie* was in Chile when Allende was elected. The U.S. couldn't tolerate another Socialist Government in the Americas, especially one that was supported by Castro. We had to move quickly and quietly so before any real damage was done the CIA took out Allende and installed General Pinochet. In Venezuela there are a number of matters on our priority list, but the first item is your drug interdiction training, which should be terminated immediately. The *information* that I referred to concerns the *players* and is more of a personal nature. We need to develop a database containing private and personal bits and pieces about the politicians, government ministers, admirals, generals, and the other senior officers of Venezuela's different military commands who have become your friends. In addition to safeguarding our drug shipments from Colombia, we also have to protect the oil interests of the United States. To achieve this level of protection it's important and if necessary, be able to neutralize those in government and the military forces that may oppose us and refuse to toe the line. To do this we've got to have detailed and specific information about the admirals and generals, their wives, girlfriends, overseas bank accounts, kids, you know all the personal stuff. I want to know where their children go to school, where they have bank accounts, where they have homes in Venezuela and overseas, personal home telephone, and cellular phone numbers. We know that many times you've been invited into their homes for private dinners and attended social events when a lot of these heavyweights have been around. We also know that Mike is friendly with the kids of the officers and because he reads and speaks Spanish fluently, could prove to be a good source of critical intelligence."

Alarmed at the thought of young Mike being placed under surveillance,

"You've been watching Mike? I doubt very much that what he talks about with the kids would have any bearing on the diplomatic relations between Venezuela and the United States."

Vela, detecting Mark's concern shot back,

"For some time both you and Mike have been persons-of-interest. Hey, you'd be surprised what we can learn from the mouths of children. When they are together without mom and dad looking over their shoulders they sometimes can provide a wealth of information. Anyway for now let's forget about the kids. What we need that's of vital importance is knowing the connection and relationships between the officers who command individual paratroop and armored units and the officers of Flag rank in all the armed services, particularly information concerning their political party affiliations. I'm specifically interested in knowing exactly which senior officers are involved and what their status or connection is with the Movimiento Bolivariano Revolucionario 200, you know the Bolivarian Revolutionary Movement the MBR-200. It's important that we identify those who are supporters and those who aren't. Hugo Chàvez is with us and recruiting a growing number of followers both in the private and military sectors; we need to know exactly who these people are.

It's essential that we know who's for and who's against so we can deal with each case individually."

After devouring the last morsels on his plate Vela stood and returned to the buffet coming back to the table with more food.

"Look you should realize that the CIA is all-powerful, if you are willing to work with us I'm in a position to make your cooperation extremely rewarding. The CIA has access to confidential funding and would pay you handsomely, but only if you cooperate and provide the information that's needed."

Mark, surprised with the mention of confidential funding,

"Hold on a minute, the confidential funding you're talking about in plain English means the dirty money that the CIA's been identified with in the past. Unless I'm badly mistaken your slush funds have been declared to be illegal."

"Forget about what you read in the papers. There's a lot of illegal stuff that goes on in Washington, but it's only illegal if you get caught. I can assure you that whatever you receive in payment for your services will be confidential, tax free and deposited in an offshore numbered account that can't be traced. You'd have nothing to worry about except how you choose to spend the money."

Now focusing on a plate filled with a collection of desserts Vela looked up,

"You needn't be concerned with breaking the law because the CIA is beyond the law. To give you an example the Directorate of Operations has a policy mandating that CIA field agents are forbidden to get personally involved with local men or women while they're posted to overseas stations. When I was working out of our embassy in Mexico City I met this gorgeous Mexican lady whose father was a heavy-weight with one of the big Mexican breweries. Well, one thing lead to another and we secretly got married and have lived happily ever since. In your case you'll quietly get your money and no one will ever be the wiser." Without looking up from a diminishing piece of Black Forrest cake Vela went on,

"How much has it cost you personally to conduct the training in Venezuela?"

"I donate my time and pay all my own out-of-pocket expenses. I guess if I would have billed for my time at the normal rate of a naval architect, with the hours I've expended so far the cost could be $80,000 or $90,000. As you know when I stay in Caracas I stay at the Euro Building and pay the bill myself. Outside of the Capital, and depending on where the training takes place, if it's near a military installation the Venezuelan Navy provides me with accommodation and my meals. This hasn't happened more than half a dozen times so most of the costs I've paid for personally. I would guess that so far I may be out of pocket around $20,000."

Vela smiled,

"$20,000, that's petty cash. You'll be paid a lot of money after you start giving us the information we need. In 1991 when you were requested to undertake the Venezuelan Initiative you moved quickly and produced incredible results. Less than five months later you had done such a bang-up job the Venezuelan Navy commissioned you with the rank of Captain and gave you a big job reporting to the Commandant. We kept you in our sights as a person-of-interest especially after you took the delegation of senior Venezuelan Navy Officers to the Roosevelt Roads Navy Base for training and then another group to the USCG Auxiliary National Conference in California. You seem to be under the impression that in September 1992 it was the U.S. Coast Guard who promoted you to the rank of Captain and designated you the Department Chief of Pan-American Auxiliary Liaison, not so, it was the CIA who engineered your promotion the Coast Guard was only the messenger."

"How could the CIA get me promoted?"

Vela smiled,

"Don't ask. In February 1992 our sources told us that in March the Venezuelans were going to commission you with the rank of Captain in the Coastguard Command of the Navy and the Commandant was going to name you his National Policy Advisor. American Citizens can't become members of the military of a foreign government so the CIA paved the way. Didn't you ever wonder why you were able to accept an officer's commission in Venezuela's military? If you would have thought about it you should have known that something was in the works when neither the U.S. Government nor the Coast Guard had any objection to your being commissioned a naval officer in the service of a foreign government."

"I must admit I found it a bit strange that I didn't get any flack from the Coast Guard or for that matter the State Department after Washington was notified of the commission. When I didn't hear anything, I though it best to let sleeping-dogs-lie especially when a few months later I was told that I was in line for promotion to flag rank."

Vela smiled.

"That's right you've been selected for promotion to Rear Admiral because its part of Operation Divine Guidance. The promotion will not be the work of the Coast Guard it's the CIA that's the moving force behind your becoming a Flag; as before the U.S. Coast Guard will only be the messenger. Because you'll be working for the CIA the Coast Guard can't and won't officially offer you any payment for the work you'll be doing because you'll be working for us. Any promotion you receive will actually cost the U.S. government nothing because the payments will be made from our funds. You've risen to great heights, but with Flag Rank, especially one who has been awarded the Honor Merito will add even greater prestige to the Venezuelan Initiative. A Rear Admiral will definitely have increased exposure to Venezuelan government ministers and the military's *inner-circle* with access to the sensitive information we need. After you accept our proposal we'd immediately go to work to pave the way for your promotion. If we can agree to put everything together on what's needed, I'll work out the details when I return to Caracas and make the necessary arrangements with my superiors in Washington."

Finishing a double piece of Key Lime pie Vela gently placed his hand on Mark's arm,

"The CIA and the Coast Guard know you have done an outstanding job in being accepted as a trusted member of Venezuela's Navy and the other armed forces. You enjoy a unique position that permits you to operate covertly within the military as a well placed informant. What you'd be doing would be for the benefit of the United States of America and would make you one of our country's true patriots."

Reaching across the table to grab a large prawn that was left on Mark's plate Vela said,

"Your help and cooperation is extremely important to the Venezuelan Initiative and to the affairs of the United States. We set up and backed Chàvez in the February coup and believed we had all the bases covered, but soon realized we'd made some serious miscalculations. After CAP, Carlos Andres Perez was impeached the country, from a political perspective was in a mess. It now appears his political adversary Rafael Caldera is gaining strength and political momentum and we're pretty sure he'll win the December election. But even if he wins the popular vote may not have the support of the military. There's growing discontent with the current state of affairs and we're convinced that some of your friends in the armed forces are just waiting to see what transpires after the election next month. If they're opposed to a Caldera administration, assuming he wins, there could be a rogue attempt to overthrow the government. A government controlled by a military junta that's outside our control would put us in the same untenable position that we're faced with now, or even worse. On the other hand Washington is firmly convinced that if Chàvez was to take control of the government there could be another coup led by a *junta* made up of the Admirals of the Venezuelan Navy and the Generals of the Air Force and the outcome may not be favorable to U.S. interests….."

Interrupting Mark started to speak,

"But…" Vela cut him off,

"Please, let me finish. We've got two important issues that must be resolved and you're in a position to help us. First is to insure the unimpeded flow of our shipments out of Colombia by stopping the Coastguard's drug intervention activities. The second is helping us get Chàvez into the Miraflores Palace without a military rebellion. The CIA believes that if a defiant military junta opposed to Chàvez were to seize control of the country they could seriously compromise America's interests by cutting off the flow of oil. Before this happens we need to continue the process of destabilizing the present government, neutralize the opposing military, and create chaos which will pave the way for Chàvez to take power. Our sources inside the Venezuelan Senate are secretly trying to arrange for Chàvez's early release from prison. If Caldera is elected he'll be inaugurated in February and if we can pull it off, Chàvez will be freed in March. There was a slim chance we might get Chàvez out of prison before the December 1993 elections, but because of too much opposition we know that's not going to happen. There are other forces working behind the scenes in the country that you wouldn't necessarily know about such as the National Endowment for Democracy. To make sure there aren't any problems the NED is quietly making a significant contribution to the success of CIA Operation Divine Guidance. What the CIA did covertly in the past the NED does today, openly. This is not the time or the place to tell you about the inner workings of the NED, but while being cloaked in secrecy the organization is funded, effective, and has the unequivocal backing and support of the U.S. government. The NED want what we want and have the means to insure that we both meet our objectives. The military groups we'd organized to support Chàvez in the February coup backed out at the last minute and blew our plan, we'll not make the same mistake this time. We had a mole inside the government's political circles, but he proved to be unreliable so we dumped him. Then you surfaced. After the Ambassador told me of what you had accomplished I immediately went to work on Operation Divine Guidance. As the CIA Station Chief I knew the timing was perfect, but first had to submit my idea to the Agency's National Clandestine Service for review. Special activities involving covert political action and paramilitary special operations must have the approval of the Special Activities Division and the Special Operations Group. Once SAD and SOG approved, I finalized the details and was given permission to move forward with Divine Guidance."

According to Vela the CIA had carefully planned and set the stage for another coup and Chàvez's early release from prison. Admiral Dicker was clearly involved because Vela emphasized he had worked closely with the Coast Guard Attaché McBride and his replacement, Commander Gary Soy. Mark was curious,

"In addition to Admiral Dicker who else in the Coast Guard knows about your Divine Guidance and the CIA's activities in Venezuela? Did the CIA arrange for Soy to be transferred from Honolulu to replace McBride?"

"Don't ask this doesn't concern you. When you come on board we'll fill you in on a need-to-know basis. You're being given an opportunity to get a star on your uniform and become a legendary hero in the Coast Guard while making some good money to boot. I've already pulled everything I need for your security clearance, so we're ready to roll."

"I'm flattered by the importance that you feel I have attained in Venezuela, but what you're suggesting sounds a bit too easy. For a little spying you'll pay me a lot of money and get me promoted, it seems too simple, what's the downside? If my spying activities were to be discovered and I was arrested could I rely on the U.S. government to get me out?"

"Nope, you'd operate as a NOC, a spy with *No Official Cover*. If you got caught you'd be on your own. The U.S. government would deny any knowledge of your activities because if they didn't we could be faced with an international incident of serious proportions. The publicity surrounding the exposure of a CIA spy in their military would be disastrous and surely destroy the relations between the two countries and maybe even shut off the flow of oil."

"You said the promotion would come right away, what's right away and what about the money?"

"The wheels are in motion. You're already a Captain in the Auxiliary. The next step is for your promotion in the Reserves from Commander to Captain which might take around 60 days. Once you get the four stripes it might take maybe another 90 days for the star. Here's what's on the table for the money side. Once you're onboard the Agency will set up a numbered account with the Swiss UBS Bank in Nassau in the Bahamas. You'll receive an initial payment of $30,000.00. In return I'll expect a monthly flow of information to begin with what you know right now. On the 15th of each month $75,000.00 will be deposited into your account in Nassau. In addition to the personal stuff I want the specific details of the Coastguard's scheduled surveillance and

interdiction operations between the Gulf of Venezuela and Isla
Margarita. Since you began the training in drug interdiction
Blanes has become even more confident that the Coastguard will
prevail. If Admiral Blanes is allowed to crush the Unidad
Maritima it would seriously impact and cripple our shipments
through Venezuela. Once you come on board with us you will
immediately stop the interdiction training. Just in case you might
be followed you should never come to the Embassy when you're
in Caracas. In the event something urgent comes up and you need
to contact me, call this number in the U.S. (703) 285-3111 and
only make the call using a public telephone. If it's during normal
working hours and the operator answers, ask to speak with the
Bishop and she'll connect you. If it's after hours and you get a
voice mail recording leave a message for the Bishop that the
Reverend called. From here on out you'll only be known as the
Reverend."
Vela, passing a notepad across the table,
"The information you gather should be compiled in a monthly
report and sent by FedEx to this address in Langley, Virginia. To
avoid any possible surveillance by their intelligence services you
should never call me at the Embassy, only use the number in
Langley. If something develops where I need to contact you I'll
send you a letter addressed to The Occupant. The letter will be
sent in the Diplomatic Pouch from Caracas and mailed to you
from Washington the following day. The envelope will have a
return address of the Venezuelan-American Chamber of
Commerce. The stamp placed upright means that I'll meet you at
the next scheduled Navy League meeting at Rosy Roads. If the
postage stamp is inverted it means that something has come up
and I need to see you right away and we'll meet at the Coast
Guard Base in San Juan. I'll fly to Puerto Rico and when I arrive
call your cell phone and ask for the Reverend. When you answer
your response will be sorry, wrong number, but you'll know it's
me. The call will let you know that I'm at the Coast Guard Base
and you should come right away. Any questions Reverend?"
"Nope, the only problem is with the money. If I'm to work as a
NOC and I'm on my own, and my cover gets blown I could have
a real problem. There will be undeniable danger and effort

required to prepare the monthly reports compiled for I'll call the *Book of Revelations.* If the Reverend is ordained to prepare the *Revelations*, his holiness will require $50,000.00 for the advance payment and a minimum of $100,000.00 a month. Amen..."

Vela was not amused. "Sounds like his holiness is a bit greedy, aren't those of the Cloth supposed to be pious and self-sacrificing for the good of mankind?" Mark smiled, "Mr. Vela, please understand the only Cloth that I'm contented with is Cloth sold by Burberry or Armani. Your Reverend is unquestionably pious, but hasn't taken nor is he committed to the vows of poverty. What the good Reverend is doing is not for mankind, the only good that's being done is for the good of the CIA. That's the deal take or leave it."

Vela frowned,

"I'm not authorized to agree to anything like you've suggested. We need you to help us, but I'll have to get approval from Langley for any changes. I'm scheduled to fly to Maiquetia tomorrow, but I'll change my return and call my superiors to see what they say. Let's meet in the Food Court at the Navy Exchange at 1400 tomorrow."

The following day Mark arrived early at the Navy Exchange to collect some uniforms he'd left at the dry cleaners and to pick up some pipe tobacco. Vela arrived promptly at 1400 and sat down. Mark asked,

"Is it a go?"

"I think so. I spoke with my superior and he's a bit upset about the money and would like you to reconsider. We need your help, but he doesn't want any problems. He's told me to fly to Washington and meet with him and another officer from the Directorate of Intelligence tomorrow. I'd like to tell them that you're okay with what's on the table so we can get the Operation rolling."

"Mr. Vela there's nothing to reconsider. I'll do what you ask, but it's either $50,000 up front then $100,000 per month thereafter or I'm not interested. Hey, if *The Company* is short of cash tell your boss to add a couple of kilos to the shipments of cocaine you've got coming out of Colombia. The way I figure it the Reverend will only need a few months to compile the information for the

Book of Revelations and unless his holiness gets caught before the *Book* is completed there'd be no need for any more Divine Guidance. Sorry, but you can tell your superior that the Reverend isn't interested."
"Commander please don't close the door just yet, I'll see them tomorrow, let's meet on Friday at the Coast Guard Base in San Juan say 1500 hours?"
"I've got a meeting in San Juan with a client at 1300 hours so 1500 would be fine with me."

————

Joseph Vela took the direct flight from San Juan to Dulles and arrived in Langley early on Thursday morning. In attendance at the meeting with Vela were Roger Doyle and Bert Downing who were overseeing Operation Divine Guidance. As the senior of the group Doyle was the first to speak. Looking at his secretary,
"Mary, please bring us some coffee and grab us some of those croissants from the cafeteria."
"Joe what the hell is going on with Kelly? I think the money we've offered him is more than reasonable for what he's got to do, maybe he thinks he's got us over a barrel. Should we wait and see if he changes his mind?"
Then Downing spoke,
"Roger I think we've got to be careful. Kelly is in a position to really screw up our shipments from Colombia. If he continues to push the interdiction training with the local Coastguard it would be disastrous. If the Minister of Defense and the Coastguard Commandant see an increase in seizures or worse yet more reports of Guardia Nacional interference people are going to start asking questions and once the media gets wind of it they'll surely start pressing for answers, exposure of the people on our payroll could prove costly. Kelly's on the inside and can get the personal stuff we need on the military commanders. With his information any opposing forces could be neutralized if they were to mobilize and could cause us some serious problems when Chàvez is ready. I say let's pay him what he wants."
Vela nodded in agreement.
"Roger I think Bert has a good point. If he's with us we're in a

position to get everything we need. He's a do-gooder and knows his interdiction training clearly won't stop all the drugs flowing through Venezuela, but would definitely have a positive effect in slowing the flow. It's clear that he knows of our shipment points at Castillets at Laguna Cocinetas for deliveries to Aruba and Curacao and our competition with the Arabs for the stuff moving out of Margarita. Kelly could be dangerous especially because he knows precisely what's going on and where it's all happening. With this information and as the Commandant's National Policy Advisor he's got the clout and he's in a position to increase surveillance over these areas. From what I've found everybody loves the guy. With a commission as a Venezuelan Naval officer, then receiving a prestigious military award he's looked at like a knight in shining armor. Kelly's well connected and I'm sure he has a lot of sources that we don't even know about. I don't know where or how he got it, but somehow Kelly found out that General Davila is on our payroll and knows about our storage bunker at Maiquetia airport and that its Davila's troops who guard it until the stuff is loaded and shipped out of the country as freight."

Doyle shook his head and looking at his colleagues,

"Looks like there isn't much of a choice, when are you seeing him again?"

"Tomorrow at 1500 hours at Base San Juan."

"Okay, tell our Reverend that he'll get his $50,000 and $100,000 a month thereafter, but I want results. If he doesn't produce we'll kill the son-of-a-bitch. No, don't tell him that, but impress on him that we don't take failure lightly. I saw in the preliminary report you've established the methods of contact for you or if he should need to call us here. He doesn't need to have or know the names of the players involved here or in the Coast Guard. If the son-of-a-bitch gets out of line or creates any problems, he'll have a fatal accident. Get my drift?"

Pressing the intercom,

"Mary, please get me Derek Mathews at UBS in Nassau."

"Yes sir, just a moment."

Moments later,

"Mr. Doyle, I have Mr. Mathews on line 5."

"Hello Derek, I need a numbered account for a deposit we'll be making in the next few days. No name, just a number. Thanks, I'll hold...... alright go ahead. Let me read it back, okay, got it, thanks. Please let me have the PIN. Okay, I'll read it back, SAILOR 2020, thanks, I've noted it. How's the weather in Nassau? Been awfully cold and wet here, Jean and I are long overdue for a visit. Sure, as soon as I can get a break from chasing the bad guys I'll let you know. Best regards to Gwen, see you soon. Bye."

Passing a Post-it note pad to Vela,

"Joe here's the account number at the UBS Bank in Nassau and the PIN. His contact at the UBS will be Derek Mathew. The account is identified by number only and no one knows his name. If Kelly agrees to come on board, $50,000 will be transferred to the account on Monday and $100,000 on the 15th of each month thereafter while the Operation is underway. I've written Derek's direct phone number in Nassau below the account number. When our Reverend calls Derek to confirm the first and subsequent deposits tell him that he should not use his name. When Derek answers the phone the Reverend should only give the PIN, SAILOR 2020, Derek will then respond with the transactions. After you meet with him tomorrow please call me on my private line to confirm, use one of the secure phones on the Coast Guard Base. After you tell me it's on, I'll arrange for the first deposit. If you have any problems with the Reverend - kill him."

"Roger, I'm confident there won't be any problems. I'll call you tomorrow late afternoon."

Joe Vela and Bert Downing then left the meeting.

———

Main Gate: United States Coast Guard - Greater Antilles Section (GANSEC) - La Puntilla, Old San Juan, Puerto Rico.

Commander Mark Kelly stopped and returned the sentry's salute, "Good afternoon Sir, I see your windshield sticker has expired, you might like to visit the admin office to get your renewal."

"Thanks Chief, I'd forgotten about it, I'll get the new sticker before I leave today. Have a nice day."

After obtaining the windshield sticker from the Base

Administration Office Mark went to the Exchange Cafeteria and grabbed a cup of coffee. As he sat down Vela entered.

"Hi Commander it's been a hectic couple of days, but I'm happy to say that your request has been approved."

Checking that no one was sitting close to them, in hushed tones Vela spoke,

"A numbered account has been set up for you with the UBS Bank in Nassau."

Passing a Post-it-note across the table,

"This has the name of your contact at the Bank, his direct phone number, the account number, and your password. The account is identified only by the number the Bank does not know your name. When you call to confirm the transactions on the account and the gentleman answers only give him the password. If you confirm your participation now, the first deposit will be made on Monday."

"If the amounts have been agreed, then let's get the ball rolling."

"Welcome aboard Commander. I'm looking forward to working with you."

Vela and Mark stood and left the building. As Mark left the Base he stopped briefly at the main gate.

"Chief, thanks for the heads-up about the sticker. I'll remove the expired one and put the new on when I get home."

Returning the Chief's salute, Mark drove away.

Later that afternoon he visited Bird Travel in Fajardo.

"Hi Lucy, next week I'll be returning to Caracas, but instead of taking the direct American flight I'd like you to book me on the first morning flight from San Juan to Miami with a connection to Grand Cayman. The business I need to take care of in George Town will only take me a few hours so please book me on the afternoon flight through Kingston to Piarco in Trinidad that connects with the first available Aeropostal flight to Maiquetia. The return can be booked a week from Wednesday on the direct American flight from Maiquetia to San Juan. I'll pick up the tickets from you on Saturday."

Noting the itinerary Lucy Bird acknowledged the arrangements, then asked,

"No problem Mark. Will Mike be staying with us while you're

gone?"

"Yes please. I'd appreciate if you and Poncho would look after him while I'm away. I've got a lot of stuff to do and the trip wouldn't be much fun for Mike having to keep up with me running through a bunch of airports before we'd even get to Venezuela. In any case, I'll only be away just over a week."

In Grand Cayman Mark took a cab to the Cayman National Bank on Elgin Street in George Town where he opened a numbered savings account. With a few hours to kill before his flight to Kingston he decided to take a cab to Jed Foster's Dive located on Seven Mile Beach just outside of town to see his friend Reggie Calvert. Reggie, of British extraction had engaged Mark to help in the design modifications and reconstruction of a large catamaran that had suffered damage as a result of a storm that hit Cayman the year before. Following Mark's redesign, the modified catamaran proved to be an important element to the success of the dive business and the two had become good friends. Entering the Dive Center Mark smiled,

"Good afternoon Julie, is Reggie around?"

"Hi Mark, yes, Mr. Calvert is on the Calypso over at Sting Ray City. I'll call him on the radio to let him know that you're here. What brings you to Cayman?"

"Just a quick trip for a little banking business, then I'm off to Venezuela."

"Are you still doing that training thing for the Venezuelan Coastguard?"

"Yep, still at it."

A short time later Reggie arrived and they talked about the increase in the number of dive customers and how well the catamaran was performing. After having afternoon tea, Reggie drove Mark to the airport. The flights were on time and Mark arrived at Maiquetia at 2300 hours and took a taxi to the Euro Building. The following morning without looking at the clock he jumped from the shower to answer the phone. He saw it was still dark outside.

"Mark, Jim McBride here. Sorry about the time, but I know you're an early riser. Tonight I'm having a little get together at my place in honor of Admiral Wildling's visit to Caracas, as you know Paul Wilding is the Coast Guard's Atlantic Maritime Commander. I realize its short notice, but unless you've got something else planned, I'd like you to come."

Rubbing a towel over his face Mark responded,

"Sure Jim, what time?"

"Things starts pretty late here so were asking people to come around 8 o'clock. Later this morning when I get to the office I'll leave the directions to my place on your voice mail at the hotel."

The taxi took about 30 minutes to reach the garden apartment of Jim and Kathy McBride, 10 minutes of actual driving and 20 minutes in bumper to bumper traffic getting out of the city. Mark had decided to attend McBride's party in his Venezuelan Coastguard uniform and was glad he did when he found that the other officers were also in uniform.

"Hi Mark I'm glad you were able to make it. Allow me to introduce my wife Kathy, now how about a drink?"

"It's nice to meet you Mrs. McBride and thanks Jim, a Coke would be fine."

In addition to the uniformed military officers there were also a number of suit-and-collar types undoubtedly from the Embassy as they were easily identifiable by their close cropped regulation haircuts required for all those employed by the U.S. Government. Like a flock of sheep a number of the suit-and-collar types were clustered together on the balcony of McBride's apartment located in an upscale section on the hillsides overlooking the city. McBride was obviously in his niche and in addition to having a fondness for tennis felt right at home being the effervescent host especially when the bill was being picked up by the U.S. government, courtesy of the American taxpayer.

Colonel Graham of the U.S. Air Force and Captain Hill the U.S. Navy Attaché, oblivious to the other guests had secluded themselves in a corner swinging their arms in an animated display resembling a golf swing. The last swing caused Colonel Graham to stumble throwing him off balance, not necessarily from the weight of his imagined club, but due to the excessive levels of Johnny Walker whisky he'd consumed. Fortunately Captain Hill caught him preventing his air force colleague from an ungraceful nose dive that would have surely resulted in a crash landing.

Other than Kathy McBride, there were only one or two unremarkable ladies present who appeared to be bored to tears. Obviously this was not meant to be ladies night, but purely a man's *gathering of eagles*. McBride later told Mark that every month or so each branch of the armed services would find some reason to have a cocktail party that could be charged off to the Embassy. With only a few exceptions when these get-togethers were planned the same people attended, mostly Colonels and Captains who wore Eagles as uniform insignias and a few lower grade officers like McBride. Jim later told Mark that if you don't invite the Air Force or the Army then they wouldn't invite you to their *gathering of eagles*, tit-for-tat.

"Mark Kelly, what are you doing here?"

The high-pitched voice cut through the air like a hot knife through cold butter and unquestionably was that of Paul Blaine. Mark had come to know Captain Blaine of the U.S. Coast Guard when he had served as the Commanding Officer of the Coast Guard's Greater Antilles Section in San Juan, Puerto Rico. Turning as Blaine approached,

"Hi Paul it's nice to see you, but if I may ask, what are you doing here? After you left GANSEC I heard you were warming a desk in Washington." Blaine smiled and said, "You tell me first."

"Last September Jim McBride asked if I'd be interested in accepting an assignment to reorganize and train the Venezuelan Coastguard Reserves and Auxiliary. In March after it had been approved by Washington the Coastguard Commandant, Admiral Blanes promoted me to the rank of Captain and named me his National Policy Advisor."

Blaine grimaced,

"But as an American citizen you can't serve in the armed forces of a foreign government especially as an officer, it's not permitted by the U.S."

Blaine said, rolling his eyes in obvious displeasure.

"Sorry Paul, I can't tell you how it came about, but as I'm wearing the uniform of a Venezuelan Naval Officer at a party thrown by the U.S. Embassy's Coast Guard Attaché I can assure you that it did come about. Now what's your story?"

Blaine clearly taken aback picked up the conversation,
"While I was in Washington I was offered the opportunity to become Chief of Operations for the Coast Guard Atlantic Maritime Area reporting to Vice-Admiral Wilding, the Atlantic Commander. I don't understand why I or Admiral Wilding hadn't been told of this training program in Venezuela or of your commission as a Captain in the Venezuelan Coastguard."
Captain Blaine then introduced Mark to Admiral Wilding who obviously knew more about the Venezuelan Initiative than his Chief of Operations was aware of. By his demeanor it was also apparent that Wilding didn't want to talk about what was going on in Venezuela in front of Blaine so Mark dropped the subject. He was confident that Wilding had been fully briefed about the Venezuelan program, but found it strange that Blaine as his Chief of Operations hadn't been told. It was surprising that with Blaine's extensive military and government contacts in Washington he was unaware of an operation that had been endorsed by the Central Intelligence Agency, the State Department, two Commandants, a gaggle of admirals, and was taking place in his own backyard.
A short time later while munching on some finger-food and sipping from a glass of Coca-Cola, Mark watched as the dignified Admiral Blanes quickly finished his normal two whiskies, no doubt in preparation of his gracious withdrawal. After the Admiral said his good-bye's Mark too thanked Jim and Kathy McBride's for their cordial hospitality feigning early morning training exercises. Anxious to remove himself from this patronizing group of military-politicos Mark realized in descending the steps he hadn't arranged for taxi.
"How are you getting back to the Euro Building?"
The voice from the shadows was that of Admiral Blanes. Being a bit startled Mark quickly turned,
"Admiral sorry I didn't see you. I forgot to order a taxi, but I'll go back and ask McBride to call one for me."
Raising his hand the Admiral said,
"No problem, I can have my driver drop you off at your hotel it's on my way home."
The traffic was light and their journey to the Euro Building took

only a few minutes during which time they engaged in small talk. "You know Captain, I hate these embassy parties and my wife dislikes them even more and why she seldom attends. With the exception of the Spanish and French the rest are boring."

So as not to offend, Mark cautiously acknowledged the comment, telling the Admiral that he too wasn't really the party type and had only attended at the insistence of McBride who said that Admiral Wilding had indicated that he wanted to meet him personally.

"You've never met Admiral Wilding? This is surprising because in speaking with him recently I expressed my admiration for the work you're doing in Venezuela and he appeared to know you very well. I'm surprised you say that you hadn't met him previously. And by the way, you're not supposed to know this, but Wilding told me that Washington is planning to award you the Coast Guard Administrative Merit decoration for your work with my Command."

As they approached the hotel the Admiral asked,

"How is Mike? Please do send my best regards to him when you return to Puerto Rico. I'm sorry he's not with you as my son enjoys his company. We're looking forward to seeing you at my home for dinner tomorrow night. I'll have my driver collect you at 1900 hours. In any case you know where I live and have my home and cellular telephone numbers, if needed."

Opening the car door and turning, Mark said,

"Thank you sir, I'll look for your driver tomorrow at 1900."

Out of courtesy the following week Mark sent a letter to Admiral Wilding expressing his pleasure in having the opportunity of meeting him in person along with a brief synopsis of the recent training exercises. A few days later Mark received a reply.

Dear Captain Kelly, Thank you for the information on your work in Venezuela. I'm glad to hear of the progress you've made since we last met. Just as in the United States, I see a great potential and need for Coast Guards in Latin America.

The letter was signed Paul A. Wilding, Vice-Admiral United States Coast Guard. Mark wondered if his Chief of operations, Captain Paul Blaine had now been briefed on Operation Divine Guidance. The following month Mark returned to Venezuela to conduct training in the eastern area of the country. The city of Puerto La Cruz located in the State of Anzoátegui was the home of Coastguard Auxiliary Grupo Delfin and was commanded by 1st Lieutenant Leo Caldaria, who a dozen or so years earlier had emigrated from Italy. In addition to volunteering more than 30 hours a week for Coastguard duty Leo operated two schools, one of which taught computer skills and the other languages, he was fluent in at least a dozen languages. In spite of running a successful business enterprise Leo was totally committed to his adopted country and its Coastguard. Under his command the Coastguard Auxiliary in Puerto la Cruz went from strength to strength while at the same time his language school flourished and became so successful that it caused the local Berlitz franchise to close.

As the Aeropostal 727 jetliner circled on its final approach to Barcelona, the airport that serves the eastern Venezuelan city of Puerto La Cruz, looking out the window he was always fascinated by the dry and desert like topography of the eastern sections of Venezuela. The area around Barcelona was in sharp contrast to the lush tropical countryside found in the country's interior and the jungles of the Bolivar province to the south.

"Mark, Mark, over here."

The voice was unmistakably that of Leo Caldaria calling amidst a crowd of people waiting to meet the flight from Caracas. The handsome, olive skinned Italian at 5'11" and a trim 160 lbs had a charismatic personality. While he could have easily been a movie star, an opportunity declined in his early years, his engaging and cheerful manner had led him into sales. After completing his college studies in Rome, Leo successfully applied his people-skills as a door-to-door encyclopedia salesman. Within a short period of time his employers, the publishers of the Encyclopedia Britannica recognizing his management skills elevated him to the position of general sales manager. After a number of years working 12 hour days and making a pot full of money he decided to set out and seek his fortune in the new world; in spite of having relatives in the United States Leo chose to move to Venezuela.

"Mark let's first get you checked into the Hotel Melia. I've scheduled a meeting for us with Capitán de Navio Saùl Pérez Altuve the Commanding Officer of the Coastguard base at Guanta. The Capitán is anxious to get the training programs started so they can expand their coastal patrols. Altuve has a growing problem with illegal drugs that he knows are moving along the coast to Margarita and Trinidad; drugs that are being transported on yachts and ships which he's sure are under the protection of the Unidad Maritima."

Unlike the desert characteristics of Barcelona, Puerto la Cruz is surrounded by a lush landscape. This modern and beautiful city was built much along the same lines as Fort Lauderdale, in Florida with numerous man-made canals that fringe the coast adjacent to the tranquil Caribbean Sea. The canals are bordered by lavish and expansive condominiums, villas and Five-Star hotels. The Melia, a luxury hotel located on the eastern side of Puerto la Cruz is a favorite of business executives and Senior Military Officers because of its peaceful ambiance and superb restaurants and bars.

"Let me see K-E-L-L-Y, yes Capitán, we have your reservation for five nights at the official military rate."

Accompanied by Leo, Mark proceeded to his room on the 5th floor that he would call home for the next few days. His room was actually a suite that provided a spectacular view of the harbor, the hotel's white sand beach and the out-lying islands located a short distance offshore. Putting his bags on the bed Mark turned,

"Leo the room is magnificent. Thanks for making the arrangements. Okay let's go see Capitán Altuve and get things rolling."

The Coastguard base was only a short drive due east along the coast just outside the city and was situated near the PDVSA-LAGOVEN oil terminal.

"Capitán Pérez, may I introduce Captain Mark Kelly the coordinator of training that the Commandant spoke to you about."

Pérez stood and with a broad smile extended his hand,

"Captain welcome to my Command. I have been anxiously awaiting your arrival and looking forward to meeting you. If we can increase my effectiveness in our war against the traffickers I will be eternally grateful. In the event you should need to contact me after hours here is my home address and private home and cellular telephone numbers."

Passing the notepad across his desk Altuve added,

"Please, I want you to feel free to call me at anytime."

Capitán Pérez Altuve, a 30 year veteran of the Navy was clean shaven, no more than 5'4" and corpulent weighing in the region of 300 lbs. Observing professional courtesy in anticipation of Mark's arrival he had worn his Class A dress uniform. In the oppressive heat of the day he was red-faced and perspiring profusely while his abundant body mass appeared to be desperately trying to release itself from the captivity and restraints of his tightly buttoned and undersized uniform. With the exception of his bald head, clean shaven face and white uniform rather than red, a visitor's first impression was that of Santa Claus in a sub-tropical environment. Much like the legendary Mr. Claus, he had a warm smile and a kindly disposition that immediately produced a pleasant atmosphere. Mark immediately liked him. As Mark's wet hand slipped from Altuve's perspiring grasp,

"Captain I understand that in spite of the on going difficulties with the Unidad Maritima that your drug interdiction training programs are still being given in other areas of the country. I'm confident that with your support and the efforts of Leo and the Grupo Delfin we might not completely stop the flow of drugs through the area, but at least we'll be able to slow it down. When do we begin?"

That evening starting at 1900 hours and ending at midnight in a classroom provided by the management of the LAGOVEN oil terminal, 30 coastguard sailors were assembled for training. For the next five days instruction commenced at 0800 and lasted until 1800 hours. On the last day of instruction the focus was placed on boarding procedures and small arms training. Passing out the reading assignments Mark asked that they be completed before he returned at which time they would begin actual on-the-water interdiction patrols. Before leaving Leo and Mark discussed the inherent risks and perils in boarding and disabling the crews of suspected drug boats along with the proficiency needed in the use of fire arms.

"Leo it's vital that all the students complete their assignments so we can move on to the next step. Because of the danger involved, when we start the actual boarding the crews can't leave anything to chance."

"Mark you can count on me. I'll see that your orders are followed to the letter and that all the assignments are completed. When will you be back?"

Looking at his agenda Mark said, "In two weeks."

In returning to Puerto La Cruz two weeks later Mark continued the classroom training and then began the on-the-water exercises of boarding suspected drug boats which included man-overboard drills, towing, firefighting, and first aid; another two days were spent on the firing range devoted to the use of small arms. After completing the final advanced training, it was show-time.

At dusk two unmarked 36' Inter Marine offshore racers, each fitted 500 hp MerCruiser engines were idling at the dock of Coastguard Base Guanta. Charlie Golf Foxtrot was commanded by Leo with a three man crew. The second vessel, Charlie Golf Bravo was under the command of Mark also manned with a crew of three. Along with radio gear and small arms each vessel was equipped with 24 nautical mile radars. The vessels departed under a full moon, when they were approximately six miles from the coast,

"CG Bravo this is CG Foxtrot, do you copy?"

"CG Bravo this is CG Foxtrot, affirmative."

"CG Bravo we have a bogey 3 miles at 4 o'clock running with no lights, closing."

"CG Foxtrot affirmative, we have a visual and will provide back-up. Radar target shows another vessel off bogey's starboard quarter. Have you identified this vessel?"

"CG Bravo that's a negative."

"Unidentified vessel off Puerto la Cruz, this is Coastguard CG Foxtrot, do you copy? Unidentified vessel off Puerto la Cruz, this is Coastguard CG Foxtrot, do you copy?"

"CG Bravo, no response, CG Foxtrot closing."

As CG Foxtrot got closer to the bogey, which was suspected of carrying drugs, bursts of automatic weapon fire were seen coming from the other unidentified vessel.

"CG Bravo, CG Bravo, this is CG Foxtrot. We have no radio contact, but profile of unidentified vessel indicates she is a Guardia Nacional 85' Bolivar Class patrol vessel."

"CG Foxtrot this is CG Bravo. Do you have any damages?"

"This is CG Bravo negative, boat and crew uninjured, CG Foxtrot returning to base."

After securing the vessels at the Guanta Coastguard Base, Leo called Capitán Pérez to report the incident and Mark called Admiral Blanes at home. The Admiral asked Mark to send him a full report of the incident which he would discuss with the Minister of Defense. When his report to Admiral Blanes failed to produce any action or reprimand of the Guardia Nacional Mark decided that at least for the time being, interdiction patrols off Puerto la Cruz would be suspended, while basic search and rescue training would continue.

The training paid off when a few weeks later a German flag sailboat which had come to Venezuela to stay during the hurricane season caught fire while at anchor in the harbor at Puerto La Cruz. Seeing the smoke from the burning boat the Coastguard vessel *Rescate Uno* responded rescuing two persons in the water and extinguishing the fire which saved the yacht. When Mark was advised of the rescue he was pleased, Leo had been pleased and the German and his wife who owned the yacht were pleased even more.

Knowing that that the Guardia Nacional had been corrupted and their patrol vessels were protecting the drug traffickers, Mark was troubled when the Minister of Defense asked that he consider and include training of Detachment 76 of the Unidad Maritima based at Porlamar on Margarita Island. Mark wondered was this somehow a ploy? Was the Minister of Defense also involved with Vela?

Vela had told him that the Unidad Maritima was on the CIA's payroll and involved in their drug trafficking activities, which on two occasions he'd now witnessed and experienced first hand. The previous month the Guardia Nacional had not only prevented the boarding of a go-fast, but had actually fired on a Coastguard boarding party; which if they were confronted with would surely deny. Wanting documented proof to give to the Commandant, Mark knew he'd have to be careful, but a training relationship might be a good idea. In being able to board Guardia Nacional patrol vessels he would be in a position to confirm and document their relationship with the traffickers.

The opportunity came the following month during Guardia Nacional training exercises purportedly related to boarding's for safety inspections. In scanning the horizon through binoculars on a routine surveillance patrol on board a Detachment 76, 85' Bolivar Class patrol vessel some ten miles to the west of Porlamar, Mark observed a 150' general cargo ship. The vessel had a rusted, faded blue hull and was flying the national flag of Honduras. The aging tramp with Lady Dianna painted on her transom clearly had seen better days, but was still engaged in some type of trade. The Honduran ship offered the perfect training opportunity. Riding low in the water steaming at 12 knots on a north easterly course she was the type of vessel that matched the profile of a trafficker. In U.S. maritime law enforcement circles suspected drug boats are profiled and identified through EPIC, the El Paso Intelligence Center.

Mark was soon to be able to confirm why the Commanding Officer of the local Unidad Maritima lived in a beautiful home and drove an expensive car, but never wanted to openly discuss drug interdiction. After sighting the target located approximately 10 miles off the eastern shore of Margarita, Mark suggested to the Commander of the Unidad Maritima patrol boat that the Honduran ship be contacted by VHF radio and instructed to stop her engines and hove-to, as she was about to be boarded. The Commander of the Unidad Maritima vessel, Lieutenant Carlos Sabatini refused to make the call.

Pulling Mark aside he said that this would not be a good idea as this was a protected ship and was *authorized* to transit through Venezuelan territorial waters without interference. Sabatini then told Mark that the Lady Dianna and other *authorized* vessels regularly transited the waters in and around Margarita Island and were never stopped or boarded. Being curious Sabatini had once asked his superiors where these *authorized* vessels came from and where they were going; he was told that they usually sailed from ports in Colombia, but never told where they were going.

"With all due respect Captain, it's best not to ask anymore questions."

Showing Mark a clipboard holding a sheet marked *Standing Orders* he pointed to the 7th line on a page that contained some two dozen names and the particulars of each ship. Then Sabatini said,

"You can see this ship the Lady Dianna registered in Honduras is shown here. This and the other vessels on the list have been given official clearance and are all under protective orders. Certain people have made *arrangements* with my Commanding Officer at the Unidad Maritima in Porlamar and the Regional Commander in Caracas to allow these ships to pass unchallenged as they are part of a classified operation."

Mark was curious,

"Classified operation? And certain people, what certain people Lieutenant?"

"I don't know exactly who the people are. Once or twice a week the boat commanders receive *Standing Orders* with instructions that certain ships must not be stopped or boarded by the Guardia Nacional or anyone else while they pass through Venezuelan waters."

"Haven't you asked where the lists come from and who issues these *Standing Orders*?

"I did once, but my CO only told me that it was some high ranking official in the American Embassy in Caracas."

Sabatini then softly uttered the letters, "C-I-A."

The Guardia Nacional knew in advance when, where and what ships were transporting drugs. The patrol boat commanders had orders not to interfere with these ships because the Guardia Nacional was on the CIA's payroll. Mark knew that with regular shipments from Cartagena and Barranquilla the CIA clearly wasn't interested in exporting Colombian coffee, but now had the proof through the *Standing Orders* that with the protection of the Guardia Nacional the CIA was directly involved in the business of transporting illegal drugs.

It was the American's who were providing the means for the

Commanding Officer of Detachment 76 in Porlamar and his superior in Caracas to become wealthy individuals.

As this was the documented proof he needed Mark focused on obtaining a copy of one of these *Standing Orders* which he did the following month. In subsequent coastguard training exercises held with Grupo Tiburon on Margarita Island Mark also learned that the island was not only an important transshipment point in the drug trade, but also a fund raising center for a number of Islamic terrorist organizations.

———

Following the unnerving experiences in Puerto la Cruz and Margarita, Mark as planned, returned to Puerto Rico on Wednesday. On Friday morning he received a call from his good friend Jacques Deauville, Chief of the French Narcotics Task Force in Venezuela and a former Commissaire de Police in Paris. Even though a senior law enforcement officer Jacques was officially shown as a Second Secretary in the Embassy's Commercial Section assigned to the department dealing with trade.

"Bonjour Mark. I hope you are well and busy."

"Hey Jacques bonjour to you too and yes thanks, I'm well and keeping busy. What's up?"

"Mark the Embassy is throwing a small cocktail party and dinner on the 18th to honor of the visit of André DuPont our Minister of Foreign Affairs who's coming to Caracas for an official visit. If you can arrange it, I'd like very much for you to attend. There are two other people I'd like you to meet as they're in the same business. Pierre Dumont is the Commander of the French Marine Nationale and responsible for all naval forces in Cayenne and the French Antilles. When I told Pierre about your work, he said he'd like to meet you. The other person is Dirk van der Maas, a Commander in the Royal Netherlands Navy and Commanding Officer of the DCCG, the Dutch Coastguard which is based at Parera in Curacao. Dirk is responsible for all the Dutch ABC islands and Sint Maarten. Cocktails will start flowing about 6:00 p.m. with dinner at 8. Is it possible for you to make it?"

"Of course I'd love to come. I'll schedule some training for that week so I can be in Caracas. I'll be at the Euro Building and fly in on the afternoon of the 17th. I'd like very much like to meet Dirk and Pierre and discuss our mutual interests." "Yes, meeting my colleagues could be equally beneficial. Will Mike be with you? If he is he's more than welcome to come along."

"Thanks Jacques, but over the last couple of months Mike's come with me to Venezuela probably a half dozen times and I don't think I should take him out of school again so soon. While I'm involved with the training Mike stays with the Blanes' family or at other times with the families of Generals Martinez and Suarez, but I don't want to strain their hospitality. Mike enjoys the company of the officer's children and as they all speak Spanish always has a great time. I've also taken him to a few cocktail parties, but he's been bored to tears so I promised him no more cocktail parties. Anyway thanks for offering."

"No problem, I'll send the invitation to the Euro Building so you'll have it when you check in, Au Revoir Mark."

The days seemed to fly by. Amongst the other responsibilities of a single parent there were the regular Parent-Teacher meetings at Fajardo Academy, soccer matches, two basketball games, meetings with the Navy League president, and volunteer work at the local Abandoned Animals Shelter.

Mark had previously sent three of the monthly reports to Langley, then on the afternoon of the 16th after completing his fourth report called Federal Express to arrange for the pick-up. FedEx said the courier would collect the envelope sometime around 5:00 p.m. Mark then went to a public telephone near his home and dialed a telephone number in Langley, Virginia.

"Hello."

"Are you the Bishop?"

"Yes."

"This is the Reverend."

"Good afternoon Reverend. You can speak this is a secure line, what can I help you with?"

"When I advised the Commandant that I was going to Miami he asked me to buy four Motorola Star-Tac cellular phones. He said that two were for him and his wife and the other two for General Rodriguez, the Commander of the Air Force and his wife. I thought you should know."

"Good job Reverend. When will you be in Miami?"

"Next week."

"Where will you be staying?"

"Miami Airport Marriott on Le Jeune."

"Call me when you know you'll be there. I'll arrange for one of our people to come to the hotel and put tracking devices in the phones."

"How long will it take? Will they know the phones have been tampered with?" "No more than 10 minutes. No, the devices are undetectable."

"Okay I'll be in touch."

"Bless you Reverend, bye for now."

The reports sent to Langley focused primarily on the Chain of Command beginning with the Admirals and Generals. Mark was careful and thorough in their preparation. While giving the impression and appearing to contain critical data, the reports were little more than generic information, such as private home addresses, home and cellular phone numbers. Providing the name and location of the Admiral's and General's offshore bank accounts and the location of their vacation homes was an ingenious, yet simplistic endeavor of fraudulent deception. Knowing where they had taken their holidays Mark compiled a list of the names of the various banks in the area and then simply picked the name of any particular bank located in the Cayman Islands, the Bahamas, Sint Maarten or Panama. With their bank accounts located in offshore and tax free jurisdictions they would be numbered accounts and even though having a bank's name and address or imagined account number an account's beneficial owner could never be identified.

As the information in Mark's reports hadn't been challenged it was evident that the CIA hadn't picked up on the misinformation. In any case had the CIA checked the travel history of their flights it would confirm and corroborate that the Admirals, Generals and their families had actually traveled to where their so-called vacation homes and offshore banks were located. The deception continued with the address of their vacation homes which was the street address of the resorts where they had vacationed with their families, information innocently obtained by Mike while playing with the officer's children. They didn't, but had the CIA diligently checked where Admiral Blanes had his vacation home in Grand Cayman they would have found the street address was actually that of the Ritz Carlton Resort and Spa on Seven Mile Beach. The address of the vacation home in Panama of General Rodriguez, Commander of the Air Force, was the street address of the Hyatt Regency Resort in Panama. Along with other misinformation included in his reports was that he'd found that all the Generals and Admirals had expressed their admiration and unwavering support for Lieutenant Colonel Hugo Chàvez and his MBR-200. In fact, the truth of the matter was, from the Minister of Defense down through the Chain of Command, all the armed forces strenuously opposed Chàvez and his Socialist inspired Movimiento Revolucionario Bolivariano–200.

———

On the morning of the 17th after dropping Mike off at school Mark drove to the airport in San Juan to catch the midday flight to Caracas. Later after checking in at the Euro Building, Mark went to his room and called Toschenko to let him know he'd arrived. Declining Toschenko's invitation to dinner, Mark decided that a dip in the hotel's luxurious pool would be in order. For dinner he chose to walk the short distance to a popular Argentinean Steakhouse in Las Mercedes where he indulged himself. The next day after a sumptuous breakfast of fruit and pastries he returned to his room to work on the details of his upcoming visit to Isla Margarita. At 6:15 p.m. Mark took a taxi to the French Embassy where after presenting his invitation to the doorman was welcomed by Jacques Deauville in the foyer.
"Mark it's great to see you, I am very pleased you could come. Let's go upstairs, I want you to meet Pierre and Dirk."
The two proceeded up a magnificent winding staircase with walls suitably adorned with artwork dating from the French Revolution and frequently updated with oil paintings commissioned and approved by the past and present leaders of the French Republic. Upon entering a splendid salon reserved for such gatherings a tuxedo attired maître d' offered the choice of vintages in red or

white or flutes of the finest of French champagne. Moving through the crowd of dignitaries Mark and Jacques approached two naval officers both in dress uniforms, one French, the other Dutch.

"Pierre, Dirk, I'd like to introduce Commander Mark Kelly of the United States Coast Guard who is also Captain Mark Kelly of the Venezuelan Coastguard."

Both smiled as Pierre inquired,

"Should we address you as Captain or Commander?"

"Neither, Mark is fine."

"Mark, Jacques has told us of your training in Venezuela and particularly your interest in drug interdiction. Obviously, as the Commander of French Naval Forces in Cayenne, the Antilles and working in close cooperation with the Gendarmerie Maritime, I have a keen interest in what you're doing. We have a growing problem with narcotics being smuggled into Fort de France and Guadeloupe which are then put on Air France flights that fly direct to France. We have Trident's and Vedette's based in Cayenne and Fort Saint Louis, but with limited resources our ships simply can't be everywhere. Good intelligence is the key to our success."

Dirk then spoke,

"Like the French we too have a similar situation, but with Aruba and Curacao being so close to the coast of Venezuela our problem is even greater. We have Cutters based in Parera that have been reasonably successful in seizures and the airport police are doing a good job catching swallowers. However, without reliable intelligence the go-fasts are many times getting through to Orangestad and Willemstad. Jacques tells us that he's worked with you in the past and you have a reliable network of informants who have provided actionable intelligence that's proved positive. Like the American's we have a confidential program that will pay informants for information that leads to a seizure. The informants are never identified, but they receive 10% of the value of the drugs seized. So there's no misunderstanding and because of price fluctuations between street and wholesale prices, the 10% is paid based on a value of $13,000.00 per kilo. The payment is made in cash…"

Pierre cut in,

"We do the same."

Mark was clearly interested,

"Are you confident that your law enforcement people and the politicians in local government aren't corrupt and thwarting your efforts of interdiction? If those responsible for enforcement are corrupted you're not going to reduce or stop the flow and your informants probably wouldn't live very long. I've had situations in Puerto Rico and Sint Maarten where law enforcement is on the payroll of the druggies and with their help shipments are being made without any fear of interdiction."

"I can't speak for Dirk, but Jacques and I know that our people in the narcotics branch are beyond reproach. Gendarmerie Maritime and our Navy personnel are all sent from France and fully vetted before they are assigned. They do an 18 month tour of duty before being rotated. We have some people in local government who we know are involved after the drugs reach the island in local distribution and arrange transshipments, but little by little we're catching them. No locals are involved or have anything to do with our narcotics surveillance or intelligence activities. Having worked with Jacques in the past you know and trust him, I see no reason why we couldn't develop let's say, a mutually beneficial cooperative arrangement. If you'd be willing to provide the information obtainable through your sources and work confidentially through Jacques we could set up an information pipeline. As your informants wouldn't ever be identified the 10% could be paid to you and then you'd pay the informant. Dirk, would this be acceptable to you?"

"I don't see any problem with such an arrangement. I'd need to consult with the DCCG in The Hague, but I'm sure they'd approve."

Jacques was pleased and said, "Dirk, once you receive the approval of your government please let me know. I'll speak with my contact at your embassy to set up the procedures. When payment is due as a result of your seizures he can transfer the funds to our special account and I'll wire the payment to Mark."

"Mark you have my secure numbers here at the embassy so we can keep in touch."

"Jacques I believe I can put something together fairly quickly. I'm in the process of obtaining a list of the movements which will allow me to provide you with the information of when and where the shipments are coming from and a description along with the details of the go-fast or ship that's carrying the drugs. Once I give you the details then you'll have to decide whether it'll be a French or Dutch operation based on the departure point. You can advise Pierre and Dirk and they can decide who does the seizure depending on whose assets are closer. In the meantime here's my account number at the Cayman National Bank in George Town. If we're successful the payments can be made to this numbered account and I'll pay the informants."

Taking the note with the account number, Jacques smiled and said, "Mark that sounds good to me. I believe that completes our business for the moment so if there's nothing else let's eat."

The following morning Mark was on the flight to Isla Margarita. After the plane's normal intermediate stop in Barcelona, Mark arrived at Margarita's international airport where he was to meet Javier Augustus Soto. Originally from Buenos Aires, Argentina, Javier had immigrated to Venezuela and established a successful interior design business on this prosperous and duty-free island. Immediately outside of the arrivals hall Mark spotted Javier.

"Captain welcome back to Margarita, how was your flight?"

With a broad smile and shaking Javier's hand,

"It's great to see you Javier, the flight was fine and I'm pleased that it was more or less on time."

Driving from the airport into town Mark was always amazed by the dry barren terrain of Margarita. Instead of lush tropical vegetation the landscape was similar to that of Tangiers in Morocco, but without the camels trekking along the road.

"We're going to make a quick stop for something to eat and have a drink at the Blue Topaz. It's a new fashionable restaurant in Porlamar owned by a client who commissioned me to do the interior design. Unfortunately before it was completed his cash flow got a bit tight, so I'm taking some of my fees in food and drinks as part of a barter deal. It's a beautiful place with great seafood and it's not out of our way. We're going to meet my friend, José Soto who by the way is no relation. When I told him about your problems with the Guardia Nacional he said he'd like to meet you so I suggested the Blue Topaz. José's an agent with the DISIP the Venezuelan Dirección de los Servicios de Inteligencia y Prevención. He said he's got some information that he's sure you'll be interested in. After we meet he wants us to visit Juangriego so he can show us what's going on."

As they entered the restaurant Javier cautioned,

"Watch the first step."

But unfortunately the warning was just a moment too late as Mark stumbled to regain his balance having missed the darkened first step.

The Blue Topaz was indeed quite magnificent and Javier had every reason to be proud of his work. Situated on the main street in Porlamar's commercial center the bar-restaurant had become the favored watering-hole of the local upscale crowd. It was also a popular rendezvous for wealthy Venezuelans who flew in from Caracas to spend long weekends in the many beautiful condos that fringed the island's numerous white sand beaches. Two steps down from the street a classic Italian renaissance water fountain fashioned in hand carved granite greeted customers at the restaurant's imposing entrance. Rising from the center of its small pool was a life-size marble statue of the goddess Diana. The double width glass entry doors, tinted in azure blue shielded the restaurant's subdued interior from the piercing rays emitted by the eternal sun of this Caribbean isle.

With the exception of the sun rays penetrating the darkness through the open door and a number of soft iridescent lights embedded over the bar, the interior was shrouded in obscurity. After momentarily adjusting to the darkness, Mark followed Javier to a corner table that was softly illuminated by a single Tiffany lamp. Sitting at the table was José Soto, a strikingly handsome man with tousled hair showing a touch of gray wearing a sports jacket emblazoned with the logo of the Tampa Bay Buccaneers. Standing as we approached,

"Hey Javier what's happening my man?" Shaking his hand Javier smiled,

"Good to see you José, how's Terre doing, has she recovered from the accident?"

Terre, Jose's sister had recently been injured by a hit and run driver. While she could have easily been killed her injuries were limited to a few scratches and a broken arm.

"She's a tough lady, her arm is still in a cast, but hopefully she'll be back to normal in a couple of months."

"José I'd like you to meet Captain Mark Kelly. Mark's been doing the Coastguard training and in July was made the Honorary Commander of the Tiburon Group here in Margarita."

Mark extending his hand,

"Pleased to meet you José, Javier has told me that you work for the DISIP. I'm curious about what you have that I may be interested in." After first scanning the room José began speaking in a hushed tone,

"Javier has assured me that you can be trusted, but I must insist that whatever we discuss be held in the strictest confidence."

To assure José of confidentiality Mark responded,

"No problem whatever we speak about goes no further."

"As Javier told you I'm a special agent with the DISIP. When I learned that you have some reliable contacts with a number of law enforcement agencies, I wanted to meet you. Because of your connections I have a proposal that I'm sure will be of interest. In addition to my work with the DISIP I have developed let's say a relationship and was retained by an Arab Group in Venezuela that have a base operating out of Juangriego. The Group is made up of Palestinians and Lebanese, but to conceal their true identities they're shown as *Syrians* on their Venezuelan identification cards. They pay me to provide them with confidential information about any government activities that could damage or compromise their import-export activities which is the transshipment of narcotics through Venezuela from Colombia. The payments they receive are in cash and laundered through banks here in Margarita and in Aruba, Curacao, Panama, and the Cayman Islands. The Arabs also support and fund the terrorist organizations Hezbollah and Hamas in the Middle East, when money is transferred it normally goes through Paraguay. For the wire transfers they use the Banco Confederado in Margarita or sometimes the cash is taken by courier to Cuidad Del Este. Their activity in the drug trade is increasing and appears to be unstoppable. In addition to direct shipments to the U.S. and Europe in the last two months there has also been at least ten large consignments transshipped through Margarita to Guadeloupe, Sint Maarten and Trinidad. The shipments go through without any problems because the Arabs are paying the Guardia Nacional for protection. The Arabs recently found that the Guardia Nacional was also being paid by the CIA for protection of their shipments and weren't happy to learn of their double-dipping. With the Guardia Nacional allowing drugs to be shipped by the CIA the Arabs believe the competition is hurting their business."

In hushed tones and absorbed in their conversation they were startled when from the shadows the soft voice of a demure waitress asked,

"Would you like to order something?" Javier, looking up inquired, "Mark I assume you'll have the normal cappuccino. I'll have a Polar[1], José what'll you have?"

Turning, José smiled and looking at the Venezuelan beauty said, "What I'd really like is to have is you for dinner, but for the moment two Polars and a cappuccino."

With a provocative grin the waitress responded,

"I'll get your order while you write down your phone number."

Smiling at José, Javier said,

"Wow, you don't waste any time amigo."

Obviously amused by his own possible success,

"You know Javier I once heard of a man in Caracas who was known to have stopped many beautiful women in Plaza Bolívar to ask them if they would like to go to bed with him. The story goes that he got his faced slapped many times, but he also went to bed with a lot of beautiful women."

José's prospective new love returned with the drinks and phone numbers were exchanged. Javier, either through envy or disapproval said,

"Can we please get back to business?"

Apologetically Jose tendered,

"I'm sorry Javier, but hey man, you're married. I'm not."

With his eyes once more darting around the darkened room José

---

[1] a popular Venezuelan Beer

looking directly at Mark said,

"Mark I'm ready for a change. I've been with the DISIP for 15 years working for a pittance. The only way I can live in the manner I do is because of a small inheritance that my late wife received when her uncle died and the money I receive on the side. I want to make some *big money* and then retire to Florida. I believe the *big money* can come from what I know is going on between Colombia and Venezuela, particularly in Juangriego and Porlamar. What I'm looking for is to be paid for the reliable information I can provide. Exactly how close are you to the DEA and U.S. Customs?"

"José what's the purpose of the question?"

Again, glancing around the bar José put his elbows on the table and brought his fingers together tip to tip against his mouth.

"I know from my brother-in-law in Clearwater that Customs are paying informants up to 10% of the street value of seized narcotics. He told me that he saw a story in the Tampa Tribune where a confidential tip lead to the seizure of drugs with a street value of $58 million, at 10% the tipster would have received a lot of money. If your contacts can be relied upon I can produce the information that would make $58 million seem like petty cash and do it more than once. Of course, it will be very dangerous for me and my children and something I could only do for a short time, but I'm willing to take the chance if I could be guaranteed a percentage of the seizures. When I decide it's time to leave I would want to be assured of resident alien status for me and my two children in the United States."

"José tell me more, what are the routes and methods they use for the shipments?"

"It really depends on the size. Go-fasts leave from Castilletes in the Gulf of Venezuela and normally head for Aruba or Curacao, while other times the drugs are transferred to small freighters waiting offshore. The go-fasts can carry up to 27 bales which each weigh about 100kg so their loads are normally around 2 to 3 tons. In the case of larger shipments the drugs are sometimes hidden in containers loaded at Puerto Cabello or in La Guaira. They always use old, nondescript inter-island freighters that sail to the French or Netherlands Antilles, Haiti or the Dominican

Republic. Once they arrive at the transshipment ports the containers are transferred to ships bound for Europe or the East Coast of the U.S.A. In Guadeloupe or Fort de France the containers will either be transshipped to Marseilles or broken down and sent with mules on Air France flights to Paris. When they cross the Caribbean 95% of the ships get through without being boarded. There's never a problem between Colombia and Margarita because the Arabs have the Colombian authorities and the Guardia Nacional on their payroll. When shipments that are to be broken down arrive in Margarita which is their central distribution point, they transfer the drugs from the freighters anchored offshore to a warehouse in Juangriego."

"José do you know where these freighters originate?"

"Normally from either Cartagena or Barranquilla, but the ships are never Colombian registered and normally flagged in Venezuela, Honduras or Panama. There was only one case where I saw that a freighter was registered in Cambodia. I'm sure there were probably more, but on at least three occasions they sent 1,000 kilos hidden in false keel-coolers and half-round cylinders that were welded to the hulls of containerships sailing to Le Havre and Marseilles. I've never seen an open package, but from what I've been told it's all high grade stuff from Cali. After Escobar was killed the Cali Cartel took over most of the trade from Medellin. The Arabs don't cut it, but sometimes the 100kg bales may be opened to accommodate smaller shipments, but the *bricks* are shipped out in the same packages they receive from the Colombian's. To identify the lab and the source the packages all have a distinctive marking like a zodiac, horse or a scorpion. In Juangriego the shipments may be broken down into smaller lots and the *bricks* are bundled in 5 or 10 kilo packages. The smaller packages make it easier to conceal on go-fasts and the smaller boats that are destined for islands like Sint Maarten, Martinique or Guadeloupe. Last year they set up an arrangement with a Frenchman who lives in Saint Lucia for local distribution in Fort de France, Pointe ó Pitre, St. Bart's, and St. Martin. It's a very smooth operation. The Frenchman sends go-fasts with triple engines from St. Lucia who at night rendezvous 5 or 6 miles west of Saint Vincent with the ships from Margarita. After the transfer, the go-fasts will then go to Rodney Bay or Castries. From St. Lucia the Frenchman handles the distribution from Dominica to Grenada with his own people. Some of the consignments destined for Europe are concealed in the floors or ceiling panels of 40'containers or hidden within cargo consignments. I know of other times when the drugs have been hidden within heavy goods like cases of ceramic tiles so that when the ports weight the containers nothing appears unusual. They also use mules. With help from employees of Air France and KLM who are paid according to the quantity involved, they can safely send 10 or 20 kilos in pre-screened baggage or placed in compartments inside aircraft destined for Schiphol, Orly and Charles de Gaulle. The Arab's also have people in the Dutch ABC islands that they use as swallowers who leave as passengers from Curacao on the KLM flights to Holland. They stopped using swallowers from Caracas on flights to Miami and New York because too many got caught. The Cocaine is tightly packed in a condom that reduces them to a pellet about 5cm x 2.5cm which is then swallowed. Depending on the physical size of the swallowers, who are usually young women, they are forced to swallow anywhere from 30 to 60 pellets. If they get through they're met at the airport and then taken to a flat where they're given liquids to make them drop their load which is normally in a bathtub. They get paid based on the number of pellets they carry which is generally around $5,000.00 before returning home. The swallowers were reasonably successful in getting through until one time during a flight to Holland a pellet broke and the woman died of a cardiac arrest. The medical examiner reported the cause of death to the Dutch police at Amsterdam's Schiphol Airport who then started doing random X-rays of passengers arriving from the Dutch Caribbean Islands."

"José I thought we were only talking about shipments to the United States? If you're including the Dutch and the French this could get interesting. I've recently spoken with the Dutch and have a good friend in the French Narcotics Task Force in Caracas. Both have a program to pay informants. I think I could make the right contacts with the U.S. authorities, but keeping your identity anonymous might be a problem especially if resident alien status has to be part of the deal and would only work if the DEA or Customs would agree to put you in the witness protection program. To make sure everything you're asking can be agreed, I'll do some checking when I get back to Puerto Rico. As the resident alien status is going to take some time to organize, I'd suggest we begin with the Dutch and the French. One of the problems all drug enforcement people have with informants is that the information they provide is many times unreliable. There have been a number of cases where Customs has received information on something that's coming down, but after they organize a strike team involving boats and sometimes helicopters they then find that the information is bogus. This happens because the informant provides false information to law enforcement who set up an operation in one place only to find that the actual delivery is coming down somewhere else. The traffickers are smart and know how to play the game. Then there's the other side of the coin where an informant provides good information, Customs make a bust then reneges on the payment. It's something to think about. As an example I have an informant on Dutch Sint Maarten who had access to critical information on shipments to Puerto Rico and the Virgin Islands. The informant was close to the Colombian king-pins who had set up shop on the island, after he gave me a rundown on what he had to offer I organized a bust with Customs in San Juan. As a test case to establish his creditability he agreed to provide information on a shipment of 1,000kg of cocaine that would be on a particular twin engine go-fast that would leave Sint Maarten at a specific time. The informant agreed to provide a full description of the individuals on board, the name and boat's registration number, the make and horsepower of the engines, and the amount of fuel they carried. Based on the sea state, weight of the boat and fuel, how much cocaine was being carried, which in this case was 1,000kg, and the horsepower of the engines I calculated the time it would take the boat to reach Fajardo and gave all the information to Customs. This was only a test case to prove that the informant was for real, but if the information was good and the specific boat and contraband was seized the informant wouldn't receive any payment, but his credibility would be established. For future seizures U.S. Customs agreed to pay the informant 10% of the value at $13,000.00 per kilo of the narcotics that were seized based on his information. It's the same scenario that your brother-in-law told you about and the procedure you'd have to follow to make it work. Give Customs a freebee and if it's good, you'd be put on the payroll."

José briefly pondered his options, but quickly realized there really weren't any.

"Okay José, we've discussed the generalities let's get specific."

"Mark like I said the shipments sent from the Mainland and Margarita travel in a number of different ways. The Arabs are meticulous and pay close attention to their shipping methods, packaging and concealment to avoid detection. Their methods are under constant scrutiny and subject to change depending on the perceived danger of discovery at any particular port. Hassan knows that only a small percentage of containers are inspected when they arrive at mainland U.S. Ports. He also knows they have a free ride especially when they are transshipped through Trinidad and other Caribbean ports like Haiti and the Dominican Republic...."

Mark interrupted, "Whose Hassan?"

"I'll explain who the players are when we get to Juangriego. I can tell you where and when the go-fasts are moving out along with their destinations. If it's a ship with containers, I can give you the name of the ship and the container numbers that will make them easier to track. I have access to this information because Hassan oversees and controls the container movements. Depending on the final destination they'll generally use a number of different 40' containers going to same port. Before they reach the departure port where they're loaded on the ships the hidden cavities are stuffed with drugs. At the departure port they pay the crane operators to stagger the loading of the containers so they're out of sequence when they're put on board the ship. While there's always a chance that one or two may be detected the others will get through. When they have containers that are being transshipped through say, Trinidad, bound for Miami and they want to leave a quantity of drugs in Port-of-Spain they have devised a method of being able to open a container without breaking the customs seal. Hassan knows that the standard practice in shipping is to place the custom's seal only on the right door of the container. By slightly bending the center plate between the doors they are able to open the container's left door, remove the narcotics for the local market and then close it again without damaging the seal on the right door. Customs in Trinidad aren't aware that the container was opened nor are Customs in Miami because the seal hasn't been broken or tampered with. The tool they use is quite simple, but very effective. Hassan likes using Trinidad for shipments to the U.S. and Europe because he's got people which he refers to as 'family' working for him in Port-of-Spain. In some cases he'll send consignments bound for Europe via West African ports. After arriving in places like Dakar or Agadir the drugs are hidden on trucks that then go overland to Tangiers in Morocco and cross the Straight of Gibraltar to Algeciras in Southern Spain. I've also heard them mention that some of these shipments have been cut down and concealed in cars or small trucks that cross from Tangiers to the Spanish port of Tarifa on the fast ferries. Hassan believes this is a good route because no containers move through Tarifa and the Spanish customs in Tarifa aren't as thorough as they sometimes are in Algeciras."

"José you've obviously got a lot of information that could be very useful. What's the next step?"

"I want to show you what I'm talking about in Juangriego, but it wouldn't be wise for me to be seen with two strangers driving around Juangriego because the local police and the Arabs all know me. Javier, your Ford Bronco has dark tinted windows; could we all travel in your car?"

Javier cleared the back seat of the Bronco which was piled with sample books used to display tiles and wall coverings to his clients. José positioned himself low in the back while Mark sat in front on the passenger side. About halfway to Juangriego while passing through the town of La Asuncion José reaching over the seat, taped Mark on the shoulder,

"Mark, Javier tells me that you're originally from California, how did you and your son end up in Puerto Rico?"

Without turning Mark answered,

"Actually he's not my son, Mike's my nephew. I took the responsibility of raising him after my sister and brother-in-law died. Mike and I were living in Sint Maarten on the Dutch side, but after he'd finished the 6th grade we were faced with the problem of his further education. When children in Sint Maarten finish their first level of schooling which is the 6th grade, the parents usually pack their bags and send the kiddies off to a boarding school in Holland. Even though as a single parent the idea was tempting, I feel that young children should be brought up by their parents or in my case a family member, not by a disinterested headmaster that's 6,000 miles away. I didn't want to live in the States so I began looking at different cities in Latin America and the Caribbean. My searches lead me to Puerto Rico and a particularly good private school in Fajardo located on the eastern end of the island. After making the decision we pulled up the anchor and sailed to Fajardo. The pulling up the anchor is actually what happened because at the time we lived on a 43' Hatteras motor yacht moored in Simpson Bay. Over the years I've met a number of truly wonderful people in Puerto Rico, but early adjustment to the island's *banana republic* attitude is necessary in order to maintain your sanity. While the Commonwealth of Puerto Rico is part of the United States the local politicians act as if Puerto Rico were a sovereign country. In a demonstration of their stupidity the Puerto Rican government once tried to sign a bilateral trade agreement that included Castro's Cuba, when Washington found out they told the mental dwarfs in San Juan to drop the idea. There's a high level of unemployment because many Puerto Ricans get more money from government hand-outs than they can from holding a job. Having to work every day doesn't go down well with the *Borinquen'*. Humorists' in the U.S. have a number of Puerto Rican jokes, but one of the favorites asks the question, what's the difference between a Puerto Rican and a Dominican? The answer, 'one gets welfare - the other doesn't.' But much like anywhere else you have to weigh the good with the bad."

"Okay, so Puerto Rican politicians and the government aren't honest or too bright, but what in actuality is really the bad side?"

"Crime, corruption and the high cost of living, the per capita murder rate, armed robberies, muggings, and car theft puts Puerto Rico in the top ten in the United States, and crime isn't just limited to the lower classes. Many of the islands politicians are either in jail or under indictment for fraud or embezzlement of government funds. The investigations involving corruption and RICO violations keep the FBI and other federal law enforcement agencies busy. The U.S. government attorneys always have a full case load bringing the bad guys to justice. Strangely it doesn't seem to bother the locals too much who appear to believe that a bit of graft and corruption should be the norm for Latinos. Based on past experience the Puerto Ricans also know that when the local coffers run dry Washington always sends more money. The state and local police are really a joke. At least half the cops in the eastern and southern parts of the island are in jail for transporting or selling drugs, stealing cars or receiving stolen property."

"Sounds pretty bad, what's the good side?" Still looking forward Mark said,

"A year round temperature of about 75°, Roosevelt Roads Naval Base which is close by, and thanks to American Airlines a first class airport with connections to anywhere in the world." José grimaced then asked,

"If the local government and the cops are crooked, how's that leave me if I'm providing, let's say, sensitive information?"

"José if I can put something together it wouldn't involve any contact with the Puerto Rican police. In any case because of the high level of corruption the federal authorities seldom share important intelligence with them. If the DEA or the Customs Service is interested in what you have to offer you'd work directly with their agents. The Feds have such a distrust of the local cops that they don't let them in on anything that's coming down. In many cases the Feds are the ones that arrest the Puerto Rican cops and sometime even the judges. As you want to obtain Green Cards the Puerto Ricans wouldn't be involved because residency status would only be a matter for the U.S. Agencies and that may take a little time. Until we know if the Feds are interested in your offer and depending how soon you can start the flow of information, I think we should get things rolling with the Dutch and French."

José replied,

"I'm ready to start now. Hopefully getting the Green Cards won't take long, but in the meantime I'll be patient while you try and work things out with the right people because if there was a leak I could quickly be dead meat. For the time being I think you're right about putting the gringos in a holding pattern and in the meantime move forward with the Europeans."

Turning into the main square of Juangriego José poked Javier with his finger,

"Make a turn at the next corner and go slow."

The Bronco maneuvered around a stalled car while slowly passing a number of tourist shops with their gaudy displays of t-shirts and inflatable beach toys hanging from improvised wire mesh racks. As José slid still lower in his seat he told Javier,

"Okay slow down, see the red Mercedes parked on the left? The guy standing next to the driver's door is Johnny Hassan, he and his brother Mohamed Abbas the guy sitting down are the ones who run the show. Both drive new Mercedes 450s which doesn't come from selling t-shirts and the other cheap crap they offer to the tourists. I don't know how he got the name Johnny it probably was just a nickname he picked up along the way. Both Hassan and Abbas were born in Lebanon and have close ties with the large Lebanese community in Cuidad Del Este in Paraguay."

Johnny Hassan was a dark skinned man of about 45, slender in build and short, being no more than about 5'2". He was wearing a plain white shirt with blue trousers. The two Arabs appeared to be little more than unremarkable shopkeepers who were simply discussing the business of the day, not the treacherous drug lords described by José. Hassan, his eyes squinting from the smoke rising from the cigarette dangling from his mouth was flaying his arms in the air in some type of an animated explanation while Abbas looked a bit like Yasir Arafat, but without the traditional head scarf. His bald head had some nasty scars and he too was smoking as he rocked back and forth in a plastic garden chair resting on its two back legs. Neither of the men appeared to pay much attention to the Bronco as it slowly passed.

"If you should ever come to Juangriego and pass the shop never drive by more than once. Hassan has a photographic memory and if he thinks someone looks suspicious or appears to be watching him he'll have me or the municipal police run the license plate to see who the person is and why they're in Juangriego. Hassan is a very nervous type who distrusts everyone except for his brother. Javier, continue down the street, at the gas station take a left turn. I'll show you the warehouse they work out of."

On a dusty, non-descript side street leading to the waterfront José pointed to a two story concrete block building set back about 100' from the road. The outer perimeter was surrounded by a ten foot cyclone fence. Situated about thirty feet from the building was an inner enclosure protected by an eight foot high steel cyclone fence topped with barbed razor wire. Surveillance cameras and large spotlights were mounted at each corner of the outer fence. Two guards in green uniforms both holding sawed-off shot guns were sitting in chairs positioned on each side of the expansive entrance door of the building. The door, as the building's sole point of entry was of a sufficient height and width to accommodate a large truck. Directly above the door a sign proclaimed in English that this was the building of VENEZ Import-Export. Below the English name was a collection of letters in Arabic.

"José what happens here?"

"When a shipment arrives it's taken off the ship by a feeder boat, which I'm going to show you in a minute. After the packages are off-loaded from the boat they then move them to the warehouse in that black truck parked alongside the building. The driver and three armed guards watch while six to ten guys transfer the tightly wrapped bundles from the pier to the truck, after it's loaded the truck returns to the warehouse. Abbas and another Arab by the name of Ahmed are always on hand to monitor the transfer. Hassan, Abbas and Ahmed are armed and carry 9mm weapons. The municipal police are on Hassan's payroll and when the shipments are moved which is usually late at night, they watch from a respectable distance to make certain everyone stays away and there aren't any prying eyes. My job is to make certain that the local cops stay honest and that there's no interference from the federal authorities in Caracas. Hassan pays me for information I'm his eyes and ears. I'm on the payroll to let him know if there might be any chatter that could affect the operation."

Driving further down the road the Bronco approached the Bahía de Juangriego. Tied alongside a small pier was an aging 40' ex-crew boat that had clearly had seen better days when she was servicing the oil rigs out of New Orleans.

José with a smirk on his face said,

"That's what Hassan calls his Dream Boat, when I asked him how he picked the name he said, because of that boat all his dreams would come true."

Taking a last look at the boat the trio continued along the road leading away from Juangriego towards the village of La Galera, Mark asked,

"José how often does our Mr. Hassan use his Dream Boat?"

"It depends on the number of ship arrivals, but at least three or four times a week. Hassan always knows the, who, what, where, and when because he plans and organizes the stuffing, shipping and scheduling of the containers originating in Barranquilla, Cartagena, Puerto Cabello, and La Guaira. The warehouse is only a temporary storage area that's used after the drugs come off the ship. If the consignment has to be cut down it normally only takes one or two hours before it's repackaged and moved out. Everything is carefully planned to insure that the consignments never remain in the warehouse more than 24 hours. In the last two years there was only one case where a ship, after she had been loaded experienced engine problems and was delayed for two days while they did the repairs. Hassan is an edgy type who always keeps his gun handy in an ankle holster, he's left handed so the holster is fastened with a strap under his trousers on the inside of his left ankle. There are always two guards with shotguns at the bottom of the stairs leading to his office who are there to protect him because he keeps a lot of money in a safe in the warehouse. Abbas is normally the courier who carries the money in a black 22' roll-on that he keeps with him from Maiquetia to Sao Paulo where he connects with a flight to Foz do Iguaçu, which is near the border with Paraguay. At Foz do Iguaçu

Abbas always stays at a hotel called the Bourbon where he is met by his Lebanese contact and driven across the open border between Brazil and Cuidad Del Este in Paraguay. In Cuidad Del Este the cash is turned over to a guy who's the banker for the Hezbollah organization. When Hassan transfers large amounts of money by wire he normally uses the Banco Confederado in Margarita, but not exclusively. Last month I was in his office waiting to get paid and overheard him speaking to someone in the Cayman Islands about money being transferred to a bank in Beirut. On another occasion while he was in the toilet and I was alone in the office I saw wire transfer instructions on his desk for the transfer of $2 million to the BNP bank in Paris."

"José I know of the connection between the Guardia Nacional and the CIA, but why is Hassan concerned? If he's getting protection from the Guardia Nacional why should he worry about the CIA and their shipments?"

"Mark it's really quite simple. Allowing the CIA to ship drugs under the protection of the Guardia Nacional is hurting Hassan's business and cutting into his profits. Hassan thought that he was the only one paying the Commanding General of the Guardia Nacional in Caracas and wasn't pleased when he learned that he was double-dipping. When I told him that the General was actually being paid by both him and the CIA he was furious and said the competition had to stop. Hassan pays the General in Caracas and knows he then pays both the Guardia Nacional Commander in Maracaibo who controls their post at Castilletes, and the Lieutenant Colonel who commands Detachment 76 in Margarita because both areas are major transshipment points. Maracaibo is particularly important because of the large quantities of drugs which are brought by truck across the open border with Colombia near Castilletes. Believing that the CIA might be moving almost as much as he was, he promptly arranged a meeting with the General in Caracas. I'm not sure, but I think the General may have used the meeting as an opportunity to get more money from him because according to Hassan the General acknowledged that the CIA was paying him, but said the payments were *irregular*. The General said when the CIA needed him they would give him the name of the ship and where

and when it would sail to ensure it was on the list of ships that wouldn't be interfered with. The General said that his involvement with the CIA was small in comparison and assured Hassan that he was his biggest client. Hassan has never let on about how much he pays the General, but it's got to be a fairly sizeable amount. Through my DISIP contacts in Caracas I have access to information about CIA shipments and can assure you they aren't *irregular*. The General lied to Hassan. Apparently the General told Hassan that he had no intention of dropping the CIA's business and if he didn't like it, too bad. So at the moment it seems like nothing's really changed. It's just as it's always been, the CIA is still in the picture and Venez Import-Export continues with their monthly payments, wiring the General's commission in U.S. dollars to his bank account in Aruba. I don't know what the commission is, but considering the increased number of movements it's got to be pretty sizeable. Hassan said that with the information he has about the General and his bank account in Aruba he wouldn't hesitate to use it as blackmail if he doesn't end his CIA connection. He also told me that if the General doesn't play-ball he'll have him killed. I think him telling me this may have been meant as a subtle warning for me as well. To make things even worse, last month I was with Hassan when he learned that the CIA had used a stolen sailboat to move a small quantity of narcotics through Venezuela and got caught by the Guardacostas. He was furious that the Guardia Nacional and their CIA clients would do such a stupid thing. Hassan couldn't understand why the General would compromise a very profitable business enterprise for the sake of a little side business that couldn't have amounted to much. After the sailboat incident Hassan told me that the CIA surely wouldn't last because they were little more than a bunch of stupid Yankee cowboys."
Javier was shaking his head while Mark was frantically trying to write everything down. It was clearly time for a break,
"Wow, that's quite a story. Let's stop somewhere and have something to drink."
"Okay, but let's wait until we are well away from Juangriego it would be too dangerous for me to be seen with two strangers

especially when Hassan didn't know I was here. Let's go to the Bodega Tampico on the road outside Pampatar. It's on the way back."

Located on the outskirts of town the Bar Tampico was like a scene or caricature out of a Hemmingway novel based in Havana in the 1950's. Six plastic tables and matching chairs emblazoned with faded red and white Coca-Cola decals fronted a bar counter that had been fashioned from a display counter which had obviously been long over used by a now closed supermarket. The establishment was empty except for an aging, toothless proprietor who struggled to balance a tray carrying three Polar beers to our table. While sipping on the lukewarm beer Mark finished writing down the information that José had provided. He then carefully explained the arrangements with the French and Dutch for the flow of information and the payment that José would receive.

"Every two or three days I receive the *list* with the details of the various shipments which I'll fax to you. If something comes up and you need to speak with me please call my sister Maria in Tampa, I've written her phone number on the notepad. I'll tell her that if you call, she's to call me and I'll call you from a public telephone. I don't think the DISIP is monitoring my cell phone calls, but just in case, a call from my sister won't mean anything. I'll fill in Maria so she'll know what's going on."

"José this is how it'll work, as soon as my French contact receives the payment he'll transfer the funds to my account in the Cayman Islands. I'll then transfer the money to your sister's account in Florida then call her so she can let you know. No one will know your name or have any details so nothing can be traced back to you."

Passing the notepad across the table José continued,

"Mark here's the name of the bank, address and the number of my sister's account in Florida. Because this is only coming together with your help I want you to keep half of the payments. The other half can be deposited into my sister's account. I'm still hoping that you can put something together with the DEA or U.S. Customs so I can get thc Green Cards, but in the meantime we'll get started with the others."

"Okay José this is workable, but there's really no need to give me anything. I'm just glad that I'm in a position to help. When you speak with your sister tell her she should never say my name. I'll only say I'm calling for *El Gato Negro* and hang up so she'll know to call you."

"Mark I wouldn't be able to make any money without you and insist that you take at least 50% of the payments, and by the way, *El Gato Negro*? What's this?"

"José from here on out - no names, when I call your sister you're *The Black Cat*. We've both got to be very careful and watch our backs." "Mark, if I need to speak with you what do I call you?"

"There's no need for you to call me anything. I'm the only person that answers my cell phone, so you'll know it's me you're speaking with. No names."

After arriving in the town center and shielded from any prying eyes, José got out of the Bronco in a back alley a block away from the Blue Topaz. That evening Mark returned to Caracas. The following morning he called the French Embassy.

"Bonjour Jacques, I've got some good news for you, are you sitting down?"

"Hi Mark, yes, I'm sitting down, what's the news?"

"I don't want to get into any details over the phone, but if Pierre and Dirk are ready I've got a wealth of information for them. I'm on the American flight back to San Juan this afternoon, but if you've got a bit of time and when we're done you could have one of your drivers take me to Maiquetia, I'll come over?"

"No problem. Will you come right away?"

"I'll check out and be with you in 45 minutes."

45 minutes later a taxi dropped Mark at the steps of the French Embassy.

"Hello Mark, how about some coffee?"

"Thanks Jacques, black please. I've had a very positive and rewarding trip. During my visit I met with an individual who has detailed information on the major drug shipments that are flowing from Colombia through Venezuela. My source, two or three times a week will provide me a *list* with everything that's on the move. This includes the go-fasts, small coastal freighters and the containers used for transshipment. I expect to have the first *list* in the next few days and as soon as I receive it I'll send it

to your private fax. Depending on the points of departure you can advise Pierre and Dirk, so they'll be able to coordinate the logistics of interdiction. Once the seizure is made and the quantity is determined you can let me know how much will be deposited into my account in the Cayman Islands, I'll then transfer the payment to the informant. Which brings up the question, how long will it take you to make the transfer?"
Jacques smiled,
"It sounds as though you've nicely assembled all the pieces of the puzzle. As to the payment, once we know the size of the seizure and calculate the payment I'm confident that the transfer could be made in two or three weeks. Sorry about the delay, governments always ask for promptness when they're owed money, but are a bit slower when they pay their bills. You can be assured that if the operation is successful I'll keep the heat on for quicker payment. In the meantime I'll alert Pierre and Dirk and look forward to receiving the first of the *lists*. I've got a driver standing by to take you to the airport."

———

Mark returned to Puerto Rico and spent the following week attending to the assignments received during his absence. Dealing with the marine losses in the Dominican Republic and the Virgin Islands where a bit mundane considering what was coming down in Venezuela, but at least temporally took Mark's mind off the activities of *El Gato Negro*. A few days later while preparing for his return to Venezuela he received the first of the *lists* which he promptly faxed to Jacques.

———

On the return and sitting *up-front* they had an enjoyable flight to Caracas and both thanked the American Airlines' flight attendants as they left the plane. Walking towards immigration Mike said to Mark, "You know flying *up-front* is really great. It's nice when American gives us an upgrade because flying *common class* really sucks."
"You're right, being in the Business or First Class cabin is always a nice experience, but don't forget I had to fly 2 million miles in

what you call *common class* to qualify for Elite Platinum Status that provides the privileges of upgrades. You know Mike, calling it *Common Class* makes you sound like a real snob."

As usual Toschenko was there to greet them as they entered the arrivals hall.

"Hola amigos, welcome back to Venezuela! Tonight my wife has invited you both for dinner. We live in the La Trinidad section of Caracas. I'll pick you up about 1830 hours on my way home from the office."

"Sounds good to me we'll look forward to seeing you at 1830."

While waiting for Toschenko in the hotel lobby Mark and Mike had a *fatherly* discussion about the growing problems with drugs and how it was ruining the lives of so many people both young and old. Toschenko was on time and the traffic was bearable, while driving he said,

"I'm truly pleased that you'll be coming to my home for dinner. My son and daughter are looking forward to meeting you both. Nicholas is 17 and Alexandra is 16."

Mark looked at Toschenko and with a slight grin said,

"Nicholas and Alexandra, hmm, I guess there's no question of the Russian origins of this family."

A beaming Toschenko acknowledged the comment,

"That's for sure. But I want you to meet my mother she too is a real Russian. We'll stop by her house on our way so I can introduce you and Mike. I've told my mother a lot about you and she's looking forward to meeting you."

The home of Toschenko's mother was situated in a beautiful suburb on the outskirts of Caracas. Set back from the road a graveled path passed manicured gardens shaded by flowering trees and latticed arbors placed alongside a large fishpond leading to an imposing château reminiscent of the antebellum architecture found in America's Deep South.

"Captain it is such a pleasure to finally meet you in person, Nicholas has often spoken about you and your work with the Guardacostas. I would like to introduce my sister Katrina, Nicholas's aunt."

"It's is a pleasure to meet you both and please allow me to introduce my nephew Mike."

"Madame Toschenko Nicholas has often spoken about you and I too have been looking forward to having the opportunity of meeting you personally."

"Mother I think it would be a good time to sample a bit of your vodka." With a sheepish grin on his face Toschenko continued,

"My mother makes her own vodka in the cellar which is the best outside of Mother Russia and the smoothest in the world. I'm sure that if I were to ask her kindly she might even give me a bottle or two to take home."

"Nicholas of course you may have a bottle to take home, but first let us enjoy a drink together with the Captain and Mike."

Mike declined a sample of the best and smoothest opting instead for orange juice. Pouring plentiful doses of the clear liquid from a former wine bottle Mrs. Toschenko raised her glass,

"Like the British say, Cheers."

Following the Cheers the charming 80 year old matron downed a sizeable portion of the high-octane spirits then Nicholas only seconds behind his mother emptied his glass. Deciding to err on the side of caution Mark slowly sipped the potent fluid.

"No, no, Mark good Russian vodka is not meant to be sipped, but taken all at one time."

"Nicholas if I were to swig the contents of the glass you'd have to carry me out to the car."

Toschenko smiled,

"But in the movies John Wayne always knocked his whisky back in one swig."

"You're watching too many movies Nicholas."

After exchanging some small talk about their visits to Venezuela and what life was like in Puerto Rico, Nicholas stood saying,

"Mother I'm sorry, but we must be going as my lovely Daniela has prepared a sumptuous dinner for our guests and we must not be late."

Expressing their thanks and Nicholas with two bottles of his mothers Vodka held tightly in his hand they left. At Toschenko's home while turning the key in the lock and pushing on the door,

"Daniela, Daniela, we're here."

From the kitchen Daniela emerged wiping her hands on a towel as she approached. Nicholas inquired,

"Where are the children?"
Kissing her husband on the cheek she responded,
"They're in the bedroom playing games on the computer."
Daniela then called out,
"Alexandra, Nicholas, please come, your father's home."
Alexandra was a striking girl with long black hair and beautiful eyes that belied her 16 years. Young Nicholas too was a handsome lad with tussled hair wearing a t-shirt emblazoned with the logo of the New York Yankees. After the introductions were made Mike, Alexandra and young Nicholas disappeared into the bedroom where they quickly became immersed in a video game concentrating on a super hero that was taking out all the bad guys with what sounded like a battery of AK-47's and a never-ending supply of ammunition.
With a limited command of English Daniela described in Spanish what she had prepared for dinner then called on Nicholas to translate,
"My wife says she hopes that you like pork as she has prepared a lovely roast."
Mark responded, "Gracias Señora Toschenko, cerdo asado es muy bueno."
In broken English she gracefully replied,
"Please, my name is Daniela there is no need to be formal amongst friends."
Daniela was clearly a warm person who in spite of having endured extensive chemotherapy in treatment of breast cancer made everyone around her feel welcome. She declined joining Nicholas and Mark for a round of his mother's vodka opting instead for a glass of Argentinean Concho y Toro Chardonnay. With the exception of some unidentified root vegetable that had the taste of partially cooked cardboard, the dinner was excellent. The distortion of Mike's face when he tasted the brownish vegetable quickly vanished upon receipt of Mark's subtle kick under the table. On the drive back to the hotel Mike was quiet while Toschenko and Mark conversed about the usual Coastguard business and the appalling state of affairs caused by the country's disgraced President Carlos Andres Perez.
"Captain, I'm very pleased that you could come to my home for

dinner tonight. It really means a lot to me. Daniela is very sick and has been weakened further as a result of the chemotherapy. With me being away so much because of my work with the Coastguard it's nice that she has now had the opportunity to meet you and Mike."

Putting his hand on his shoulder,

"Nicholas it was our pleasure to have dinner with your family. I know and understand what you're talking about in being away so much which is why when I travel I always try to bring Mike with me as much as possible. I don't have a wife to consider, but children grow up very fast. I think it's important for parents and family to be around as much as possible, especially during a child's formative years."

"Mark you're a good man and an excellent role model for young Mike. All of us in Venezuela greatly appreciate you efforts and the time you have given to help us with the Guardacostas. Yesterday I learned something at headquarters that you will find most interesting. You must however keep this confidential. Admiral Blanes told me in private that after the Coast Guard in Washington received his letter commending you on your work in Venezuela for the Navy he was told that you were going to be promoted to Rear Admiral."

"Thanks for letting me know Nicholas and for sure it will go no further." Back at the hotel Mike was less restrained.

"Dad that's great news you'll be an Admiral with all those gold things on your shoulders?"

"You got it kid Rear Admirals do have all those gold *things* on the shoulders which are called shoulder boards. Lot's of gold things in addition to a single star on top."

"Wow, my Dad is going to be an Admiral. That's fantastic!"

"Hey, not yet, I agree its good news, but for the moment I just need to concentrate on being a good Captain."

"Dad there's something else, that brown stuff at dinner was awful. Do you know what it was?"

"No, but you're right it was pretty dreadful, however as guests we don't complain about the food."

"Okay, but please don't ever again ask me to eat something that's likely to make me sick."

From the gargantuan breakfast he consumed the next morning Mike didn't get sick and they agreed that no permanent internal damage had been done. Mark's work with the Venezuelan Navy continued and a few days later he received further recognition at a reception hosted by the Honorable Gloria Marrero, Consul General of the Republic of Venezuela in San Juan. During the reception Mark was honored when the Consul General presented him with an award and a plaque for his work with the Venezuelan Navy on behalf of the Foreign Affairs Ministry. Along with a number of U.S. Coast Guard officers those in attendance included Venezuelan Navy officers, Captain Nicholas Toschenko and his wife Daniela, 1st Lieutenant Eric Lopez and his wife Beatrice, a 2nd Lieutenant, Captain Carlos Luis De Camas Bauer and his companion Veronica, and Captain Carlos Proscenia Jared.

A similar, but less inspiring afternoon reception was hosted by the U.S. Coast Guard Greater Antilles Section in San Juan. Unlike previous Commanders who had been admired and respected the self-centered and egotistical Captain Greg Margo was looked upon as someone best avoided. Mark hadn't recalled if Margo attended the reception hosted by the Venezuelan government, but if he was there, even briefly, he was noticeably silent which wouldn't be unusual considering his serious lack of communicative skills. Initially Mark had believed that Margo was a friend, but soon found that he wasn't when he tried to torpedo Mark's promotion to Rear Admiral. Unfortunately for Margo, he wasn't aware of the CIA's influence in his promotion. Greg Margo was interested only in himself and had great aspirations of promotion past the grade of Captain, but was never promoted. Many of those who served with or under him were able to see him for what he was and hopefully were able to do so before he'd thrown them to the sharks for his own self-interest. His subordinates viewed him as cold and ruthless whose sole pursuit was personal recognition and promotion.

To follow up with helping José Soto, Mark telephoned a good friend, Jean-Claude Daman, a French narcotics agent assigned to the Joint Task Force working out of the U.S. Coast Guard base in San Juan. Jean-Claude answered the phone,

"Bonjour amigo, any good tips on the new vintages coming in to

Guadeloupe?"

"Mark it's been a while, how have you been my friend, still working in Venezuela?"

"Yeah, the beat goes on, everything is fine and we're seeing good results from the training. I'm also working with Jacques Deauville on a program that may prove interesting. Jean-Claude I know your line is secure, but I'm not sure that mine is. There are some interesting things happening that I'd like to tell you about, but not over the phone. Are you planning to be on the Base sometime soon?"

"In fact I'll be out on Saturday to do a bit of shopping at the Navy Exchange."

Because of his concern with possible bugging, only on rare occasions would Mark discuss sensitive information on the telephone. Any meetings with government agents or his law enforcement contacts were always conducted in the safety of the Roosevelt Roads Naval Station. The Base offered maximum security and could only be accessed by those persons with government identification or others who had been given security clearances by the Navy or the Department of Defense. The Base provided Mark with a secure feeling that whomever he met and what they discussed would not be overheard or observed by the general public. Outside meetings in restaurants and other public places or being seen with persons who might be identified as federal agents was always avoided as it might prove harmful to his health. Saturday morning Mark waited in the restaurant of the Navy Exchange. After making his way across the Food Court to the booths situated against the inner wall a smiling Jean-Claude sat down.

"Hi Mark sorry I'm a bit late, but the traffic getting out of San Juan was murder. What is it you'd like to discuss?"

"Jean-Claude through my contacts within the Venezuelan Coastguard I've met someone who has some important information that he'd like to share, but wants to receive some compensation in return."

"Compensation, exactly what kind of compensation is he talking about?"

"He knows that the U.S. Customs Service will pay 10% of the

street value of seized narcotics to informants who can supply the necessary intelligence that leads to a successful bust. In addition to a monetary payment he also wants to obtain the agreement of Customs that if everything works out as planned he can get resident alien status, namely Green Cards for him and his children. He's a widower and bringing up his children as a single parent. I'm working with Jacques in Caracas, but as his information also involves shipments of narcotics through Guadeloupe and Fort de France that end up in France, I thought you might also have an interest."

Listening intently the Frenchman took out a small black note book and began writing.

"Tell me more."

"For the moment let's call him Charlie. He was introduced to me by a friend who is also in the Venezuelan Coastguard. My friend is reliable and even more important, Charlie trusts him. Charlie works for the DISIP, the Venezuelan Security Service, but on the side he provides cover for a Lebanese drug lord who has a thriving business sending narcotics to the United States and Europe. I was introduced to Charlie on my last visit to Venezuela. After he gave me a run-down on what he had to exchange for his *compensation* we drove around and he showed me where everything is coming down. He knows a lot and I'm confident that he's for real."

"Sounds interesting, but why not call Customs or the DEA?"

"Jean-Claude, they definitely would have an interest in what's being offered, but as you know there's always a scramble and the inter-agency rivalry to contend with. Customs, DEA and the Coast Guard are always fighting to ensure their agency gets the credit and the publicity surrounding high profile seizures to make sure that when budget time comes around their agency gets the funding. I just don't want to get Charlie tied up with bunch of clowns who primarily are only interested in their own personal glory and might cause problems for him. Because of shipments that are going to mainland France through the French Antilles and considering I'm already working with Jacques I thought you'd be best for the first contact. If you were interested you could sort of be the lead in bringing the others into the act. I trust you, I don't trust the others."

"Thanks Mark, you're a real friend. You're right, if Customs or DEA come across something they first fight amongst themselves and then either throw me a bone at the last minute or cut me out completely. As I'm sure Jacques has told you the Gendarmerie has a program that will pay informants a reward for actionable information. The payment is normally a percentage, but in some cases we can also do a lump sum. If there's anything that's coming down in the areas where I'm working, we could either pay him the 10% or a lump sum, whichever the informant prefers. I also have a friend in the DEA who I owe a favor to so I might cut him in for a piece of the pie in case we have any jurisdictional issues. I'm sure he'd be interested."

Mark then provided Jean-Claude with an outline of the information that he had. They devised a code and agreed to keep in touch. Monday morning Jean-Claude called,

"I've spoken with the pharmacist and both your prescriptions will be ready on Tuesday morning at 10:30 at the pharmacy on the Base. For identification you must bring your papers with you to collect the medications. Please contact me if this is not convenient. Good-bye."

To ensure that telephone calls made over Mark's telephone, if monitored would have little significance, the message contained simple codes. The pharmacist was the Drug Enforcement Agency. The pharmacy was the aspirin and pill section immediately behind the cash registers in the check-out area of the Navy Exchange. The two prescriptions indicated that Mark was to look for two DEA agents. A single prescription would have meant for Mark to look for only one DEA agent. The papers for identification would be a copy of the *Lloyd's List* newspaper which is printed on pinkish paper which Mark was to carry in his right hand. While anyone else might be carrying a local newspaper or one of the other stateside papers which is printed on white or buff paper it was a good bet that no one on the Navy Base would have a copy of the *Lloyd's List* and Jean-Claude knew that Mark was a subscriber of the London based shipping newspaper. Mark arrived at the exchange at 10:00 and moved through the tobacco section briefly looking at different pipe tobaccos and cigars before meandering over to where the aspirin was located where he was approached by two men.

"Are you Mark Kelly?"

"Yes."

"I'm Larry Compton and this is Bob Weaver – DEA"

Moving into the seating section of the Food Court, Compton and Mark sat down while Weaver remained standing.

"How do you take your coffee?"

"Black please."

While waiting for Agent Weaver to return with the coffee, Compton got right to the point.

"Our boss has spoken with Jean-Claude and we understand you have some information that may be of interest to the Agency."

Without revealing his name or location in Venezuela Mark provided the two DEA agents with an outline of the information that was being offered and what the informant wanted in return. After taking a sip of his coffee, Compton, who appeared to be the senior of the two, spoke,

"Mark the information sounds very intriguing. I feel confident that it will be of great interest, but you must understand that I'm not authorized to agree to anything at this point. You'll have to give us the full details so we can submit it through channels to see if the demands of the informant can be met. The biggest hurdle is going to be the resident alien status for the informant and his family, this could be a problem. Also if there were a number of successful seizures the informant would have to appear in court and testify."

With annoying arrogance Compton recited the words as if he was reading from the *Wannabe -DEA Agent Lesson Plan 101,* which no doubt was part of his curriculum at the Federal Law Enforcement Training Center in Georgia. The pompous and supercilious novice acted as if he was doing him a favor, not the other way around. Mark was angry, but restrained himself, then went right to the heart of the matter,

"First, let me make it abundantly clear, unless all the conditions are met which includes the payments for the information and Green Cards for the informant and his family there won't be any seizures. If and only if, he was put in the witness protection program might he consider appearing in court, but this could be a problem because he wants to live in Florida. I realize that his acceptance in the witness protection program would need to be cleared beforehand by the U.S. Marshals Service who would determine whether or not his relocation to Florida would be acceptable, but I'm sure for what he's got to offer the DEA could pave the way. Florida shouldn't be a problem, being Hispanic he and his children would go unnoticed and better assimilate in Florida instead of someplace like Iowa. If you weren't willing to get him a new identity I can't believe that you would even ask that he agree to testify in court because it would never happen. You might as well ask him to commit suicide. I think you guys have been watching too many 'B' movies. Thanks gentlemen, this has been a total waste of my time."

Mark got up and left. From a pay phone outside he called Jean-Claude.

"What a couple of clowns. These guys haven't got a clue as to what's going on in the real world. Jean-Claude maybe you should try someone at Customs to see if they might be interested because as usual the DEA is hopelessly lost in never-never land."

The following day Mark received another coded call from Jean-Claude to advise him of a meeting with U.S. Customs. This time instead of meeting a pharmacist the rendezvous would be with a shipping company that had his order which was to be collected in the uniforms department of the Navy Exchange. Mark met with a Senior Customs Agent and repeated the story of Charlie. Unfortunately Mark got the same run-around and ended the meeting.

At home that night around 10:30 p.m. the phone rang.

"Hey dad can you grab the phone I just want to finish folding the laundry. If it's Carlos Gonzalez, please tell him that I'll call him back in 15 minutes."

Carlos, one of Mike's close friends was in his class at Fajardo Academy, but it wasn't Carlos who was calling. Hearing coins being dropped into a pay phone Mark answered,

"Hello."

"Captain Kelly?"

"Yes, who is this?"

"There's no need for you to know my name. I have something to tell you that I'm sure will be of interest. Have you had your phones swept, are they clean?"

"Why are you asking about my phones…"

"Don't ask, just tell me."

"I had a friend sweep them this afternoon and yes, they're clean."

"Please listen very closely because what I have to tell you is very important about what you're doing in Venezuela and might just save your life."

"How do you know what I'm doing in Venezuela?"

"Let's just say I read it in the papers. If what I am about to say is revealed it could get me in a lot of trouble and as it's my nickel just listen because I'm only going to say it once. If what I tell you is made public or repeated in anyway the wrong people might figure out where it came from. Agreed?"

"Okay, mums the word, but who are you?"

"My name's not important, but you can consider me a friend. I know exactly what you're doing and that you're involved with some of the most powerful and dangerous people in the U.S. government, unless you're careful they'll bury you."

"Bury me? What do you mean by that? Who are *they*?"

"You're obviously a smart guy and you know precisely who you're working for. You were put on *The Company's* payroll to infiltrate the Venezuelan military because the U.S. government wants Hugo Chàvez to become the President of Venezuela. They're going to get him out of jail and continue dumping money into his MBR-200 to keep it alive and well. The CIA and NED are pumping millions into a conspiracy that will put dear Hugo in the Miraflores Palace to ensure their drugs and the oil continues to flow. They're sure that the political hacks who are opposed to Hugo wouldn't follow Washington's agenda and the military would quickly squash another coup lead by Chàvez. They brought you on board to spy on the military, but not before you got the Coastguard and Navy all fired up with drug interdiction training which is hitting them hard in the pocket book. You'd better be extremely careful because if you continue what you're doing they'll kill you. Hang on a minute; I've got to feed this thing."

Mark was curious. Was the unidentified caller trying to somehow set him up? The lady on the phone was articulate and guessing from her voice sounded like she was probably in her mid 30's. By her matter-of-fact demeanor, choice of words and explanation of *bury me,* she clearly had intimate knowledge of Operation *Divine Guidance.* As she knew what was going on Mark wondered if she might be a Para-legal or maybe a lawyer in the CIA, Coast Guard or even the State Department. After hearing a number of coins being dropped Mark asked,

"But why are you doing this considering the risk you're taking?"

"I graduated from school believing in the rule of law. The United States is a country that is based on the premise of law. When the rule of law of our great nation is violated I get upset. From what I've seen you've done a great job in Venezuela, but I'm disgusted knowing that the CIA is a drug pusher. I don't know if you're somehow involved with them in the narcotics business, but I don't think so because since they put on the payroll under Operation *Divine Guidance* their business has collapsed. At this point I'm not certain exactly how you did it, but it appears that you've successfully torpedoed the CIA before they knew what hit them. That makes you a good guy in my book and why I want to help you, if I can."

"I really appreciate you giving me a heads-up, but I'm wondering if you're maybe setting me up. I know it may sound a bit crude, but if you're for real, I guess I should consider you as my *Deep Throat.*"

"Deep Throat is a bit crude, but it's also true. Had the original Deep Throat not come forward and provided Woodward and Bernstein with the nitty-gritty on Watergate, Nixon would never had been forced out of office. You might like to know that before Vela made the first contact with you he had to get the security clearance that you needed in order to work for the CIA so he pulled all your personal background information in an effort to find something you might be ashamed of and could use to blackmail you. To his dismay he couldn't find any skeletons in the closet that you'd be ashamed of or could use if you became a problem. You were shadowed and followed everywhere to keep tabs on your drinking habits and see if you were womanizing;

you disappointed them when they found that you only drank 7UP when everyone around you was sucking on a Heineken. The Agency also discovered that you didn't do drugs and weren't a womanizer because you were either home alone, doing what you do on boats or with Mike in tow when you went out. One CIA report to the Directorate suggested that you might be a closet gay, but later had to admit that they couldn't find any evidence to support this. Even though they said you didn't attend church regularly the reports described you as a choir boy in diapers whose single parent activities were limited to working, eating and when you slept, it was always alone."

"Hmm, I've never been labeled a choir boy before and assure you I don't wear diapers…"

"Hey Captain, that's the CIA's assessment, not mine."

"I appreciate what you've told me and hope you're on the up and up. Can you call me again in a few days in case anything else surfaces?"

"I don't know if I can do that, but I've got to go now. Stay vigilant and keep your eyes open. If you don't, you'll be dead, good bye and good luck."

The line went dead. Mark continued to hold the phone in disbelief wondering if he had only imagined what had just taken place. Thanks to the call Deep Throat had confirmed that the seizures by the French and Dutch had not gone unnoticed and had become a serious problem for the CIA.

———

As the drug seizures had drawn the attention of Roger Doyle, he called Joe Vela,

"Joe, this is Roger. What the hell is going on in Venezuela? I'm sure Kelly is up to something that we don't know about. For the last 4 months he's been sending the confidential stuff about the military and from what you've told me he's stopped the interdiction training. To date we've paid him $450,000 so we've met our part of the deal. Now all of a sudden our shipments are continually being busted by the French and Dutch, Kelly's got to have contact with these people. I don't know how he's getting the information, but just in the last few weeks we've lost 12 shipments. I'm sure that somehow Kelly's got the Frogs and the Cheese Heads involved and with these losses he's becoming a dangerous liability."

"Roger I don't know of any connection with the Dutch, but he's friendly with a guy named Jacques Deauville who's a Commercial Attaché at the French Embassy. The guy I've got tailing him says he only occasionally visits the Embassy, but because he's never there very long we assume these are just social visits."

"Holy Christ Joe, that's the connection. I don't know how he's finding out about our movements, but as the French and their Dutch counterparts are making the seizures he's got to be their source of intelligence. I want Kelly removed, permanently out of the picture. Kill the bastard!"

———

"Mike I'm going back to Venezuela on Wednesday, do you want to come along? The Commandant has invited me to a naval graduation ceremony at the Circulo Militar in Caracas and there's no training or work scheduled, only a bit of play so it should be fun."

"No thanks Dad. I've got a Spanish test coming up on Wednesday and I can't miss it, but if you would, please bring me back a couple of the GUARDACOSTAS T-shirts." As always Toschenko was waiting at Maiquetia when he arrived.

"Hola Mark, I really appreciate you coming down for the graduation ceremony, everyone is looking forward to your attending. I'm not supposed to tell you, but during the ceremony the Commandant is going to present you with another engraved wall plaque for the services you've rendered to the Navy."

At the Euro Building Mark found a message from Mayo the Coastguard's Chief of Operations asking if while he was in Caracas he could meet with the Commanding Officer of a Coastguard Reserve Unit based in Valencia in the State of Carabobo. If acceptable Mayo said he'd arrange for one of his staff, a Navy Lieutenant by the name of Armando Aguilar to drive him to Valencia. Later Mayo telephoned Mark at the hotel.

"Mark because of the traffic and the driving time to Valencia, if it's okay, I'll have Aguilar pick you up in front of the Euro

Building at 0530 hours."

"Sure that's fine. What kind of a car will he be driving?"

"He's asked if he could use his personal vehicle and put in for mileage reimbursement, I approved the request. He has a dark green 2-door Mitsubishi Trooper."

The following morning before leaving the hotel's lobby Mark picked up two go-cups of coffee, one for himself and the other for the Lieutenant. At precisely 0530 a dark green 2-door Mitsubishi Trooper drove around the hotel's entrance and stopped as the passenger door swung open. Saluting, the Lieutenant said,

"Good morning Captain."

"Good morning Lieutenant, how about a coffee? I'm not certain how you take it, but it's got a little milk and here are three sugars."

The traffic was light as they passed by the University and the Plaza Venezuela on the freeway to the west.

"You know Lieutenant this is probably the only time I've ever driven through Caracas where the traffic has been bearable."

Smiling he replied,

"Most people don't get up this early."

Traveling at a high speed the Mitsubishi made good time leaving the metropolitan area. When they were a few miles from the city of Maracay the sun began emerging on the horizon behind them.

"Lieutenant do you mind if I smoke?"

"No, carry on sir."

In reaching over the back seat to get his briefcase, which contained his pipe and tobacco pouch, Mark noticed a dark colored Chevrolet sedan about 100' behind them that appeared to have tires hanging alongside the passenger doors. Then momentarily before he'd turned away the Chevrolet increased its speed and was now in the passing lane a short distance behind to the left of the Mitsubishi. Mark was then able to confirm that the dark colored sedan did in fact have two tires tied along its passenger side.

"Lieutenant look...." But before Mark had time to alert the Lieutenant to look at the car to the left and see the tires, the sedan slammed into the driver's side of the Mitsubishi. The Lieutenant shouted,

"Coño! Pendejo!"

While trying to release the holster clasp and take hold of his weapon the Lieutenant struggled to maintain control of the Mitsubishi as the Chevrolet rammed into the side of their car trying to force it off the road. At the speed they were traveling had the Mitsubishi been forced from the right hand lane it would have ended up in a deep ditch that paralleled the road and because of the trooper's high profile most likely would have landed upside down. The large dark sedan kept moving to and fro as the driver repeatedly slammed into the side of Mitsubishi while the Lieutenant held tightly to the steering wheel. No more than maybe 200' ahead was a slip road leading to a gasoline station on the right.

"Lieutenant, try and make it to the gas station!"

The Mitsubishi entered the forecourt of the gas station at almost 70 mph barely missing one of the pumps before bouncing over a curb and coming to a stop. With two tires still hanging along its passenger side the dark sedan sped away and continued down the highway.

"Lieutenant, are you Okay?"

"Yes I'm fine Captain, how about you?"

"I'm okay, but I think that somebody out there doesn't like us very much."

Clearly shaken they both entered the gas station's shop and while the Lieutenant called the police Mark bought two more coffees. 20 minutes later two police officers entered the shop and the Lieutenant told them what had happened. Seeing both were uniformed Naval Officers the policemen appeared to have a little more than the normal interest, but said there wasn't much they could really do. Their report simply indicated that a large dark colored car which may or may not have been a mid 1970's Chevrolet sedan, with two tires tied along the passenger side had been involved in a hit and run accident with a Mitsubishi Trooper. The police were told that the dark sedan was reasonably clean, but the rear license plate was obscured as it had been covered with dirt or mud. The drivers' side of the Lieutenant's Mitsubishi Trooper displayed a number of black marks from the tires and the driver's door and both fenders were caved in with an assortment of small dents that the Lieutenant said hadn't been there before.

Looking closely at the damages, other than the crushed fenders and the partially caved in driver's side door there was little real evidence of what had happened. The Lieutenant gave the police his Venezuelan Navy ID number and produced his driver's license and the Mitsubishi's registration papers. After the two police officers left, over coffee Mark and the Lieutenant pondered whether they should proceed to Valencia or abort the meeting. As there were people waiting for them they decided to continue, but agreed that they would definitely return before dark. They laughed, adding that they would also keep a close watch for cars around them, especially those with tires tied to their doors. About two miles further along the highway towards Valencia they saw the police car parked on the side of the highway next to two large tires. Seeing the Mitsubishi the police officers waved them to stop.

"There's no sign of the car, but we found the tires."

Holding up pieces of a light polypropylene line still tied to one of the tires the officer remarked,

"They used this line to tie the tires to the car probably to prevent them from making a metal to metal contact with the Mitsubishi and damaging their car or leaving any paint marks. I'm afraid that there isn't much more we can do. We have your contact information Lieutenant so if anything comes up we'll get in touch with you."

Albeit a bit delayed they completed the meeting in Valencia and safely returned to Caracas without being attacked by any other tire adorned Chevy sedans. When he got to his room at the Euro Building Mark found a hand written note that had been pushed under the door. *Mark, tomorrow during the day I have some work I must to attend to, but let's plan to have dinner. I'll pick you up at the hotel at 8:00.* The message was signed by Nicholas Toschenko. The following morning Mark took advantage of the free time to catch up on his paperwork when the phone rang. The call was from Commander Mayo, the Chief of Operations.

"Good morning Mark, I've just spoken with Aguilar who told me what happened yesterday. Are you Okay?"

"Yes I'm fine, just a bit shaken from the experience. We were both very lucky. There's no way that a car with two tires tied along its side would coincidentally be driving along the highway at exactly the same time as we were and try to run us off the road by mistake. This was no accident, someone had obviously marked our car and tried to hurt or kill us."

Mayo, clearly concerned picked up the conversation,

"I've got an investigation underway and intend to get to the bottom of it. I'll let you know what I find out."

Mark then called the French Embassy,

"Bonjour Jacques how about a coffee this morning?"

"For you my friend, the pot is always on."

"Great, I'll see you in 20 minutes."

At the Embassy Mark told Jacques about his experience while driving to Valencia.

"Mark you were lucky that you didn't end up in the hospital or worse yet in the morgue. It's obvious that someone knows your movements and was following you. Do you really trust your informant?"

"My informant is totally trustworthy. He wouldn't be involved or do anything to take me out because he needs me. In any case I've got a pretty good idea who the culprits are."

"I'm glad to hear this because his information is producing phenomenal results. In the last month alone the *lists* have resulted in over a dozen seizures. Because I told you that it may take a number of weeks for the payments to be made, you may not be aware, but late last week I transferred $11 million to your account in the Cayman Islands. At my insistence and because of its success Paris has agreed to establish a separate fund for the operation. As soon as Pierre confirms the number of kilos seized during the last 10 days and sends me the verification I'm authorized to immediately transfer another payment to you."

"Jacques that's fantastic news, you're right, I didn't expect anything this soon so I haven't bothered to check with the bank."

"Your informant is a gold mine of information. The results he's producing will negatively impact the cartels which will undoubtedly be confirmed when we see an increase in the street price. I haven't received the updated report from Pierre as of yet, but if it's anything like the last one you should check with your bank because you'll be receiving another few million or so. Next time we have dinner I'll expect you to pick up the tab, but in the meantime I'd suggest that you keeping looking over your shoulder."

"Good advice. I'll be in touch."

Returning to the Euro Building Mark continued to work until lunch then went down for something to eat. After a sumptuous fruit salad at the poolside restaurant he stopped at the hotel's gift shop where he bought copies of the New York Times and Herald Tribune. Returning to his room he found a message printed on the hotels notepaper that had been slipped under the door. The time stamp showed 12:15 p.m. and was from the Concierge: <u>Message from Captain Toschenko.</u>

To save a bit of time I would appreciate if you could meet me at the hotel's entrance on the main road to save me having to enter the hotel's parking area. Please be at the street entrance to the hotel on Las Mercedes at 7:45pm.

Just after 5:00 p.m. the phone rang. "Mr. Kelly this is the concierge desk, I would like to confirm that you received the telephone message from Captain Toschenko about meeting him tonight at 7:45 p.m.? The message was delivered to your room earlier today."

"Yes I did, thank you."

After closing and locking his briefcase Mark decided to go for a swim in the hotel's pool before meeting Toschenko. At 7:30 p.m., dressed in civilian clothes he took the elevator to the lobby and started walking down the sidewalk towards the Las Mercedes entrance to the hotel. Rounding a slight curve in the road leading to the intersection of Las Mercedes two shots rang out hitting the pavement in front of him. With a high concrete wall on his right and the open road to his left there was no place to take cover. Mark quickly turned and began running up the slight incline leading to the hotel's main entrance. While running with his head down he looked to his left towards the grassy hillside adjoining the road, but couldn't see anyone. Twenty or thirty feet from the entrance he dropped behind one of the cars parked near the lobby entrance, shielded from view from behind the car he saw the road was empty.

The silence was deafening, no one was around. Using the car as cover he saw that the only place the shooter could have been would be on a small knoll about 200' above and overlooking the parking area to the left of the main entrance road. Crouching he waited another few minutes to watch the area from where he believed the shots had been fired. If a person or a car attempted to leave through the main entrance leading to Las Mercedes or by means of a second access road to the left they would have to pass the hotel's main entrance, but no one left the area. A few minutes later the owner of the BMW he was using as cover returned and after looking at him wondering what he was doing, drove away. Mark went inside the hotel lobby. At the concierge desk Mark identified himself as a guest in the hotel and said he wanted to report a shooting that had just happened.

"A shooting, are you injured?

"No I'm not, but please call the police."

The flustered concierge said he would immediately summon the police asking Mark to wait in the lobby until they arrived. Just as he turned away from the concierge Toschenko entered the lobby.

"Mark, are you ready to go?"

"Hi Nicholas, there's been a bit of a problem. Someone fired two shots at me as I was walking down the road to meet you, fortunately they missed. I received your message to meet you at Las Mercedes and when I was about half-way down the entrance road the shots were fired, I think they came from an area on the left hand side of the road."

"Someone tried to shoot you? What message? I said I'd pick you up at 8:00 p.m. in front of the hotel, why were you walking to Las Mercedes?"

"I received another message that asked me to walk to Las Mercedes so that you wouldn't have to enter the parking area."

"I didn't leave you a second message I only left you one message that I'd pick you up at the hotel. I never asked you to walk to Las Mercedes."

A few minutes' later three police officers entered the hotel and walked to the front desk and spoke with a receptionist who pointed towards Nicholas and Mark sitting in the lounge area. After the police officers had been told what happened two of them went outside to look around the area while the third took Mark's statement. The policeman showed little interest and began explaining that each week Caracas had between 30 and 40 murders, many of which were simply attempted robberies that had gone bad. Mark wasn't pleased,

"No one tried to rob me and there was no one around or near me. The shots were fired from a distance, no one approached me."

It was obvious that the police weren't interested even after Toschenko told them that Mark was an officer in the Venezuelan Navy, an American Citizen and a U.S. Coast Guard Officer. Much like the tire incident the day before the police officer said he'd file a report with the same run-around, don't call us – we'll call you.

"How do you feel Mark? Do you want to maybe forget about La Estancia and have dinner here?"

"Are you buying? If the invitation is still on, let's go to La Estancia. I don't and probably never will know who the bastard was that shot at me, but I do know that he needs a lot more target practice. My only hope is that he'll take his practice shots at someone else. Let's eat."

While trying to present a positive appearance Mark found the two incidents disturbing, or maybe better said, both incidents had scared the hell out of him. As Mark was due to return to Puerto Rico on the afternoon American Airlines flight the following day, the next morning he stopped to speak with the hotel's manager, an affable German who earlier had been made aware of the shooting when he came to work. Introducing himself,

"Mr. Kohlberg I'm the guest that was shot at last night, I'd be grateful if I might ask you for your help."

"Yes, but of course, whatever you need please let me know. However, I would first like to offer my sincere apologies for what happened. Caracas is a very violent city with very ineffective police. Our internal security in the hotel is very attentive and we have roving security officers on the grounds and in the parking areas to safeguard our guests. I am very, very, sorry for your ordeal."

"Thanks, but it's not the shooting incident that I need your help with. Mr. Kohlberg yesterday after returning from lunch, I received a phone message that had a time stamp of 12:15 p.m. The problem is that the message was not from Captain Toschenko as it states. I would be grateful if you would allow me to speak with the telephone operator who took this message in case she may have noted the number of the person who called."

Reaching for his phone Kohlberg summoned the hotel's assistant manager and asked to have the department head come to his office immediately. Marta Cortez was a grand-motherly lady who Kohlberg said had been with the Euro Building for a number of years appeared terrified as she entered his office.

"Ms. Cortez this is Mr. Kelly, a guest of the hotel. Yesterday he received a telephone message that had a time stamp of 12:15 p.m. I want you to find out which of your staff took the message and who the message was from.

"Handing her the message Kohlberg said, "The message itself is not an issue, Mr. Kelly's concern is that there is no return telephone number and the caller wasn't Captain Toschenko. Ms. Cortez you are aware that the hotel policy is clear that all messages are to include the telephone number and the name of the caller. As you can see the line for the caller's telephone number is blank. Please bring the person who took this call to my office immediately."

Clearly upset Ms. Cortez stood and turned to leave,

"I'm sorry Mr. Kohlberg I don't know what happened, but I see that the call was taken by Ms. Sanchez who only joined us last month. I'll be right back."

"May I offer you a coffee while we wait Mr. Kelly? The hotel's switchboard is on the lower level so it should only be a few minutes before the telephone operator returns."

"Yes thank you, coffee would be nice."

Calling through the partially open door to his office, "Ms. Delgado, please arrange for some coffee."

From beyond the door an unseen Ms. Delgado acknowledged her master's request. A few minutes later Ms. Delgado, a stunningly beautiful woman in her late 20's gently knocked on the partially open door of Kohlberg's office announcing the arrival of the coffee. Ms. Delgado said that Ms. Cortez, accompanied by Ms. Sanchez the recently hired telephone operator, was waiting outside. Looking for my approval Mr. Kohlberg inquired,

"If it's alright with you we'll have our coffee first then speak with Ms. Cortez and hmm, what was her name...oh yes, Sanchez."

After the small cups of the strong espresso had been consumed the two telephone operators were summoned,

"Mr. Kohlberg this is Ms. Sanchez who took the call for Mr. Kelly."

"Good morning Ms. Sanchez." Handing her the telephone message,

"As you know the hotel's policy is very clear that all messages we take for our guests are to have the name and the telephone number of the person calling. Why does this message not indicate the caller's number?"

Being new and obviously having never been in the Executive Offices, particularly the office of the General Manager, Ms. Sanchez was clearly ill at ease.

"I'm sorry sir, but when I received the call the gentleman said he needn't give me his phone number as Mr. Kelly already had it. As he said that Mr. Kelly already had the number I didn't ask him again. This happens many times and I didn't think it was unusual. I do apologize for any inconvenience that I may have caused the guest."

"Thank you Ms. Sanchez. Mr. Kelly is there anything else you need from Ms. Sanchez or Ms. Cortez?"

"No, thank you Ms. Sanchez, I just needed the caller's phone number, but now understand the circumstances of why it wasn't obtained."

After checking out, on the ride back to the airport Mark decided that on future visits he'd stay at the Caracas Hilton or the Tamanaco instead of the Euro Building.

"Hey Dad, welcome home, did you have a good trip?"

Not wishing to upset Mike with the details of the incident on the road to Valencia or the shooting,

"Yeah, it was an interesting trip. Toschenko and the Admiral both send their regards. We're really making good progress and the training is moving along smoothly. How about you? Did you miss me? I got you two Coastguard T-shirts, how was your stay with Poncho and Lucy?"

On those occasions when Mike didn't accompany Mark to Venezuela he would stay with their close friends Poncho and Lucy Bird, whose home was walking distance from his school the Fajardo Academy.

"They're both fine, but still insisting that I'm in bed by 9:30, Yuk. Won't you tell them that it's okay for me to stay up until at least 10:30?"

"Hey you're a growing boy and need the rest, maybe next year."

"Dad, next year is next month so I'm going to hold you to that. Don't forget you told me that a man is only as good as his word."

Two weeks later Mark was off again to Caracas for meetings with the Minister of Defense and Admiral Blanes. In the interim period Blanes had been promoted to Vice-Admiral and was now the Comandante General de la Armada. As the Commanding Admiral of all Naval Forces his office at Naval Headquarters located in the San Bernardino section of Caracas. After Toschenko met him outside the arrivals hall at Maiquetia he drove Mark to the Tamanaco Hotel.

"I'm sorry that I won't be able to see you tonight because my wife has something planned for me to do, but I'll pick you up in the morning at 8:00. After what happened last month at the Euro Building I think you're wise moving to the Tamanaco Hotel."

Arriving at the hotel with no commitments for the rest of the day Mark decided to take a swim in the hotel's expansive pool. Later following a great dinner, he decided to walk to the Las Mercedes shopping mall to look and browse around the expansive number of shops. Collecting his pipe and tobacco from the room he proceeded through the lobby to the hotel's entrance road. The Euro Building and the Tamanaco Hotel are relatively close to one another situated in the same general area of Caracas. Each has private access roads that connect to the main boulevard of Las Mercedes which is situated below an overhead freeway. The Tamanaco's access road is bordered on both sides by flowers, well manicured gardens and lawns and no more than a few hundred yards in length. When Mark was only a short distance from the intersection with Las Mercedes Boulevard a single shot rang out ricocheting off the concrete walkway in front of him. He immediately thought to himself, Holy Christ not again. However, this time he wasn't completely alone as a taxi was proceeding up the road towards him from the Boulevard. For cover he lunged to the side of the cab while simultaneously pulling open the rear door sliding low across the back seat.

"Please take me to the Tamanaco Hotel."

"But mister you're at the Tamanaco Hotel."

"Okay then take me to the reception."

Mark gave the cabbie $10.00 for the 30 second ride which clearly made his day. Once inside the safety of the hotel he asked to speak with the manager that was on duty. A Mr. Contreras soon emerged advising him he was the assistant manager and asking if he could be of assistance.

"Mr. Contreras I was walking down the hotel's entrance road towards Las Mercedes when someone fired a shot at me. I didn't see the person, but at the angle that the bullet hit the pavement it appears the shot was fired from the hillside parking area on the left side of the road."

Removing a hand-held radio from his pocket Contreras summoned the head of the hotel's security. A moment later the security chief appeared and Contreras gave him instructions.

"Take one of your men and immediately search the grounds along the entrance road. Someone has just fired a gun at this gentleman. Who ever did this may still be on the property,"

With that the security chief speaking on his radio quickly disappeared out the front door of the hotel. Contreras turned to Mark,

"Are you a guest in the hotel?"

"Yes, the name is Kelly, I'm in room 517."

"I'm truly sorry about this and on behalf of the management do apologize for this terrible experience. As you know Caracas is a terribly violent city and many people have guns." Mark thought to himself, Holy Mother of God, here we go again, another sermon about the crime, killings and whatever.

"Mr. Contreras I know that Caracas is violent which is why I don't wander around the city alone. I'm staying at the Tamanaco because I believe you would have proper security. I strongly object to being shot at while I'm on the property and merely walking through the grounds."

"Yes, but......" Mark cut him off,

"Please Mr. Contreras let's not waste anymore time, while your security people look around could you please call the police, I'd like to file a report."

"Yes of course."

This time two police officers showed up. After first speaking with the hotels' security chief Mark told the officers about the previous incident at the Euro Building Hotel. Taking little interest in the Euro Building shooting they said that sometimes these things just happen; the complacent remark by the police did little to raise Mark's comfort level. Once the police had taken his statement and passport number they suggested that he report the matter to the American Embassy just in case something might happen to him. Quickly determining that this wouldn't be a good idea he returned to his room and decided to take a bath which he though would be relaxing. Before getting into the bath he closed the drapes and positioned a chair under the door handle. Half in jest he thought that if the assassin couldn't shoot him he or she might try an Alfred Hitchcock *Psycho* approach and cut him up in the shower or if that failed, drown him in the bathtub. After settling into bed he turned on the television to see what was happening in the rest of the world when the phone rang.

"Hello Mark, I'm sorry we couldn't get together for dinner tonight, but let's do it tomorrow."

"That's' fine Nicholas, we'll talk tomorrow."

————

Back in Langley Roger Doyle discovered he had more problems,

"Mary, please get me Derek Mathews on the phone."

Moments later,

"Mr. Doyle, Mr. Mathews is on line 5."

"Good morning Derek. I've got a bit of a problem. You'll recall a few months back we sct up a numbered account the password is SAILOR 2020. I'd like you to transfer the funds in this account back to our special account. Okay, I'll hold on... What? The account's empty! How's that possible? I transferred $450,000.00......., how can you now tell me the account has no money in it?"

In a typical British matter-of-fact response, Mathews answered,

"I'm sorry Roger, but both you and the other unnamed beneficial owner have the password which allows the account to be accessed by either principals. I see that you made the first deposit of $50,000.00 with subsequent deposits of $100,000.00 on the 15th of every month for the next four months. The day after the first $50,000.00 was deposited I received instructions to transfer $49,500.00 to the Cayman National Bank in the Cayman Islands. On the 16th of each month thereafter we were instructed to transfer $100,000.00 to the Cayman National Bank. Two days ago instructions were received to transfer the remaining $500.00 balance to the Cayman National. Sorry, but the funds in the account have been depleted."

"Christ Derek, so what you're telling me is that with both of us having the PIN the account could be cleaned out."

"Yes Roger, that's correct, it's exactly what you're trying to do now, unfortunately the other account holder beat you to it."

Extremely annoyed, Roger slammed down the phone.

"Mary get me Joe Vela in Caracas."

A few moments later,

"Mr. Doyle, Mr. Vela is on line 4."

"Joe I just got some disturbing news. In addition to dodging cars and bullets that bastard Kelly has also walked away with $450,000.00 of our money. I want you to have one of our people find the son-of-a-bitch in Puerto Rico and kill him and that kid of his, but don't leave a trace. I think a late night boat ride with a couple hundred pounds of cement chained to their legs before throwing them overboard would do the trick. Have the boat go out over the Puerto Rican Trench so unless anyone's looking for lobsters in 6,000 feet of water we'll be rid of the son-of-a-bitch forever. Joe, I want you to thoroughly search his condominium. Kelly's stolen $450,000.00 and obviously is the source of our problems with the French and the Dutch, I want to know how and who gave him the information about our shipments and have them killed too. When you're done at his condo, torch the place."

"Sorry Roger, but I've already been to his home. I sent him a letter with an inverted stamp alerting him for a meeting at Base San Juan. When I called to let him know I was on the Base and that he should come, I found his phone had been disconnected. The next day I got Bennie Garcia, our guy at the Coast Guard base in San Juan to accompany me to Kelly's condo. His car wasn't there and no one answered the door so Bennie picked the lock, when we got inside we found the place was empty. Kelly's gone. The only thing left is some furniture, a few pots, pans, and dishes. I spoke to his next door neighbor who said that Mark and Mike had moved out a few days ago, he thinks they went to Canada."

Even more annoyed, Roger slammed the phone down, again.

———

Roger was further infuriated when he watched the CBS 60 Minutes television exposé captioned, *The CIA's Cocaine…….* The 60 Minutes program exposed the drug trafficking activities of the Central Intelligence Agency while reporting that the *CIA's Cocaine* was allowed, without interference to be shipped to the United States because General Ramon Guillen Davila of the Venezuelan National Guard was on the CIA payroll.

And then there were the newspaper stories in New York and Miami…..

Venezuelan General Indicted in C.I.A. Scheme
A Federal Grand Jury in Miami has indicted a Venezuelan General who was in charge of a Central Intelligence Agency counter-narcotics program. Following an investigation that lasted more than five years, the grand jury handed up a sealed indictment earlier this week against
General Ramon Guillen Davila who was the chief of the program set up by the CIA with the Venezuelan National Guard. The CIA Station Chief in Caracas was recalled to Washington, while another CIA officer resigned……….

———

Shortly before he left Caracas Mark saw a story in *El Universal,* along with gruesome photographs of a DISIP agent who was naked with his outstretched arms and legs tied spread eagle on a wooden pallet. The mutilated body was found on a beach on Isla Margarita. The agent had been castrated, his tongue cut out and his ears cut off; along with his genitals everything had been stuffed into his mouth. Ice picks protruded from his eyes. Mark did not return to Venezuela. After executing the necessary paperwork his accountant became the owner of the condo and his Mercedes. Mark contacted the Cayman National Bank and transferred $19 million, exactly half the balance in the numbered Cayman account to José's sister's bank account in Florida. He then called to tell Maria to check her bank account as it had money earned by *El Gato Negro*.

After completing his business affairs Mark and Mike took a cab to the airport in San Juan and flew to Guadeloupe. In Guadeloupe they were met by Jacques Deauville and driven to the headquarters of the Gendarmerie Maritime where both were given new French passports. Mark and Mike Kelly became Alain and Jean-Paul DuPont, Citizens of the French Republic.

After flying from Guadeloupe to Orly the DuPont's then boarded a flight to Dubai. The flights were all in First Class. They were met in Dubai by the French Consulate General and given the keys to a luxurious penthouse over looking the marina. Alain purchased a new Maserati Quattro Porto and weekends were spent on their new *SUNSEEKER* Manhattan 74' motor-yacht moored in the marina below the penthouse. Jean-Paul was enrolled in the International Diplomatic School where he was learning French along with Arabic.

Nothing in life is so exhilarating as to be shot at without results.
Winston Churchill

Made in the USA
Charleston, SC
02 May 2012